DISCIPLING
the
NATIONS

DISCIPLING
the
NATIONS

Richard R. De Ridder

BAKER BOOK HOUSE
Grand Rapids, Michigan

Library of Congress Catalog Card Number: 75-157077

This edition, August 1985, reprinted with the permission
of the copyright owner, is available only from the
author at: Calvin Theological Seminary, 3233 Burton St., SE,
Grand Rapids, Michigan 49506

Formerly published under the title, *The dispersion of the people of God.*

Printed in the United States of America

To Adrianna:
my wife,
my partner in life, ministry, and goals.

Index

"One small step for man; one giant leap for mankind." These words from earth's satellite, the moon, commemorate together with an indelible imprint of a man's cleated boot on the spongy lunar soil the drama of man's first small beginning toward freedom from his planet. A plaque records the names of the men who successfully completed this mission and the place where man first set foot on the moon. It was a small beginning; its full consequence will never really be measured.

Centuries ago an unrecorded step was taken by some unknown "Follower of the Way" across the national boundaries of Israel into the vast Gentile world. No one recorded the step. No one knows what border was crossed. But there came a moment, a place in redemptive history in which God's universal covenant with mankind started its immeasurable march through the nations of the world. An unknown disciple on a distant and remote frontier made a beginning by challenging a fellow man to join him as a member of the disciple fellowship of Christ. Only God knows where this happened, by whom that step was taken, with what fruit the witness was crowned. Its full consequence will not be measured until "the sovereignty of the world has passed to our Lord and his Christ," when men purchased "for God of every tribe and language, people and nation" are made "a royal house, to serve our God as priests" and shall „reign upon the earth," when the "vast strong, which no one could count, from every nation, of all tribes, peoples, and languages" will shout together, "Victory to our God who sits on the throne, and to the Lamb! ... Amen! Praise and glory and wisdom, thanksgiving and honor, power and might, be to our God for ever and ever! Amen!" (Rev. 11:15; 5:10; 7:9-12 – NEB). That day will live in eternity as a day among countless others in which through the power of the blood of Christ a man was set free from his bondage to death and made a new creature in Christ. Who brought the message of liberation? Who was liberated? We do not know. We know only the Liberator.

The campaign for world-wide proclamation of liberation was commanded by the Liberator, who himself is and remains the great missionary.[1] He continues

---

1   Cf. Rom. 8:21 (N.E.B.): "The universe itself is to be freed from the shackles of mortality and enter upon the glorious liberty of the children of God." Jesus spoke of his work as that of a Liberator – comp. Isa. 61:1 with Luke 4:18. See Johannes Verkuyl, *De Boodschap der Bevrijding in deze Tijd* (Kampen: J. H. Kok, 1970), for a current application of the concept "liberation" to our day and time.

to work, as one ending of Mark's Gospel states, "while the Lord worked with them and confirmed the message by the signs that attended it" (Mark 16:19), and yet another ending of the same Gospel, "After this Jesus himself sent out by means of them, from East to West, the sacred and imperishable proclamation of eternal salvation" (Mark 16:8 f.).[2] He had said, "Lo, I am with you always, to the close of the age" (Matt. 28:20).

No student of missions can long escape the necessity of examining the Old Testament antecedents to the Christian mission. Christianity was born in Palestine from Jewish antecedents. The emerging Christian church, schooled in the Old Testament and nurtured by the Gospel of the Kingdom of God declared by Jesus Christ, very soon (by the end of the first century) became a Gentile movement. What occasioned this unparalleled success? How is it that Judaism, whose proselyting efforts in the centuries preceding and immediately following the time of Christ were by no means feeble, failed, whereas the Christian mission continues unabated? Is the success of the Christian mission explainable only in terms of commission? Did it owe nothing to Judaism? What was the framework of reference for the disciples when Jesus spoke this word of commission – only the words of Jesus or also the Jewish practices and propaganda with which they were familiar?

The Christian mission did not arise in a vacuum. It received the legacy of the Jewish proselyting movement, an enterprise of considerable extent. These Jewish antecedents conditioned the Christian church's prosecution of its task, gave content to its Lord's commission and determined some of the questions which troubled it. The first disciples were men of their day and cannot be separated from the times and events in which they lived.

That this is so is confirmed by Jesus' words in Matt. 23:13-15 (NEB) – "Alas for you, lawyers and Pharisees, hypocrites that you are! You shut the doors of the Kingdom of Heaven in men's faces; you do not enter yourselves, and when others are entering you stop them. Alas for you, lawyers and Pharisees, hypocrites! You travel over sea and land to make one convert; and when you have won him you make him twice as fit for hell as you are yourselves." These words show that there was a movement in the Judaism of Jesus' day to gain converts, in spite of tensions which existed in the community regarding the questions of admission, rites to be observed, the legal position of the proselyte, etc..[3] The Talmud and rabbinic literature as a whole may be shown

---

2 The supporting evidence for the various endings of the Gospel of Mark can be examined in the critical apparatus of Ernest Nestle, *The Greek New Testament*, 25th ed. (Stüttgart: Wurtembergische Bibelanstalt, 1963), *sub loco*. Whatever position one adopts regarding these variant readings, together they constitute proof of the mind of the early church regarding the presence of Christ in the mission task, if not the inspired statement of the editor of the Gospel record.

3 The Talmud contains extensive references to the masters (Hillel and Shammai) of two schools contemporary with Jesus and their differences in the treatment and reception of proselytes. William George Braude, *Rabbinic Attitudes Towards Proselytization*

to contain all shades of opinion from the statement that the dispersion of Israel was for the purpose of making converts[4] to the saying of R. Chalbo that proselytes are to Israel as an eruption on the body.[5]

These tensions continued in Judaism until long after the birth of the Church; today a vigorous apologetic is still carried on in Jewish circles defending the position of today's Jews not to carry on mission work.[6] This modern attitude is in stark contrast to the proselyting movements in Judaism which gained rather than lost impetus after the destruction of the Temple and Jerusalem in 70 A.D.[7] Later something very curious took place in Judaism. "It gradually became a kind of special glory even, and one of the ways it (Judaism) differed from Christianity, that it made and sought to make no converts. What was once a compelling necessity imposed by force from without now became an excellence derived from within."[8] E. G. Homrighausen described the present dilemma of

(Providence, R. I.: Brown University, 1934), henceforth to be cited as *Rabbinic Attitudes*, an unpublished dissertation, maintains that opposition to proselytization centered in the teachers of the Haggadah. The teachers of the Halakah put the proselytes on a level almost equal to that of the native Israelites and in effect opened the doors to the influx of proselytes. Providentially the apostle Paul was schooled by Gamaliel (Acts 22:3), who was a pupil and successor of Hillel, who took a more lenient and embracing view of the proselyte. For a full treatment of and quotations from the traditions of the Rabbis regarding Hillel's views, see David Max Eichhorn, *Conversion to Judaism: A History and Analysis* (New York: Ktav Publ. Co., 1966), p. 44ff., henceforth to be cited as *Conversion to Judaism*.

4 *B.T.*, Pes. 87b. (All references from the Babylonian Talmud are to the Epstein edition and the abbreviations follow the standard of that edition. The Jerusalem Talmud references are from the Ehrman edition. Unless otherwise noted, the references are always to the Babylonian Talmud). See also William Gordon Braude, *Jewish Proselyting in the First Five Centuries of the Common Era* (Providence: Brown University, 1940), p. 137, henceforth to be cited as *Jewish Proselyting*, for complete statements of the rabbis.

5 *B.T.*; Yeb. 47b, 109b; Kid. 70b.

6 The literature is extensive. Dr. Israel Isidore Mattuck's article, "Why the Jews Have No Missionaries," *Papers for Jewish People*, XXXI, (Jewish Religious Union), 44-53, is representative of this viewpoint. Commenting on Dr. Mattuck's article in the same issue of this journal, Frank S. B. Gavin, "Jewish Views on Jewish Missions," pp. 5-43, responds with a question from the Melichta on Exodus 18:27, ed Horowitz, p. 200, "Of what benefit is a light except in a place of darkness?" He also deals with the differences between the orthodox and liberal Jews in our day. These differences remind one of the differences between the schools of Hillel and Shammai and in part of the questions relating to the reception of Gentiles into the Christian Church as reflected in the book of Acts. See also Jakob Jocz, *Christians and Jews: Encounter and Mission* (London: S.P.C.K., 1966), pp. 45-46, henceforth to be cited as *Christians and Jews*.

7 The nature of the propaganda shows a marked change after the initial success of the Christian mission. Reffering to I Thessalonians 2:16 where Paul remarks that the Jews hindered them "from speaking to the Gentiles," William G. Braude, *Rabbinic Attitudes*, p. 32, remarks that this does not mean that the Jews sought to prevent all means to reach the Gentiles. In fact the first century Jews wanted proselytes (Matt. 23:15). What the Jews wanted was that the heathen should be directed in their own and not in the heretical way of the Christians.

8 Frank Stanton Burns Gavin, "Jewish Views on Jewish Missions" in *Papers for Jewish People* (Jewish Religious Union), XXXI, 15.

the Jewish people in this way: "they sense the universality of the Old Testament revelation, and yet they cannot be missionary because it involves winning proselytes to their racial and national heritage. Judaism cannot express its Messianic nature because it is not fulfilled. The religion of the Jews is universal, but they do not know how to implement that universality except in their own Judaism." It is Jesus Christ who breaks through into the intended universality of the Old Testament.[9]

With reference to the days of the Second Commonwealth and the early Christian centuries, the literature testifies to the cycle of proselyters and converts and leaves no doubt where the rabbis stood. They approved of proselyting, invited it, idealized the converts of the past as well as those of their own days. All the evidence available today gives no proof, however, that they sent "missionaries" to *partes infidelium*. As the rabbis labored over the Biblical text they injected wherever possible a zeal for conversion.[10]

This raises the interesting question of the interrelationships of the pre-Christian proselyting movements and the Christian mission. Von Harnack judged that "the missionary character of early Christianity was only a repetition of the missionary spirit of the Judaism of the time which was a preparation for the Christian mission."[11] This viewpoint is representative of the older studies of the subject. But Christianity is not repetition; it is fulfillment. Pre-Christian proselyting is significant in its own right and its importance goes far beyond preparation for the Christian fulfillment. The pre-Christian movements were concerned with no less a matter than the salvation or judgment of those who received the witness, Jew or non-Jew. A position the opposite of von Harnack is expressed by Johannes Blauw, who affirms that it has been established that the missionary consciousness of the early Christian church is partly due to the intertestamentary centuries. He cautions against looking upon the New Testament mission as a continuation and strengthening of the Judaic mission consciousness: "A study of the data of the New Testament will show that the missonary consciousness of the Christian church did not fall from the air but that, on the other hand, one should be very careful about continuing the line from Judaic missionary propaganda to the Christian Church."[12]

9 Homrighausen, E. G., "Evangelism and the Jewish People," *IRM*, XXXIX, no. 155 (July, 1950), 318-329.

10 The sources are to be found in the Talmud and Mishnah. An extended survey can be found in Bernard Jacob Bamberger, *Proselytism in the Talmudic Period* (New York: Ktav, 1968), p. 174ff. Also George Foot Moore, *Judaism in the First Centuries of the Christian Era* (Cambridge: Harvard University Press, 1927), henceforth to be cited as *Judaism in the First Centuries*.

11 Adolf von Harnack, *The Mission and Expansion of Christianity in the First Three Centuries*, edited by James Moffatt (New York: G. Putnam and Sons, 1908) (henceforth to be cited as *The Mission and Expansion*); Jacob Gartenhouse, *The Influence of the Jews Upon Civilization* (Grand Rapids: Zondervan, 1943), p. 23.

12 Johannes Blauw, *The Missionary Nature of the Church* (New York: McGraw-Hill, 1962), p. 63, henceforth to be cited as *The Missionary Nature*.

At the same time it is not correct to think of Judaism and Christianity in terms of a kind of historical, straight-line of succession. Fulfillment does not mean succession in place of something else. In the case of the Christian church and the Jew

> baptized Gentiles are not the legal successors of God's chosen people, Israel. Only together with Israel are they worshippers of one Father, citizens of God's Kingdom, members of God's household (Eph. 2:18-19). There is only one Christian Church: the church from Israel and from Gentiles.[13]

The words of Jesus, "When you go, make disciples of all nations . . . baptizing . . . teaching . . ." were not unique in the sense that this had not been done in some way before, but rather the radical, revolutionary, unique thing is that the man from Nazareth acted as though he were God Himself and issued commands, promulgated a covenant and made promises which were prerogatives of God alone. The offense which he constituted to Judaism lay in the unique authority which he claimed. His enemies correctly concluded that by his deeds and words he made himself equal with God. The claim that he was Lord became everywhere and to all peoples a rock of offense and a stumbling block.[14]

The Christian mission was tremendously successful. The reasons for this success are often sought in the general religious situation of the pagan world. Reference is commonly made to the "fulness of the times" (Gal. 4:4) and emphasis placed on such matters as the expectation of the Jewish and pagan worlds, the breakdown of national religions, the pax Romana, the development and spread of the mystery religions, the spread of the ideas of monotheism und universalism.[15] Describing the condition of the Mediterranean world as facilitating the spread of religious cults of every sort, Derwacter believes this also applied to Christianity:

13   Markus Barth, *Israel and the Church* (Richmond: John Knox Press, 1969), p. 83. Rom. 9-11, it should be remembered, speaks of the Gentiles as having been "grafted in".

14   Cf. Rom. 8:33 and compare I Cor. 1:23 with Acts 5:31-33 and Luke 5:21. A careful study of the trials of Christ demonstrates that the central issue of these trials, the one issue that would not down, was that of the Lordship of Jesus. He made himself "equal with God" (John 5:18; Mark 14:63, 64). He was charged before Pilate as making himself a King (Luke 23:1), and his cross bore the superscription, "King of the Jews."

15   John Peterson, *Missionary Methods of Early Judaism in the Early Roman Empire* (Chicago: Chicago Divinity School, 1946), pp. 146-155, henceforth to be cited as *Missionary Methods*, writes in detail of the attractive features of Judaism, summarizing the literature on this subject under 5 heads: 1) ethical monotheism, 2) righteousness and morality, 3) humane laws, 4) an attractive cosmology, 5) eschatological hopes. See also Kenneth Scott Latourette, *A History of the Expansion of Christianity* (7 vols.; New York and London: Harper & Bros., 1937), vol. I: "The First Five Centuries," pp. 1-44, who discusses the background out of which Christianity came and the environment into which it was born. A. von Harnack, *Mission and Expansion*, p. 19ff., also gives his list of external conditions that favored the world-wide expansion of Christianity.

The age of the mystery religions is one of the astonishing periods in religious history, a period characterized by religious migration and experiment in the search for religious satisfaction such as has found no parallel to this day. Christianity appeared in this world, launched, we might say, on the crest of the wave and swept to a speedy recovery.[16]

It is legitimate and necessary to describe and evaluate the nature of the world in which Christianity arose. It is quite another thing to conclude that these conditions account for its success. The simple fact is that Christianity did not receive its impetus and spirit from either the pagan world or Jewish expectation. Its compelling motive was the fulfillment of God's universal covenant and election in Jesus Christ which was "good news" for all men. The Christian mission is a work of God. This does not mean, however, that man is free from responsibility in the task. Paul S. Minear illustrates the relationship of God and man in the work of mission in a reference to a custom in the diocese of Dornakal, where at baptism each person places his hand on his head and repeats the words, "Woe is me if I preach not the Gospel." [17]

Jewish history and contemporary movements did indeed furnish Christianity with a record of success and failure in a comparable movement. The Christian mission inherited great riches from its Jewish past. It cannot be denied that in its first few decades, which Filson calls "three crucial decades," [18] Christianity escaped the pitfalls in which Judaism floundered. Christianity's success is to be ascribed to the work and presence of the Holy Spirit in the midst of the redeemed community.[19] The Christian church did not supplant true Judaism; it was God's means for the fulfillment of His goals for mankind. Georg Vicedom expressed this as follows:

> There would be a mission even if we did not have a missionary command. For God always grants to his disciples through the working of the Holy Spirit a faith which is not passive, dumb, simply contemplative or selfish, but a faith which produces in the Christian a restless concern for the salvation of others, a "living and active thing", a faith which lifts the believer out of his own self-edification and makes him a building stone *and a* builder. Thus the apostles "could not but speak" (Acts 4:20).[20]

Markus Barth puts the emphasis right where it belongs when he says that

16 Frederick Milton Derwacter, *Preparing the Way for Paul* (New York: The Macmillan Company, 1930), pp. 15-16.

17 Norman Goodall, ed., *Missions Under the Cross* (New York: Friendship Press, 1953), p. 65, quoting D. T. Niles. See also I Corinthians 9:16.

18 Floyd Vivian Filson, *Three Crucial Decades* (Richmond: John Knox Press, 1963).

19 Harry R. Boer, *Pentecost and the Missionary Witness of the Church* (Franeker: T. Wever, 1955), develops the place of the Holy Spirit in the church in detail.

20 Georg F. Vicedom, *The Mission of God*, translated by Gilbert A. Theile (St. Louis: Concordia, 1965), p. 83.

we are carried abroad by the Gospel rather than that we carry it. The Gospel makes us to be something we were not before. It makes us move, go, dare, stand imperturbably.[21]

A special problem concerns the influence of Hellenism upon both the Jewish proselyting movements and the Christian missionary movement. Even if it be granted that Hellenism was not without its influence on Palestinian Judaism (a concession which Louis Ginzberg is not ready to make), it may not be forgotten that the Jewish people had a genius for assimilating foreign matter by impressing upon it its own individuality. Hence it is the Hellenized Judaism that might have had some share in the mental make-up of the Palestinian Judaism and not Hellenism, pure and simple. The Hellenism of the Diaspora Jew may have been of great importance for the development of Christianity in the second century, but it can be disregarded in the study of the rise of Christianity.[22] The motivation of mission must be found elsewhere and this will require us to look to the Old Testament and especially to the prophets.

How succesfull were the prophets of Israel in motivating the rank and file in ancient Israel to share their faith? It was no easier then than it is now to squeeze a grand ideal into a small soul. Eichhorn questions:

> Did the ordinary citizen of Tekoah or Jerusalem, the man-on-the-street in Anathoth or Bethel, the average dweller at Ramah, Gilead or Galilee swallow whole the propaganda, intended or incidental, of the books of Ruth and Jonah? Did they really believe that Moabites and Ninevites were deservedly as cherished by God as were Israelites? Did they entirely agree with Amos that the Hebrews were in God's sight merely the equal of the Ethiopian, the Phoenician, and the Syrian? With Isaiah that Egypt was also His people and Assyria the work of His hands? With the Psalmist that anyone with clean hands and a pure heart may ascend the hill of the Lord? How popular among the returning Jewish exiles was Ezekiel's scheme of counting proselytes as natives and assigning them land of their own in Judea? Or the priestly injunction that the ger must be to you as the native, and you are to love him as yourself? How enthusiastically did they take up their divinely appointed task of being "a light to the Gentiles"? Or observe the ordinance that there be one and the same law for the native and the convert? That there was, on the part of the common man, some resistance even to the simplest of these requirements we may suspect from the curious fact that the elementary rule, "You must not injure or maltreat a ger" occurs no less than six times in the Law and frequently in the Prophets. The commandment, "There shall be one and the same law for homeborn and ger," also

21 Markus Barth, *The Broken Wall* (Chicago: The Judson Press, 1963), p. 176. His statement is based on a suggestion that perhaps the daring metaphor used in Ephesians 6:15 to describe the Christian soldier ("shod with the Gospel of peace") means that the Gospel carries the Christian evangelist.
22 Louis Ginzberg, "The Religion of the Jews at the Time of Jesus" in *HUCA*, I (1924), 307-321, esp. p. 308ff.

occurs six times. If these rules were generally observed in the performance rather than in the breach, what need for all this emphatic reiteration? Telltale also is the fact that, when the Torah commends the ger to the people's compassion, he is often placed in the sad company of those traditional objects of pity and exemplifications of defenselessness, the poor, the widow, and the orphan. What the plight of an ordinary, poor proselyte's widow or orphan must have been is not pleasant to conjure with.[23]

There were men of small souls then just as there are today. Then and now they find it hard to share their legacy with others. They simply did not understand how much there was to share. The Jews did not understand that giving away one's faith is the only way to keep it. Yet something can be learned from these ancient Jews. Despite their deficiencies there were some, in fact, "a host of prophets, priests and psalmists who provided an abundance of spiritual telescopes through which men might look out upon wider vistas, higher virtues, holier splendors."[24]

> It is surprising that a religion which raised so stout a wall between itself and all other religions, and which in practice and prospects alike was bound up so closely with its nation, should have possessed a missionary impulse of such vigor and attained so large a measure of success.... Judaism as a religion was blossoming out by some inward transformation and becoming a cross between a national religion and a world religion.[25]

From its Jewish antecedents Christianity gained the shape and power of a community that is capable of a mission to the world.

What is the purpose of God for the Gentiles? The Old Testament is basic to this.[26] There has been a shift in emphasis and understanding in recent years concerning God's purpose for the Gentiles. In the past the search for the motive and meaning of mission employed the Old Testament only by way of introduction or else confined the answer to a listing of non-Israelites who were incorporated into Israel or shared its faith. Others searched the Law and the prophets and discovered confirmation for their ideas of mission, not realizing to what extent they had allowed eisegesis to determine their answers. What was forgotten in all the emphasis on the dependence of the Old Testament on its environ-

---

23 D. M. Eichhorn, *Conversion to Judaism*, p. 30.
24 *Ibid.*, p. 32.
25 A. von Harnack, *Mission and Expansion*, p. 9.
26 Harnack, in commenting on the relationship of Old and New Testaments, wrote: "The Old Testament of itself alone could not have convinced the Graeco-Roman world. But the converse question might perhaps be raised as to what results the Gospel would have had in that world without its union with the Old Testament. The Gnostic Schools and the Marcionites are to some extent the answer. But they would never have arisen without the presupposition of a Christian community which recognized the Old Testament." Cf. Adolf von Harnack, *The History of Dogma*, (7 vols., London: Williams and Norgate, 1894), I, p. 43, n. 1.

ment was the special vocation of God's elect and covenant people in the midst of their environment.[27] It is the divine, not the human, activity that stands in the foreground in the Old Testament. And "the evangelization of the world is not a matter of words or of activity but of *presence:* of God in the midst of humanity, the presence of God among his people."[28] John Piet, agreeing with this statement, adds, "This is true, but the hidden activity must be revealed and the Presence explained. This the church does by declaring the Gospel, or by preaching." [29] The meaning of that Presence must be defined in relation to the human activity in order to avoid the extremes to which either alternative leads. The purpose of Israel's election looms large once again in such a study.

The "I am with you" of God's presence is one of the great keynotes of the Old and New Testaments. H. Berkhof stated his conviction in this way:

> We are called to join God's work, not so much by saying that there were or are mighty acts of God in this world, but first by being a sign of them so that our message is "not in plausible words of wisdom, but in demonstration of the Spirit and power" (I Corinthians 2:4), in expectation of new acts in the coming years and of the time of the mightiest completing acts of all, which the Father has fixed in his own authority.[30]

The social conditions under which the chosen (elect) community of Israel lived are important for an understanding of the background of the nature of the *missio Dei.* The beginnings of Christianity demonstrate how socially conditioned this beginning was, a fact not always appreciated.[31] The early Christian mission cannot be regarded as a "spontaneous, ecstatic religion," as Shirley Jackson Case maintains. Christian missionaries were forced to compete for a place in occupied territory, but did so as fulfillment and not as substitute.[32] The main problems with which the early Christian Church had to cope and which it was called to solve as well as the conditions under which it had to exist were furnished ready-made by the communities in which it spread. It has been estimated that at the time of Christ the Jews constituted one-tenth of the total

27 J. Blauw, *The Missionary Nature,* p. 15. Gerhard von Rad, *Old Testament Theology,* translated by D. M. G. Stalker, (Edinburgh: Oliver and Boyd, Ltd., 1962) deals with this subject in vol. I, pp. 4-6, 69ff.

28 J. Blauw, *Missionary Nature,* p. 42. Recall also the promise of Matthew 28:20, "I am with you always."

29 John H. Piet, *The Road Ahead* (Grand Rapids: Eerdmans, 1970), p. 47. Robert Martin-Achard, *A Light to the Nations* (Naperville: Allenson, 1962), p. 79.

30 Hendricus Berkhof and Philip Potter, *Key Words of the Gospel* (London: SCM Press, Ltd., 1964), pp. 47-55.

31 Though the basic assumptions of the author are conditioned by his evolutionary conception of the origins of Christianity, the work of Shirley Jackson Case, *The Social Origins of Christianity* (Chicago: University of Chicago Press, 1923), will be of help in further exploring this phenomenon.

32 Shirley Jackson Case, *The Evolution of Early Christianity* (Chicago: University of Chicago Press, 1960), p. 178ff.

population of the Roman Empire, only two and one-half million of whom lived within the political boundaries of Palestine.[33] The rest of the Jews lived in the Diaspora, a term used to designate all Israelites who lived outside of Palestine. There is an element of national feeling in the term.[34] Only in recent years has the vast extent of this diaspora in pre-Christian times been realized. No one in ancient times recorded either the extent and causes of the diaspora or the numbers involved. In more recent times, no one has gathered all the available materials on this important subject. The fact remains, however, that when Christianity spread in the world of that day, its missionaries had to compete in what was essentially occupied territory.[35]

It is important to ask what influence this diaspora had on Judaism and as preparation for the Christian mission. Battenhouse concluded that "the Jews of the Diaspora formed the bridge across which Christianity entered the Roman world. The open synagogue, already established there, offered the Christian apostles an inviting door of access to every Jewish community. There too the first Gentile converts declared their faith in Jesus."[36] The Diaspora, as we shall show, was of much wider extent than the Roman world, began very early in the national history of the people of Israel, had several causes, and is of great significance for displaying the character of the Jewish people in their

33 D. M. Eichhorn, *Conversion to Judaism*, pp. 35-36. Solomon Grayzel, *A History of the Jews* (2nd ed., Philadelphia: Jewish Publication Society of America, 5728-1968), p. 138, estimates the distribution of the Jews around the Eastern Mediterranean in the first century A. D. as follows:

> Cyrenaica = 100,000
> N. Egypt = 1,000,000
> Judea and Palestine = 2,500,000
> Mesopotamia = 1,000,000
> Asia Minor = 1,000,000
> Italy = 100,000 (Rome = 50,000)
> 40% of the population of Alexandria

For other summaries see: Samuel Sandmel, *The First Century in Judaism and Chrisnianity* (New York: Oxford University Press, 1969), p. 14, henceforth to be cited as *First Century*; Erwin I. J. Rosenthall, *American Jewish Yearbook*, 1949, p. 319ff.; V. Avigdor Tcherikover, *Hellenistic Civilization and the Jews*, translated by S. Appelbaum (Philadelphia: Jewish Publication Society of America, 1959), pp. 202-205, 504-505, n. 86, henceforth to be cited as *Hellenistic Civilization*; Enno Janssen, *Juda in der Exilszeit* (Göttingen: Vandenhoeck und Ruprecht, 1956), pp. 25-39; Frederick Abbott Norwood, *Strangers and Exiles* (2 vols., New York: Abingdon Press, 1969), I, p. 141ff.

34 Judith 5:19; II Macc. 1:27; John 7:35; James 1:1; I Peter 1:1. Giuseppe Ricciotti, *The History of Israel*, translated by Clement Della Ponta and Richard T. A. Murphy (2 vols., Milwaukee: Bruce Publ. Co., 1958), 2nd ed., I, p. 169.

35 S. J. Case, *The Evolution of Early Christianity*, p. 33. See also F. W. Derwacter, *Preparing the Way for Paul*, pp. 14-19; Jan Leunis Koole, *De Joden in de Verstrooiing* (Franeker: T. Wever, n.d.) also summarizes the causes and extent of the dispersion. Almost all authors limit their summaries to the Roman Empire and/or Babylonia.

36 Henry Martin Battenhouse, *The Bible Unlocked* (New York: London: The Century Company, 1928), p. 406. Joseph John Williams, *Hebrewisms of West Africa* (New York: Biblo and Tanne, 1967), p. 355.

relationship to non-Jews. Koole believes that the real strength of the Jewish people in the days of the Roman Empire did not lie in the lands of Judea and Galilee but in the synagogues, the Jewish diaspora.[37]

Additionally, the Old Testament shows that when God chose and elected a man or a people, this meant dispersion, a giving up of home and land. Abraham, e.g., lived in the promised land "as in a foreign land" (Heb. 11:8-10). The people of Israel were never permitted to ignore the fact that the Promised Land was given by God's redemptive act of deliverance from Egypt's bondage (Ex. 20:2).

This diaspora of the people of God is an important consideration for the New Testament Church. The church lives not only in assembly but also in dispersion. It has two forms of existence, as David Paton shows: "that of the ecclesia, the assembly, and that of the dispersion, the diaspora."[38] What this means for the true role of the laity will be demonstrated when the meaning of Jesus' words, "When you go, make disciples . . ." (Matt. 28:18-20) are considered. The mission of the Church of Jesus Christ must be considered in relation to the Kingdom which it proclaims. An illegitimate dualism is created when the church is conceived of as a local assembly and the Kingdom of God as diaspora. These considerations gave rise to the title of this study: "The Dispersion of the People of God." Blauw observes, "There is no other church than the Church that is sent into the world. And there is no other mission than that of the Church."[39]

On what basis is salvation proclaimed to the world? Does the Sinai covenant suffice for the proclamation that "every one who calls upon the name of the Lord will be saved" (Rom. 10:13), or that "whoever believes in him will have eternal life" (John 3:15,16)? What promise did Peter have in mind when he said in the Pentecost sermon, "The promise is unto you and to your children and to all that are afar off, even as many as the Lord our God shall call unto him" (Acts 2:36)? Otto Michel and Joachim Jeremias have done great service with their exegesis of Matt. 28:18-20 by pointing out the parallels of this proclamation to enthronization hymns in other parts of Scripture.[40] Unfortunately, they have not recognized the covenant structure contained in these verses. Having emphasized the proclamation, they did not give sufficient attention to the universal, covenant perspectives of the purpose of God, as will be

---

37 J. L. Koole, *De Joden in de Verstrooiing*, p. 5.

38 Charles C. West and David M. Paton, *The Missionary Church in East and West* (London: SCM Press, Ltd., 1959), p. 109, henceforth to be cited as *The Missionary Church*.

39 J. Blauw, *The Missionary Nature*, p. 136. See also Ferdinand Hahn, *Mission in the New Testament* (Naperville: Alec R. Allenson, 1965), p. 169ff.

40 Otto Michel, *Der Brief an die Hebräer* (Göttingen: Vandenhoeck und Ruprecht, 1966) — see under Heb. 1:5-14, p. 116ff. Joachim Jeremias, *Jesus' Promise to the Nations: Studies in Biblical Theology, No. 24* (London: SCM Press, Ltd., 1967), pp. 38-39, henceforth to be cited as *Jesus' Promise*; Otto Michel, "Der Abschluss des Matthäusevangeliums", *Evangelische Missionszeitschrift*, X (1950-51), pp. 16-26, on Matt. 28:19-20.

shown. When was a universal covenant with all flesh promulgated and made effective? This question must be carefully considered. Its answer will provide one of the links that forms the unity of Old and New Testaments, Old and New Covenants, and the basis for the offer of free salvation for all.

One final matter requires comment at this time and concerns the words and example of Jesus Christ. Jesus during his life-time forbade his disciples to preach to non-Jews. "Go nowhere among the Gentiles, and enter no town of the Samaritans, but go rather to the lost sheep of the house of Israel" (Matt. 10:5 ff.) is one of his puzzling instructions to the disciple group. If he came to make salvation possible for all, why did he place this restriction on their mission? On another occasion he said, "I was sent only to the lost sheep of the house of Israel" (Matt. 15:24); that remark was made when a Canaanite woman appealed to him for help! The solutions that have been proposed to this problem will be reviewed, especially since after his resurrection Jesus commanded his followers to "make disciples of all nations" (Matt. 28:18-20). The answer will require a detailed look into the nature of the apostleship of Jesus and his disciples.[41]

But what of today? In what sense is it the duty of the disciples of Christ who recognize that God has come in the Person of his Son, Jesus of Nazareth, and that God has made his Son Lord of all things, who is always present as the Lord of life and action, to bring everything under his control?

> All education, all work, all aspects of life – political, social and economic – and all aspects of such life – intellectual, cultural, recreational and emotional – belong already to him. To make good his claim and to bring it home to all men everywhere and to every interest of each man is the task of mission. .... It really is a dangerous Gospel.[42]

Just to study history can be an interesting pursuit. But it is not enough.

> History is a teacher in God's school of wisdom. It is well worth our while to study history closely. Unless we do, the past ... will resolve itself in our memory into a meaningless mass, and we shall fail to learn the lesson which God means to teach us in this chapter of the history of his church.[43]

How must the present be assessed, and how ought the church to conceive of

---

41 A careful reading of the logia of Jesus in the Gospels nowhere gives us reason to believe that Jesus believed and taught a kind of exclusivism of salvation. To read into Jesus' sayings that salvation was for Jews only is to practise eisegesis. Jesus' words and deeds point to salvation for all men, sometimes even dramatically as in John 12:20-26. See Johannes Blauw, *Goden en Mensen* (Groningen: J. Niemeijer, 1950), p. 109ff., for a treatment of various views on this subject.

42 Frank Stanton Burns Gavin, *The Church and Foreign Missions* (Milwaukee: Morehouse Publishing Company, 1933), pp. 14, 19.

43 This quotation is taken from my lecture notes of the late Dr. Samuel Volbeda, formerly professor at Calvin Seminary, Grand Rapids, Michigan.

itself today? The chief concern of the believing community must be to "make disciples" or what is the same thing, "to preach the Kingdom of God." It has to develop a theology concerning itself that is commensurate with the purpose of its existence. This procedure will force God's people to look to God and to the world which he has created and then to themselves as a people of God in the world, people who are agents of his reconciling work. And if the challenge to mission brings the church closer to the writers of the New Testament than to the Reformers, or forces it to enlarge the vision of its thinking, let it be so, because the challenge of mission was the context in which the New Testament church did its work.[44] The sons of God with the heritage of the Reformation are called to build in today's generation on the foundation laid for them in Christ Jesus.

44 J. H. Piet, *The Road Ahead*, p. 12.

Chapter I   *The Old Testament background*

J. H. Bavinck once observed that "at first sight the Old Testament appears to offer little basis for the idea of missions," adding that "that entire pagan world is portrayed more as a constant threat and temptation to Israel than as an area in which God will reveal his salvation."[1] However, when the Old Testament is more thoroughly studied, it soon appears that there is much concern for the future of the nations and that God's plan of salvation has the whole world in view. Any account of missions in the Old and New Testaments must take account of the fundamental principles found in the revelation of God. The perspective of Holy Scripture is from the beginning universal, ecumenical and missionary.[2] The first concern of the Bible is not with Hebrews but with humanity. The Bible does not begin with the birth of Abraham, father of this people, or with Moses, prophet of God, but with the creation of the world and the advent of man.[3]

A. *Genesis 1-11*

"The key to the understanding of the whole of Scripture is found in Genesis 1-11," says Johannes Blauw. "It is a theology of history. Philosophical terminology and modes of thinking must be dispensed with in order not to lose sight of the true intentions of the narrative."[4] Beginning with the creation of the world and of man in the image and likeness of God, the Bible continually demonstrates the supreme importance of man to God both before and after man fell into sin. The Biblical viewpoint, contrasted with the viewpoints of other religions, emphasizes that God created the world and mankind distinct from himself and yet dependent on him. The world and its tribes are not an emanation of deity and therefore a part of God himself as taught in many of

---

1 Johann H. Bavinck, *An Introduction to the Science of Missions*; translated by David H. Freeman (Philadelphia: The Presbyterian and Reformed Publishing Company, 1960), p. 11, henceforth to be cited as *Science of Missions*; cf. also the book by the same author: *The Impact of Christianity on the Non-Christian World* (Grand Rapids: Eerdmans, 1949), p. 125ff., henceforth to be cited as *Impact of Christianity*.
2 C. C. West and D. M. Paton, *The Missionary Church*, p. 96.
3 D. M. Eichhorn, *Conversion to Judaism*, p. 12.
4 Johannes Blauw, *The Missionary Nature*, p. 18.

the ancient myths.[5] Most Gentile nations have their own ideas of the origin of the world, man, suffering, sin, death. Often they regard themselves as descended from divine ancestors.[6] Other peoples are excluded because they do not share the heritage of divine origin. Nor does the Bible teach that the world has come into existence alongside of God or in antagonism to him, existing as a dualism or force opposed to God. The Biblical position alone maintains that the world is God's "very good" creation,[7] created for his glory, and that man is the image and likeness of God.[8] Paul the apostle summed up this teaching of Scripture on the unity of the human race in this way: "He created every race of men from one stock, to inhabit the whole earth's surface. He fixed the epochs of their history and the limits of their territory," and adds that God's purpose in all of this was that "they were to seek God" (Acts 17:26,27 – NEB). Because man was created distinct from all else in God's creation and yet was a part of it, man stood in the relationship of fellowship with God and under his Lordship. This privileged relationship, which determines man's duty, has not changed because man fell into sin.[9]

This knowledge has come to man through revelation. The revelation man received established for him the "genuine correlation between the really other-worldly God and really this-worldly world." History in a sense different from that which most nations conceive it to be is now possible. There arises a history of which no inkling is found in classical myths: the revelation and history of covenant. There is a future: this is the distinctive characteristic of Biblical history. The natural myths of the classical worlds could only speak of perpetual recurrence.[10] The revelation of Scripture is not to be thought of as being static. The Old Testament is a unity in growth and development. Each stage of the development has its own uniqueness and must be considered in the light of the whole. Social history in the Old Testament is interpreted religiously, i.e., in terms of the activity of God.[11]

5 J. H. Bavinck, *Science of Missions*, p. 12. J. Blauw, *The Missionary Nature*, p. 19.

6 As an illustration we can choose the Japanese people whose indigenous religion traces their origin to the Sun Goddess.

7 Gen. 1:31; Ps. 104:24.

8 G. F. Vicedom, *The Mission of God*, pp. 15-18, develops this idea fully and expresses man's relationship to God as a "vis-a-vis" relationship. He finds in this relationship the distinctive element in the nature of man which makes possible the divine communication and universal covenant of salvation.

9 The probationary command (Gen. 2:16, 17) illustrates the sovereign lordship of God over man, as does God's act of setting man in the Garden to "till and keep it" (Gen. 2:15). God in a very immediate and real way is continuing to exercise his sovereignty in spite of man's rebellion.

10 This section was adapted from Ethelbert Stauffer, *Christ and the Caesars*, translated by K. and R. Gregor Smith (Philadelphia: The Westminster Press, 1955), p. 25. Modern illustrations of religions that teach cyclic recurrence can be found in Buddhism and Hinduism.

11 This thought is developed more fully in Harold Henry Rowley, *The Faith of Israel: Aspects of Old Testament Thought* (Philadelphia: The Westminster Press, 1956),

The concept of creation as taught in the Scripture is the basis for the proclamation of God's sovereignty over the whole world, including its peoples. David could sing, "The earth is the Lord's and the fulness thereof, the world and those who dwell therein; for he has founded it upon the seas, and established it upon the rivers" (Ps. 24:1,2). This is a constantly recurring theme in the Psalms of Israel. People sing only of things that are closest to their thoughts and hearts. This formed the basis for the constant challenge Israel in its songs threw out to the nations of the world to recognize and honor Yahweh. "By the waters of Babylon . . . our captors required of us songs, and our tormentors mirth, saying, Sing us one of the songs of Zion!" And of what did these homesick captives sing? Of Yahweh's sovereignty and of creation! God made the world and he made it good! The tribes of earth are held accountable to God who at no time relinquishes his authority over them, who presides as their judge, and who uses them to his purposes. The apostle asks, "Is God the God of Jews only? Is he not the God of the Gentiles also? Yes, of the Gentiles also, since God is one" (Rom. 3:29). One of the surprises in store for the pagan when he reads the book of Genesis is the discovery that all mankind traces its genealogy to one common ancestor, "Adam, the son of God" (Luke 3:38). All peoples belong to one family. Genesis strips away the peculiar pride of heathenism — its self-deification — and reveals man as he is: wretched, fallen, guilty, but by grace and mercy redeemable. It is no wonder that Bavinck calls the Bible "a Book for the Mission Field" and stresses the importance of the Genesis accounts.[12] Not only do all nations come from Yahweh; they are used by him as his instrument and must bow to his judgment.[13]

While other religions in the ancient world taught that the gods had chosen their tribe and people exclusively, Israel continued to declare that while Yahweh whom it served had chosen Israel for his people and set his name upon them, this did not mean that Yahweh was a local deity, bound to a single place or nation or land. Pharoah of Egypt may not agree with Moses and Aaron that "the LORD, the God of Israel" had the right to command him to let his people go that they might serve him and have a feast to him in the wilderness ("Who is the LORD, that I should heed his voice and let Israel go? I do not know the LORD, and moreover I will not let Israel go" — Ex. 5:1,2), but this does not change the purpose of God which was far greater than merely a controversy with Pharoah about the question of sovereignty over the people of Israel. The Lord said, "For this purpose I have let you live to show you my power, so that my name may be declared throughout the earth" (Ex. 9:16).

p. 14; also in Paul Sevier Minear, *And Great Shall Be Your Reward* (New Haven: Yale University Press, 1941), p. 1ff.

12 J. H. Bavinck, *The Impact of Christianity*, p. 123.

13 See Albrecht Alt, "Die Deutung der Weltgeschichte im Alten Testament," *ZThK*, 56 (1959), pp. 129-137. The decalogue in forbidding idolatry stresses this same claim. On this see Walther Eichrodt, "Gottes Volk und die Völker," *EMM*, 86 (1942), pp. 129-145.

That this was the result of the great wonders done for the deliverance of Israel is testified to by Rahab who tells the spies, "We have heard how the LORD dried up the water of the Red Sea . . . for the LORD your God is he who is God in heaven above and on earth beneath" (Josh. 2:10-11) Their LORD could be served wherever men turned to him in truth.[14] Nor did the revelation of Yahweh at any time indicate that he had chosen Israel and Jerusalem to the exclusion of all other cities, lands and nations.[15]

Solomon was conscious of this, for in his dedicatory prayer he acknowledged that "heaven and the highest heaven cannot contain thee; how much less this house that I have built" (II Chron. 9:18). His prayer also included a significant paragraph for the foreigner who seeks God that he may be heard and accepted (II Chron. 7:32-33). Jonah's words, "I am a Hebrew; and I fear the LORD, the God of heaven, who made the sea and the dry land," struck terror in the hearts of superstitious and endangered sailors when he confessed that he was disobediently running away from Yahweh (Jonah 1:9,10); the sailors and later Nineveh turn to the Lord. Assurance is given Cyrus and the the people of Israel in Isaiah 45 in terms of Yahweh's creative work and continuing providential government of all things; no gods of the heathen can be compared to him (Isa. 46). Ezra, having separated the returned captives from all foreigners and led them in confession of sin, began his prayer with the thought of the incomparable greatness of Israel's God in this way, "Thou art the Lord, thou alone; thou hast made the heaven, the heaven of heavens, with all their host, the earth and all that is on it, the seas and all that is in them; and thou preservest them" (Neh. 9:6). One cannot possess such a revelation without something happening in the working out of a man's or a people's destiny. Without a foundation such as this, no mission, Old or New Testament, would have any meaning.

Significantly, although a large part of the Old Testament is concerned with

14 J. L. Koole, *De Joden in de Verstrooiing*, p. 12. See also II Chron. 6:14 and especially Acts 10:34, "Truly I perceive that God shows no partiality, but in every nation anyone who fears him and does what is right is acceptable to him."
15 See II Chron. 7:11-22. God indeed accepts the temple and Jerusalem as the place where he will meet with and dwell among his people, toward which they may pray, where they may sacrifice, but the enjoyment and fulfillment of this promise depends on their faithful obedience in response to his grace. Israel was also warned that the house, the city, the land and the people could be abandoned in strict accord with his justice and righteousness and as a testimony to the nations (vs. 20). What is important to see in this entire passage is that David may have planned and Solomon may have builded, but the designation and acceptance of Jerusalem is repeatedly ascribed in the narrative to Yahweh's sovereign choice. It is this choice by God which provided Israel and the nations access to him. Man does not first come to God: God first comes to man (Gen. 3:8). This does not escape the attention of the Queen of Sheba who recognized that Solomon was king because God loved Israel (II Chron. 9:8). See also Jacques Ellul, *The Meaning of the City*, translated by Dennis Pardee (Grand Rapids: Eerdmans, 1970), pp. 94-112.

the redemptive work of God through Abraham and his seed, Israel, one cannot escape the conclusion that Yahweh is not Israel's God exclusively. He is concerned with the fate of all mankind. It does not matter how distant they were, as far away as the isles of the sea or neighbors on Israel's borders, God set their bounds and he did so in relation to his people Israel (Deut. 32:8). Although this verse has the clear sense of a special care of God for the people of Israel, it is as much concerned to make clear that the God who has a heritage and portion in his people also maintains a claim to the inheritance he has for the nations. The rabbis recognized this, for in the Talmud it is said that the Torah was given in the wilderness, in a no-man's land, so that Israel could not claim it as its own and withhold it from others. Also, so that the other nations could not have an excuse for not accepting it, God gave it in the wilderness so that everyone who desires may accept it.[16]

The significance and importance of this cannot be overstressed. God did indeed elect from among the nations of the world the nation of Israel to belong to him. He allowed the other nations to remain under the bondage of their self-chosen disobedience and under servitude to the demons to whom they sacrificed.[17] But he also elected Israel, called and set it in the midst of the very nations who had disobeyed him. God's election of Israel may not be thought of either as an arbitrary act in which God left all the other nations to themselves in order to show preference to Israel or as an abandonment of these nations without concern for them. Israel's election is God's service to the nations, his love to the world. Through election other nations were included in the promise (Gen. 12:1 ff.). O. Weber observes, "The Bible does not begin with the God who elects but with the God who is the Creator and therefore the God who can elect."[18] God called Israel into his service for the service of the nations.

The book of Genesis is the biblical account of the opening acts of the world drama in which Israel and the nations were involved in their days and we in ours.[19] Referring to the creation of man, D. T. Niles says:

> Man is the only creature God has made whose being is not in himself and who by himself is nought. The "dogness" of the dog is in the dog, but the

16 Mekiltah Bahodesh I in the *J.T.*, (62a and 72a). See also Jacob Z. Lauterbach, "The Pharisees and Their Teachings", *HUCA*, VI, 69-139, especially p. 134.

17 Compare Deut. 32:17 and I Cor. 10:20. See also F. Hahn, *Mission in the New Testament*, p. 18, especially n. 2.

18 Otto Weber, *Bibelkunde des Alten Testaments* (Tübingen: Furche Verlag, 1947), p. 42. This is also referred to in G. F. Vicedom, *The Mission of God*, p. 48. Vicedom summarizes the position of Johannes Blauw with respect to the relationship of God's people to the world and Israel's attitude toward the heathen; see pp. 47ff.

19 D. M. Eichhorn, *Conversion to Judaism*, p. 13. See also Charles Franklin Kraft, *Genesis* (New York: Women's Division of Christian Service, Board of Missions, The Methodist Church, 1964), p. 4.

"manness" of man is not in the man. It is in his relation to God. Man is man because he reflects God, and only when he does so.[20]

Not only is Yahweh the God of all men; Jesus Christ is also the Savior for all men. The question of the missionary nature of the church which Christ has appointed to proclaim the universal covenant of salvation will not be solved, as Johannes Blauw states, "until we have investigated the relation between Israel and the nations of the earth. Genesis 1-11 is fundamental to this understanding."[21]

This question occupied the foreground in the very first recorded communication of God with Abram: ". . . In you all the families of the earth will be blessed."[22] The prophets were given increasingly clearer understanding through revelation of the relationship of Israel and the nations.[23] The repeated phrase in the New Testament, "Jew and Gentile," reminds us that at the time of the beginning of the Christian mission the problem had still not been solved. A large part of Paul's letter to the Ephesians deals with the subject.[24] The story of the development of the Christian mission as told by Luke in the Acts indicates the need for clarification of the relationship for the early church. The indissoluble unity of all men, Jew as well as Gentile, in Christ was put into effect only after long and strenuous discussion, occasioning even differences of opinion and practice between apostles.[25] In the New Testament the subject of Israel and non-Israel, Jew and Gentile, involves the question of the significance both of the Old Testament covenant and of the universal covenant in Christ.[26] No single fact so aroused the enmity of the Jews as to be told that God sent the apostles to bring salvation to the Gentiles.[27]

It is important for this discussion to remember that the table of nations makes no mention of Israel. Von Rad says about this, "Israel is hid in the loins of Arpachshad."[28] Israel is not the focal point of the nations. When Israel looked back into history, she could only conclude that she was but one of the historical

20 Daniel Thambyrajah Niles, *Studies in Genesis* (Philadelphia: Westminster Press, 1958), pp. 60-61.

21 Johannes Blauw, "The Mission of the People of God" in C. West and D. M. Paton, *The Missionary Church*, p. 91.

22 Genesis 12:1-3. I shall not enter at this time into the question of the reflexive form of the verb in this passage. This will receive attention at a later time in this dissertation (cf. n. 41, chap. I). R. Martin-Achard, *A Light to the Nations*, p. 33ff.

23 Attention is called to Isaiah 2 as representative of a large number of prophetic utterances of similar character.

24 For an analysis of the question of the unity of the church and Israel as taught in Ephesians, see M. Barth, *The Broken Wall*, pp. 123-136. Also, Arthur Gabriel Hebert, *The Throne of David* (London: Faber and Faber, 1940), pp. 234ff.

25 Consider the controversy of Peter and Paul as told in Galatians 2:11-16.

26 F. Hahn, *Mission in the New Testament*, p. 17.

27 Acts 6 & 7; 11:1-3; 13:46-50; 21:19-22; 22:21-22; 26:19-21; 28:28.

28 G. von Rad, *Old Testament Theology*, p. 162. See also Gen. 10:22. Johannes Verkuyl, *Breek de Muren Af!* (Baarn: Bosch & Keuning, 1969), pp. 16-22.

nations. Israel was the first people to think of itself as nation. All others (Egypt and Babylon, e.g.) thought of themselves as the world.[29]

> It is in this idea of the nations, in which no nation enjoys preference over another, that ancient Israel most widely diverged from the ancient Mesopotamian ideas of the universe. The cosmic order in which Old Babylonia stood was that of the state in which the whole universe was built up of and beneficially governed by the gods. Its state was a "cosmic empire" inasmuch as the whole state was itself a universal order, an original cosmic datum.[30]

This was not the case with Israel. Israel was one of many, and the universal sovereignty of God extended to all.

The importance of God's creative act for all men finds startling emphasis in the early Christian Church. A brief survey of the prayers of the disciple group in the first months and years after Pentecost reveals how frequently the church appealed to God as Creator. When Peter and John report what happened to them when they were arraigned by the Sanhedrin, the church prayed, "Sovereign Lord, who didst make heaven and the earth and the sea and everything in them . . ." (Acts 4:24).

When the apostles and others addressed audiences comprised of Jewish people predominantly, they frequently started with a reference to Abraham or to some other person or event in Jewish history,[31] but when they addressed predominantly non-Jewish groups, they generally began their speech with reference to creation and/or the unity of the human race.[32] Fellowships composed of believers from among both Jews and Gentiles were generally reminded of the fact that there was no longer a distinction among those who were in Christ.[33] The Bible has no plural form for the name Israel, because there cannot be two peoples of God. The whole human race belongs to God, who has never surrendered his claim to man.[34] His salvation has meaning only if it is inclusive of mankind.[35] What is so tragic about the world is that man always

29 Gerardus van der Leeuw, *Religion in Essence and Manifestation* (London: Allan & Unwin, Ltd., 1938), p. 270.

30 G. von Rad, *Old Testament Theology*, p. 162.

31 Acts 2:16; 2:29 3:13; 5:30; 7:2; 13:17; 22:14; 24:14; 26:6; 28:17, 23.

32 Acts 10:34; 14:15; 17:24. See also F. Hahn, *Mission in the New Testament*, p. 135, n. 1, who has a very fine bibliography for those who would like to pursue this further.

33 Acts 10:34; 11:12; 13:26; 13:46; 15:9; 20:21.

34 This must be affirmed, it seems to me, in opposition to those who take the claims of the Evil One too seriously and forget the whole emphasis of Scripture. Man's rebellion accomplished nothing effective in terms of limiting God's sovereignty. Even in the temptations when Jesus is offered the kingdoms of the world, his reply shows that he does not acknowledge Satan's claim to them. He makes his own counterclaim in the way of obedience to the one true God and his will.

35 It should be remembered that in this dissertation the words "for all men," "all mankind," "universal," "inclusive," etc. when used with respect to salvation in Christ do not mean that all men will be saved, but that mankind as a race is offered salvation.

seeks a unity of his own (e.g., at Babel), a unity in disobedience. God promises man unity in the universal covenant through Abraham (Genesis 12). At no point is humanity more broken than at the point of its separation from God's people.[36]

A true understanding of the world as created by God gives us a world-wide perspective. A Christian can never view the world except in the context of God as the God of all men, the whole world as subject to him and history as the sphere of his redemptive activity. While it is true that the nonbeliever is not without some kind of world perspective, it is impossible to discover the proper historical relationship of world events apart from faith in and reference to the God to whom heaven and earth belong. In the Bible God tells men of himself, not as a God in abstraction from his creation but one who loves the world, who wills, plans and works in his world, who will be known by men when they believe in him, will be experienced when they love and serve him and are taken by grace into his universal covenant. Man's new deeds of violence and disobedience are always met in history with more grace, more goodness. Even at Babel God (whom Blauw in this context describes as the "shattering and scattering God") disrupts in order to restrain man's sin (Gen. 11:6-8).[37] Babel becomes the place of non-communication, the place where man is prevented from effective communication with other men, where his rejection of God's will results in his dispersion and confusion, and an end to his building. Babel becomes a symbol of man's inability to finish anything, to make anything last so long as he does not take into account his relationship to his creator. Men had to learn that it is only when God says "Come" and gathers them in His gracious will for their salvation that mankind can really be gathered again from its dispersion and wandering into a lasting city that has foundations, eternal, in the heavens. And this experience of God's grace does not depend on whether he is a Jew or a non-Jew.[38]

Nor does this allow men to think or talk of God and the world without becoming personally involved as though he may legitimately by the use of abstract and general terms discuss man's relationship to God. Markus Barth has demonstrated from the book of Ephesians that

> what knowledge God has given us of men makes us recognize God's mercy for men, and our solidarity with even the most renegade and obstinate sinners forbids us from presuming to be God's appointed state's attorney

36   J. Jocz, *Christians and Jews: Encounter and Mission*, pp. 44-45; C. C. West and D. M. Paton, *The Missionary Church*, p. 92.

37   Johannes Blauw, "The Mission of the People of God" in C. C. West and D. M. Paton, *The Missionary Church*, p. 92.

38   For a full treatment of the character of man's rebellion and failures at Babel see Jacques Ellul, *The Meaning of the City*, chapter 1: "The Builders," pp. 1-43. J. Verkuyl, *Breek de Muren Af!*, p. 22, speaks appropriately of mankind's "solidariteit in schuld" ("solidarity in guilt").

> against them .... We will be faithful to God and act according to our
> salvation when we plead before God as if we were *their* attorneys.[39]

Conclusion: The teaching of Genesis that God is the creator of the world and of man in his image is foundational to missions. Because God "has made from one every nation of men to live on all the face of the earth" (Acts 17:26), no individual or race may consider itself above others. Rather, the election by the Creator is for special service to all mankind. Man has been created by God, is dependent on him, is answerable to him, in rebellion against him, but at the same time is the object of God's redemptive, seeking love. History in the Bible is the record of God's redemptive activity for the sake of humanity.

B. *The Universal Covenant: Genesis 12*

A new period of salvation history begins with Abraham (Gen. 12 ff.). A close relationship is established between the nations and the forefather of the Chosen People (Gen. 12:3).[40] At the very outset the emphasis lies on the importance of God's redemptive purpose for all mankind in the patriarch Abram. "In you all the families of the earth shall be blessed" (Gen. 12:3).

This declaration is repeated in somewhat different forms in other places.[41] Paul in Gal. 3:8 calls this promise the Gospel: "And the Scripture foreseeing that God would justify the Gentiles by faith, preached the Gospel beforehand to Abraham, saying, In you shall all the nations be blessed." He follows the translation of the LXX here which renders the Hebrew as a passive not as a reflexive. No matter which translation is accepted for Gen. 12:3, it is undeniable that Abraham has an important role in God's redemptive plan for all mankind. If the reflexive form is accepted, (as found in the text of the RSV), then the meaning is that Abraham's world-wide reputation results from Yahweh's blessing of Abraham and his descendants. Abraham and his seed only respond

39 M. Barth, *The Broken Wall*, p. 261ff. Although Barth discusses this in relationship to the question of universalism of salvation, his argument serves as a challenge to the church today with respect to the spirit in which we carry forward our witness and the manner in which we pray for the world.

40 R. Martin-Achard, *A Light to the Nations*, p. 35, observes that Gen. 12:1ff. "marks a turning point – a beginning as well as an end: with it the history of the primordial period (Urgeschichte) – Gen. 1-11 – comes to a close, and with it the age of the promise (Gen. 12ff.) begins."

41 See the following: Gen. 18:17, 18; 22:18; 26:4; 28:14. In three of these passages the Hebrew uses the *niphal* (Gen. 12, 18, 28) while in two places the *hithpael* is used (Gen. 22 and 26). Variations in these texts are also of interest, although none changes the basic meaning of the first revelation. Gen. 18 speaks of "all the nations." Gen. 22 states that the nations shall bless themselves "by your descendants," as does Gen. 26. "By you and your descendants" and "all the families of the earth" are the phrases used in Gen. 28.

in obedience to the divine initiative. If one takes the passive form (as found in the footnote of the RSV), the divine initiative is still in the foreground since God's activity in Abraham's election is for the good of all the nations of the earth. "Abraham is chosen, not just for his own glory, the good fortune of his descendants, or the misery of his enemies; rather, with him Yahweh begins a new chapter in the history of man. Abraham is the instrument for the redemption of the world." [42] The curse upon mankind at Babel becomes the blessing through Abraham. The God who dispersed mankind by the confusion of language now commits himself to gather them again into an elect community through the Gospel of the promise.

This gathering of and the salvation of the Gentiles is represented in the New Testament not as the covenant to the fathers but the case of the Creator (Acts 14:15-17; 17:22-31).[43] It was necessary to remind the Jews that Abraham was God's means to an end: the salvation for all mankind. Gentiles had to see in Christ the claim of the Creator. Gelin finds in the promise of Gen. 12 a divine purpose: "The promise 'in thee shall all the nations of the earth be blessed' lies behind the whole Bible and makes it the book of hope." [44] When in the later unfolding through the prophets of God's great vision for mankind this blessing for all nations was revealed in the form of a Golden Age, it was tacitly recognized (see especially Deutero-Isaiah) that there could be no Golden Age for Israel unless the world, shared in it.[45] From Abraham onward history would unfold under the sign of the blessing offered all men through Abraham. What is said about Abraham is later transferred to his seed (Gen. 22:18). This was the oath to the Fathers for which Yahweh set his love on Israel (Deut. 7:7,8).[46]

But why Abraham? Jewish writers also asked this question. The question arose most naturally in later years, especially in the proselyting Judaism of the Dispersion. Would-be proselytes enquired why God selected Abraham to be the

---

42   R. Martin-Achard, *A Light to the Nations*, p. 35.

43   F. Hahn, *Mission in the New Testament*, p. 135.

44   Albert Gelin, *The Key Concepts of the Old Testament*, translated by George Lamb from the French *Les Idées Maîtresses de l'Ancient Testament* (New York: Sheed and Ward, 1955), p. 36.

45   H. H. Rowley, *The Faith of Israel*, p. 180.

46   It is important to observe in this text (Deut. 7:7-8) that Israel, a holy (i.e., separated) nation, was freed from bondage in order to provide the means whereby God might fulfill the oath to the fathers. Blessing and curse are likewise emphasized in the context, but in this case it becomes clear that the enemies do not merely hate Israel but the Lord who chose Israel (vs. 10). Gerhard von Rad, *Das erste Buch Mose*, (4th ed., Göttingen, 1956), p. 133ff., holds that the promise in Gen. 12:3 is more than just a promise to Abraham and his descendants. He stresses the relation of this text to the previous chapters (Genesis 1-11) and concludes that Gen. 12 represents a program of action in which Yahweh reveals his plan for mankind. Gen. 12 is the connecting link between the primordial period and the history of Israel. See also R. Martin-Achard, *A Light to the Nations*, p. 36, who says that "Genesis 12 has universalistic implications."

father of the chosen people while the born Jew simply took this for granted.[47] Joshua had suggested the answer a long time before (Josh. 24:2, 3), emphasizing the sovereignty of the divine initiative and recalling the idolatry of the fathers beyond the Euphrates before God called Abraham. The rabbis did not fail in later centuries to call Abraham the first proselyte.[48] Eichhorn states that today twice a year in the synagogue the Jews recite Deut. 26:5 to recall that Abraham was not born an Israelite, adding that "from the inception of this folk and faith, the religion of Israel was born with and born by converts."[49] Julius Lewy has supplied some erudite evidence showing that etymologically the word "hebrew" is not a proper noun designating a specific people, but that it was a widely used general Semitic term signifying a resident alien, an immigrant, refugees, uprooted peoples, displaced persons.[50] The choice of this term in Gen. 14:13 as a designation for Abraham emphasizes the sovereign election by God of whomsoever he wills. It is also a remarkable demonstration of how one who was himself dispersed by the command of God ("Go from your country and your kindred and your father's house to the land that I will show you" – Gen. 12:1) became the gracious instrument by which those who had been dispersed by judgment ("So the LORD scattered them abroad from there over all the face of the earth" – Gen. 11:8) will again be brought back to the only source of life, and into unity with each other. And this unity will be expressed in a common life.

God performs this act of grace by means of covenant. "Every divine-human covenant in Scripture," says Meredith Kline, "involves a sanction-sealed commitment to maintain a particular relationship or follow a stipulated course of action. In general, then, a covenant may be defined as a relationship under sanctions."[51] Philip Potter defines covenant with reference to the purpose, "Covenants in the Near East were a means by which relationships were entered into by unrelated persons or peoples on a basis of community of interests and purpose in order to maintain these interests and fufull the purpose."[52] He points out, however, that the covenants in Scripture differ in significant ways from the eastern covenants even though they follow the general pattern of the semitic covenants: (1) Covenants were never made between gods and people

47 Wilfred Lawrence Knox, "Abraham and the Quest for God," in *Harvard Theological Review*, XXVIII (January 1935), pp. 55-60.
48 Cf. *BT, AZ*, 44-45; Suk. 232; Hag. 8.
49 D. M. Eichhorn, *Conversion to Judaism*, p. 14. *BT, AZ*, 44-45.
50 Julius Lewy, "Origin and Significance of the Biblical term 'Hebrew'" in *HUCA*, XXIV (1957), pp. 1-13.
51 Meredith G. Kline, *By Oath Consigned: A Reinterpretation of the Covenant Signs of Circumcision and Baptism* (Grand Rapids: Wm. B. Eerdmans, 1968), p. 16, henceforth to be cited as *By Oath Consigned.*
52 H. Berkhof and P. Potter, *Key Words of the Gospel*, p. 25. See also M. G. Kline, *By Oath Consigned*, p. 14. Walther Eichrodt, *Theology of the Old Testament* (Philadelphia, 1961), I. Eichrodt assigns the central and unifying place to the covenant in the religious development of the Old Testament.

24

among non-Israelite nations; (2) in the Old Testament God is always the subject of the covenant and he lays down the conditions;[53] (3) God's actions are based on his free sovereign will; and (4) God's benefits are for all and not a select few.

These considerations make it possible to see how the covenant of God in its various administrations works to the salvation of God's people. The suzerains of the semitic covenants were not able to guarantee the fulfillment of the promises, the implementation of the covenant conditions, or to preserve the loyalty of their subjects. But Yahweh is the God who is the sovereign Lord of creation and therefore of election and grace, who is indeed not only able but desirous of guaranteeing the eternal blessing of the covenant to his people. Therefore, Kline writes, "God's covenant with man may be defined as an administration of God's lordship, consecrating a people to himself under the sanctions of divine law," and adds, "The overall unity of the covenants will be provided by the concept of the kingdom of God of which they are so many manifestations."[54]

Examining the meaning of the words "bless" and "curse," Philip Potter brings all these ideas together in this translation of Gen. 12:1-2

> I will make you a powerful and extensive community. I will be with you and support and strengthen you, so that you can support and strengthen others. I will strengthen those who acknowledge and accept strength, and he who refuses to have fellowship with you, who turns away from you, who treats you with contempt, I will abandon him and let him perish. Through you all the families of the earth will find their true being and strength. In a word through you will I fulfill the purpose of man's creation.[55]

53 Quoting Eichrodt, M. G. Kline, *By Oath Consigned*, p. 14: "The idea that in ancient Israel the b'rith was always and only thought of as Yahweh's pledging of himself, to which human effort was required (is) proved erroneous."

54 M. G. Kline, *By Oath Consigned*, pp. 36-37. Kline feels that the terms "Covenant of Works" and "Covenant of Grace" are both deficient and prefers as a general unifying term "the Covenant of the Kingdom," the two major divisions of which would be "Covenant of Creation" and "Covenant of Redemption," both of which unfold the concept of God's lordship. This absolute sovereignty of God prevents the covenants from degenerating into a *quid pro quo* contract (referring to W. Eichrodt, *Theology of the Old Testament*, I, p. 44).

55 H. Berkhof and P. Potter, *Key Words of the Gospel*, pp. 25-28. On the nature of semitic covenants see Meredith Kline, *Treaty of the Great King* (Grand Rapids: Eerdmans, 1963), pp. 27-46; M. G. Kline, *By Oath Consigned*, pp. 13-18; Walter Brueggemann, *Tradition for Crisis* (Richmond: John Press, 1968), pp. 1-96. Each of these volumes is amply documented by references to the latest scholarship in German and English with respect to covenant structures. Martin Buber, *Kingship of God*, translated by Richard Scheimann from the German, *Das Königtums Gottes,* (New York and Evanston: Harper and Row, 1967), p. 125, points out that B'rith is not limited to an agreement which establishes a "community of interest" between two parties until then strangers to each other. It may also alter an existing relationship, compress, clarify, occasionally just sanction it, grant it sacred protection, re-establish one that has been broken, or consecrate anew one that has been called into question.

The ultimate destiny and blessing of the nations takes place in the events that happen to Abraham and his seed. Abraham and his family stand at the cross-roads of history.[56] Grayzel states this effectively in this way:

> The history of the Jews is not an isolated adventure, nor a life lived far away from the crowded highways of civilization. On the contrary, hardly an important event happened in the history of the world but that Jews played some part in it. Sometimes the event affected them after it happened; sometimes they themselves helped to bring the event about; but at all times they were there, anxious and eager participants in humanity's struggles and progress.[57]

God's redemptive program for mankind is moving forward and although from necessity this will require that the narrative will appear to become more and more exclusive (Abraham-Isaac-Jacob-Judah-David-Christ, e.g.) this does not mean that the purpose of God has therefore been altered. God neither surrenders his claim upon the nations, nor does he abandon his purposes for the nations. The divine blessing is mediated to the world through Abraham and the chosen people.

In this early covenant for the nations the essential features basic to the missionary task are to be found. Although, as many have observed, there is here no command to evangelize as is commonly thought of in the New Testament sense,[58] that chapter of redemptive history that begins with Abraham positively affirms the Lordship of Yahweh over all the nations, (for he has created them and directs their history), that God has a purpose for all nations which he is working out through Abraham, and that election is for service, not merely personal advantage.

A word must be said concerning the treatment of Abraham and God's purpose through him as he is represented in various sources – the Scriptures, apocrypha, pseudipegrapha, Josephus, Graeco-Roman writers, Philo, Talmud, etc.[59] The rabbis taught that Abraham was the first proselyte,[60] and that he

56 Theophile James Meek, "The Interpenetration of Cultures as Illustrated by the Character of the Old Testament Literature," *JR*, VII, no. 3 (May, 1927), 244-262, says on p. 244, "If history has taught us anything it has taught us this: nations never lived in water-tight compartments in splendid isolation from each other; and least of all did the Hebrew nation, situated as they were on the great highroad between East and West. . . . Instead of developing their unique characteristics because of isolation from the world, it was actually because of it."

57 S. Grayzel, *History of the Jews*, p. 1.

58 F. Hahn, *Mission in the New Testament*, p. 20, says, "We may say that in the Old Testament there is no mission in the real sense. There is an absence of a divine commission for the purpose of any conscious outgoing to the Gentiles to win them for belief in Jahweh."

59 The best, most extensive and inclusive collection of these materials I have found is in Samuel Sandmel, *Philo's Place in Judaism: A Study of Conceptions of Abraham in Jewish Literature* (Cincinnati: Hebrew Union College Press, 1956), henceforth to be cited

made converts and brought them under the wings of the Shekinah.[61] The persons whom Abraham and Sarah had gotten in Haran (Gen. 12:5) were said to be people whom they had converted from idolatry.[62] In their exegesis of Gen. 12:8 the rabbis extolled him as a great missionary who "caused all creatures to proclaim the name of God."[63] In one place Abraham, Isaac and Jacob are described as repulsing Timnah (Gen. 36:40) who became the concubine of Esau's son Eliphaz and the mother of Amalek. The affliction of Israel by Amalek was ascribed by the rabbis to this repulse given Timnah when she wanted to be a proselyte. It is interesting to note that in this story Timnah sought the patriarchs and not vice versa.[64] In the rabbinic literature in general the rabbis read back into the career of Abraham their own interests and concerns. They picture Abraham in such a way that whoever imitates Abraham would by that token be conforming to the highest of rabbinic standards and be an executor of rabbinic laws.[65] Abraham is therefore not so much an example of a man whose faith compelled him to witness as he is an example substantiating the rabbinic ideals of work righteousness. The rabbis did remind the people that the fact "that Israel had a covenant does not make Israel more precious than proselytes, for the 'homeborn' of Abraham also had a covenant."[66]

That Abraham occupies a significant and central role in the history of redemption cannot be disputed. The New Testament references to him in this role are numerous. That place, however, is not first of all understood and revealed as being for himself but for the true Israel that would be born by faith as he was.[67]

---

as *Philo's Place*. Unfortunately the main title is a bit restrictive and misleading since the author's material is far broader than a study of Philo. See also Louis Ginzberg, *Legends of the Jews*, translated by Henrietta Szold, (7 vols., Philadelphia: The Jewish Publication Society of America, 1909-1928). I have omitted references to the Church Fathers as being outside the scope of this paper. The Talmud is included, however, since as Jacob Bernard Bamberger observes in *JBL*, 68 (1949), 115-123, "The ascription of a statement to a particular rabbi gives us only a *terminus ad quem*, since the rabbi may be quoting much more ancient material." The full text for all these sources can be found in Theodore Reinach, *Textes d'auteurs grecs et romains relatifs au Judaïsme* (Paris: E. Leroux, 1895), henceforth to be cited as *Textes*.

60 Hag. 8. This judgment concerning Abraham is based on an interpretation of Ps. 47:10. See alzo AZ 44-45, Suk. 232.

61 Cf. Genesis 17:13. Makilta, Mashpatim 18.

62 AZ 44-45.

63 W. G. Braude, *Jewish Proselyting*, p. 26.

64 San. 674.

65 See S. Sandmel, *Philo's Place*, p. 95.

66 *Ibid.*, p. 85.

67 J. H. Piet, *The Road Ahead*, p. 79, writes: "Abraham stands for two things (in Galatians 4): he is at one time both an individual and the embodiment of all Israel. Abraham is the latter in the sense that when he, in obedience to God's command, left his ancestors, he was the first Israelite and the incorporation of all Israel both as a nation and as a religious group. Like Adam and Christ, he is an individual, who incorporates the many. Paul himself describes Abraham as 'our father according to the flesh' (4:1)

Albrecht Alt has provided a very helpful interpretation of the Scriptural phrase, "I am the God of Abraham, Isaac, and Jacob." Alt has compared this epithet with similar divine epithets in Transjordanian inscriptions of the Nabataean age. He concludes that the phrase "the god of so-and-so" means the same thing in Scripture as it does in these inscriptions: this is the first man (in that social group; in Scripture, Abraham and his seed) to worship this deity; this god formerly unknown has revealed himself to this man; therefore, this god is designated among his descendants as his god. He says,

> There sprouts into growth the first bud of a totally different phenomenon from that which we find in the local and nature deities: no attachment of the divine being to a large or small parcel of earth, but its alliance to human life, at first to an individual and later through this to a whole group.[68]

The meaning of the covenant sign of circumcision is important for reaching an understanding of the purpose of Israel in the redemptive plan of God. This is necessary because the question of the necessity of circumcision was often at the very heart of the question of the manner in which non-Israelities were to be admitted to the fellowship of the people of God. In the early church no little controversy was stirred up over the question whether Gentiles needed to be circumcised in order to be saved (Acts 15; Galatians). The charges against Paul by the Jews of the Diaspora concerned reports that he taught "all the Jews among the Gentiles to forsake Moses, telling them not to circumcise their children or observe the customs" (Acts 21:21).

The covenant sign of circumcision was given to Abraham and his seed in the ritual of covenant ratification found in Gen. 17. Circumcision was not unknown among the Western Semites. Egyptians, Syrians and Phoenicians all practiced the rite.[69] Among Abraham's family and descendants this was to serve as a covenantal sign (Gen. 17::1-27), administered to those born in the house, slaves of the household, and slaves acquired by purchase. Meyer summarizes this as follows:

and 'the father of many nations' (4:17). A. G. Hebert, *The Throne of David*, p. 73, says, "The justification of mankind by faith in Jesus was integral to God's purpose from the beginning." Five times this appears in relation to Abraham: Gen. 12:3; 18:18; 22:18; 26:5; 28:14.

68 Albrecht Alt, *The God of the Patriarchs*, p. 41, quoted by Marin Buber, *The Prophetic Faith*, translated from the Hebrew by Carlyre Witton Davies (New York: The Macmillan Co., 1949), p. 41.

69 Rudolf Meyer, περιτέμνω in Gerhard Kittel, *Theological Dictionary of the New Testament*, translated by Geoffrey W. Bromiley (Grand Rapids: Eerdmans, 1965ff.), VI, 72-84, henceforth to be cited as *TWNT*. One fine feature of the English translation is that with but occasional slight variations the volume and pages follow the German original, facilitating reference to either edition. A brief summary of Egyptian practices in relation to Israel can be found in Clarence J. Vos, *Woman in Old Testament Worship* (Delft: Judels & Brinkman, 1968), pp. 51-59.

> If all the descendants of Abraham are distinguished from those around them by circumcision, Israel is itself distinguished from kindred tribes by the fact that through circumcision its people are set in covenant with God in the true sense, so that the promises apply to them alone, vs. 4-7.[70]

Jacob's sons in Genesis 34 insisted that the men of Shechem be circumcised before intermarriage would be permitted. The Shechemites understood this as an amalgamation of two peoples into one (vs. 23). Later, in the Mosaic legislation God required that any *ger* (a stranger, resident alien) among the people, resident in Palestine, who desired to keep the Passover with the people of Israel, had to be circumcised together with all the males of his house (Ex. 12:48). Israel's re-circumcision in the time of Joshua (Josh. 5) included all the descendants of all the males who had come out of Egypt. This included obviously those from the mixed multitude. A careful reading of the Old Testament legislation concerning circumcision leads to the conclusion that this rite was intended to mean the incorporation of the person into a special relationship to God.

It may not be an idea entirely foreign to circumcision in its symbolic sense that it was performed on the male organ of generation to symbolize the cutting off of a man's life in his descendants, as McCarthy suggests.[71] Children are therefore given by grace to a man so cut off and his real heritage and that of his seed is found in God's covenant. Circumcision obviously meant more than separation from the world. It included the positive element of separation to God and his service as well. Its administration was tribal at first (among Abraham and his household), and later became national (at Sinai and in the Promised Land). In later centuries the question whether non-Israelites who became attached to the synagogues and communities of the Diaspora required to be circumcised was raised and its administration extended.

Our conclusion is that circumcision also had reference to the descendants of the person who swears the covenant oath. The children at one and the same time belong to the man circumcised but also to the God of the covenant. In the case of Abraham this was prominent in his circumcision. He had no heir. His circumcision symbolized the cutting off of his descendants so as to leave him without heir or name in the kingdom. But Yahweh provides. Abraham was twice given his son as it were from death: first in Isaac's birth from one "as good as dead" (Heb. 11:12), and second in the ram which was provided as a substitute for Isaac when it is said "figuratively speaking, he did receive him back (from the dead)" (Heb. 11:19-20).

70 *TWNT*, VI, 77.

71 Dennis J. McCarthy, *Treaty and Covenant* (Rome, 1963), p. 196; see also M. G. Kline, *By Oath Consigned*, p. 87. It is interesting to note that to the Romans circumcision was comparable to castration. Even the Talmud forbids an Israelite to be circumcized by a heathen because he might be accidentally castrated by him (AZ, 132). The rabbis spoke of circumcision as "being born again": see Strack-Billerbeck, *Kommentar*, II, p. 423; also O. Cullmann, *Baptism in the New Testament*, p. 57.

The descendants, therefore, were consecrated along with the recipient of circumcision to the Lord of the covenant. Thus, God commanded that the descendants, already consecrated in their father(s), should themselves be circumcised the eighth day, thereby being consecrated again and individually by the direct application of the sign of consecration to them.[72]

Circumcision played a far more important role than merely as a sign differentiating Jew from non-Jew. It was at heart an integral part of covenant ratification, a sign of admission into God's redemptive covenant. It involved the acknowledgement of Yahweh's lordship as a matter of faith and life. In God's plan there had to come a time when an Abraham would appear, when God through one man would certify anew his purpose for all men. In his obedience (which was a matter of faith)[73] he did not act as an individual but as the householder of the special community God was creating out of fallen humanity for the purpose of redemption. Although he speaks to a different context Louis Finkelstein summarizes the Jewish faith with respect to the covenant in this way: "there is no need for any ceremony to admit a Jewish child into the faith of Judaism. Born in a Jewish household, he becomes at once a 'child of the covenant.'"[74] The covenant does not consist of the rite of circumcision. The covenant means that the Jew is to serve God and be holy as God is holy. Circumcision is the external sign of this covenant.[75]

C. The Election of Israel

Any discussion of missions compels one to consider the election of Israel. Johannes Blauw has pointed out that the election of Israel stands in the foreground in the Old Testament and determines Israel's relation to God, to the land and to other peoples (see Deut. 6:10 ff.). Commenting on Deut. 7:6-8 Blauw summarizes the meaning of Israel's election under these points: (1) Israel is chosen by God for his possession; (2) this distinguishes Israel from all other nations (peoples); (3) Israel is a people that honors the Lord; (4) God has no other point of contact in Israel besides this election; (5) there is no other reason to choose any other than Israel; (6) God elects only out of love; (7) God maintains (in election) the covenant with the forefathers; and (8) the election accomplished the deliverance from Egypt. The Bible cannot be said to concern

72 M. G. Kline, *By Oath Consigned*, pp. 86-88, who demonstrates this also in connection with the circumcision of Moses and his son, and that of Israel at Gilgal (Joshua 5).

73 See Romans 4:11 and its context.

74 Louis Finkelstein, *The Jews: Their History, Culture and Religion*, (2 vols., New York: Harper and Bros., 1955), II, p. 1328. Finkelstein bases this conclusion on the fact that the covenant at Sinai was promulgated with all those present and bound their descendants as well.

75 D. M. Eichhorn, *Conversion to Judaism*, p. 15.

itself with "nationality" in our modern sense; it is concerned with "the people of God" which can apply to any group that is characterized by alliance to God, overagainst any group that does not know God and serves other gods (cf. Jer. 10:25; I Thess. 4:5).[76] John Piet states his understanding of Israel's election and its importance in this way:

> The origin of what the church thinks of itself and its election has its roots, naturally, in the Old Testament .... The issue between the Testaments is not whether God elects, but whom He chooses. The New Testament insists that the purpose God once entrusted to Israel has passed now to the church. ... This question has two parts: the one looks backward and asks, "What compels God ... to choose Israel?" The others looks forward and asks, "To what end?" The first deals with the necessity for election, and the second with what God hopes to accomplish by means of those whom He chooses. Israel answers the first part in Genesis 1 through 11 and gropes for an answer to the second throughout her long and checkered history.[77]

The questions that arise in this connection are forced on one by the fact that God made a universal covenant for all men with Abraham. Very soon this covenant took the form of a particular administration whose seal was circumcision. How are these covenants related? Also, why was it even necessary at all to bring into existence a new people, Israel? What was the purpose of its existence, the significance of its election, its relationship to the nations, and what was its mission? Has this mission terminated with the establishment of the New Testament Church? When later the public ministry of Jesus will be considered, the question will be posed in a different format: why was Jesus sent to the lost sheep of Israel? What is meant by the statement that the Gospel is for the Jew first? All these forms of the question reduce to two main considerations: what is the necessity for election, and what did God intend to accomplish through it?

The first form of the question has already been answered from the study of Genesis 1-11. These chapters are on the one hand a series of pictures of rebellion and judgment. They contain on the other hand a brilliant display of grace and mercy in the way of election. Unfortunately, election is often thought of in terms of its past reference only, in terms of privilege and honor, and of the elect as chosen to be saved and given an eternity of bliss, neglecting the real glory which is a divine purpose in redemptive plan for the future as well as the present. Election is always for a purpose.[78] The uniqueness of God's

---

76   J. Blauw, *Goden en Mensen*, pp. 5-18, especially p. 11.

77   J. H. Piet, *The Road Ahead*, p. 38. J. Blauw, *Missionary Nature*, p. 129, says, "Whoever is offended by the election of Israel will be offended by the church of Jesus Christ." J. Verkuyl, *Breek de Muren Af!*, p. 32, speaks of Israel's election as having been accomplished by God "with his eye on humanity."

78   J. H. Piet, *The Road Ahead*, pp. 38-40. Harold Henry Rowley, *The Biblical Doctrine of Election* (London: Lutterworth, 1948) treats the subject of Israel's election

choice of Israel was the uniqueness of the work which God planned to accomplish through Israel. It was his purpose to reveal himself and his will through his people; for this he also uniquely qualified and prepared them. Israel was to be Yahweh's repesentative among the peoples. As far as can be ascertained, there was no comparable concept among the nations of that day.[79] God had a purpose in choosing Israel and he would fulfill that purpose. Precisely how Israel was to be used to be a blessing to the nations was only gradually developed and made clear. From the beginning, however, this one duty was clearly stated: obedience to God (Gen. 17:1,9). The New Testament in I Pet. 2:9-10 reaffirms the election of Israel as the agent in universal redemption by applying this to the body of Christ which is the partaker of the New Covenant in Christ's blood,[80] but points out this difference: the new Israel must *"declare the wonderful deeds of him who called ... out of darkness into his marvellous light"* whereas the Old Testament Israel displayed this to the world.

Therefore, God created a new people from the very bosom of the peoples of the world. There were others who feared and believed in God in that day (e.g., Melchizedek). But God chose Abraham, "a wandering Aramean" (Deut. 26:5) out of an idolatrous family (Jos. 24:2), i.e., he was a true representative of the *fallen* race. When God's election was fulfilled in the history of Israel, the people of God continued to be a sign of the human estrangement from God which is overcome by his gracious election. In actual working out this meant that Israel was confined to the gracious dealings of God in its history and election; the heathen were to be concerned with their relationship towards Israel and its God. Johannes Blauw states that it is clear from Gen. 12:3 that the whole history of Israel is nothing but the continuation of God's dealings with the nations, and that therefore the history of Israel is only to be understood from the unsolved problem of the relation of God to the nations.[81] This is also demonstrated by the fact that redemption in its eschatological reference always meant more than the redemption of Israel; it also concerned the renewal of the world.

> The children of Israel are a people only insofar as they are a people of God. This means that neither a natural bond nor human will and realization has linked these people together, but only the establishment of a fellowship. It

in full; also in his *Missionary Message of the Old Testament* (London: Carey Press, 1945), p. 57, and especially chapters 2-4, henceforth to be cited as *Missionary Message*. Although Rowley's works are oriented toward an evolutionary development of Israel's faith and of the Hebrew religion, they are at times brilliant analyses of the questions raised.

79 George Ernest Wright, *The Old Testament Against its Environment* (Naperville: Alec R. Allenson, 1955), p. 62.

80 Cf. Samuel Sandmel, *Old Testament Issues* (New York, Evanston and London: Harper and Row, 1968), p. 33.

81 J. Blauw, *Missionary Nature*, p. 19; H. H. Rowley, *Missionary Message*, pp. 24-26; H. H. Rowley, *The Biblical Doctrine of Election*, pp. 65-67; C. C. West, *The Missionary Church*, pp. 91-93.

means further that to this nation the option is not open to want to become a nation like other nations, since it did not become a nation the way other nations did. It means finally that this nation lives – should it wish to become a nation like others – under the threat that God will cease to call it "my people" and will call it "not my people." If God should recognize this nation as His no longer, then it becomes a non-people, for only as the people of God did they become a people, or remain so.[82]

Jocz, who says that "it is only in the perspective of a covenantal relationship that we can rediscover the Biblical connection between Israel and the world and church and mission," also warns against an all too common dichotomy in the history of revelation. When the function of Israel is regarded as having terminated with the coming of Christ, that Israel ends where the Church begins, Israel becomes an isolated entity entirely separated from the world rather than the particular people where God acts on behalf of the world.[83]

Election, therefore, is not co-extensive with redemptive covenant, a point that is important for the understanding of Israel's election and the promise of redemption of the Gentiles. The difference between election and covenant has been shown by H. H. Rowley to be as follows: election has as its corollary service; covenant demands obedience.[84] Both election and covenant are theocentric, however, as E. Jacob has said: "Election carries service as its necessary corollary; to be the *°am* of Yahweh involves being His *°ebed*: the two terms are always put in parallel."[85] For this reason the non-Israelite can be said to meet his Creator first of all in terms of covenant which demands the obedience of faith. Having done this, he is ready to share in the election of the people of God to service of the nations. This will be more fully demonstrated when the commission to carry the Gospel of the Kingdom to the world (Matt. 28:18-20) is considered. The redemptive covenant with the nations was not annulled by the covenants mediated through Moses. Rather, the promise was renewed in them. And there was added this additional feature: God promised and covenanted redemption to a particular people whom he had created *within* the context of his universal covenant with all men.[86] The task of the chosen people

82 K. Emmerich, "Die Juden," *Theologische Studien und Kritiken*, VII (1939), 20; J. Blauw, *The Missionary Nature*, p. 141, n. 24.

83 J. Jocz, *Christians and Jews*, p. 1ff.

84 H. H. Rowley, *The Biblical Doctrine of Election*, p. 69-94; especially chapter 3, "The Limitation and Extension of Israel's Election"; R. Martin-Achard, *A Light to the Nations*, pp. 40-41. For the materials that are concerned with the concepts of election and covenant one can consult a number of specialized works by authors such as W. Eichrodt, E. Jacob, M. Kline, O. Procksch, G. von Rad, T. C. Vriezen.

85 E. Jacob, *Theology of the Old Testament*, translated by A. W. Heathcote and P. J. Allcock (London: 1958), p. 204; R. Martin-Achard, *A Light to the Nations*, p. 40, n. 3.

86 M. G. Kline, *By Oath Consigned*, pp. 31-35, makes some very pertinent observations with respect to this matter. He says, "Covenant theology has exhibited a strong bent towards a reduction of covenant to election. To do so is to substitute a logical ab-

becomes, as Cullmann has suggested, to tell the world of an actual fact of which it is totally unaware: that the God whom Israel serves is actually Lord of all.[87] This task can now be specifically defined as (1) communicating to the world the divine oracle received from God; (2) speaking in the name of Yahweh; and (3) testifying under this Lordship in obedience of faith. Israel's eschatological mission becomes nothing other than accepting for its task the offices of prophet, priest, and king.[88]

The world will encounter its God in the people of Israel, the youngest of the peoples of the East. And this will depend on the divine initiative only. Through Israel as a sort of mediator Yahweh will bring the nations into communion with himself. Therefore, Israel's task before the world is to live within the universal covenant as a chosen people, a royal priesthood, a people for God's own possession. Because there is only one true God there can be only one religion; therefore, Israel's faith must one day be the religion of all mankind. Israel is to be a light to the nations so that God's salvation may be as wide as the world. The German phrase *ein Gott, ein Volk, ein Kult* sums this up quite satisfactorily. The demand for *Kultuseinheit* is completely in keeping with the demand that Israel as *ein Volk* should worship *ein Gott*.[89] Just how God would save the fallen world only gradually became clearer with the unfolding of his revelation.

Israel was not free to withdraw from this covenant. It had been sovereignly ordained and instituted. It would also be sovereignly administered. Israel's covenant is unconditional and not one from which she may feel morally free to withdraw any time she pleases. When she chose to break the covenant, this did not mean that God had by that same token repudiated her election. God's purpose included the extension of his long-suffering patience and mercy toward a stiff-necked and hardhearted people (Heb. 3:7-11). Those who lay beyond the bounds of the covenant people might also possess the heritage by accepting the covenant.[90]

Any reading of the Old Testament, therefore, which neglects God's purpose for the nations and insists that God was interested only in Israel is a misreading of the divine revelation. In the time of Abraham the worship of God was limited to his family alone. Taking into consideration the period from Abraham

straction for the historical reality and to shunt systematic theology from its peculiar end of synthetic summation." Cf. also G. F. Vicedom, *Mission of God*, p. 48; Karl Barth, *Church Dogmatics*, translated by G. T. Thomson, *et alia* (Edinburgh: T. and T. Clark, 1936ff.), II 2, p. 217.

87 Oscar Cullmann, *Christ and Time*, translated by Floyd V. Filson (Philadelphia: Westminster Press, 1961), p. 186ff.; Ralph P. Marten, *Carmen Christi* (Cambridge: University Press, 1967), p. 243, n. 1.

88 R. Martin-Achard, *A Light to the Nations*, p. 75.

89 See Isaiah 42:1ff.; 49:1ff. This is more fully discussed in G. F. Moore, *Judaism in the First Centuries*, p. 228ff. Also see Ernest Wilson Nicholson, *Deuteronomy and Tradition* (Philadelphia: Fortress Press, 1967), p. 55ff.

90 H. H. Rowley, *The Biblical Doctrine of Election*, pp. 49, 68, 140.

to Moses, mention must be made of Abraham's relatives in Padan-aram, Melchizedek of Salem, Job with his three friends and Elihu, Moses' father-in-law, Jethro, priest of Midian. Scripture does not say how long the knowledge and worship of the true God continued among other peoples, for Scripture is only concerned with revealing to us how God worked out his plan through an elect, covenant people.

Today it is still true, as Kaufmann Kohler (a Jewish theologian) reminds us, that the election of Israel is "the central point of Jewish theology and the key to the understanding of Judaism." The idea of a people of God, called to live under his rule, looking forward in the hope of the coming of the Kingdom of God is one of the unifying themes of Scripture. Election is also the link that inseparably binds Old and New Testament together: God has his people.[91] What today's Jew will not acknowledge is that Israel's election is subservient to that of God's universal covenant. The modern Jew would reverse this: only by becoming part of Israel can one participate in the promises. The Jewish people have completely misunderstood their election and its purpose! This is not just a modern development. In the second Christian century Justin, conversing with some Jews, reports that "they were astounded to hear me say that we too (the Gentiles) were children of God." [92] The word of Ignaz Maybaum in our own day is quite representative of present Jewish attitudes, "As Jews we are separated. Election is selection, segregation from others." Jewish apologists continue to limit the Jewish mission to survival as a separate people: "The mission of the Jew is to be a Jew." [93]

This development in Jewish thought only serves to underscore the necessity of clear, Scripturally-conditioned thinking on the matter of covenant and election if the Christian mission is not to go wrong. Paul makes it very clear regarding Abraham (cf. Rom. 4:9ff.) that he was saved before he was circumcised. Paul also states that the purpose of this was "to make him the father of all who believe without being circumcised and who thus have righteousness reckoned unto them." In verses 14-15 of the same chapter he states that it is not just the adherents of the law who are to be the heirs ("inherit the world"). The Christian Church is under a great debt of gratitude to the people of Israel. But neither Israel nor the Gentile believer should ever forget that they are saved by the one universal, redemptive covenant. "There is only one Mediator between God and man ... who gave himself as a ransom for all" (I Tim. 2:5,6). It is Israel's glory that of her "according to the flesh, is the Christ, who

91 Kaufmann Kohler, *Jewish Theology* (New York: 1928), p. 239; Joseph Bonsirven, *Palestinian Judaism in the Time of Christ*, translated by William Wolf (New York, Chicago, San Fransisco: Holt, Rinehart and Winston, 1964), p. 42. Frensch title = *Le Judaisme Palestinien au Temps de Jesus Christ* (Paris, 1934), henceforth to be cited as *Palestinian Judaism*.

92 Justin, *Dialogue With Trypho*, CXXIII.9, quoted in J. Bonsirven, *Palestinian Judaism*, p. 77.

93 J. Jocz, *Christians and Jews*, p. 46.

is God over all, blessed forever" (Rom. 9:5 – RSV footnote). The Christian church constantly faces the same temptation to which Judaism succumbed when it rejected its fulfillment: the purpose of God's covenant is greater than our personal salvation; it is a taking of us up into the service of God in his plan for mankind.

D. *The Exodus: Birth of a Nation*

If God the Creator is one of the poles about which Jewish thought turns, then Israel is the other and provides orientation for a number of Biblical concepts necessary for the understanding of Old and New Testaments.[94]

> Three peoples of antiquity have dated the beginnings of their history. Rome's history begins with the building and fortification of a city. And this is what Rome wished to remain, the fortress and the Capital of a power, of an ordered, penetrating system out of which a world is ruled and toward which a world is expected to turn its gaze.
>
> The land of Greece counts its years from the first of the communal games for which the cities of its regions came together (Rome was 'the city'; Greece had its cities). They assembled to see how their men might measure the strength of body and mind, and in order to become conscious of the individuality given to each of the cities and to all of them together. This was the life of Greece; this was Hellenic existence. They saw with a curiosity of genius. Out of their conceptions humanity received an everlasting profusion of riches. Such was the gift of this people, to be spectators and authors in a 'theater for gods and man.'
>
> The people of Israel counted its time from the exodus from Egypt, from the redemption that set them free to walk the way of history. Israel was not a structure, like Rome, in which a power sets its foundation, and not a contest in which a people views its talents. Israel conceived of something completely different: the great freedom. It was admonished to conceive of a drama, with itself as the active and suffering hero .... And in its own drama it came to learn of the drama in which all humanity finds its history. Israel's history was thus set upon its foundations when the reckoning of its time, though achieved after much wavering, extended itself to the farthest reaches of humanity. Finally, it counted the years from the creation of the world. This, too, arose out of the great decision and the great negation which the exodus from Egypt demanded.[95]

94 J. Bonsirven, *Palestinian Judaism*, p. 42.
95 Leo Baeck, *This People Israel: The Meaning of Jewish Existence* (New York: Holt, Rinehart and Winston, 1964), p. 42. This is part of a larger section "Rome, Greece and Israel: A Comparison."

The reminder found in Num. 14:19 shows clearly that the Exodus marked the birth of a nation, for in this passage we have the dating of Israel's history, "From Egypt until now." The importance of this will be seen if it is remembered that God's people always live in a provisional state of the Kingdom. Their life, witness, and ministry must always be performed under the sign of the coming Kingdom and in hope.[96]

The Exodus is a manifestation of Yahweh's unconditional sovereignty. It is not a point of departure for an automatic history of salvation which runs comfortably and inevitably from it, a kind of history that holds Yahweh the captive of Israel's own existence, a feature of the history which the people make for themselves. Instead, the Exodus is the act of the world-God who thereby in no way qualifies or limits his sovereign freedom. Israel has no special status among the nations other than what God has given to her. Other nations have also had their "exodus" (Amos 9:7). The focus of attention becomes not just *what* God has done but *why* he acted in this way for his people Israel.

It is significant how often the deliverance of Israel from Egypt is referred to by God when his covenant with the people is in view. Gerhard von Rad has demonstrated how the earliest and clearest expressions of Israel's historical memory were preserved in the cultic confessions of the people.[97] Deut. 26:5-9 brings together these memories: (1) the wanderings (diaspora) of the fathers; (2) the deliverance from Egypt; and (3) entrance into the promised land:

> And you shall make response before the LORD your God, "A wandering Aramean was my father; and he went down into Egypt and sojourned there, few in number; and there he became a nation, mighty, and populous. And the Egyptians treated us harshly, and afflicted us, and laid upon us hard bondage. The we cried to the LORD the God of our fathers, and the LORD

96 G. von Rad, *Old Testament Theology*, p. 6, observes that strictly speaking the name "Israel" can only be applied to the Twelve Tribes after the Settlement in Palestine. It should be noted that the relatively short period of Israel's monarchy (only about 400 years) may not be regarded as normative for its history and mission. What is striking about the Old Testament history of Israel is the many forms under which Israel lived from the time of Abraham to Christ: patriarchal (Abraham, Isaac, Jacob); bondage in Egypt; tribal (period of the Judges); national unity and disunity (the kings); Captivity and Diaspora alongside of national form part time in the period of the Second Temple. It appears that at no time was any single form intended to remain permanent but that each was used by God to advance his purposes for all men. For the nation, therefore, the Exodus served not only as a reminder of redemption but also as a focal point of God's work in and through them. The temporary character of each period is demonstrated by the fact that the law of the king was already defined at Sinai (Deut. 17); the Davidic kingship (though often understood literally) was really a non-worldly kingship (Ps. 110:1; II Sam. 7:13-16; John 18:36; Acts 2:34-35); Jerusalem as the religious center for the worship of God would also be superceded by a new order (John 4:21).

97 Gerhard von Rad, *The Problem of the Hexateuch and Other Essays* (London: Oliver and Boyd, 1966), pp. 1-78; W. Brueggemann, *Tradition for Crisis*, p. 15ff.; James Luther Mays, *Amos* (Philadelphia: Westminster Press, 1969), p. 148.

heard our voice, and saw our affliction, our toil, and our oppression; and the LORD brought us out of Egypt with a mighty hand and outstretched arm, with great terror, with signs and wonders; and he brought us into this place and gave us this land, a land flowing with milk and honey."

It is important to note concerning these events that they are experiences of the community, events that occurred in history, and that they all concern things God had done for Israel.

When Israel has confessed this faith, she has made her basic affirmation about the nature of reality and about the character of her own life. Israel understands herself as the object, recipient and beneficiary of the gracious sovereign actions of God. She is not one who makes history but one for whom God does history. Her memory reminds her that her destiny in life is to respond fully and faithfully to these actions.[98]

When later Israel reflected on this (see especially Ps. 136:4-9), then the conclusion is inevitable: the God who saves men is none other than the God who made the world! What this means for Israel's mission in the world is not made clear at this point. God must confirm to them the nature of the life he would have them live. This took place at Sinai.

The Sinai covenant brought Israel and Yahweh into a kind of relationship to one another that is entirely new. It had to correspond to the essentially new situation that now existed: there has appeared a people, Israel, in process of national formation. Yet Israel was a different kind of people. Other nations were the offspring of their gods. Israel was taken into partnership by its God in a sacral-legal, reciprocal covenant. This can only happen when a people can act and work as a unit, i.e., when it is nationally-politically constituted. The Sinai covenant is a kingly covenant (taking the word *melekh* in its original folk-political meaning). "Yahweh is not just the exclusive Protector-God of the group; he is its exclusive, political head."[99] The point at issue is once again: divine lordship. In the exodus event God showed that he had chosen Israel to be a special people that would stand in a unique relationship to him. In the Sinai event God made provision for the continuation and consolidation of this special relationship. God's election, as in the case af Abraham, had its continuation in covenant. The election was an act of his sovereign will. But men are not automatons. God gave man a will and provided him the sphere in which this will must operate if man is to be free and no longer slave.

This covenant was with a people. It is unfortunate that in our atomistic, individual approach to both election and covenant we have lost sight of the Old Testament concept of "people" and the New Testament counterpart in the

98 W. Brueggemann, *Tradition for Crisis*, p. 16. I am indebted to this author for clarifying this and other similar relationships.
99 M. Buber, *The Kingship of God*, pp. 124-216.

term "body" of Christ.[100] God commands the *community* at Sinai. What he says in effect is, "If you wish to live in covenant fellowship with me, this is what you must do." But from the side of the people this is not a *do ut des* relationship.[101] Nor is this "law" in the sense in which law is often understood in the Western sense. It is *Torah*, i.e., the direction the covenant Lord gives to his people. The Sinai legislation is not rules or laws for the ordering of the cult or society in general. They are the will of God for the people, the conditions for a continuing relation which have their origin in the will of the covenant Lord. Though they cover a variety of subjects, they have as their single intention to bring all of life under the immediate, direct, and radical lordship of this God. They function to define what it means to be the people of God. No area of life is free from his purpose and his will.[102] At the same time the life of the people of God is spared every caprice and whim of men and institutions, for collectively and individually everyone stands under the will of God.

Whenever Israel declares that she lives in a covenant relationship, she acknowledges that she may not become a nation like the other nations. Her charter is found in Ex. 19:3-6.

> And Moses went up to God, and the LORD called to him out of the mountain, saying, "Thus you shall say to the house of Jacob, and tell the people of Israel: You have seen what I did to the Egyptians, and how I bore you on eagles' wings and brought you to myself. Now therefore, if you will obey my voice and keep my covenant, you shall be my own possession among all peoples; for all the earth is mine, and you shall be to me a kingdom of priests and a holy nation."

Obedience to her covenant relationship, the divine redemptive act of God, Israel's uniqueness among the peoples and the purpose of her existence find a clear expression in this passage. Other nations came into existence differently than Israel. Israel alone owes its existence and calling among the nations to her God. When the people wanted to be like the other nations by having a king to rule over them, this was judged as disobedience and a rejection of God's lordship (II Sam. 8:4-9). To have a king was not wrong in itself. We have observed already that the Deuteronomic code provided for this eventuality. This in itself was not displeasing to God so long as the king was the man of God's choosing, a king after God's heart (Deut. 17). But to do so in order "to be

100 This is not intended to deny the teaching of individual election, but rather to point out that the emphasis in Scripture falls on corporate election. Both Old and New Testaments also teach individual election. Cf. J. H. Piet, *The Road Ahead*, p. 45, who says, "Individual election is not an isolated thing. It takes place within the context of God's people, and its purpose is to implement the intention of God for his people."

101 A. Gelin, *The Key Concepts of the Old Testament*, p. 38.

102 W. Brueggemann, *Tradition for Crisis*, p. 20 states that no conception of law similar to this can be found in the ancient Near East and that "this legal material is theological in a decisive way."

like all the nations" was a rejection of God as king over them. The first king set over them proved to be pre-eminently "the king after man's heart," fitting *their* specifications, not God's, of what Israel's king should be like.

The uniqueness of Israel is set in conjunction with the Hebrew word *bahar* (to choose or elect), first used in the book of Deuteronomy.

> Did any people ever hear the voice of a god speaking out of the midst of the fire, as you have heard, and still live? Or has any god ever attemped to go and take a nation for himself from the midst of another nation, by trials, by signs, by wonders, and by war, by a mighty hand and an outstretched arm, and by great terrors, according to all that the LORD your God did for you in Egypt before your eyes? To you it was shown, that you might know that the LORD is God, there is no other besides him — Deut. 4:33-35.

Israel's existence determined her conduct. This theme can be seen running through the entire prophetic revelation.

The Sinai experiences of the people of Israel have significance for Israel's task in the world and for the Christian mission in one other respect. Moses was the recipient of a considerable mass of divine revelation. It is at Sinai that the collection of this material into a book or books began, setting the stage for the wide dissemination of the Scriptures so characteristic in later years of the Jewish Diaspora and in the advance of the Christian mission. It is impossible to overrate the significance of this development. At Sinai the nation Israel became a people with a Book. At the very time that the knowledge and service of God was apparently at the point of dying out among other peoples, the preservation of God's revelation through written records was advancing among his chosen people. There was guaranteed to the world, therefore, the identical revelation which Israel was first privileged to see, enjoy, preserve, according to which she must live, and which it was to share. God remembers his universal covenant.

It is surprising, in a certain sense, that there is so little knowledge of the contents and nature of revelation in the pre-Mosaic period. The largest portion that we do have is concerned with the covenants and the patriarchs with one possible exception — the book of Job.[103] This book is obviously a non-Abrahamic tradition significantly different from the rest of Scripture. It displays a degree and kind of knowledge of God and his works not found in the rest of the ancient Scriptures. Though written in poetic form, it is not too much to say concerning its content (the bulk of which consists of speeches by Job and his friends on the basis of their knowledge of God, creation and history) that its references to creation and to the antediluvian and post-diluvian periods almost equals the amount found in Genesis 1-11. It is of a different order from that of Genesis and displays a remarkable grasp of man's

---

103 It is outside the scope of this study to go into the questions concerning the authorship of the book of Job, the period in which Job lived, etc. The reader should consult the literature on this subject.

moral character and responsibility, as well as of divine righteousness and justice. It is perhaps the only authentic remnant of a non-Abrahamic tradition that has been preserved. In the book of Job God appears as the God of all men. One of its singular contributions is to present this truth in the context of man's accountability to God. Peter's words, spoken so very much later, could be applied to the book: "Truly I perceive that God shows no partiality, but in every nation any one who fears him and does what is right is acceptable to him" (Acts 10:34,35). The book of Job makes no mention of a specially chosen people of God, such as is found in Israel's birth as a nation. In terms of this present study it must be concluded that it is based on God's universal covenant.

E. *Israel in the Promised Land: A People Among the Nations*

The conquest of Canaan and the development of the tribal and national forms under which Israel would live from that time onward meant that Israel faced an entirely new situation and an accompanying new set of questions. Previously Israel had lived as a *ger* (a stranger, resident alien) in the land of Egypt (Ex. 22:21; 23:9; Lev. 19:34). Even her existence in Canaan was described as that of a *ger*, for God forbade them to hold the land "in perpetuity, for the land is mine; for you are strangers and sojourners with me" (Lev. 25:23). Israel would occupy Palestine, but other peoples and tribes would continue to live in or occupy the land also (permanently and temporarily). What status would Israel give the *gerim* (the plural form of *ger*) in her midst? What part did the *ger* have (if any) in the inheritance of Israel and under what conditions? What responsibilities did Israel have to the non-Israelites?

This was the first time that the separated people entered upon the world stage as a nation. These new conditions brought with them new problems and dangers. On the one hand, syncretism with pagan faiths of the surrounding areas was a constant threat which Israel did not always successfully avoid. On the other hand, insularity easily became as complete a repudiation of her election as was the turning to other gods. The history of the tribes shows that both of these extremes became reality at different periods.

Israel was set in a postion that was not that of an observer but that of a participant in world affairs. Israel did not just live in the midst of the nations; the peoples of the world were also right in her midst. When the bondage of Egypt was broken for her, a mixed multitude went out with the Israelites (Ex. 12:38). The conquest of the occupying tribes and possession of their lands took a very long time. Palestine was never really completely subjugated and its peoples replaced by Israelites. The deception of the Gibeonites meant the reception of a foreign people as permanent residents within the land (Josh. 9). The Kenites (Moses' relatives) were another tribal group which attached itself permanently to the land and fortunes of Judah (Judges 1:16); in this case we have an illustration of a specific invitation to a tribe to join its fortunes to that of Israel (Num. 10:29-32). Even Jerusalem, so very close to Israel's point of entry into Canaan, did not come into Israel's possession until the days of David and remained its possession for only 400 years after David conquered it and Solomon rebuilt it sumptuously.[104] Evidence for the continued existence of other non-Israelites, some in places of responsibility, is found in the books of Samuel. Mention is made there of Doeg the Edomite (I Sam. 2:17), Uriah the Hittite (II Sam. 11:3), Araunah the Jebusite (II Sam. 24:23), Zelek an Ammonite (II Sam. 23:37), Elnaam and Ithmah, Moabites (I Chron. 11:46). The list of the mighty men of David's army contains a number of men of various tribes (I Chron. II:26-47). Raisin points out that David's entourage included Cretans, Philistines, Itureans, Arameans, and Hittites ("gebborim").[105] When Solomon took a census of all the aliens resident in the land of Israel, they were found to number 153,600 (II Chron. 2:17). Their status appears to be that of servitude, however. The Mishnah, Naso viii. 4, says that Solomon used such large numbers of strangers (proselytes) "to inform us that the Holy One, Blessed be He, brings nigh those that are distant and rejoices over the distant just as the nigh." These foreign peoples must always have been a considerable number. In Josh. 8:33 they are specifically referred to and called "all Israel, sojourner as well as homeborn," a reference hardly necessary if they were only few in number or excluded from the covenant privileges and obligations.

As will appear from the legislation regarding this class of people, God always envisioned that strangers would be found among his people in their land. In Lev. 19:34 the keynote of Israel's attitude is sounded: "The stranger who sojourns with you shall be to you as the native among you, and you shall love him as yourself." Much later in the time of Ezekiel and the Babylonian captivity Israel is rebuked for its ill-treatment of the gerim because "the sojourner suffers extortion in your midst ... without redress" (Ezek. 22:7,29). Later when instruction is given for the resettlement of the country after the end of the captivity the people are told,

> You shall allot it as an inheritance for yourselves and for the aliens who reside among you and have begotten children among you. They shall be to you as native-born sons of Israel; with you they shall be allotted an inheritance among the tribes of Israel. In whatever tribe the alien resides, there you shall assign him his inheritance, says the Lord God (Ezek. 47:22-23).

The conquest of the land was to be carried out under the strict orders which God had given. Before Israel was permitted to use its sword against any distant city it was about to besiege, it was first to offer terms of peace to the city and its people allowed to live, but as servants to Israel. If these terms were rejected,

---

104 Martin Noth, *The Laws of the Pentateuch*, translated by D. R. and P. Thomas (Philadelphia: Fortress Press, 1967), p. 261.

105 Jacob Salmon Raisin, *Gentile Reactions to Jewish Ideals* (New York: Philosophical Library, 1953), p. 119, henceforth to be cited as *Gentile Reactions*.

the city was cut off by the slaughter of its males. This regulation did not apply, however, to certain specified tribes to whom Israel was to be God's instrument of justice because of their sins (Deut. 20:10-18; also 9:4,5).[106]

Not only was Israel affected internally by the presence of other peoples whom it absorbed or alongside of whom it lived, the development of the kingdom meant foreign alliances as well. That of David and Hiram of Tyre is well known (II Sam. 5:11,12). These alliances constituted no little problem for Solomon whose myriad marriages led the wisest of men to build temples for his heathen wives and to worship in them himself (I Kings 11:1-8). Godbey has shown from Scripture (II Kings 23:13) and other sources that these pagan cults persisted on the Mount of Olives even in Josiah's time. He also documents from Assyrian and other sources the persistence of pagan cultic forms and of continued Iranian migrations into Palestine throughout the days of the monarchy.[107] The true religion was never the sole religion of Palestine, nor was it ever confined to Palestine.[108] The large number of figurines and small plaques of the Canaanite fertility and mother goddessess found in Israel shows the widespread syncreticism practised there.[109] The books of Judges, Samuel, Kings, and Chronicles detail many foreign interferences in the life of the chosen people. Israel lived at the crossroads of history, and this forced her to look at herself in relation to the nations and their faiths. The similarities or points of contact between the Old Testament religion and the neighboring religions are such that the Jews and the native religions of the land must have deeply influenced each other.[110]

Later the contacts of Israel with the world in the dispersions of her people will be detailed. It will suffice at this point to say that no place on earth was

106 Julius Morgenstern, "Jerusalem - 485 B. C.," *HUCA*, XXXI (1954), 1-30, refers to the passage in Deuteronomy 20:10-14a as "as a body of war legislation" and details its significance with respect to Israel's relation to the nations and God's purposes for the peoples.

107 Allen Howard Godbey, *The Lost Tribes A Myth* (Durham, N.C.: Duke University Press, 1930), pp. 106-110, henceforth to be cited as *Lost Tribes*. This work by Godbey is very well done. Unfortunately the title "Lost Tribes" is misleading. The book has a far broader scope than the question of the ten lost tribes, which the title suggests.

108 This is detailed by James William Parkes, *The Conflict of the Church and the Synagogue* (Cleveland and New York: The World Publishing Co., 1961, p. 5ff.

109 James B. Pritchard, *Palestinian Figurines in Relation to Certain Goddesses Known Through Literature* (New Haven: University Press, 1943); G. E. Wright, *The Old Testament Against its Environment*, p. 24.

110 Consult Stanley Arthur Cook, *The Old Testament* (New York: Macmillan, 1936), pp. 62-100, for a detailed presentation of the points of contact between Old Testament religion and the neighboring religions. The author's bias will be immediately apparent, but his source material is invaluable for this question. See also II Kings 17:11, 26ff. Cf. also William Oscar Emil Oesterley, ed., *Judaism and Christianity* (3 vols., London: The Sheldon Press, 1937), I, p. 255ff. article by S. H. Hooke. Of very great significance for today is the fact that the problem of Palestine and Israel and the nations continues to confront the Church and the world. See footnote 7, Chapter IV, of this dissertation.

comparable to Palestine so far as being advantageous for contact with the rest of the world. God favored his people when he set the bounds of the nations with reference to Israel (Deut. 32:8). Excavations in Yemen (S. Arabia) show that as early as 4,000 B.C. an extentive trade was begun and continued to be carried on through the millenia with the lands we now know as India and Greece. This region was an important base for the spread of Jewish trade and colonies down into the Christian era. Not a few Jewish colonies throughout the seas and the continents of Africa and Asia traced their origins to the Yemenite Jews.[111] It is the combination of all these circumstances that confronted the Jews with the question, "What about the *gerim*?"

At Sinai the basic legislation was laid down. It concerned the place of the *gerim* among the people and within the boundaries of the promised land. Everything concerning this legislation need not be detailed.[112] A summary will suffice to show the relationship to the fulfillment of mission to the world. What was the legal position of the *gerim*?

Regardless of where he originated or what was his ancestral faith, elemental morality was expected of every resident in ancient Israel. For the utter alien whose disassociation from Israel's faith and freedom of life was total Scripture employs precise designations, such as the Hebrew words *ben nechar*, *nachri*, *zar* and *achar*, the meaning being that of travellers or aliens (Deut. 14:21; 15:3; 23:21; 29:21; Ex. 12:43; II Sam. 22:45ff.; Ezek. 44:9). He is without rights, although passages such as Ex. 20:20ff. and 23:9 show a milder attitude than was generally shown among other peoples.[113] But the *ger* was always to some degree at least incorporated into the community of Israel. This implied religious fellowship. The varying degrees of affiliation were not clearly defined or categorized in Biblical antiquity. However, when the *ger* assumed all the group obligations – ethnic, social and religious – he became a full-fledged member of the congregation of Israel and his descendants were legally indistinguishable from other Israelites.[114] In Josh. 8:33 he is described as being part of "all Israel."

It is important to understand this in the light of and against the background of the semitic religions of the day. Religion did not exist among the Semites

111 A. H. Godbey, *Lost Tribes*, p. 174ff.

112 A number of authors have given considerable attention to these data. Some of the principal works that may be consulted are: Alfred Bertholet, *Die Stellung der Israeliten und die Jüden zu den Fremden* (Leipzig: J. C. B. Mohr, 1896), henceforth to be cited as *Die Stellung*; D. M. Eichhorn, *Conversion to Judaism*; F. Derwacter, *Preparing the Way for Paul*; W. O. E. Oesterley, *Judaism and Christianity*; J. Peterson, *Missionary Methods*; E. Shürer, *Geschichte*; Joachim Jeremias, *Jerusalem in the Times of Jesus*, translated by F. H. & C. H. Cave (London: SCM Press ,1969); German title = *Jerusalem zur Zeit Jesus* (Göttingen: 1937).

113 Karl Georg Kuhn, προσήλυτος, *TWNT*, VI, p. 728; D. M. Eichhorn, *Conversion to Judaism*, p. 9; A. Bertholet, *Die Stellung*, is frequently used by Kuhn as one of his sources.

114 A full treatment of this subject can be found in D. M. Eichhorn, *Conversion to Judaism*, p. 3ff.

for the saving of souls but for the preservation of society, as William Smith shows.[115] Every man had to take his part in whatever was necessary to that end. The alternative was to break with the domestic and political community to which he belonged. It was therefore impossible for a man to change his religion without changing his nationality. The nationalism of the Semite was religious.[116] When a man changed his religion, he had to foreswear his own kindred and be received into a new circle of civil as well as religious life. Consistent with this the rabbis spoke of the proselyte "as a child newly born." Another rabbinic statement concerning the legal status of the *ger* says "the heathen has no father."[117] The parable of the stag admid the sheep and goats is quoted by Abrahams with this rabbinic application, "so we must treat with tender consideration a *ger* who has forsaken his family and his father's house, who has left behind his people and all the peoples of the world and has chosen to come to us." The parable stated that the stag would not sleep in the wilderness with others of its kind, but associated with the flocks instead. The owner held it especially dear, just as God loves the proselyte because he has left his family, home, people and the Gentile nations and has come over to the Israelites. In yet another place the Mishnah and Talmud lay down this principle: "one must not say to descendants of proselytes: recollect the deeds of your forefathers for it is said in Ex. 22:21 thou shalt not vex, neither shalt thou oppress them." The Talmud adds, "If a proselyte desires to learn the Bible, say not to him, Shall the mouth that ate carrion recite the words spoken from the mouth of Power?"[118] At this stage of Israel's history we have no record of any ritual requirements marking the formal admission to citizenship other than the requirement that he and his house must be circumcised if he is to partake of the Passover.

What were the mutual responsibilities of *gerim* and Israelites? To answer this question it is necessary to observe that originally the word *ger* had a geographical connotation. Even Jews living outside of Palestine were called *gerim*.[119] Although the LXX generally translates this term by προσήλυτος, the religious sense did not gain prominence until the Babylonian exile when the Jews, themselves *gerim* in the sense of strangers in Babylon, became convinced that it was their duty to make *gerim*, in the sense of proselytes, of their fellow countrymen. This later development was accompanied by the understanding that

115 William Robertson Smith, *The Religion of the Semites* (New York: Meridian Books, 1956), pp. 29-37.
116 G. van der Leeuw, *Religion in Essence and Manifestation*, p. 270.
117 *BT*, Yeb. 131; J. Jeremias, *Jerusalem in the Times of Jesus*, p. 323, who quotes the Mek. on Exodus 12:49, 7c. Jeremias in this volume has an exhaustive study of the legal rights, descent, rights of inheritance, etc. of the proselyte.
118 *The Mishnah*, Naso viii.2; Israel Abrahams, *Studies in Phariseeism and the Gospels* (2 vols., New York: KTAV, 1967), pp. 7, 116; Karl Georg Kuhn, προσήλυτος, *TWNT*, VI, p. 738.
119 F. Derwacter, *Preparing the Way for Paul*, p. 21; cf. also p. 21, n. 20.

faith or non-faith alone made one a member of the community of Israel or an alien.[120] The translation "stranger" for the Hebrew *ger* is unfortunate. The *ger* was a guest, a resident alien, under the protection of the law of the land. When later the religious sense came to dominate, προσήλυτος was an adequate translation, meaning literally "one who came over." The term in this sense adequately fits the real attitude and activity of Israel concerning whose efforts it is preferable to speak of the "reception of the Gentiles" rather than of "Gentile mission." [121]

Because there was no sharp distinction between the religious and secular in the life of Israel, it is difficult to separate the purely legal status of the *ger* from his spiritual privileges and duties. There was to be one law for the *ger* and for the native: this was God's command (Lev. 19:34; 24:22; Ex. 12:49; Num. 9:14; 15:15,29). There was no favoritism for either the alien or the native born: both enjoyed religious and social equality. The *ger* not only enjoyed but was entitled to full freedom with justice (Lev. 19:10; 23:22; Deut. 24:19ff.; Lev. 25:6; Deut. 14:28ff.; 26:12ff.; Num. 35:14ff; Josh. 20:9).

The same moral and ceremonial commands and prohibitions applied to the *ger* as to Israel. Forbidden to him were unchastity (Lev. 18:26) and idolatry (Lev. 20:2; Ezek. 14:7ff.; Num. 15:30). The same ritual requirements were made of him. He was obligated to observe the same taboos (Num. 19:10), might not eat blood (Lev. 17:10) or any animal that died of natural causes or was torn by beasts (Lev. 17:15); the same procedures were required of him in sacrifices (Lev. 17:8; 22:18; Num. 15:14,26). The sacred days had to be observed by him: Sabbath (Ex. 20:10; 23:12; Deut. 5:14), Day of Atonement (Lev. 16:29), Feast of Tabernacles (Deut. 16:14), and Pentecost (Deut. 16:11). The Passover prohibition of leaven applied to him also (Ex. 12:19).[122] If the full-fledged male *ger* wished to partake of the passover, he and his family had to be circumcised (Ex. 12:48). This completed his incorporation into the religious union with God's people. He had to enter formally into the covenant in order to share the responsibility of the election.

This, in brief, is the legislation of the Scriptures regarding the *ger*. When he accepted fully the responsibility of Israel's faith, he was in every respect an Israelite with the same privileges and obligations as the native-born sons. He,

120 E. Schürer, *Geschichte des Jüdischen Volkes in Zeitalter Jesus Christi* (4th ed., 5 vols., Leipzig: 1909), Vol. II, Div. II, (E.T.), p. 317, n. 315, calls attention to II Chron. 15:9 and II Chron. 30 where he believes we have the first Biblical use of the word *ger* in the religious sense; henceforth to be cited as *Geschichte*; K. G. Kuhn, *TWNT*, VI, 728-730.

121 Ernst Lohmeyer, "Mir ist gegeben alle Gewalt," *In Memoriam Ernst Lohmeyer* (Stüttgart: Evangelisches Verlagswerk, 1951), p. 43; also J. Jeremias, *Jesus' Promise*, p. 23, n. 2.

122 This passage (Exodus 12:19) is especially interesting since it is part of the preparatory instructions for the first observance of the Passover and mentions the *gerim* as being a part of Israel, sharing equally in the promise of deliverance as well as equally under the curse for disobedience.

in short, could become a son of God and a joint heir of the promise. There is no data from any source to substantiate whether or not the Jews in the days of the judges and kings actively sought to convert the *gerim* living in their midst to the worship of Yahweh. However, when it is remembered that every ancient cult was exclusive, that none but members of the family participated in the worship of the tutelary gods, that no foreigner was able to sacrifice to the deities of the cities, the legislation under which Israel's covenant life was lived is seen as being unique in that ancient world. The pagan world knew nothing comparable to the Torah of Israel which gave full recognition to the resident alien and made specific regulation for his full incorporation into the life of the people. Finkelstein retells the experience of Orestes, who, masked as a stranger, returns to his ancestral home and asks permission to take part in the religious ceremonies, qualifying his request in this way, "If strangers may sacrifice with citizens." He further adds that in the fifth century B.C. the Athenians considered it a "calamity" for a person to have an alien father.[123]

Summary: God's universal, redemptive covenant continued to be worked out. The non-Israelite, too, could share in the salvation through the obedience of faith in the God who has chosen to live on the world stage as a participant in Yahweh's drama of redemption. The bond that held Israel together as a people was more than racial: Israel was bound to Yahweh by a covenant bond. For this reason it was always possible for individuals of other nations to be admitted as members of the particularistic covenant with Israel and join with Israel in the service required by her election.[124] The non-Israelite met in Israel the demand of obedience to the God who in redemptive grace was working out by means of Israel's election his universal covenant with mankind.

John Piet describes this function of Israel (and the Church) in a reference to I Peter 2:9. In this passage (based on Deuteronomy 10:15 and Exodus 19:5) the apostle speaks of "a chosen race, a royal priesthood, a holy nation, God's own people that you may declare the wonderful deeds of God." Piet remarks:

> The word "declare" is crystal clear in this epistle. It describes the duty of a messenger who brings news from within. In classical Greek the individual who performs this function on a Greek stage tells the spectators what goes on in the house or behind the scenes, which means he directs his declaration outward to an audience which is not part of the acting group.[125]

There is always a double concern, however, in this calling. For one thing, it is always important to a society that all its members should be in harmony with God's will since an individual could involve a community in dishonor or

---

123 L. Finkelstein, *The Jews: Their History, Culture, and Religion*, I, p. 76.

124 A. G. Hebert, *The Throne of David*, p. 96.

125 J. H. Piet, *The Road Ahead*, p. 33. See also G. Kittel, *TWNT*, I, 69, where Julius Schniewind defines ἐξάγγελος as "a messenger who proclaims abroad . . . what is concealed from the gaze of the spectators."

suffering (e.g., Exodus 20:5,6; Achan at the time of Israel's defeat at Ai –
Joshua 7:1). Rowley states,

> No man could be indifferent whether his neighbor walked in God's way or
> not, and there could be no delusion that a man's religion was merely his own
> affair .... Nor can any individual be wisely indifferent to the sin of those
> around him. That was why the prophets were tireless in calling men to
> walk in the way of God. It was because this was their truest service to
> themselves, to their fellows and to God. And since the nation was but a part
> of the wider society of the world, Israel could not be indifferent to the
> foreign peoples .... It is important that we ... should recognize that this
> developed (note the concern of Isaiah, Jonah, Amos for the peoples of the
> world) from the fundamental thought of the Old Testament on the nature
> of man as created in God's image ... as a member of a corporate society ...
> ultimately concerned with the life of the nations other than their own.[126]

It is necessary at this point to give consideration to the message of the
prophets. Israel is settled in her land. She is set on the world's stage. A people
of God has been brought into being. The Gentiles must be identified with this
people if they are to be saved. In the prophets God will be met instructing,
challenging, warning, and comforting his people, and interpreting his will for
them and for the world.

F. *Vision: The Age of the Prophets*

> The world will be perfected under the kingdom of the Almighty, and all
> the children of flesh will call upon thy name, when thou wilt turn unto
> thyself all the wicked of the earth. Let all the inhabitants of the earth
> perceive and know that unto thee every knee must bow and every tongue
> swear. Before thee, O Lord our God, let them bow and fall; and unto thy
> glorious name let them give honor; let them all accept the yoke of thy
> kingdom, and do thou reign over them speedily, and forever and ever ....

Concerning this prayer from the Mussaf, W. G. Braude observes: "...Prayers
of this kind were not suspended in mid-air. Actions consonant with their spirit
must have preceded and followed them." [127]

The prayer underscores what the teachers of Israel had repeated in an endless
variety of ways and in all conceivable contexts: there is salvation for the Israel
according to the flesh; there is an equal hope of salvation for the *gerim*.

Prophet, priest and psalmist possessed a patient, tireless pedagogic course

---

126 H. H. Rowley, *The Faith of Israel*, p. 99ff.
127 W. G. Braude, *Jewish Proselyting*, p. 17, from which the prayer preceding is
also quoted.

that made them remind Israel again and again: you are all *gerim* before God .... He loves the alien .... Therefore, you too must love the *ger* .... Let him be to you as the homeborn and love him as you love yourselves ... for many nations will join themselves to the Eternal and become his people .... He who gathers Israel's exiles in says, "I will yet gather to them those who were gathered against them." [128]

This age of the prophets and the purpose of the prophetic revelation has been studied and debated extensively. Some find in the prophets a clear apologetic calling Israel to mission; others feel just as strongly that the missionary motivation and purpose is quite limited.[129] Whichever position one adopts, the prophetic message of pre-exilic and post-exilic periods contains significant challenges and promises to Jew and Gentile. One will not find a call to missions in the sense in which mission is often understood in the present day, that is, a centrally governed missionary initiative. Rather than being a movement in which the whole community conceives of a corporate task to fulfill on behalf of humanity, Jewish proselyting movements were individually undertaken and concerned largely with individuals.[130] Aalen says,

> There is no real missionary conception in these writings if we understand by mission a message or missionary initiative going out from the center, striving to reach the Gentiles where they are, and meeting them just as they are for their own sake. The doxa is inseparably bound up with Israel and Jerusalem. No one can share in it without "coming to it," becoming a proselyte, i.e., without becoming a Jew.[131]

Such judgments as the above statement may not be taken to mean that Jews did not make far-reaching, significant and effective attempts to win others to their faith. Their record is too clear to say that. Even though it is true that no one has found in the Old Testament a direct, unmistakably clear divine commission

---

128 D. M. Eichhorn, *Conversion to Judaism*, pp. 31-32.

129 Representatives of both views are numerous. For a sample of those who find strong missionary appeal in the Old Testament the works of the following authors may be consulted: A Bertholet, H. H. Rowley, E. Sellin. For representatives of the position that the missionary purpose of the Old Testament is limited, consult the bibliography for the works of S. Aalen, R. Martin-Achard.

130 Thus, e.g., Sverre Aalen, *Die Begriffe "Licht" und "Finsternis" im Alten Testament, im Spätjudentum, und im Rabbinismus* (Oslo: I Kommisjon Hos Jacob Dybwab, 1951) says, p. 218, "Eine Sendung an die Völker liegt nicht in der Prophetenstellung Israels." Also see A. Causse, "La sagesse et la propaganda juive a l'epoque perse et hellenistique," in *Werden und Wesen des Alten Testaments, ZAW*, No. 66, (Berlin: 1936), p. 148ff., cited by R. Martin-Achard, *Light to the Nations*, p. 5, n. 18, to the effect that "proselytism is more frequently rooted in 'Wisdom' than in 'Prophecy,' and advocates a monotheistic humanism."

131 S. Aalen, *Die Begriffe "Licht" und "Finsternis,"* p. 205; Johannes Münck, *Paul and the Salvation of Mankind* (Richmond: John Knox Press, 1959), p. 270ff.

calling to a mission of consciously going to the Gentiles to win them for God, this does not mean that the Old Testament is indifferent to such activity. In fact, the whole fabric of the revelation is woven through with the golden threads of divine covenant promise for all peoples. There is the clearly discernible outlook on mission in the Old Testament which is unambiguous in its revelations as to what God expects from his people.[132]

1. The City of God

A distinctive feature of the period now under review was the designation of the city of Jerusalem, not only as the capital of the united tribes and later of the Kingdom of Judah but as the holy, central city of the first commonwealth, the cultic center for Israel and of the worship of Yahweh.[133] The designation of Jerusalem was made by Yahweh himself (I Chronicles 21:18–22:1; II Chronicles 6:6) in fulfillment of his promise (Exodus 20:24). Zion became the center of unity. It is the center to which Israel must gather; it is the center to which the Gentiles are seen as coming in the message of the prophets. King Jeroboam I found it necessary to designate the shrines at Bethel and Dan as substitutes for Jerusalem, for he feared the reunification of the tribes if Jerusalem continued to be used by his subjects as the cultic center (I Kings 12:26-30). That Jeroboam's fears were not unfounded is shown in the incident recorded in II Chronicles 30. Hezekiah of Judah invited "all Israel" to celebrate the Passover in Jerusalem. Many of his messengers were mocked by some of the tribes, but many of Ephraim, Manasseh, Issachar and Zebulon came to keep the Passover unto the Lord in Jerusalem. Jerusalem was the spiritual capital. The pilgrims came from all over the diaspora. Here God promised to gather the outcasts of Israel (Ps. 147:2). Yahweh said through the prophets, "This is Jerusalem; I have set her in the center of the nations, with countries round about her" (Ezekiel 5:5).[134] "Nations shall come to your light, and kings to the brightness of your rising" (Isaiah 60:3). "The earth shall be full of the knowledge of the LORD as the waters cover the sea" (Isaiah 11:9). "Behold, you shall call

132 Walter Eichrodt, "Gottes Volk und die Völker," in *EMM*, 86 (1942), 129-145, in his synthesis of Old Testament revelation shows that God says both "yes" and "no" to his people as well as to the nations. Their rejection or acceptance is ultimately resolved in Christ.

133 Cf. Samuel Kalman Mirsky, *Jerusalem as a Religious Center* (New York: Mizrachi Organization of America, 1950), p. 8; E. W. Nicholson, *Deuteronomy and Tradition*, p. 97; A. G. Hebert, *The Throne of David*, pp. 92-93. Nicholson ignores the divine activity in the selection of Jerusalem, declaring that "the centralization of the cult (in Jerusalem) was probably accepted (by the people) simply in the interests of cultic purity and as a means of countering the widespread syncretism which had pervaded the cultic shrines." See also J. Koole, *De Joden in de Verstrooiing*, p. 49.

134 Ernst Lohmeyer, *Lord of the Temple*, translated by Stewart Todd (Richmond: John Knox Press, 1962), p. 22. See also Ps. 37:1, 2, 5, 6.

nations that you know not, and nations that knew you not shall run to you, because of the LORD your God and of the Holy One of Israel, for he has glorified you" (Isaiah 55:4-5).

In the New Testament this is altered by the fulfillment. The center of unity for the people of God is no longer a city, Jerusalem, but a Person, Jesus the Christ, and his Kingdom. He becomes the gathering point as promised, "The root of Jesse shall stand as an ensign to the peoples; him shall the nations seek" (Isaiah 11:10). From the time that he was "lifted up from the earth," he drew all men unto himself (John 12:32). In the gathering in of the elect they will come to the Son of Man and find him (Mark 13:27). Jesus explicitly stated to the Samaritan woman at Jacob's Well that the time was coming when both Jerusalem and Gerizim would be superceded by Jesus himself as the gathering point of the worshippers of God (John 4:21-24). Events would move to that great climactic day of crucifixion with its noonday darkness symbolizing the gross darkness of the peoples upon whom a great light shines in the victory of Christ over sin, death, and man's rebellion. Nations which were once summoned to Zion are now summoned to be gathered to Christ.[135]

Today geographical Jerusalem is no longer the center of the unity of the people of God. Its symbolic, typical character has been completed. It is now the heavenly Jerusalem, the City of God that we approach (Hebrews 12:22-24). This culminates in the vision of Revelation 14:1 where the Lamb is surrounded by the 144,000 who follow him "wherever he goes, who have been redeemed from mankind." Where the Lamb is, there is Zion.[136] In these revelations is found the fulfillment of the Old Testament prophecies which speak of the Gentiles coming to Zion.

The significance of the new form of unity for the people of God must not escape us. In Christ, the Head, with his Body, the Church, a form of unity has appeared that is capable of gathering into itself all the diversities among men and peoples without leveling them to a featureless uniformity. Theologically there is no problem: all are one in the Christ to whom all men must be gathered. The practical problem is the area of our difficulty. When his people are one (John 17:20,21), then in that very unity the world will have an undeniable demonstration that the Gospel of God's grace is for all men, for the unity includes not only those who are his disciples from among the Jews but also all those who will believe on him through their word. The form of the Christian message is such that it must of its very nature be universal.

Jerusalem served yet another function. Not only would "all the nations flow into it, and many peoples come ... to the house of the God of Jacob that he may teach us his ways and that we may walk in his paths" (Isaiah 2:2-4), an activity that is due to God's working through Israel among the nations, but

---

135 A. G. Hebert, *The Throne of David*, p. 231. James C. De Young, *Jerusalem in the New Testament* (Kampen: J. H. Kok, 1960), pp. 117-164.

136 A. G. Hebert, *The Throne of David*, p. 225ff.

the ultimate destiny of all men (Jew and non-Jew) was determined by the events that took place in the City of God. The Servant of the Lord had to set his face toward Jerusalem, for it was an impossibility that a prophet should perish anywhere else. So too in preparation for the great day of salvation and judgment the face of the nations would be turned toward Jerusalem in order that they might bathe in the light that would shine on them and share the blessings of the law and the word that would go out from there and the salvation worked there. Jerusalem served as the great center for instruction. Here the great Hillel came to study. At Jerusalem Saul of Tarsus sat at the feet of Gamaliel. From Jerusalem many scribes went out to teach in the Diaspora, as the numerous inscriptions testify. In more ways than one, therefore, the Word of the Lord went out from Jerusalem.[137]

It is still a question, as Martin-Achard suggests, whether Jerusalem has a role to play in the future. "This role should be defined with precision and the question as to how the gathering of mankind together round about Christ fits in with the eschatological function of the City of David ought to be investigated."[138] The Church does not only inherit the mission of the Old Testament people of God, this author suggests. It is through the Church that the mission of the people of God finds its fulfillment.

This substitution by Jesus Christ of himself and his Kingdom as the center in place of the city God had chosen is extremely important. The implications of this are just as great as the substitution of the Supper in remembrance of him for the Passover in remembrance of Israel's deliverance out of Egypt, or of baptism in his name as the mark of discipleship for circumcision in obedience to God's command. K. Schilder has correctly observed that the one phrase that epitomizes and precisely designates the activity of the God of revelation as it operates in Israel's trekking through the world, the one formula that is the compendium of all liturgical ordinances and accomplishment is this: "the Bible constantly stresses the thought of creating a memorial in remembrance of the name of the Lord . . . . The whole purpose of the busy, colorful worship among them is just this: God causes His Name to dwell there."[139] When Jesus appeared, claiming to be the Servant of the Lord, he caused his name to be remembered. Two alternatives are open: either this is idolatry (and hence worthy of the curse), or else it is obedience (and demands faith). It is sheer blasphemy, satanic rebellion for a mere man to set aside any of God's ordinances and to direct men's attention to himself instead. As Schilder says, "The

137 J. H. Waszink, et al., Het Oudste Christendom en de Antieke Cultuur (Haarlem: H. J. Tjeenk Willink, 1951), p. 549; Schifra Strizower, Exotic Jewish Communities (New York and London: Thomas Yoseloff, 1962), p. 125.

138 R. Martin-Achard, A Light to the Nations, p. 78, n. 7. See also Chapter IV, n. 7, of this dissertation.

139 Cf. Klaas Schilder, Christ in His Suffering, translated by Henry Zylstra (Grand Rapids: Wm. B. Eerdmans Publishing Co., 1938), p. 231ff., on whose presentation this paragraph and discussion are based.

issue is one of eternal right or wrong, a question of all or nothing, of being a servant or of being a rebel." But when Christ established a memorial at Passover to himself in the Supper, he was establishing a memorial for the name of God. When he commanded men to become his disciples, he was himself the obedient Shepherd (Jeremiah 17:16). When men were baptized in his name, they became part of the Kingdom which he will at the end of the age give into the hands of the Father so that God may be all in all. He is in his own Person the Temple of the Living God but also the Priest of that Temple. He supplied God's altar with the one redeeming sacrifice that was efficacious. Where he is, there is God's Temple and the true Jerusalem.[140] To this the prophets of the Old Testament bore consistent witness and foretold as the Scriptures record: "The latter splendor of this house shall be greater than the former, says the LORD of hosts; and in this place I will give prosperity" (Haggai 2:9).

Perhaps something of the reason why the Jews are today repelled by Jesus can be found in this: "He destroyed Israel," said one of their great philosophers; "he was received by the Gentiles and became the center of a new Israel in the earth." [141] Unwittingly, one of their own high priests, speaking prophetically, had said to the Council of the Jews,

"You know nothing at all; you do not understand that it is expedient for you that one man should die for the people, and that the whole nation should not perish." He did not say this of his own accord, but being high priest that year he prophesied that Jesus should die for the nation, and not for that nation only, but to gather into one the children of God who are scattered abroad (John 11:49-52).

2. *The Message of the Prophets*

One can expect when giving attention to the message of the prophets that the prophets would speak in this revelation concerning the place and purpose of Israel among the nations. And this is so. There are a number of differing opinions as to the purpose of this revelation, as has been indicated. The question is usually posed in some fashion such as this: Did God through the prophets intend to challenge Israel to a world-wide witness or mission? Or was his purpose merely to affirm that Gentiles might be saved but that his people need feel no responsibility to exercise themselves in any way to make this a reality

140 No single book in the Scriptures makes these identifications so clearly as the book of Hebrews. See especially chapters 8-10; on the place of Jerusalem see Hebrews 12:22.

141 Quoted by E. G. Homrighausen, "Evangelism and the Jewish People," *IRM*, XXXIX, no. 155 (July 1950), 318-329, especially p. 318.

for the nations? When we search the Old Testament for a command to evangelize the nations, we find none.

To approach the prophets with this limited viewpoint is not legitimate. The prophetic message addressed itself to the life of the people in its wholeness. It may not and cannot be fragmented into so many parts as one pleases. At times the prophetic message was corrective; at others eschatological. Sometimes it is for comfort and hope; at other times it is a message of judgment. In all circumstances the whole life of the people is addressed in terms of the day in which they lived. The prophets addressed a people who knew from the record of God's great works that they owed their life and existence to the graciousness of Yahweh. In contrast to her neighbors, Israel's religious idiom had to be different because man cannot manipulate God who sovereignly holds all things together. Israel knew that men are not spectators to the capricious, unpredictable behavior of immoral deities but that men are caught up in a divine drama which forces from them a decision. This their prophets taught them.

The prophets attempted to work out in various historical situations the implications of the covenant liturgy for the life and destiny of Israel. They affirmed that the grace of God and the claim of God are inseparable and can be known in the covenant. The prophets of the pre-exilic period called attention principally to the dangers that lay within the nation. Syncretism with other religions, Baalism, intermarriage with heathen peoples, foreign alliances instead of trust in Yahweh – these are in large measure the background against which the prophets spoke. Brueggemann summarizes this nicely when he says, "The central concern of the prophets was to communicate to Israel what it meant to be Israel," and adds:

> To say it in contemporary language, they were concerned with the nature and mission of the church. The covenant liturgy had made it clear that Israel's primary *loyalty* was to this gracious God who had confronted her in her moments of despair and need. Concerning her *purpose* in life, Israel had vowed to give herself to Yahweh through the keeping of the covenant commandments. But in working out her loyalty and her purpose, Israel had turned away from the focus of covenant, which meant she had denied the very foundation of her existence. It is to this dishonoring of covenant that the prophets address themselves. It is an urgent concern for related to it is the question of Israel's historical survival.[142]

How must we conceive of the role of the prophet? He is mediator, one who stands between two covenant parties so that they may relate to each other. He may not speak just any word but he may speak only the word which God bids him (Numbers 22:35). The words of the prophet are therefore in the service of the covenant and depend on the situation of the covenant in his day. At the same time covenant with Yahweh is grounded in a distinctive world-

142 W. Brugggeman, *Tradition for Crisis*, p. 25.

view which holds that life is whole and joyous where there is perfect obedience to Yahweh's purpose.

It is in this consideration that we can find the importance of the covenant message of the prophets for our purpose. It may perhaps best be seen against the recurrent disobedience of Israel to the covenant when she turned to the service of idols and the peculiar phenomenon known only in Israel of the "false prophet." The first of these Brueggemann defines af "false cult." He says,

> False cult is found when Israel goes through the motions of covenant but does not intend covenant. Such false worship is characterized by: the assumption that the worshipper leaves the sanctuary just as he came, without being changed in any way; liturgy which avoids all decision-making and responsibility; a pre-occupation with the worshippers wellbeing; a disregard for the purposes of the covenant Lord; the assumption that this is our worship and we are answerable to no one; and, therefore, worship which permits and sustains "business as usual." Worship which has no integral relation to the covenant by which it is measured is false worship. It is worship which has forsaken the political-secular-historical-social idiom and has reverted to the religious idiom of Israel's neighbors.[143]

With respect to the false prophets, who may or may not be linked to the cult (this is not essential), they are prophets who do not speak within the context of covenant. They affirm that Yahweh is in the midst of his people, but they teach that the people are safe from any harm. Von Rad points out how they speak of well-being when Yahweh is bringing judgment.[144] The issue is the control of history. The true prophet compels men to confront Yahweh who is in charge of all history. The false prophet allows and encourages Israel to think that Yahweh can be appeased, manipulated, influenced, bought off to work Israel's will, that Israel's own purposes count most. The result is that Israel becomes a self-enthroned lord, master of the covenant relationship.

These matters bring us to the heart of the prophetic tradition and its significance for the development and working out of the universal covenant. Read in this light, the passages in the Prophets and Psalms which have been taken to speak of the wider vision that embraces Jew and non-Jew into one mean simply that the most powerful witness God has is an obedient, covenant-keeping people living under his sovereignty.[145]

---

143 *Ibid.*, p. 101.

144 G. von Rad, "Die falschen Propheten," *ZAW* (1933), 109ff., and Eva Osswald, *Falsche Prophetie im Alten Testament* as cited by W. Brueggemann, *Tradition for Crisis,* p. 157, n. 27; see also pp. 102-103 of Brueggemann.

145 E.g. Isa. 2:2-4; Mic. 4:1-4; Hab. 2:14; Zeph. 3:9ff.; Jer. 12:15ff., 13:17; 16:9ff. Passages implying universal acceptance of Israel's God listed by H. H. Rowley, *Missionary Message,* are these: I Kings 8:41ff.; Isa. 55:6; Jer. 3:17; Ps. 86:9ff.; 102:15ff.; 22:27ff.; 67; 68:31ff.; 47:8; 72:8ff.; Zech. 9:9ff.; 8:20ff.; Ps. 18:49ff.; 55:6; 117; 96:1, 7ff.; Isa 66:18ff. In most of the above passages Israel is the passive agent in God's hands

A corollary of the above is that Yahweh who addresses Israel through his true prophets addresses the world through Israel. He is God of the nations. Perhaps no prophet makes it so clear that Yahweh is God of the nations as the prophet Amos. Yahweh had acted in the history of the Philistines and the Arameans (9:7). He sends his fire of judgment on the nations that oppose his authority (1:3–2:3). He summons one nation as the instrument of his wrath against another (6:14). Even world disasters serve his purposes (7:1,4; 4:6-11). His authority extends even to Sheol (9:2-4). In 9:7 the Exodus is cited as an instance of his control of history and set in the context of international history. "In the high points of Hebrew prophecy, the sovereign rule of God is not separated from his sovereign, spiritual presence." [146]

Moltmann recognizes this as a central element in the history of Israel. He shows that the lordship of Yahweh is not displayed in the history of Israel as a wordly kingship over the natural world around man, but leadership towards the land of promise, and thus a historic lordship which shows itself in unique, unrepeatable, startlingly new, purposeful events. The world and all nations become his universe, his kingdom and his praise. "The universal expectation has its ground in remembering the particular historic reality of his sovereign action in Israel." [147]

Through Israel the world would learn and discover the greatness of Israel's God. Confronted by the unmistakable transformation of Israel into a People of God, elect and precious, the nations would give God the glory that is his due. The redemption of Israel becomes the arena in which Israel confronts and subdues the nations. The battle will not be fought with swords and spears nor with the use of swift horses and chariots. The word of God will be the sword (Isaiah 49:2) and the dusty feet of the swift messenger will be beautiful upon the mountains as they carry the news of God's triumph and publish peace (Isaiah 52:7).

In this sense the role of the Messenger of the Covenant (Mal. 3:1) must be understood. His mission is prophetically tied to Jerusalem and Temple. His task is to bear the judgment of God and before Israel and the world to work the redemption which will become good news for all the peoples (Isaiah 53). [148]

---

for the fulfillment of his purpose. Other passages which speak of the nations sharing the faith of Israel and entering into her religious heritage are: Isa. 2:2-4; Mic. 4:1ff.; Isa. 11:9ff.; Hab. 2:14; Isa. 11:1ff.; Zeph. 3:9ff.; Jer. 31:31, 33ff.; Mal. 1:10ff.

146 J. Arthur Baird, *The Justice of God in the Teaching of Jesus* (Philadelphia: Westminster Press, 1963), p. 56, henceforth to be cited as *The Justice of God.*

147 Jürgen Moltmann, *Theology of Hope*, translated by James W. Leitsch (New York and Evanston: Harper and Row, 1965), pp. 216-218.

148 Joachim Jeremias, *The Eucharistic Words of Jesus* (Oxford: Basil Blackwell, 1955), p. 148, tells us that we must distinguish between pre-Christian and post-Christian Judaism's interpretation of Isaiah 52 and 53. Post-Christian Jewish exegesis rejected the interpretation of pre-Christian Jewish scholars that these passages refered to the Gentiles. The passages, which were so important to the church, suffered greatly from the anti-

Blauw observes that "all the emphasis falls on the fact that the world of nations is a gift to the Messianic Servant; there is no reference to the world of nations as the 'missionary territory' of the Servant."[149]

> The ultimate destiny of the world depends on the existence of Israel in the midst of the nations: in living by Yahweh the Chosen People lives for mankind. Such is the missionary outlook that emerges from the oracles of Deutero-Isaiah. The concrete form that the mission of Israel to the world has to assume it that Israel should be the People of God.[105]

When the nations come to Yahweh, they will not lose their national identities. They shall not become Israelites; they will remain members of their own peoples. But they will be recognized as servants of God (Zechariah 2:11).[151] What Karl Barth writes about the church applies equally well to Israel:

> As the community goes to the nations, calling them to discipleship, it does not remove frontiers and differences between them. Nor does it sanction them. It rather constitutes right across them a new people in which the members of all peoples do not merely meet but are united. Gathered to it, men are first members of this new people, i.e. Christians, and only then, without disloyalty to their derivation but above all without compromising their unity, are they members of the different nations.[152]

It is not clear whether the Jews consciously addressed themselves to the conversion of the Gentiles in the light of the messages of the prophets. Many have combed the literature, sorted out the doctrines taught in the Old Testament and found in the literature of the Jews, asking us to believe that the author of some individual book or statement represents both himself and his audience, that his attitude reflects either a broadly held antecedent position or else that it permeated virtually the entire community. The fact is that Scripture represents God's will for his people and the world, and in ancient days as truly as today that will is only imperfectly carried out. Sandmel opines that "virtually all the evidence available concerning outsiders joining themselves to Judaism deals with passive reception . . . . What remains elusive is the question of a Jewish missionary movement."[153] The belief that the true religion must in the end be

Christian Jewish polemic. The pre-Christian exegesis included Jew and Gentile alike in the promises.

149 J. Blauw, *Missionary Nature*, p. 49. A similar opinion is expressed by R. Martin-Achard, *A Light to the Nations*, p. 31.

150 R. Martin-Achard, *A Light to the Nations*, pp. 31, 32.

151 Louis Finkelstein, *The Pharisees*, (3rd ed.; 2 vols.; Philadelphia: The Jewish Publication Society of America, 1962), II, p. 506.

152 K. Barth, *Church Dogmatics*, IV:3, *p. 899.*

153 S. Sandmel, *The First Christian Century*, p. 21; Jean Juster, *Les Juifs dans l'Empire Romain: leur condition juridique, economique et sociale* (2 vols.; New York: B. Franklin, 1965), I, p. 388ff., henceforth to be cited as *Les Juifs*.

universal was enough to make Israel a missionary people and Judaism a missionary religion.[154]

In order to avoid being repetitious, the developments in the pre-exilic period that are regarded by some as laying the foundations for the development of the synagogue, which became a significant institution for Jewish and Christian propaganda, will be passed over for the present.[155] Israel must first be seen as it spread among the nations in the early diaspora. The revelation of God's purpose for Israel and the nations became increasingly clearer and the foundations laid which eventually led to the proselyting movements that prepared the way for the spread of the Christian message. While in the home-land the divine revelation was being reduced to writing and incorporated into the sacred Scriptures, out in the Diaspora the People of God were learning to live among the nations.

3. The Diaspora: A People in the Midst of the Nations

The survey of the Old Testament antecedents and background of the Christian mission has thus far witnessed the appearance of Israel on center stage in God's redemptive drama, observed by the nations, bathed in the light of grace that shone on it through election and covenant. A no less important development of the pre-exilic period involved the movement of significant numbers of the people of Israel into the midst of the nations. From earliest times Palestine was not the exclusive and only home of the Jews although it was the main cultic center. The early dispersions of the Jews were largely voluntary, undertaken for varied reasons, and of great significance for the later dispersions and proselytism. The complete story has never been told; only the broad outlines can be drawn.[156] In tracing the movements of the Jewish people into the world it is sometimes difficult, as Sandmel observes, to weigh the distinction between an ethnic group with religion as its basis and a community that is primarily a religious community.[157] The Jews never lost their ethnic sense, no matter how far they wandered from the ancestral lands. Because they were scattered through

154 G. F. Moore, *Judaism in the First Centuries*, p. 229.

155 For a full treatment of the pre-exilic antecedents of the synagogue see Louis Finkelstein, "Origins of the Synagogue," *Proceedings of the American Academy for Jewish Research*, I, 49-59; A. Menes, "Tempel und Synagoge," *ZAW*, L, 268-76; Salo Wittmeyer Baron, *A Social and Religious History of the Jews* (3 vols.; New York: Columbia University Press, 1937), I, p. 109ff. For the further treatment of this subject see pp. 76-77 of this dissertation.

156 Several scholars have documented what is known of the various Jewish movements and these will be cited. On the problem of a complete picture see S. W. Baron, *A Social and Religious History of the Jews*, p. 128; Thomas Torrance, *China's First Missionaries: Ancient Israelites* (London: Thynne and Co., Ltd., 1937), p. 16; J. H. Waszink, *et al.*, *Het Oudste Christendom en de Antieke Cultuur*, p. 537-560.

157 S. Sandmel, *The First Christian Century*, p. 81.

the world some account had to be taken of the rest of humanity, which in some way necessarily tempered the ethnic sense. According to the Talmud the rabbis wrestled with the question of the proselyte and his relationship to Israel, but it was the ethnic problem that appears most difficult for them to solve: when and under what conditions did the proselyte receive full, legal status as a Jew?

The ancient world was characterized by continued movements of peoples. The settlement of Judaeans and Israelites in foreign lands is not a unique nor an exceptional phenomenon of that age. There are ancient parallels among many of the peoples, e.g., the Phoenicians and the Greeks. The Assyrians established commercial colonies in Cappadocia as early as 1850 B.C.[158] With respect to the Jews the earliest Scriptural references to trade and commerce with other nations occurs in the context of the preparations for and building of the First Temple. Hiram, the king of Tyre and close friend of both David and Solomon, sent his servants to Solomon to teach them the sea-routes of the Mediterranean and the routes from Ezion-Geber and Eloth to Ophir (I Kings 9:26,27; II Chron. 8:27). It appears that prior to the building of this great fleet the Israelites were not great sea-farers. But the alliance thus formed led eventually to the absorption of the Phoenicians by the Jews. The Greeks thought of and referred to the Phoenicians and Jews as being one people and applied one name to them.[159]

From the list of materials used in the construction of Solomon's Temple one catches just a glimpse of the extent of this commerce.[160] The Jews reached India or at least carried on extensive contacts with that land in this period, for all products listed in I Kings 10:22 are of Indian origin. The Hebrew word for "peacock" (*tukkiyyim*) is a word of Dravidic origin.[161] Raisin maintains that the Jews had a great influence on the development of the South Indian alphabets.[162] One may not draw the conclusion from the above that the Jewish Diaspora was largely oriented to commerce.[163] Josephus tells us that not a few

158 Robert Henry Pfeiffer, *History of New Testament Times* (New York: Harper and Bros., 1949), p. 166. Pfeiffer also gives a fully documented summary of the Jews in the lands of their dispersion.

159 S. W. Baron, *A Social and Religious History of the Jews*, I, p. 138; Michael Delafosse, *The Negroes of Africa* (Port Washington, N. Y.: Kennikat Press, 1968), shows how the Jews followed the Phoenicians in all areas. Nahum Slouschz, *Travels in North Africa* (Philadelphia: Jewish Publication Society of America, 1927), p. 212, says "The Greeks could not distinguish between the Hebrews and Phoenicians."

160 See I Kings 9:26-28; 10:11, 15, 22, 27. Levi Herzfeld, *Handelsgeschichte der Juden des Altertums* (Braunschweig: John Heinrich Meyer, 1878), henceforth to be cited as *Handelsgeschichte*, details the extent of this commerce and the origin of the varied commodities, p. 90ff.

161 Thus the *Jewish Encyclopedia*, VI, 581-582; S. Strizower, *Exotic Jewish Communities*, p. 88; A. H. Godbey, *Lost Tribes*, pp. 317, 329-330, traces the linguistic associations with South India in detail.

162 A. H. Godbey, *Lost Tribes*, p. 330; J. S. Raisin, *Gentile Reactions*, p. 23.

163 This is the conclusion that L. Herzfeld drew (*Handelsgeschichte*, p. 202ff.),

Jews served as mercenaries under Alexander the Great. In fact they were much sought after for this purpose.

> Generals, soldiers, policemen, government officials, tax-farmers, estate owners, agricultural laborers, slaves, craftsmen, merchants, money-lenders, physicians — all these types of people were to be found in the Diaspora, and if we had more numerous sources at our disposal we should certainly discover a still greater variety.[164]

One is astonished at the extent of the trade. Herzfeld has detailed the trade carried on by the Babylonian, Syrian, Cyprian, Egyptian, Cyrenian, Ethiopian, Arabian, Asia Minor, and European-Asia Jewish colonies. The list of materials produced and traded is like the goods found in any great Middle Eastern market today: cereal grains, rice, wood, wines, olives, olive oil, dates, various fruits, vegetables, balsam, salves and medicines, spices, honey, wax, animals and various cattle, animal products, fish, luxury goods, raw materials of varied kinds, cloth, clothes, jewelry, weapons, tools, implements, writing materials, salt, and other items for daily use.[165] All of this demonstrates how in a thousand and one ways the Jewish people were thrown into daily contact with their environs, and along with his goods the Jew frequently carried his religion.

Beginning with the Far East and China the lands and areas to which the Jews migrated will be briefly surveyed. China was known to the Jews in the days of Isaiah, being mentioned in Isa. 49:12 by the name Sinim.[166] Silk is mentioned in Ezek. 16:10,13. That the Jews had early contact with silk and China is evidenced by the fact that among the tombs belonging to a Jewish merchant colony in Southern Russia near Kertsch, where the important Pontus trade had its center in Roman times, remants of silk stuff have been discovered, traced to the third century B.C.[167] The existence of Jewish colonies in China dates from very early times. Place names associated with the Jews of China parallel the ancient overland silk routes that extended from Palestine across Asia to the Pacific Coast and Northwest India.[168] The Jews reached China by

basing his claim largely on a list of important commercial centers in which Jews resided from very early times. However, V. A. Tcherikover, *Hellenistic Civilization*, p. 333ff., refutes this thesis in a well-documented study saying, "The list of important cities in which Jews settled can be countered by an equally long list of small villages."

164   Josephus, *Contra Ap.*, I. 22; V. A. Tcherikover, *Hellenistic Civilization*, p. 343.

165   L. Herzfeld, *Handelsgeschichte*, p. 90ff., all of which is documented by this author from Scripture, Talmud, and other sources.

166   There are some who do not accept this identification of China with "Sinim," preferring instead to relate this to a place "Syene," a city in Southern Egypt towards Ethiopia, now called Aswan. Silk came only from China. See on "Sinim," *The Jewish Encyclopedia*, article "China," IV, pp. 33-38.

167   Kaufmann Kohler, "The Jews and Commerce," *The Menorah*, III, (October 1887), 211-217; L. Stephani, *Comptes Rende pour 1878* (St. Petersburgh: 1881), p. 134.

168   A. H. Godbey, *Lost Tribes*, see map on p. 366. Also see the maps by William Charles White, *The Chinese Jews: A Compilation of Matters Relating to the Jews of*

other routes also and in different periods. Some colonies of Chinese Jews came by way of India and Ceylon, from there finding their way to China and forging a final link with those who had come by the overland routes. These Jews have left their traces all along the Southern coasts of Asia, in Ceylon, and in the Eastern Archipelago.[169] Some form of contact was maintained with Indian Jews, for the Black Jews of the Malabar Coast had a list of sixty-five Jewish colonies resident in India, Tartary, and China, all of whom were represented as composed of "Israelites."[170] Others entered China by way of Bactria and Parthia in the days when those ancient kingdoms were under the sway of Antiochus the Great.[171] Later, when Parsee fanaticism in the third and fourth centuries A.D. drove large numbers of Jews out of Babylon, they turned to the existent colonies of India and China and settled permanently around the chief centers of the silk culture, attracted by the trade of Jewish predecessors. They settled in the great cities, including Honan which for awhile was the capital of China.[172]

Oral tradition establishes the only datable early migration to China as taking place during the Han dynasty (206 B.C.–221 A.D.). In favor of the early date for some of these settlers is the fact that when contacted by Christian missionaries in later centuries they knew about Jesus Sirach but had never heard of Jesus Christ. Also, the building known as the Synagogue of K'ai-feng Fu resembled more the pattern of Solomon's Temple than the pattern of the synagogue structures, although the Jews there did commemorate the destruction of the Temple in 70 A.D.[173] Few settlements in Asia surpass them in antiquity, though so far as we know they never reached the size of other colonies. Torrance who has studied the Chiang people of Western China in Western Szechuan (between China proper and Tibet) concludes that these people are definitely not of Chinese stock and that the many similarities between the Old Testament and the customs of these people points to a B.C. origin from a Semitic group. The people themselves claim to be descendants of Abraham. Taking the reference of II Esdras 13:40-45 as referring to the early dispersion of Jews eastward into Afghan, this is a possibility.[174]

K'ai-feng Fu (2nd ed.; Toronto: University of Toronto Press, 1966), pp. A-D, henceforth to be cited as *The Chinese Jews*. Also, A. K. Glover, "The Jews of the Chinese Empire," Part V, *The Menorah*, V (July 1888), 11-15. The most complete and recent bibliography of all matters relating to the Jews of China can be found in Rudolph Löwenthall, "The Jews in China," *Chinese Social and Political Science Review*, XXIV, no. 2 (Peking, 1940).

169 A. Kingsley Glover, "The Jews of the Chinese Empire," *The Henorah*, IV (April 1888), 359-365.

170 A. K. Glover, *The Menorah*, IV (March 1888), 239-249.

171 Sidney Mendelssohn, *The Jews of Asia* (London: Kegan, Paul, Trench and Trubner, 1920), p. 133 (chapter 9); J. Peterson, *Missionary Methods*, p. 137.

172 K. Kohler, "The Jews and Commerce," p. 213.

173 *Jewish Encyclopedia*, IV, p. 33; A. K. Glover, "The Jews of the Chinese Empire," parts 3 and 4, *The Menorah*, IV (May 1888 and June 1888), 439-440, 520-524.

174 T. Torrance, *China's First Missionaries: Ancient Israelites*, p. 17ff. This conclusion drawn by Torrance is by no means certain.

It is of interest that in China alone of all countries the Jews are characterized by a name, *Tiao Kiu Kiou* ("the sect which extracts the sinews"). The name calls attention to an ancient practise based on Gen. 32:33, a custom of great antiquity. Nowhere else is this practice used to give a local name to a race.[175] Adjoining the northern wall of the synagogue of K'ai-feng Fu there was a recess in which the sinews were extracted from the animals slain for food, a remarkable fact since nowhere else is it known that the synagogue was chosen for this practice.[176] All the facts tend to show a long and peculiar development as well as social life of the Jewish community in China.

The synagogue at K'ai-feng Fu is of special interest, for it is in that place that the contact of Christian missions with remaining colonies of Jews in China took place in more recent centuries. The building itself was rather large, being 300-400 feet by 150 feet, having four courts, facing Jerusalem (1 Kings 8:38; Dan. 6:11). The elevated chair in this synagogue was called "the chair of Moses."[177] The colony celebrated the New Moon (which also indicates a pre-Talmudic origin). In the Hall of Ancestors a golden censor was assigned to each patriarch and great man whose memory was perpetuated there. Ezra was included among this group. The history of the group is best known from the inscriptions found there. One says, "Adam the first man was from Teen-chou in the West . . . . Our religion comes originally from T'heen-chuh (= India or Ceylon) . . . . During the Han dynasty this religion entered China." Perhaps there was more than one migration to this place for the tablets are not consistent with respect to this date. In the earliest inscription it is said that a party of seventy families reached China in the Sung dynasty and were invited by the emperor to settle at Piem (modern K'ai-feng). The second says the Jews reached China in the Han dynasty, while a third dates this in the Chou Kingdom or before the year 250 B.C. (1027-256 B.C.).[178]

Western knowledge of the colony came about in this way. In June 1605 a member of the colony, Ai Tien, came to the Jesuit Father Matteo Ricci in Peking to inquire about the religion of which he had heard. W. C. White tells the story in this way:

175 S. Mendelssohn, *The Jews of Asia*, p. 141.

176 *The Jewish Encyclopedia*, IV, p. 36. The author also comments that this shows a very early origin for the colony since "Rabbinic Judaism would have suggested more distinctive peculiarities of the Jews to the Chinese."

177 Muslim travellers mention the Jews in chronicles dated 851. Marco Polo (1286) also spoke of their powerful commercial and political influence and of their synagogues at K'ai-feng Fu and Hangchow. See J. Peterson, *Missionary Methods*, p. 137. On the direction of prayer toward Jerusalem see Franz Landsberger, "The Sacred Direction in Synagogue and Church," *HUCA*, XXIV (1957), pp. 181-204, who shows how very ancient this practice of prayer toward Jerusalem was. "The chair of Moses" is still a common fixture in today's synagogue and is mentioned by Jesus in Matt. 23:2.

178 For full details see *The Jewish Encyclopedia*, IV, article "China," pp. 33-38; the series of articles in *The Menorah* by A. K. Glover; W. C. White, *The Chinese Jews*; S. Mendelssohn, *The Jews of Asia*.

On this occasion Father Ricci asked Ai if he had any knowledge of the Christians and he could say nothing about them under that name. But when he made signs to him, he said that there were certain foreigners in the same city of K'ai-feng, and also at Lin-ching and in Shan-hsi, who had come to China with their ancestors and worshipped the cross, and that part of the doctrine which they recited was from their [Jewish] books which they too recited – this would be the Psalter.[179]

Down to modern times a synagogue still furnished a contact point for the Christian mission!

The K'ai-feng Fu synagogue inscriptions display a loyalty to China in these words, showing how completely the Jews had accepted China as their homeland.

Although our religion enjoins worship thus earnestly, we do not render it merely with a view to securing happiness to ourselves, but, seeing that we have received the favors of the Prince and thus enjoy the emoluments conferred by him, we carry to the uttermost our sincerity in worship with a view to manifesting fidelity to our Prince and gratitude to our country.[180]

Here in China, as elsewhere in the Diaspora, Jerusalem remained their holy city, but they were for generations citizens of the lands of their birth, as Philo said.[181]

The emigration of the Jews to India is even more difficult to assess. The colonies claim various origins, some as early as the captivities; others as late as the destruction of the city of Jerusalem by Titus in 70 A.D.[182] Godbey demonstrates commercial contacts as early as 900-1000 B.C. This does not mean settled, permanent colonies, however.[183] A very early migration is indicated by the Black Jews of the Malabar Coast who possessed few manuscripts and practiced traditions different from those of neighboring Jews of later origin. Their traditions as to their origin date their ancestors to the time of the Babylonian Captivity. Many of the Jews who did not return after the Exile continued to move farther and farther eastward and formed permanent settlements in Central Asia and India. Alexander the Great's conquests were another means of spreading the Jews more widely in the East than ever before. The Jews always seemed to follow on the heels of conquering armies.

The Jews of India down to modern times evidence distinct differences among themselves, in part the result of the various times in which they came to India

---

179   W. C. White, *Chinese Jews*, p. 32ff.

180   A. K. Glover, "The Jews of the Chinese Empire, Part 5," *The Menorah*, V (July 1888), 10-19. The full text of all inscriptions is given here by Glover. Also by the same author "Manuscripts of the Jews of China and India, Part VI," *The Menorah*, V (September 1888), 144-151.

181   Philo, *Flaccum*, 7.

182   S. Mendelssohn, *The Jews of Asia*, p. 98 (chapter 9: "India").

183   A. H. Godbey, *Lost Tribes*, p. 332ff.; see also map on p. 366 showing the trade routes and locations of principal centers.

with different traditions, in part due to the circumstances of their settlement, and in part because of the emergence of distinct characteristic resulting from intermarriage and proselytization (including manumission of slaves). An interesting name for the group which called itself the "Bene-Israel" and which and which settled in the Bombay area, tracing their descent to the ten tribes, was *Shanwar Teli* (literally: "Saturday oilmen" or "a caste of oil pressers who do not work on Saturday").

A very large migration, said to number 100,000 and reported in an ancient Hebrew manuscript, went to India after the destruction of the Second Temple by Titus.[184] Godbey tells of the association of certain Jews who became resident in India with the arrival of Thomas, the first recorded Christian missionary who in the first century reached India with the Gospel. He also mentions that the Craganore Jews showed the early Dutch traders a letter which they claimed was a copy of those reported in Esther 8:9 to their ancestors in North India authorizing them to protect themselves.[185] From Persia some Jews (seventy families) under Joseph Rabban went to the Malabar Coast. By treaty they were given permission to erect synagogues and to convert Hindus to Judaism; in general, to practice and propagate their religion. Many slaves were acquired and admitted to Judaism, receiving their freedom. What is so singular about this instance is that a treaty would be sought not merely to allow the Jews to continue unobstructed in their faith, but permitting them to propagate that faith as well.[186]

The association of the Jews with Arabia goes back a very long time, to the times of Solomon and the Queen of Sheba. The West Coast of the Peninsula was early associated with Jewish trade and shipping. Many Jewish colonies in other lands trace their origins to the Yemen. The region was of great importance for the spread of Jewish trade and colonies both before and after Christ. In 1 B.C., one hundred and twenty large vessels are recorded as leaving the port of Aden to trade in India and the headlands of Ethiopia.[187] The Jews of Yemen had come to love the region so much that when Ezra the scribe sent them a message inviting them to come up to Jerusalem because the the Lord had taken pity on his people through Cyrus, king of Persia, who had liberated them from the Babylonian Captivity, these Yemenite colonies refused. They argued that the Second Temple would also be destroyed and Israel would be dispersed again. Ezra, the traditions say, became very angry and cursed them, prophesying that they would experience great misery and never know lasting happiness. This did happen, and wretchedness and proverty was often their lot.

184 A. K. Glover, "The Jews of India," Part. I of the series "The Jews of the Extreme Eastern Diaspora," *The Menorah*, IV (March 1888), 239-249; S. Strizower, *Exotic Jewish Communities*, pp. 48-124.

185 A. H. Godbey, *Lost Tribes*, p. 332.

186 S. Mendelssohn, *The Jews of Asia*, p. 102; J. Peterson, *Missionary Methods*, p. 137. The Craganore Jews report, "For many centuries our ancestors had a virtually independent principality in Craganore and they were ruled over by a prince of their community." Cf. S. Strizower, *Exotic Jewish Communities*, p. 90.

187 A. H. Godbey, *Lost Tribes*, p. 174.

The tradition helps to explain the hostile attitude of the region's Jews to Ezra.[188]

Stone tablets recovered in the Yemen give evidence of the process by which the royal household was gradually judaized, reaching its height in the sixth century A.D. when a Jew, Yuseph Dhu Nuwas, became king. The Christian Church was also very powerful in this region, very likely experiencing its great advances as the result of the Jewish presence which preceded it. The early Yemen Jews lived in the very heart of their communities, as their occupations show. They were builders, carpenters, diggers of cisterns, potters, tailors, weavers, leather workers (shoes and water skins), manufacturers of ornaments and utensils of gold and silver, makers and repairers of farm implements, manufacturiers of armaments. The list of their crafts includes fifty different trades. As early as the commencement of the African trade with Palestine, the Jewish religion had spread itself far into Arabia and made considerable progress far into Africa.[189]

In addition to colonies voluntarily settled in Assyria, Babylonia and Persia, the forced deportations of large numbers of Jews into these regions by the kings of these lands are well known from the Scriptures. According to the Jewish sages the Assyrians "mixed up the world" by their systematic policy of deporting whole nations for security reasons.[190] This had its benefits, as Godbey notes, for "religious influence of Israelite colonies in the 'Cities of the Medes' would extend as far as the political and commercial activity of the Medo-Persian and Parthian protectors. Iranized Yahwism would not be Talmudic."[191] The Jews in Persia were from a very early date connected with the silk trade with China.

188 S. Mendelssohn, *The Jews of Asia*, chaps. 10 & 11, pp. 164-180; S. Strizower, *Exotic Jewish Communities*, p. 12; Itzhak Ben-Zvi, *The Exiled and the Redeemed* (London: 1958), pp. 23-25.

189 S. Mendelssohn, *The Jews of Asia*, p. 164ff., deals with Judaism in the Yemen.

190 Ben Zion Dinur, *Israel and the Diaspora* (Philadelphia: The Jewish Publication Society of America, 1969), p. 3. This Assyrian policy was especially important in the judgment of the Rabbis who concluded that because the world was so mixed up it was no longer possible to identify the nations which by Biblical proscription were not permitted to come under the wings of the Shekinah (e.g., Ammon, Egypt). They taught that all men should be accepted. In the *BT*, Ber. 168, Judah, an Ammonite proselyte asked to be admitted to the *Beth Ha-Midrash*. The question was raised regarding the prohibitions of Deuteronomy 26:4. It was decided that the Ammonites and Moabites no longer live in their ancestral homes, and "Sennecharib, king of Assyria, long ago went up and mixed up all the nations . . . and whatever strays from a group belongs to the larger section of the group." W. G. Braude, *Jewish Proselyting*, p. 55, says, "The rabbis of the pre-Christian centuries and the first Christian century did all they could to lessen the burden of discrimination imposed on the Ammonite proselytes by scriptural authority." The dispersions by the Persians are documented by J. Peterson, *Missionary Methods*, pp. 134-139. A. H. Godbey, *Lost Tribes*, p. 366, has a good map locating the migrations and deportations. E. Janssen, *Juda in der Exilszeit*, pp. 25-39, also details these deportations and the numbers of Jews involved. Cf. also R. H. Pfeiffer, *History of New Testament Times*, p. 166ff.; V. A. Tcherikover, *Hellenistic Civilization*, pp. 202-205, 504-555.

191 A. H. Godbey, *Lost Tribes*, note on map, p. 366.

Historians have disputed whether or not during the many centuries in which the large Jewish population maintained itself in the various provinces pertaining to Persian power Judaism influenced Iran's religious development. From a very early date there was interchange between the religions, however. The deportations of Sargon (721 B.C.) to Media spread the Jews still further over large areas. In the nineteenth century A.D. all Jews domiciled in Persia declared that they were descendants of the first exiles from the Kingdom of Israel. Jews had been settled in Khurdistan by Tiglath Pileser (738 B.C.) The prophet Nahum seems to have had first hand acquaintance with Nineveh and may have lived there. Here Ezra the scribe died on his journey from Jerusalem to King Artaxerxes. There is no doubt that the Jewish religion of the Persian Empire was an official religion, "The Established Church" for all Jews.[192]

The commercial activities of the Jews in Babylon are well documented. The records of one commercial firm ("Murashu & Sons Bank") show this firm as having dealings with Persians, Medes, and Arameans and numbers of others in the international trade.[193] Large numbers of the Jews in Babylon were farmers, serving for Jews as well as non-Jews. Many were poor. Others were the artisans, while others excelled in brewing beer.[194] During and after the Exile Babylon emerged as a center of Jewish religion and learning. It is there that we find the development of the synagogue, sanhedrin, Jewish apostolate, and from there great Jewish scholars came. One of the greatest treasurers of Judaism is the Babylonian Talmud.[195] Some believe that at least one of the Jewish colonies in Babylon erected a copy of the Temple of Jerusalem.[196] At the time of Christ Babylon is estimated to have had a Jewish population of 1,000,000 or more, as did Syria, Egypt, and Asia Minor.[197] Babylon assumed

192 Article "China" in the *Jewish Encyclopedia*, IV, p. 33ff.; K. Kohler, "The Jews and Commerce" in *The Menorah*, IV, 211; S. Mendelssohn, *The Jews of Asia*, pp. 73-97 (the Jews in Persia), p. 181ff. on Khurdistan. Hermann Vogelstein, "The Development of the Apostolate in Judaism and its Transformation in Christianity," *HUCA*, II (1925), 99-124, especially p. 100 where the author refers to the Elephantine papyri and the Pesach epistle of Darius II.

193 G. Ricciotti, *History of Israel*, II, p. 63.

194 Ely Emanuel Pilchik, *Judaism Outside the Holy Land: The Early Period* (New York: Block Publishing Co., 1964), p. 106, henceforth to be cited as *Judaism*. Many mercenaries from among the Jews received estates and lands on the borders of the countries in which or for which they served. It was common practice to seek their compatriots in Palestine, who were willing to emigrate, to work these lands for them, thus strengthening and enlarging the Jewish community.

195 E. M. Pilchik, *Judaism*, p. 103ff. Ezra came from Babylon, as did the Great Hillel, teacher of Gamaliel the teacher of Paul; so too Rabbi Chiyya, co-editor of the Mishnah.

196 James William Parkes, *The Foundations of Judaism and Christianity* (Chicago: Quadrangle Books, 1960), p. 6ff., refers to Ezekiel 20 which some authors take as a reply to the community of Kasiphia.

197 S. W. Baron, *A Social and Religious History of the Jews*, I, p. 132; S. Grayzel, *A History of the Jews*, p. 138; F. A. Norwood, *Strangers and Exiles*, p. 141.

great importance for Judaism of the Diaspora and constituted one of the principal strands of a network which included Jerusalem and Alexandria and almost completely enveloped the ancient world in its web. Later, Antioch would constitute a fourth center.[198] When Judaism waned elsewhere in the third century A.D., it continued to flourish in Babylon.[199] It was in Babylon that the word *ger*, which formerly had a geographic connotation, first assumed a religious significance. It was there that Judaism first divested itself of the last shred of blood and soil and proclaimed that faith alone renders one an alien or a member of the community of Israel. It was the old but still loyal Babylonian families who gave tone to the Jewish community and who could speak and write on Judaism in Aramaic and thus familiarize others with the doctrines of their religion, a step in the direction of proselytism. These Jews accepted full citizenship in the lands in which they and their forefathers had lived for centuries while at the same time remaining for the most part loyal to their faith. Philo says, "We hold sacred the holy city, but we regard as our fatherland the land of our birth." [200]

It was in Egypt that the people of Israel grew to nationhood and there the Jewish nation was born at the time of the Exodus. Commercial relations with Egypt were carried on long before that time, however. Abraham lived there (Gen. 12:10); Sarah had an Egyptian maid as her personal servant (Gen. 16:1); Joseph was sold as a slave to Egypt by way of an Ishmaelite caravan (Gen. 37:25); Jacob emigrated to Egypt at God's revelation (Gen. 46:3). We have already noted that a mixed multitude went out of Egypt in the Exodus and that they had identified themselves with Israel religiously as well as nationally. It is not necessary to chronicle the contacts between Israel and Egypt as shown in the Scriptures. Isaiah does mention ambassadors from Nubia, a land "buzzing with insects" (Isa. 18:1), and Isa. 19 tells of five cities of the Egyptians that would "speak the language of Canaan and swear allegiance to the LORD of hosts" (19:18). In Isa. 27:12 Jews are mentioned as living there. Alexander the Great forced many Jews to settle there. Some scholars have found remarkable parallels between the proverbs of Amenope who lived in Solomon's time and Prov. 22:17–23:11.[201] The trade routes followed by the Jews down the Nile have been documented, and at a very early date served as staging areas for the Westward march of the Jew and Jewish influence across the heartland of Africa to the Atlantic Coast where they were joined with similar commercial activities which crossed the Sahara and followed the Northern and Western Coasts by way of the Mediteranean.[202] It is simply impossible to define the

198 G. Ricciotti, *History of Israel*, II, p. 63.

199 E. M. Pilchik, *Judaism,* p. 103.

200 J. L. Koole, *De Joden in de Verstrooiing*, p. 9.

201 A. H. Godbey, *Lost Tribes*, p. 189-193; 205; T. J. Meek, *JR*, VII, no. 3 (1927), pp. 247-248.

202 Maps detailing this can be found in A. H. Godbey, *Lost Tribes*, p. 256; M. Delafosse, *The Negroes of Africa*; J. J. Williams, *Hebrewisms*, p. 323ff.

beginnings of Hebrew influence in Africa, but it was very early and of considerable extent.

Ptolemy I granted the Jews a separate section of the city of Alexandria "so that they might not be hindered in the observance of their laws by continual contact with the pagan population." Eventually the Jews came to constitute 40% of the population of that great city and ⅛ of that of the country. Under this great king the Jews became so numerous that "at length no other country besides Palestine contained so many individuals of the nation."[203] Many of the Jews who settled in Egypt were mercenaries, although this term does not always mean soldiers and can include traders who went along with the troops. Not all of the Jews remained true to the faith of the fathers for the tomb inscriptions show that some took the names of the erotic deities, Aphrodite and Isis, e.g.[204] At Elephantine a temple was built, but the papyri show deviations from the pure worship. Onias of Leontopolis received permission to build a temple which continued from 160 B.C. to 73 A.D. (Isa. 19:19?). It must be noted that Jerusalem continued to be the center of Judaism, even for the Jews of Egypt. The Temple of Onias was neither a full temple in the sense of the Jerusalem structure, nor was it merely a place of assembly. It was less than a temple but more than a synagogue. It was a *bama*, a high place where sacrifices could be brought and made. The high places were never intended to be permanent or central places of worship. The history of the Jews indicates quite clearly that after the buildings of Solomon's Temple the presence of other places of worship divided the people. Kings are charged with less than full obedience to the Lord because the high places were not removed from the land (I Kings 15:14, II Kings 15:4, e.g.). It is possible that the reference may be to the continued existence of pagan shrines, although there likely were also such high places to Yahweh. Certainly Deut. 12:21 permitted the slaughtering of animals outside the cental place of worship whenever the latter was not of easy access.[205]

Ezekiel laments the fact that in the Exile period some of the Jews became pagan missionaries who "hunted the souls as birds" in the hope that they would

203 Sidney Mendelssohn, *The Jews of Africa* (London: Kegan Paul, Trench, Trubner, 1920), p. 35; S. Grayzel, *A History of the Jews*, p. 138. The very best bibliography detailing the presence, history, and influence of the Jews in Africa is found in Mendelssohn's book, pp. 191-196. D. M. Eichhorn, *Conversion to Judaism*, pp. 35-36.

204 J. L. Koole, *De Joden in de Verstrooiing*, p. 31.

205 E. M. Pilchik, *Judaism*, p. 21ff.; William Foxwell Albright, *From the Stone Age to Christianity* (New York: Doubleday, 1957), p. 349ff. has a complete survey of the latest material on the presence of the Jews in Egypt, especially after the fourth century, B. C.; S. W. Baron, *A Social and Religious History of the Jews*, I, p. 104ff. On the Leontopolis temple see J. H. Waszink, *et al.*, *Het Oudste Christendom*, p. 546. For a discussion of the Elephantine papyri, consult Laurence Edward Browne, *Early Judaism* (Cambridge: University Press, 1920). Our chief source of information on the temple of Onias is Josephus (*Bell. Jud.* 1.1.1, 7.10.2-3; *Ant.* 13.5.1, 13.9.7, 20.10.3). See also S. A. Hirsch, "The Temple of Onias," *London Jews College Jubilee Volume* (London: Luzac and Co., 1906), pp. 36-80.

thus save their own souls. These, especially the women, cowed the hearts of the righteous by their divinations and strengthened the hands of the wicked by distributing among them handfuls of barley and crumbs of bread in return for their willingness to admit that they had seen the light of paganism (Ezek. 13:18ff.).[206]

Egyptian Judaism made important contributions to the Jewish and Christian missions. Here the apologete Philo lived and wrote, whose great contributions to the Jewish apologetic are well known. The third century B.C. literature is characterized by the production of numerous histories of the Jews, displaying a kind of national pride and interest.[207] Although Philo respresents to Sandmel a Judaism that is the result of as complete a hellenization as was possible for a group which retained its loyalty to the Torah and the separateness of the group, "he represents with his associates a marginal, aberrative version of Judaism, of which ultimately only Rabbinism and Christianity have survived to our day."[208] It is to the Hebrew scholars from Egypt that the people of God owe the production of what was probably the greatest single factor in spreading the faith and preparing the way for the fulfillment in Christ: the Septuagint version of the Old Testament.

Jewish presence in Africa was not limited to Egypt and environs. On the coasts they engaged in overseas commerce, a traffic begun in the days of Solomon and Hiram. When they moved inland their principal occupations were preparation of tiles, roofing, earthen vessels and pottery of all descriptions. In Abysinnia and Ethiopia the legends consistently refer to a Jewish kingdom of greater extent than that of Solomon. The Abysinnians who in large numbers were converted to Judaism possessed the entire Old Testament except the Book of Esther although they did not observe the Feast of Purim. Nor did they know the Talmud or Mishnah, all of which points to a B.C. origin of their faith.[209] The histories of the times tell us that on the eve of the Roman invasion, there existed between Elephantis and Ethiopia autonomous Jewish colonies which were military, agricultural and industrial in character, with a republican form of government and which exercised a civilizing religious influence on the natives of the country.[210]

" Somewhere in the dim past, a wave, or more probably a series of waves, of Hebraic influence swept over Negro Africa," says Williams, "leaving unmistakable traces among the various tribes, where they have endured to this day." [211]

---

206 J. S. Raisin, *Gentile Reactions*, p. 131.

207 For a survey and bibliography of these histories see G. Ricciotti, *History of the Jews*, II, p. 199ff.; R. H. Pfeiffer, *History of New Testament Times*, pp. 197-230 surveys the histories of the Maccabean period.

208 S. Sandmel, *Philo's Place*, p. 221.

209 S. Mendelssohn, *The Jews of Africa*, pp. 1-30; J. Peterson, *Missionary Methods*, p. 138.

210 N. Slouschz, *Travels in North Africa*, p. 213. See note 207 above.

211 J. J. Williams, *Hebrewisms of West Africa*, p. 319. This is a very valuable book.

At the beginning of the Christian era there was a prosperous Jewish diaspora spread over the whole of Northern Africa as far as the shores of the Atlantic.

> Proselyting had won over many Berber Tribes, not only of the coast but also of the hinterland. And it would be difficult at this distant point to distinguish these Judaized Berbers from the colonized Hebrews with the infusion of Berber blood that was entailed by their early associations and subsequent intermarriages. For all practical purposes in religious matters they acted as a unit, especially in opposition to Grecian and Roman paganism, and the prosperity of what we might call Jewish Colonial Africa was at its height.[212]

The migrations across the Sahara of large bodies of Hebrews and of more or less Hebraized tribes was met from the South and East by similar migrations from the headwaters of the Nile. Williams summarizes the result of these contacts as follows:

> The Supreme Being not only of the Ashanti and allied tribes, but most probably of the whole of Negro land as well, is not the God of the Christians which, at a comparatively recent date, was superimposed on the various tribal beliefs by ministers of the Gospel: but the Yahweh of the Hebrews, and that too of the Hebrews of pre-exilic times, that either supplanted the previous concept of divinity in the African mind, or else clarified and defined the original monotheistic idea which may have lain dormant for many centuries, or even perhaps been buried for a time in an inexplicable confusion of polytheism and superstition. It was the triumph over the darkness of error of the original monotheistic idea, that had existed previous to the lapse from grace of the parents of the Human Race, and the reawakening of this primitive concept was the fruit of the Diaspora of the Chosen People of God that was to pave the way for Christianity.[213]

Mendelssohn makes this observation:

> Although many were unobservant of many Jewish customs, ... in short, they were not orthodox Jews, ... there can be little doubt that many of the Berber tribes embraced Judaism, and that the troglodyte villages still existing in Tripoli are inhabited by the descendants of sons of these Jewish converts who retain some of the traces of Judaism. Many of these people have the tradition that their forebears came from Palestine or from the countries in

---

An extensive bibliography is found on pp. 357-409. On p. 320 the author summarizes the influences he has discovered and expresses his belief that "diffusion is the only plausible explanation for these trait-complexes" (p. 321). A nondiffusionist might interpret the data differently but some explanation will have to be given to account for the mass of evidence. See also A. H. Godbey, *Lost Tribes*, map on page 256 and notes.

212 J. J. Williams, *Hebrewisms*, p. 323; N. Slouschz, *Travels in N. Africa*, P. 274.
213 J. J. Williams, *Hebrewisms*, p. 355ff.

the vicinity of the Holy Land. Little is known, however, regarding the history and customs of these primitive Jews, among whom, it has been contended, Rabbinical Judaism was not known.[214]

In the regions of Tripoli there are ruins of synagogues, troglodyte villages and Jewish catacombs or subterranean mortuaries from the early B.C. period of the Jewish diaspora. With respect to Tunisia the records of Jewish colonies in Carthage go back to very early times, some to the building of the first temple, some after the destruction of the First Temple (587 B.C.). The Jewish presence in Algeria is certain after 587 B.C. In Morocco, some of the Jews in the area of the Atlas Mountains say that their ancestors did not go into the Babylonian Captivity and that they possess many ancient writings. Many of the tribes are reported as possessing legends and traditions connecting them with such early Jewish settlers.[215]

A similar story can be told for Europe. Godbey places colonies of Jews on the Middle Danube as early as 400 B.C., north of the Black Sea in the Persian Period, and says that Yahwism was found in the Lydia-Caria area (seven churches of Asia Minor) from Jehoiada's time (836 B.C.).[216] Jehoiada, it is known, used Carian temple guards (II Kings 11:4). The colonies in Southern Russia associated with the silk trade have been mentioned previously. Synagogues were located in Yugoslavia, Decia, and Dura-Europos.[217] The colonization of Asia Minor, Greece, Italy and the Iberian peninsula are well known.[218] Much of this was voluntary, but not all. Among the sins of the peoples of Gaza, Tyre, Edom mentioned by Amos is that of selling large numbers of the people of God into slavery (largely to the Greeks) in the catastrophe of 485 B.C.[219]

The extent of the Diaspora is shown by the many lands listed as receiving from the Romans a copy of their treaty with Simon Maccabeus, protecting the Jews in their right to worship God. In 161 B.C. the Jews had received the status of *peregrini* in the Roman Empire, ennabling them to be judged by their own laws and follow their own customs in marriage and inheritance. In 110 B.C. this status was secured for Jews everywhere in all states and kingdoms controlled by or allied with Rome. Previously under Medo-Persian power Ezra

214 S. Mendelssohn, *The Jews of Africa*, p. 64.

215 *Ibid.*, pp. 64, 80, 105, 142. A list of sources is given by the author on p. 191-196.

216 A. H. Godbey, *Lost Tribes*, map on p. 316.

217 S. W. Baron, *A Social and Religious History of the Jews*, III, p. 52, n. 15.

218 Max Radin, *The Jews Among the Greeks and Romans* (Philadelphia: Jewish Publication Society of America, 1915), is a well-documented survey. See also Josephus, *Ant.*, XIV.10, and Philo, *Legatio*, 36. Harry J. Leon, *The Jews of Ancient Rome* (Philadelphia: Jewish Publication Society of America, 1960-5721), details what is known of the Jewish community in Rome. On p. 259 he says, "We have more information about the Jews of Rome than about any other community of the Diaspora in ancient times." Leon's book includes an extensive bibliography and is an important source for our knowledge of this community.

219 Cf. Amos 1; J. Morgenstern, "Jerusalem in 485 B.C.," *HUCA*, XXXI, p. 16.

was given authority to govern all Jews beyond the Euphrates (7:24), including the right to punish.[220] As a result the diaspora communities were largely self-governing, possessed considerable judicial, fiscal, and administrative autonomy, and controlled all matters of entry into the community and the personal rights and status of their members. The apostle Paul testifies to this power and autonomy of the communities when he tells us that he had five times received thirty-nine stripes from the Jews (II Cor. 11:24). It was Julius Caesar who had said that "Jews might live according to their Torah," implying two things: (1) recognition of the Torah as part of the public law of the Empire, and (2) acceptance of any Jewish community anywhere within the Empire as part of a single Jewish people. This was a unique concession.[221]

Ricciotti summarizes as follows:

> When Sulla was waging his campaign against Mithradaites in 84 B.C. the Jewish nation had "already made its appearance in every city and it would not be easy to find a place on the inhabited earth which has not given refuge to this people and which has not been occupied by it." Agrippa's letter in 40 A.D. to the emperor Caligula: "Jerusalem is the metropolis not only of the region of Judea but of very many others because of the colonies she has sent out on different occasions to neighboring lands: to Egypt, Phoenicia, to Syria, and the so-called Coelesyria, to the remote territories, Pamphylia, Cilicia, to many parts of Asia up to Bithynia and to the remote corners of Pontus; likewise to Europe, Tessaly, Boetia, Macedonia Aetelia, Attica, Argus, Corinth, to the more populous and better parts of the Peloponnesus. Not only are the continents full of Jewish colonies but also the more important islands, Euboea, Cyprus, and Crete. I do not speak, however, of all the lands on the other side of the Euphrates; expect for a small area, all the satrapies, Babylonia and the others which have a surrounding fertile country, contain Jewish inhabitants."[222]

All of which agrees with what Philo said about the Jews: "They frequent all the most prosperous and fertile countries of Europe and Asia." And Strabo is quoted by Josephus as saying, "It is hard to find a place in the habitable earth that has not admitted this tribe of men, and is not possessed by it."[223]

---

220 J. S. Raisin, *Gentile Reactions*, p. 158, gives the list in full. See also Josephus, *Ant.*, XIII.9.2, XIV.10.22; I Macc. 8:22; J. W. Parkes, *The Conflict of the Church and Synagogue*, p. 8. G. Coleman Luck, *Commentary on Ezra and Nehemiah* (Chicago: Moody Press, 1969), p. 57.

221 J. Juster, *Les Juifs*, I, pp. iii; 252, n. 1; 440ff.: J. W. Parkes, *Foundations*, p. 104; E. Schürer, *Geschichte*, II:2 (E.T.), pp. 291-295, lists the privileges given the Jews by the Romans.

222 Josephus, *Ant.*, XIV.7.2; *Bell. Jud.*, II.16.4, VII.3.3; Philo, *Flaccum* 7; G. Ricciotti, *The History of Israel*, II, p. 173.

223 Philo, *Flaccum* 7, cited by F. M. Derwacter, *Preparing the Way for Paul*, p. 76, n. 3. Josephus, *Ant.*, XIV.7.2.

The civic status of the Jew in the Greek world was not always uniform. For one thing, although

> theoretically the Jewish community was open to every Jew who had come from another country to settle in the place where that community existed, the continual emigration from Palestine, which caused the flourishing of the communities in various countries, also caused a division in the community itself. The civic status of the Jews in the Greek world was not the same for all members of the community; those that had come first enjoyed certain rights, while the new immigrants were looked on as foreigners. Within the community existed aristocratic groups which constituted the upper stratum of society, and side by side with them the broad sections of the population, including chiefly those immigrants who arrived later. Sometimes several communities existed in one city, the reason for their separateness from one another cannot now be determined.[224]

The Greek world also granted a special status to the Jew, although (1) this was not uniform and the extent of the Jew's rights depended on when, how and for what purpose they came to a given community outside Palestine, (2) The organized Jewish community as a whole stood juridically outside the Greek city and the Jews who lived in it had no civic rights there, (3) Isolated Jews could acquire civic rights individually. The focus of Jewish life in the Diaspora must be found in the privileges of the Jewish communities, not in citizen rights in the Greek towns. The Jews lived as a true *ger* outside the Promised Land.[225]

The case of the proselyte was different and often difficult. The Romans did not always treat proselytes to Judaism in the same way in all periods. A Jew who was excommunicated from the synagogue lost all his legal privileges as a Jew, and his situation could be extremely burdensome. Even when the Jews regarded the proselyte as a full Jew, this did not mean that the authorities were prepared to accord him such status.[226] In this respect Christianity's freedom from Jewish privilege was an advantage to the Christian church. As late as 80-90 A.D. Jewish Christians still frequented the synagogues until the Jewish anti-Christian propaganda sought deliberately to exclude Christians from participation in the synagogue worship. The break was finalized after the Bar Cochba revolt when a Christian bishop was installed in the city of Jerusalem.[227]

224 V. A. Tcherikover, *Hellenistic Civilization*, p. 297; E. Schürer, *Geschichte*, III, 81ff. on Rome. Tcherikover deals with the Jewish community in its relationship to the Greek cities and the ways in which the Jews enjoyed peculiar privileges to live according to their ancestral laws; cf. Part. II, chapter 2 with its full documentation from the sources.

225 V. A. Tcherikover, *Hellenistic Civilization*, pp. 331-332.

226 *The Biblical, Theological and Ecclesiastical Encyclopedia*, VIII, p. 659, details the sufferings and problems of converts to Judaism and the disfavor in which they were often held.

227 J. W. Parkes, *The Conflict of the Church and Synagogue*, pp. 61-79. Jerome, Justin and Eusebius make reference to a letter from the Jewish Patriarch in Palestine to all the Diaspora synagogues warning them not to have dealings with Christians. Al-

Judaism remained something incomprehensible to the Roman world. Parkes observes, "It would have been astonishing that philosophers did not appreciate it had they not been quite unaccustomed to the combination of ethics which they could approve, with ritual and theological presuppositions which they associated only with superstition."[228] Philo does judge, however, that "the daily uninterrupted respect shown them by those to whom they have been given" created widespread respect on the part of the Gentiles for Jewish laws.[229] It is sufficiently clear from the anti-semitic literature of the pre-Christian era that Jewish religious customs such as circumcision, Sabbath, festivals, and dietary laws were the first things to attract the attention of the Gentiles and served as signs which made the Jews immediately recognizable.[230] It was largely this literature which prompted the production of the Jewish apologetic works, as Aptowitzer has pointed out.[231]

The Jewish apologists answered the attacks and accusations of the pagans by pointing out the ridiculousness and absurdity of the fables regarding the origin of the Jewish people, declared that the exclusiveness of the Jewish people was a necessary precaution and protection against the immorality of the pagans and against their idol worship, and showed that the Jews, despite their exclusiveness and rejection of emperor worship, were yet loyal citizens of the state and were loyally devoted to their rulers. They refuted the charge they were godless by pointing out the loftiness and reasonableness of the Jewish worship of God, and the baseness and unreasonableness of heathenism. Concerning this question, they did not limit themselves to defending the Jewish religion but they actually carried the attack over to their opponents, and initiated a violent attack

though we do not have the letter, it is possible to define certain details that were included in it. The letter included instructions for (1) the daily cursing of Christ in the synagogues; (2) excommunication of Christians; (3) avoidance of discussion with Christians; (4) denial of Christian teaching about the Person and death of Jesus. See also Harm Mulder, "Ontstaan en doel van het vierde evangelie," *Gereformeerd Theologisch Tijdschrift*, 69 (1969), pp. 251-252.

228 *Ibid.*, p. 23.

229 Philo, *De Vita Moses*, 2.5.

230 V. A. Tcherikover, *Hellenistic Civilization*, p. 345ff., has a complete summary and critique of this anti-semitic literature. The attacks on the Jews did not concern their religion only; the economic, religious, and political affairs of the Jews were also foci of attack.

231 V. Aptowitzer, "Asenath: the Wife of Joseph — A Haggadic Literary — historical Survey" in *HUCA*, I (1924), 239-306. This book is a study of the Haggadic material *re* Asenath who merits great distinction in the Haggadic tradition. The author concludes that the book comes from the period characterized by a strong inclination towards Judaism on the part of the heathen world, the period of "Jewish propaganda, of the conflict between Judaism and paganism, the period of mass conversions to the faith of Israel, when the heathen population flocked to Judaism in great numbers. It was the period in which Philo could say regarding the Jewish laws, 'they attract everybody and win them over easily — barbarians, Hellenists, inhabitants of the mainland, inhabitants of the islands, the population of the Orient and of the Occident, Europe, Asia, the entire inhabited world, from one end to the other.' "

against idol worship, a conflict replete with bitter and acrid polemics. Even if the apologetical and polemical purposes which these writers served are not considered, from a positive point of view they were carrying on a propaganda in behalf of the faith of Israel.

Ricciotti describes the development in this way:

> In the beginning, when the Diaspora was still an inconsequential thing, the strange Jewish race must have aroused only a neutral curiousity. When this strange race spread throughout the world without fusing with its environment, when Jewish colonies (communities) everywhere formed impenetrable spiritual citadels, and especially superior to the surrounding worshippers of Jupiter and Artemis, and shunned all moral contact with their neighbors — although they were themselves often rude and uncultured — then the reaction set in.[232]

4. The Significance of the Diaspora

Jer. 29:1-7 contains a copy of the letter Jeremiah sent to the elders, priests, prophets and people in the Babylonian exile. This letter constitutes a kind of charter for the continuation of Israel's religion outside the Holy Land. Verses 4-7 read:

> Thus says the LORD of hosts, the God of Israel, to all the exiles whom I have sent into exile from Jerusalem to Babylon: Build houses and live in them; plant gardens and eat their produce. Take wives and have sons and daughters; take wives for your sons, and give your daughters in marriage, that they may bear sons and daughters; multiply there, and do not decrease. But seek the welfare of the city where I have sent you into exile, and pray to the LORD on its behalf, for in its welfare you will find your welfare.

The same prophet tells the nations in 31:10 that the scattering of the people was the work of Yahweh, God of Israel, but that he did not forget his covenant and would also gather them again. The scattering of the people among the nations had been prophesied as an inevitable consequence resulting from their rejection of Yahweh and disobedience to his covenant (Lev. 26:33; Deut. 4:27; 28:64; 30:3; Jer. 9:12-16). Although the scattering of Israel was often looked at as punishment for sin, Rabbi Eleazer said, "The Holy One, Blessed

232 G. Ricciotti, *The History of Israel*, II, p. 191. The Jews also held the pagans in contempt (cf. Josephus, *Contra Ap.*, II.6.65). Pliny called the Jews "an impious race" (*contumelia numinis insignis*) in his *Natural History*, XIII, 4:46. Appolonius Molo called them "atheists" (Josephus, *Contra Ap.*, II.14.148). Alexandria was a center of many anti-Jewish calumnies, a full documentation and analysis can be found in Ricciotti, p. 193ff. J. L. Koole, *De Joden in de Verstrooiing*, p. 28, says that Tacitus described the Jews as "een walgelijk volk" ("a disgusting, loathsome people"). Roman attitudes are also discussed by A. H. Godbey, *Lost Tribus*, p. 459.

be he, dispersed Israel among the nations in order that proselytes should be added to them." [233]

Scattered and dispersed among the nations, the Jews could maintain their existence and national features only as long as the organization of their internal life was of sufficient strength to serve as a barrier against the influences of the alien environment. The establishment of colonies marks the beginning of the extension of Judaism to the environing population. In this way the centers of the Jewish diaspora (military stations, commercial establishments, trading centers, agricultural settlements, etc.) became a nucleus for the proselyting of surrounding areas. The religion of the Jews exercised a powerful influence on the peoples with whom they were thrust into daily contact. Even in places where the Jews mingled eventually with the peoples of their adopted lands, relics of their proselytism are to be found today among many Asiatic and African peoples from China to the Gold Coast.[234] The real strength of Judaism lay in the days of the Roman Empire in the Diaspora, not in Judea and Galilee, for many of the returned exiles showed their determination to continue the association of the Jewish people with the history, the religion, and the land of Israel. It was a direct result of the Exile that the faith of Israel was transferred from the Old Testament temple-centered cult to the individual-centered faith of universal validity. In general it may be said that Israel threw off the vestment of her statehood together with her kingdom with remarkable ease and without apparent internal crisis. She could still think of herself and her dispersed children as Yahweh's people.[235]

Dispersion alone does not guarantee the perpetuation and enlargement of a community or the continuation and development of its faith. The Samaritans are a people in many respects similar to the Jews. They too were forced to leave the Holy Land and formed communities abroad in the great centers of the Empire – Tripoli, Egypt, Rome, etc. But their extreme exclusiveness and closed communities made it impossible for them to continue their Diaspora communities for very long except in Damascus, which place also they eventually quit. The most tenacious vitality of the community could not save it on foreign soil because it had "experienced neither the exile nor the prophetic emancipation of religion from its territorial roots."[236]

This is what made it possible for Judaism outside Palestine to keep the community together in days of adversity.[237] This does not deny the fact that

233 *BT*, Jes. 87b.
234 J. W. Parkes, *The Conflict of the Church and the Synagogue*, p. 7ff.; A. H. Godbey, *Lost Tribes*, pp. 105-110.
235 J. L. Koole, *De Joden in de Verstrooiing*, p. 5; J. W. Parkes, *The Foundations of Judaism and Christianity*, p. 3; G. von Rad, *Old Testament Theology*, I, p. 90.
236 S. Strizower, *Exotic Jewish Communities*, pp. 156-157; S. W. Baron, *A Social and Religious History of the Jews*, II, p. 30.
237 F. A. Norwood, *Strangers and Exiles*, p. 45; E. Janssen, *Juda in der Exilszeit*, p. 57ff.

Jerusalem remained the spiritual capital where pilgrims from all over the diaspora would gather. The Synagogue, whose significance will be considered, became the place where Israel could withstand the influences of its hostile environment. It was there in the weekly gathering for fellowship and teaching, more than anything else, that the Jew was refreshed and where he met the Gentile on the most fundamental issues of life: their mutual responsibility to the one true God.

The event that in 587 B.C. took place in Jerusalem — the defeat and captivity of its people, the destruction of the city and ultimately of the temple too — from the standpoint of world history was little more than the so ordinary fate of many other small centers of government as they were subsumed under the authority of greater powers. But in actual fact it was something quite different, for through Israel the King of kings was preparing the way by which his people would be more than conquerors and the world come to share in this victory.

5. *The Synagogue*

The return from the Babylonian Exile in 536 B.C. marked a turning point in Jewish history. The Hebrews entered captivity as a nation; they emerged from it a religious community. "The Exile may be thought of as the bridge across which Israel journeyed in its historical pilgrimage from the soil to the soul."[238] The Exile and Return mark the point in Israel's mission when proselytization began to be actively pursued by segments of the people. Isaiah 56:3 speaks of "those who joined themselves to the Lord" in the Exile, indicating that there were many in that time who had been attracted to Judaism. As Israel was dispersed among the nations and as the nations joined themselves to Israel, new forms by which the cultic life of the people could be maintained had to develop. It is this place in the spiritual life of the people that the Synagogue entered and filled. The Synagogue represented for Israel an entirely unprecedented form of religious activity: the popular worship of God, without sacrifice, and the instruction of the community in the implications of Scripture as applied to living according to Yahweh's will. The wonderful jewel Israel possessed might not be wrapped up in a napkin, hidden and buried, but needed to be displayed, offered to all to see and share. The Synagogue provided the means to that end.

In certain respects the Synagogue marked a religious revolution. The creation of a liturgy which was not concerned with sacrifice was no small change in Jewish life. It was a revolution that was inevitable and the spread of the

---

238 H. M. Battenhouse, *The Bible Unlocked*, p. 221; H. H. Rowley, *Faith of Israel*, pp. 139-140; D. M. Eichhorn, *Conversion to Judaism*, p. 33.

Synagogue made for even greater cohesion of the Jews throughout the world.[239] By the time that the Temple was destroyed the Synagogue had become so well established that conditions adjusted themselves easily. The emergence of the Synagogue came about at exactly that period when the nation was forced to make several reorientations.[240] It was developed for the needs of the believing community but was undoubtedly often consciously adapted to the needs of the foreigner.[241] "The Synagogue was a unique institution," Isaac Levy observes, adding:

> It occupies a pre-eminent place in Jewish respect and affection and has become indispensable to the life of the individual and community ... As the natural successor to the Temple in Jerusalem it inspires an exceptional measure of public devotion; it has stimulated the creation of a rational form of worship from all mystery and cultic practice, and a liturgy of prayer unparalleled in quality and wealth of content. As heir to the influence of priest and prophet, it has assumed the role of a forum for the propagation of the faith, offering scope to teachers and preachers to present the truths of Judaism in contemporary idiom.[242]

The origin of the Synagogue is acknowledged to be lost in obscurity. It is conceded by most scholars that the origin must be found in the need for secular and spiritual assemblies even in pre-exilic times among God's people.[243] Certainly the meeting together at times for some form of instruction was not an entirely new thing when the Jews entered the Exile. In II Kings 4:23 the Shunammite woman asks her husband, "Why will you go to him (i.e. Elisha) today? It is neither new moon nor sabbath," implying some form of assembly with the prophet of God on stated days and festivals. In II Chron. 17:9 it is recorded that priests and Levites went on circuits throughout the Kingdom of Judah, "having the book of the Law of the LORD with them; they went about throughout all the cities of Judah and taught among the people." This assignment by Jehosaphat shows that there was a well-organized religious activity conducted among the people outside of the cultic center of Jerusalem.

There are other and later references to similar practices. In Jer. 39:8 mention is made of the *Beth Am* (house of the people) which the Chaldeans burned down with the king's house at the time they razed the walls of Jerusalem. This title *Beth Am* was a name for the Synagogue. In Jer. 41:5 the place called "the

239   J. Bonsirven, *Palestinian Judaism*, p. 126.

240   Herbert Martin James Loewe, *Judaism and Christianity* (London: The Sheldon Press, 1937), II, p. 44; J. Peterson, *Missionary Methods*, pp. 175-177.

241   J. Derwacter, *Preparing the Way for Paul*, p. 96; J. Peterson, *Missionary Methods*, p. 174.

242   Isaac Levy, *The Synagogue: Its History and Function*, p. 1; see also the work of Harm Mulder, *De Synagoge in de Nieuwestamentische Tijd* (Kampen: J. H. Kok, 1969).

243   For the pre-exilic antecedents of the synagogue see L. Finkelstein, "Origin of the Synagogue," *Proceedings of the American Academy for Jewish Research*, I, 49-59.

house of the Lord" to which eigthy persons came in mourning from Shechem, Shiloh, and Samaria with cereal offerings could not be the Temple because by this time the Temple had been destroyed. An interesting reference in Ps. 74:8 speaks of "all the meeting places of God in the land" as having been burned by the enemy.[244] The Jewish community finds a reference to the establishment of the Synagogue in Ezek. 11:6 where the name *mikdash ma'at* (small sanctuary) is used.[245]

Whatever the antecedents of the Synagogue it is clear that some forms of assembly and places of meeting existed throughout the land even in the days of Solomon's Temple. These were not rivals of the center in Jerusalem and the worship of God like the groves and high places for the worship of the heathen deities so often mentioned in the Old Testament. Even in subsequent centuries Temple and synagogues existed side by side in Jerusalem itself.[246] Recall, e.g., the mention in Acts 6:9 of the "synagogue of the Freedmen and of the Cyrenians and of the Alexandrians, and of those from Cilicia and Asia."[247] One report places 480 synagogues in Jerusalem prior to its final destruction by Titus, while another account mentions 394, "a number probably grossly exaggerated."[248]

When the Diaspora communities began aggressively to extend Judaism to the environing population, the Synagogue was the place where Jew and Gentile met apart from the one thousand and one contacts of everyday life.

> One of the striking features of the synagogues of this period is the designation which many of them bore, a true indication of the influences responsible for their establishment. We thus read of the "Synagogue of the Alexandrians" in Jerusalem, the "Synagogue of the Roman Jews" in Mehuza of Babylon, the "Synagogue of the Babylonians" in Tiberias, and the "Synagogue of the Greek-speaking Jews" where most of the service was conducted in that language. One also reads of the artisans who had their own places of worship such as the "Synagogue of the Copperworkers in Jerusalem," where separate seating arrangements were made for members of each of the artisan guilds.[249]

---

244 I. Levy, *The Snagogue*, pp. 12-13.

245 E. E. Pilchik, *Judaism*, p. 10.

246 Jacob Z. Lauterbach, "The Pharisees and their Teaching," *HUCA*, VI, 119-126 has a fine treatment of the relationship of Pharisaism to the development of the synagogue, and discusses why synagogues were found even in the Temple. See also I. Levy, *The Synagogue*, p. 14-15, on the presence of synagogues in the Second Temple.

247 For a discussion of the meaning of Acts 6:9 see the commentaries, and J. W. Parkes, *Foundations*, p. 107; J. Peterson, *Missionary Methods*, p. 172ff.; J. L. Koole, *De Joden in de Verstrooiing*, p. 44.

248 I. Levy, *The Synagogue*, p. 23. *JT.*, Meg. 3.1, Ket. 3.1. For the number of synagogues in Tiberias and other places see pp. 21-22. Also see Josephus, *Bell. Jud.*, ii.18.7 on Alexandria; H. Mulder, *De Synagoge in de Nieuwtestamentische Tijd*, p. 6.

249 I. Levy, *The Synagogue*, p. 23ff.; *JT*, Meg. 3.1; Soph. IIa, Tosefta Meg. 11.13; *BT*, Meg. 26a and 26b; Suk. 51b.

The same was true in Rome where the names of the approximately twenty synagogues tell of the trades, nationality, and even patrons of the Jewish community. There were, e.g., the synagogues of Augustus, Agrippa, Volumnius, Herod, the Subarenses, the Campenses, the Calvarenses, the Vernaculi (*urbani* = city born), Hebrews, Tripolitania (Africa), Lebanon, etc.[250]

The significance and value of the Synagogue lay in its varied functions. As the meeting place of Jew and Gentile it did not have the prohibitions of the Temple which threatened death to any Gentile who trespassed its sacred courts. Yet more than anything else the weekly preaching of the Word in the Synagogue was an important means for acquainting the world with the true God.[251] This cannot be underestimated. To nascent Christianity, the synagogues of the Diaspora meant more than that they were *fontes persecutionum* as Tertullian complains.[252] The Synagogue also formed the most important means for the rise and growth of Christian communities throughout the Empire. The Synagogue attracted widespread interest and a variety of degrees of adherents among the Gentile neighbors, and the Diaspora Jew was ready and eager to welcome such interest and adherence. The centurion in Capernaum and the Roman Cornelius, benefactor of the synagogue at Caesarea, are examples of this (Luke 7:4,5; Acts 10:2). Paul never had to defend the right of the Gentiles to hear the Gospel – they were already listening to the Word wherever Jews gathered; his compatriots disputed what he said about the status of the Gentiles who heard his message.[253] The Synagogue was the house of prayer and public instruction on the Sabbath, Monday, Thursday, and the New Moons and Festivals.[254] These observations should not be taken to mean that the Synagogue was uncritically accepted in the Jewish world. Its subsequent development was so much a Diaspora phenomenon that it sometimes provoked the opposition of the Palestinans.[255]

That the Synagogue's purpose was broader than just a meeting place for worship is documented and described by Pfeiffer:

> It became customary among Diaspora Jews to confer the current Gentile honors – such as crown and chief seats at the synagogues (instead of the chief seats at the games) – and record them on inscribed stelae placed in the synagogue and occasionally even in the amphitheater; to dedicate synagogues to the king; to confer on women titles and honorary positions such as 'chief of the synagogue', 'mother of the synagogue', etc.; to free slaves in the

250 I. Levy, *The Synagogue*, pp. 20-21; G. Ricciotti, *The History of Israel*, p. 186ff.; H. J. Leon, *The Jews of Ancient Rome*, pp. 135-158, treats in detail what is known from the tomb inscriptions concerning eleven synagogues in Rome.
251 J. L. Koole, *De Joden in de Verstrooiing*, p. 81.
252 A. von Harnack, *Mission and Expansion*, I, p. 1ff.; Tertullian, *Scorpiace*, 10.10.
253 J. W. Parkes, *Foundations*, p. 108.
254 I. Levy, *The Synagogue*, pp. 18-19.
255 S. W. Baron, *A Social and Religious History of the Jews*, p. 109, who quotes A. Menes, "Tempel und Synagoge," *ZTW*, 50, 268-276.

synagogue with the obligation that the freedman would honor the synagogue and attend it regularly, as pagans freed slaves by fictitiously selling them to a temple.[256]

The Synagogue very early also served as a hostel for the stranger who needed accommodations while travelling. The rabbinic exhortations to hospitality are remarkably similar to that of Scripture which exhorts, "Do not neglect to show hospitality to strangers, for thereby some have entertained angels unawares" (Heb. 13:2).[257]

Both Philo and Josephus say that the purpose of the Synagogue was to promote the moral and religious education of the community.[258] Programs of study were a prominent feature of the Synagogue, and schools for instruction were from early times attached to it. Philo said there were "thousands of houses of instruction in all the towns" in which people assembled in order and respect while the learned explained the Scriptures to them.[259] Such instruction obviously centered in Torah, as James said, "For from early generations Moses has had in every city those who preach him, for he is read every sabbath in the synagogues" (Acts 15:21).[260] In ordinary speech the school and Synagogue were so closely associated that the two were not distinguished. In time the name *hazzan* for the Synagogue official came to denote also a primary school official.[261] Drazin details the curriculum, discipline, attendants, etc. of the synagogue schools and shows how these schools attracted the Gentiles as well as the Jews. For adults the schools were very important:

> From the time that the porter at the door of the college at Jabneh was dismissed, adults were permitted to enter the academy and seat themselves on the ground in the rear among the very youthful students in order to listen to the proceedings. Frequent attendance of this kind helped many people to gain an advanced education.[262]

The *Beth Ha-Midrash* or House of Study served the educational requirements

256   E. Schürer, *Geschichte*, III, pp. 91-96; R. H. Pfeiffer, *History of New Testament Times*, p. 185.

257   I. Levy, *The Synagogue*, p. 23ff.

258   J. Peterson, *Missionary Methods*, p. 171; Philo, *De Vita Moses*, ii.167; Josephus, *Contra Ap.*, ii.18.

259   Philo, *De Septenario* 6; F. Derwacter, *Preparing the Way for Paul*, p. 77.

260   J. H. Waszink, *et al.*, *Het Oudste Christendom*, p. 547. Waszink also gives a description of the early synagogue service; cf. pp. 526-528. Cf. also J. Peterson, *Missionary Methods*, p. 169ff.

261   Nathan Drazin, *History of Jewish Education from 515 BCE to 220 CE* (Baltimore: John Hopkins Press, 1940), p. 61, henceforth to be cited as *Jewish Education*. Drazin thoroughly reviews and documents the Jewish educational system and curriculum of the period. The relationships of non-Jews to the system is not covered extensively, however. A. H. Godbey, *Lost Tribes*, pp. 651-664, treats in detail the Babylonian academies.

262   N. Drazin, *Jewish Education*, p. 77.

of all sections of the community and created a large measure of good-will. "Seminaries" were also established in the large centers, not only to spread learning in Israel but also to propagate the principles of Judaism among the Gentiles.[263]

The Synagogue also became the center for Jewish charity to Jew and Gentile. The Pharisees collected funds and encouraged contributions for the support of widows and orphans from the Jews and of proselytes. Josephus tells us that the practice of charity was one of the things sympathizers with Judaism imitated.[264] The apostle Peter, writing to diaspora Christians, included repeated injunctions to charity in his letters (I Pet. 1:22; 2:17; 3:8-12; 4:7b-9).

> Where Jews and non-Jews lived together in the same city, it was decreed by the Pharisean authorities that for the sake of peace and in order to further the relations of good-will, the non-Jewish poor should be supported together with those of the Jews, and the dead non-Jews be honored like those of the Jews, and likewise comfort be offered to the sorrowing of either Jews or non-Jews; also that the collectors of alms on both sides should cooperate.[265]

A special name was given to the charity workers in the Jewish communities. They were called *Hasidim*, and their work is described as follows:

> How well organized their charity was may be learned from the Tos. Peah. 4,8-14, and that is goes back to very old times is shown by the Mishnah Kid. 4,5, according to which those in charge of the charities belonged to the old patrician families with whom alone the priests would intermarry .... The Babylonian Jewry kept up the rule of the Tos. Peah. 4,9, that there should be no community without an alms box and a soup kitchen. The collectors of charity were called Shluhe Mizwah, "those sent forth for the duty (of benevolence)," corresponding to the apostles of the New Testament who were originally collectors of charity, as were the so-called Jewish apostles also in later times, and who were always sent forth in pairs lest they be suspected of dishonesty.[266]

The Synagogue became in these ways the bridge by which Judaism made

263   I. Levy, *The Synagogue*, p. 19; J. Peterson, *Missionary Methods*, p. 178; F. Derwacter, *Preparing the Way for Paul*, p. 96; W. G. Braude, *Jewish Proselyting*, p. 18.
264   J. S. Raisin, *Gentile Reactions*, p. 159, quoting Gen. R. 28:5; *BT*, Aboth 1:12. See also Josephus, *Contra Ap.*, II.39.283; David Daube, *The New Testament and Rabbinic Judaism: The Jordan Lectures in Comparative Religions* (London: Athlone Press, 1956), p. 129.
265   Kaufmann Kohler, *The Origins of the Synagogue and the Church* (New York: The Macmillan Co., 1929), p. 152, henceforth to be cited as *Origins of the Synagogue*. H. Loewe, *Judaism and Christianity*, II, p. 45ff. has a complete resume of the relationship of the Pharisaic brotherhoods and the promotion of social service in the Diaspora communities. *JT*, Gittim 47c; Demai 24a; Tos. Gittim 5, 4.
266   *BT*, Sanh. 17b; Tos Peah. 4, 15; B. B. 8b. K. Kohler, *Origins of the Synagogue*, p. 40ff.

itself known to, interpreted God's will for, and exemplified its faith for the world. It flourished at precisely that stage of Jewish history when Judaism was thrust on the world stage through the Diaspora and Exile. The Synagogue obviously made the transition to the true faith easier for the proselyte because it offered varied degrees of affiliation. The Synagogue was wonderfully adapted to compete with other faiths, providing as it did a public forum for an apologetic overagainst the anti-Jewish propaganda and slanderous accusations of the heathen. Its schools were proof that the Jews were not enemies of culture and its works of charity demonstrations of concern and care for all men regardless of race. It was motivated by a noble purpose: to make known Yahweh's sovereignty over all the world and over the whole life of all men.[267]

6. The Scriptures

It is conceivable that an institution such as the Synagogue could be designed for the purpose of serving the Jewish community only. So long as a cult is being spread only among fellow countrymen, even though this take place far from home, the god of that people is for that people only. But when real mission work is carried on, the universal claim of a people's god is declared and insisted upon.[268] It was inevitable that the God of all men should speak to men in their own languages. The groundwork for this divine activity was laid in the Diaspora. The place where men would meet in encounter with God and hear him speak was found in the Synagogue. But not all men speak the same language. A brief consideration of the significance of the translation of Scripture for the mission of God to the nations is therefore necessary.

Within Palestine foreign forces affected conditions of life more than is generally appreciated. The varied influences to which the land was subjected throughout history have already been observed. After the exile, the same conditions continued. At the time of Christ the existence of such parties as the Sadducees, Pharisees, Herodians, and Zealots evidenced differing political outlooks and allegiances. Tax collectors and the exaction of tribute for Caesar, foreign soldiers policing Jerusalem and stationed at the very edge of the Temple courts, Roman control of the high priesthood, synagogues in the Holy City whose services were in the Greek language – all of these are only a few indications that life even in Judea was a continual adjustment to other influences. For the Jews in the Diaspora this would be even greater.[269]

---

267 J. Peterson, *Missionary Methods*, pp. 175-177, treats the importance of the synagogue as a part of the Jewish propaganda.

268 This idea is developed more fully by W. Foerster, *Herr ist Jesus* (Gütersloh: C. Bertelsmann Verlag, 1924), p. 78, and by G. F. Vicedom, *The Mission of God*, p. 11, who refers to Foerster.

269 S. J. Case, *The Evolution of Early Christianity*, p. 30.

Under these circumstances,

> this people, almost without desiring to do so, sent a messenger to the peoples. Men of its congregations in Egypt, which had become a Greek land, had translated the Holy Scriptures into the new, world language of Greek. With that this book became the greatest of apostles. It traveled road after road, and into whatever distances it reached, there this people had arrived, even without being present. The world of this people could open its portals in many lands. This people had often spoken, in exhortation, in hope, of "all peoples," those who were near and those who were far. Now it began to speak directly to all of them, and many answers came back.

> The Greek Bible translation became the great apostle, the missionary of the Hebrew Bible.[270]

It is doubtful whether the Jewish proselyting movements could have achieved any measure of success without the translation of the Scriptures into the vernacular language. The best known of these is the Septuagint. In all the colonies of the Diaspora it is remarkable how tenaciously the Jews held to their Hebrew language and script. Tablets, grave inscriptions, monuments abound wherever the Jews settled, and the use of the Hebrew in many areas was constantly reinforced by new arrivals from Palestine. However, the Gentiles, many proselytes, and even the sons and daughters of the Jews could naturally be expected to find communication in their native tongues of greater value in the understanding of the Word of God. Translation of God's will into life involves first of all communication by means which men understand.

Before the actual translation of Scripture took place, other means were undoubtedly used. Prayers, e.g., could be said in any language in the synagogue.[271] The Babylonian Talmud makes frequent reference to the practice in public worship of using "translators" when the Scriptures were read. It is said that "whoever expounds the words of the Torah in a manner which is not pleasing to the listener – it is better that he should not utter them."[272] A few references will clarify their positions:

> (The Torah) may be read to those who do not speak Hebrew in a language other than Hebrew.[273]

---

270 L. Baeck, *This People Israel: The Meaning of Jewish Existence*, p. 230. A. H. Godbey, *The Lost Tribes*, p. 621ff. It is not necessary to repeat the stories and legends surrounding the origin of the Greek Septuagint (LXX). There are many histories. A brief and adequate summary can be found in J. Peterson, *Missionary Methods*, p. 167ff. J. L. Koole, *De Joden in de Verstrooiing*, p. 60ff., calls the LXX "the foremost agent for the Jewish mission." We should not forget, however, that volumes such as the LXX and other possible translations are produced only when a community has first been convinced of the necessity of proclaiming its faith in the vernacular, both for its own sake and that of the environing community. H. J. Leon, *The Jews of Ancient Rome*, pp. 75, 126.

271 G. F. Moore, *Judaism in the First Centuries*, p. i-iii.

272 I. Levy, *The Synagogue*, p. 107, referring to Cant. R. on Cant. IV.11.

273 Meg. 110.

One may read in Coptic, in Hebraic, in Elamean, in Median, and in Greek.[274]

The translator repeated each verse (in Talmudic period) after it had been read by the reader, one verse at a time,[275] and was not permitted to raise his voice above that of the reader.[276] A mourner was not allowed to read or translate.[277] A Megillah Mishnah, referring to Esther, says that the public reading is not properly done if done in a language the reader does not understand. "It is lawful, however, to read to those who know no Hebrew in a foreign language which they understand; if they have heard it in Assyrian characters, they have done their duty." Such *Megilla* may not be cheap, carelessly made copies on poor materials, "but must be written in Assyrian characters, in a book, on good parchment, and with ink."[278] It was said by the rabbis that Moses enunciated the Torah in seventy languages. An illustration of this method of reading and address is found in Neh. 8:8 which is rendered "translating as they went" by the rabbis.[279]

The existence and use of the Aramaic Targums is well-known. In our modern times the word *targum* has been so regularly restricted in meaning to certain post-Christian, western, Aramaic paraphrases of the Old Testament that the average reader is surprised to learn that the word originally meant any translation whatever, and that such translations existed from early exilic times.[280] What is forgotten is that the scholars of rabbinic Judaism used to refer to any translation as "interpretation," a not unreasoned or inapplicable concept.[281]

The life of the Jewish people in their adopted countries, their peculiar religious observances, and their places of worship frequently aroused the curiosity of their neighbors and led to enquiry about the religion of these peculiar people. Among heathen people, e.g., to whom a weekly day of rest was unheard of, the sight of men, women, children suddenly ceasing their labors, retiring to their homes, and gathering in synagogues with order peculiar people, not infrequently led to attendance at the synagogue services. There they would hear the Scriptures read in a strange language and in their own as well. Moses

274   Meg. 110. Coptic = an Egyptian vernacular; Hebraic = a kind of Aramaic spoken by the Bene Eber on the East side of the Euphrates.
275   Meg. 140ff.; 143ff.; Sot. 194.
276   Ber. 275.
277   MK 133.
278   Meg. 110, 114, 140, 143, 153, 193; A. H. Godbey, *Lost Tribes*, p. 630.
279   Ber. 49, cited by A. H. Godbey, *Lost Tribes*, p. 629.
280   A. H. Godbey, *The Lost Tribes*, p. 628. Von Harnack asserts in "Bible Reading in the Early Church," p. 45ff., that "it cannot be proved that the Scriptures of the Old Testament were translated into any other language except the Greek before the Christian era." Godbey, who quotes Harnack in this (p. 648), correctly observes that this fails to take account of the great volume of Talmudic evidence which is always of the nature of a *terminus ad quem* and often reflects the settled opinion arrived at after long periods of discusson and development.
281   J. W. Parkes, *Foundations*, p. 112.

would be read and interpreted to those assembled. The roots of this strange and alien faith would now be seen to have found good soil in the vernacular tongues and dialects. They would hear God speak in words they could understand, and they in turn could speak to God in their own tongue for he would understand because he is Creator and God of all peoples! Raisin says,

> Perhaps they would find an entire copy of the Scriptures in the vernacular. The Talmud refers not only to the Aramaic Targum (translation), which is attributed to Ezra, not only to the Greek LXX and the translation of Akilas (Onkelos or Aquila), but also to renditions in Coptic, Median, Iberian, Elamian, Assyrian, Arabic, and Persian or Pahlavi. There was also the Peshitta in Syriac, attributed by some to a proselyte but ascribed by others to the days of Solomon.[282]

Another statement of similar import is this:

> In the Babylonian Talmud is approval of the use Holy Books in Assyrian, Greek, Coptic, Old Hebrew, Median, Iberian, Elamite, Aramaic, Syriac, Armenian, Arabic, and Persian, with the inference that any other language necessary for popular comprehension was permissible. The insistence that particular languages were necessary in particular regions is repeated, and specific reasons for the prejudice that developed against certain languages are recorded.[283]

Similarly, Theodoret, a Syrian bishop of the fifth century, asserted that an old Persian translation of the Bible existed.[284]

What is so very clear from the above survey is that wherever the Jews went, they carried their Scriptures with them. And as their roots sank deeper into the soil of their new homelands, they felt the need of speaking, praying, reading in the languages of the people of these lands. They were not against having God speak to others besides themselves and may even have welcomed and encouraged this. By this means they demonstrated that the God of the synagogue and of the Temple was one and the same God. The God who spoke to them through their prophets now spoke to the world through his people. It may not be possible to remove every shadow of doubt that surrounds the question of the existence of actual vernacular translations; what is important is that the Jews were not adverse to making known the Word of God by word of mouth in the vernacular tongues but actually felt it their duty to do so.[285]

282   J. S. Raisin, *Gentile Reactions*, p. 163.
283   A. H. Godbey, *Lost Tribes*, p. 627. In chapter 24, pp. 621-650, Godbey treats the subject, "Ancient Jewish Translations of Their Scriptures."
284   L. Finkelstein, *The Jews*, II, p. 826.
285   The existence of the Aramaic section of Dan. 2:4-7:1 has long puzzled scholars, since no Hebrew copy of the section exists. A possibility is that the Aramaic section was inserted to fill the gap created by the loss of the Hebrew section. It evidences at least the existence of a translation in a language other than Hebrew.

Commenting on the Septuagint and its importance, N. A. Dahl asserts that the greatest contribution of the Septuagint was the translation of the Hebrew name Yahweh by the Greek *kyrios* (Κύριος). "In this way it became evident that Yahweh was not a folk deity, but that Israel was the elect people of the God of the world." [286]

One can hardly conceive of more providentially supplied means for the Christian mission to reach the Gentile community. Wherever the community of Christ went, it found at hand the tools needed to reach the nations: a people living under covenant promise and responsible election, and the Scriptures, God's revelation to all men. The open Synagogue was the place where all these things converged. In the Synagogue the Christians were offered an inviting door of access to every Jewish community. It was in the Synagogue that the first Gentile converts declared their faith in Jesus. What Old Testament Israel and the nations could not know, until someone would tell them, was the exceedingly good news of the fulfillment of God's covenant in Christ.

What use did the Jews make of their opportunities? Were they interested in the conversion of the heathen? And if they were, what place was the convert given in the community of God's people?

286 Nils Alstrup Dahl, *Das Volk Gottes* (Oslo: J. Dybwab, 1941), p. 95; J. Blauw, *Goden en Mensen*, p. 103.

With the epoch of the proselytes – those who stood on the doorstep and those who entered – a new chapter of Israel's history began: a unique form of colony, the congregation, increasingly determined the history of the people. A people of congregations! It sounds like a contradiction, but it is one of those fertile contradictions out of which spirit and power are born.[1] What was the nature of these congregations? What sort of affiliations did the non-Jews maintain to them? By what were people attracted to these assemblies? Who invited them, and did the Jews welcome them? With what ceremonies were they admitted? These are a few of the questions that need an answer if we are to understand the context in which the Christian mission evolved.

A. *The Synagogue Community*

The origins of Jewish proselytism must be found in the regulations for the treatment of the stranger in the Promised Land. We have already seen that the word *ger* (a resident alien) came to mean proselyte (one who joined himself to the Lord from other nations) in the period of the Babylonian Exile. The term arose in the Diaspora where it naturally lost its geographical significance as a result of the wide dispersion of the people of God.[2]

The Diaspora, which was largely responsible for the development of the synagogue, presented a unique opportunity for the nations to attach themselves in varying relationships to the Jewish faith and people. There was the obvious group of curious persons who would inquire about this strange people and their singularly different faith. They appear to have been always welcome, but they displayed a wide range of devotion to Jewish ideas and customs. They were sincere but basically they remained pagan.[3] The Gentiles associated with the

---

1 L. Baeck, *This People Israel*, p. 233.

2 Cf. Karl Georg Kuhn, προσήλυτος, *TWNT*, VI, pp. 727-744; article by Karl Axenfeld, "Die jüdische Propaganda als Vorläuferin und Wegbereiter in der Urchristlichen Mission" in *Missionswissenschaftliche Studien: Festschrift zur 70 Geburtstag Prof. Dr. Gustav Warneck* (Berlin: Martin Warneck, 1904), pp. 1-81; L. Finkelstein, *The Pharisees*, II, p. 461; Bernard Jacob Bamberger, *Proselytism in the Talmudic Period* (New York: KTAV, 1968), p. 13, henceforth to be cited as *Proselytism*.

3 Strack-Billerbeck, *Kommentar*, on John 12:20. The Christian term "pagan" comes

synagogue were not sharply divided into those who accepted and those who rejected the true faith. Derwacter calls them "the partly informed and the partly persuaded among whom were the open-minded and the willing hearted." It is this group of persons whom Derwacter judges to be those who offered Christianity fertile soil for the gospel seed.[4]

The book of Acts provides considerable light on another class of adherents called "God-fearers" or "devout" persons (e.g. Acts 10:2 where these words are used: εὐσεβὴς καὶ φοβούμενος).[5] Cornelius the centurion of Caesarea is called "a devout man who feared God" (Acts 10:2). Paul seems to imply a mixed audience of Jews and God-fearers in his address at the synagogue in Antioch of Pisidia (Acts 13:16,26,43) as well as a non-Jewish group of "devout women" from the city (vs. 50). Lydia is called "a worshipper of God" (Acts 16:14). At Thessalonica the term "devout" is specifically applied to Greeks who frequented the synagogue (Acts 17:4,17). In Acts 18:7 the home of Titius Justus, "a worshipper of God," was next door to the synagogue and became the center of Paul's activities in Corinth after the synagogue was closed to him because of hostility. In all uses of the terms just cited it is evident that we are dealing with non-Jews who are more or less closely associated with the Jewish religious community. In one instance (Acts 13:43) the word "devout" is used in the description of proselytes. The Mishnah generally means the proselyte when it refers to "God-fearers."[6]

Is such a class of persons indicated elsewhere in Scripture? Some have taken the phrase "ye that fear the Lord" in the Psalms to indicate Gentiles in contrast to the Jewish people and the priesthood.[7] The Capernaum synagogue in the days of Jesus was built by a centurion who "loved the nation," implying that he was not a Jew (Luke 7:4). Cornelius was also such a person (Acts 10:2). Gentile writers mention a class of persons who followed Jewish sabbaths, feasts, etc. but who were not actually completely committed through circumcision as the sign of complete identity with Israel. Theophilus, for whom Luke

from the Latin *paganus* or "rural," implying that the greatest success of the Christian mission was in the urban centers. Cf. S. W. Baron, *A Social and Religious History of the Jews*, I, p. 236. E. Schürer, *Geschichte*, III, pp. 126ff., 150ff., says that "formal conversions to Judaism do not seem to have been as frequent as a loose attachment in the form of σεβόμενοι." J. Jeremias, *Jerusalem in the Time of Jesus*, p. 320ff.

4 F. Derwacter, *Preparing the Way for Paul*, p. 40.

5 See Georg Bertram, *TWNT*, III, pp. 123-128; Rudolf Bultmann, *TWNT*, II, pp. 751-754.

6 *J.T.*, Vayyikra III.2, Naso VIII.9, e.g.

7 See Psalm 115:11-13; 118:4; 135:30. The *Jewish Encyclopedia*, VIII, p. 521, takes the phrase to mean the whole group of pious persons outside of Israel. Aubrey Rodway Johnson, *Sacral Kingship in Ancient Israel* (Cardiff: University of Wales Press, 1967), p. 124, comments on this phrase at length, noting that Kirsopp Lake in *The Beginnings of Christianity, Part. I: The Acts of the Apostles*, note VIII "Proselytes and God-fearers," p. 74ff., questions the validity of this viewpoint, feeling that the phrase simply refers to a devout Israelite. See also F. Hahn, *Mission in the New Testament*, p. 17ff., and K. Kohler, *Origins of the Synagogue*, p. 160.

wrote the Gospel and Acts (Luke 1:1-4; Acts 1:1), is an interesting example of one for whom special instruction was provided in the teachings concerning Jesus Christ and his work.[8]

As an example of a Jewish community which included proselytes we can cite what is known about the Jewish community in Rome. The tomb inscriptions found there (as also in other communities of the Empire) give conclusive evidence that proselytes were found in the Jewish community. The epitaphs of seven "indubitable proselytes, two males and five females", have come from the Jewish catacombs of Rome. Proselytes were accepted as full members of the community, were regarded as being Jews in every respect, and were honored with burial in a Jewish cemetery. A class of persons who only practiced a few Jewish rites, such as the worship of One God, celebration of the Sabbath, and abstinence from pork, were not regarded as Jews and did not receive a Jewish burial. A class of persons more than casually committed to the Jewish faith and associated with the synagogues is indicated by all the evidence.[9] The position of these people was not always enviable, and it can be assumed that the proselytes and others shared in the calumnies directed against the Jews. Several of the Roman writers were cynical, others frivolous, and not a few hostile towards the Jewish community.[10]

In order to make clear what the duties of the Gentiles were the rabbis spoke of what were called the Noachian laws. These were injunctions traditionally given to Noah and therefore obligatory for all men, Jew and Gentile alike.[11]

8   F. Derwacter, *Preparing the Way for Paul*, pp. 35-39, cites many of the pagan writers. So also Johannes Adrianus Hebly, *Het Proselitisme* ('s Gravenhage: Boeken-centrum N.V., 1962), pp. 9-13. On Theophilus see Harm Mulder, "Theophilus de God-vrezende", in *Arcana Revelata: Een bundel Nieuw-Testamentliche studiën aangeboden aan Prof. Dr. F. W. Grosheide ter gelegenheid van zijn 70e verjaardag* (Kampen: J. H. Kok, 1951), pp. 77-88.

9   Thus H. J. Leon, *The Jews of Ancient Rome*, pp. 253-256. Leon takes issue with the position of J. B. Frey who includes four Roman inscriptions which show the term *metuens* and who applies these to the Jewish epitaphs. Leon says, p. 253, "none of these is known to have come from a Jewish catacomb". Frey's position is also followed by F. Derwacter, *Preparing the Way for Paul*, p. 37, referring to W. Oehler, *Monatschrift für Geschichte und Wissenschaft des Judentums*, Vol. 53 (1909), nos. 170, 192-197. 208. 261.

10   Ovid, *Ars Amatoria* 1:75:415 (cf. T. Reinach, *Textes*, p. 248), says that "one should remember to visit the Jewish meeting places of he seeks a love affair." Derwacter judges this to mean that the synagogue was a popular gathering place for the curious and the earnest; see F. Derwacter, *Preparing the Way for Paul*, p. 36. See also H. J. Leon, *The Jews of Ancient Rome*, pp. 12, 40-42, 250-253, for comments on the Roman attitudes.

11   On the Noachian Laws see the following: Solomon Schonfeld, *The Universal Bible: Pentateuchal Texts At First Addressed to All Nations* (London: Sidgwick and Jackson, 1955), p. 10ff.; J. W. Parkes, *Foundations*, p. 197; K. Kohler, *Origins of the Synagogue and the Church*, p. 161; E. Schürer, *Geschichte*, III, p. 175. Both Mishnah and Talmud make frequent reference to this class of persons; e.g. Jethro is called a Noachid and proselyte, *Misnah, Debarim* I.5; Bemidbar V.9; Tzav IX.6.

A Gentile who observed these laws, acknowledging their divine source, was regarded as a pious man who merited the Kingdom of heaven.[12] It was never taught, however, that simple observance of these ethical standards entitled a man to a place among the Chosen People.[13] Although the Talmud states that "there are thirty Biblical commandments which the nations took upon themselves," the general tradition taught that there were six prohibitions: against (1) idolatry, (2) blasphemy, (3) murder, (4) sexual immorality, (5) robbery, and (6) eating a maimed animal or portion of a living animal; a 7th injunction required justice.[14]

The greatest single obstacle to the conversion of the Gentiles was the requirement of circumcision, which became the criterion for determining the full sincerity of the Gentile convert.[15] But experience showed that the next generation often advanced to full conversion by undergoing circumcision. Juvenal tells of a father who observed the sabbath and dietary laws, worshipped only clouds and sky, but, though he was not circumcised himself, his children after him were. This all happened, he says, because the father did not like to work on the Sabbath; "trained to despise the laws of Rome, they learn to maintain the laws of the Jews which Moses transmitted in a mystic volume."[16]

It appears that a greater number of women than men affiliated with the synagogue, perhaps because the question of circumcision did not arise with respect to them. In any case, Josephus tells us that almost the entire female population of Damascus had joined the synagogue.[17] Nero's consort, Poppaea Sabina, was a "God fearer" according to Josephus.[18] The mention of women in Gentile communities and diaspora synagogues visited by Paul reflects this same situation.[19] In its proclamation Judaism relegated ritual prescriptions to the

12 Sanh. 105a.

13 J. W. Parkes, *Foundations*, p. 197.

14 Various classifications are given. Sometimes there were 6, 7, 10, and even 30! Cf. K. Kohler, *Origins of the Synagogue and the Church*, p. 161ff. In *BT*, *Meg.* 74, we are told "whoever repudiates idolatry is a Jew." E. Schürer, *The Jewish People in the Time of Jesus Christ*, II, p. 318, says that the prescription of the seven precepts of the children of Noah was "barren theory ... a casuistical theory that was never reduced to actual practice." However, the Mishnah does in retrospect apply the title to examples in the past. See note 11 above (on Jethro).

15 Greeks and Romans often would not become full proselytes because of the necessity for circumcision followed, as it was, by open derision by protagonists at every subsequent gymnastic performance by them in the stadium. *The Mishnah* frequently speaks with disfavor of Jew or proselyte who resorted to surgery to hide his circumcision. Cf. S. W. Baron, *A Social and Religious History of the Jews*, I, p. 137.

16 Juvenal, *Sat.* 14:96-106; T. Reinach, *Textes*, p. 292; E. Schürer, *The Jewish People in the Times of Jesus*, II, p. 296.

17 Josephus, *Bell. Jud.*, II, 560.

18 Josephus, *Ant.*, XX.195; *Vita*, 16; Georg Bertram, *TWNT*, III, p. 126, n. 16.

19 Examples are Lydia (Acts 16:14), the "devout women of high standing" stirred up in Acts 13:50, the "leading women" (Acts 17:4). Cf. also the later mention of Priscilla and Acquila.

background and emphasized instead a moral code. It was not easy for a man to accept the Jewish faith together with its ritual laws.

> Any convert to Judaism became a part of a nation as well as an adherent to a religion. His conversion partook, in a certain degree, of the character of naturalization. One can understand a man saying, "To all intends and purposes I am in *doctrine* a Jew, but I don't want to become a Jew in *practice*, and indeed, I am not asked to become one. Their ritual laws and religious institutions are a preserve kept exclusively for the enjoyment (or the trouble) of the Jewish people." It would be consistent, if very difficult, for orthodox Jews to say to any group of persons, "Organize yourselves as Theists; believe *our* doctrines about God ans His relation to man; observe *our* moral law; observe a weekly day of rest on any day of the week you please; and, for the rest, arrange, and devise your own liturgy own ceermonies, your own religious institutions." That would be a difficult and odd thing to say to a cultivated people; but how much more difficult and unsatisfactory would it be to say so to the heathen ... To such people a new religion must be presented as a whole: doctrine and cult, faith and practice; belief and ceremonial, in one combination or in harmony. Nor would it be very feasible to present a cult which was not, more or less, the cult of the missionaries themselves.[20]

Because the synagogue service was relatively free from cultic practices such as sacrifice (offered at the Temple in Jerusalem) the interested Gentile would not feel out of place nor would he encounter much difficulty in understanding and following the service for it was mostly communication by word and readings, often in his own tongue. Judaism had no difficulty in maintaining the ethical and ceremonial (cultic) side by side. Those in the Diaspora who could do so made the pilgrimage to Jerusalem, meeting in this way the cultic requirements. The ceremonial laws of everyday life called attention to and reinforced his knowledge of God's special purpose in the existence of the Jewish people. These daily ceremonial observances frequently elicited the ridicule of pagan writers when they noted the character of the daily life of the Jew.[21]

Within the synagogue community there was also the full convert, the proselyte, "the one who comes forward." That not all people who converted were sincere is evidenced by the reference of Arrian of Nicomedia who represents Epictetus as saying,

> when we see a man playing half one part and half another, we are accustomed to saying, "He is not a Jew, but he is playing the Jew." It is only when he has the experience of the baptized and the chosen that he really is and is called a Jew.[22]

20   F. S. B. Gavin, *Jewish Views on Jewish Missions*, p. 9.
21   Cf. F. M. Derwacter, *Preparing the Way for Paul*, pp. 96-99.
22   *Dissertations of Epictetus*, II.9:19-20; cf. T. Reinach, *Textes*, p. 154; F. Derwacter, *Preparing the Way for Paul*, p. 28.

The Talmud also recognizes that some people proselytized out of improper motivation. Anyone, e.g., who became a proselyte simply for the purpose of marrying an Israelite is "not a proper proselyte."[23] The rabbis also spoke of "self-made proselytes who were dragged in" and judaized in multitude out of fear.[24] They said that no proselytes will be received in the days of Messiah, even though idol worshippers come and offer themselves as proselytes, because they will defect in the time of Gog and Magog.[25] Although these references might be taken to mean that the rabbis did not favor proselytism (reflecting also the judgment in Niddah 88, "proselytes are as hard to endure for Israel as a sore"), the very large number of favorable references in Talmud and Mishnah to the true proselytes actually demonstrates how eager the Jews were to receive them. The negative references are easily explained and are of the same kind as those directed against apostate Jews.[26] When the rabbis labored over the Biblical text, they injected a zeal for conversion wherever possible.

That this class of converts was exceedingly zealous is indicated by the complaint of Justin, "The proselytes not only do not believe but blaspheme Christ's name twofold more than you and endeavor to put to death and torture us who believe in him."[27] In the beginning of the Christian era it appears that the Jewish apologists and the Jerusalem Sanhedrin were mainly defensive against Christianity. It was only at the end of the first century that this changed.[28] One can understand the attitude of the proselyte, for he had to give up so much when he became a Jew; a decision such as this was not easily made nor would it be relinquished readily if one had acted in sincerity. Josephus tells in detail of the hesitation of King Azates who feared the loss of his throne if he would be circumcised.[29] The Jewish proselytes in the synagogues were often the greatest antagonists of the early Christians.[30]

The existence of a class of genuine proselytes attached to the nation and synagogue is well attested in sacred and secular sources. Peter's audience on Pentecost (Acts 2:9-11) consisted of Jews and proselytes from several lands of the Mediterranean basin. The frequent mention of the proselytes in connection with the synagogues visited by Paul and his co-workers is evidence that throughout the Diaspora there was a body of persons who were willing to go all the way, break completely with their past, throw in their fortunes with the

23   Yeb. 147-148.
24   AZ 8; G. F. Moore, *Judaism in the First Five Centuries*, I, p. 337.
25   AZ 8.
26   W. G. Braude, *Jewish Proselytizing*, pp. 19, 138ff. Chapter 4 = "Utterances Misinterpreted as Unfriendly." B. J. Bamberger, *Proselytism*, p. 274; William David Davies, *Paul and Rabbinic Judaism* (London: SPCK, 1948), pp. 64-65, contains a complete summary of first century-BC attitudes to proselytes.
27   Justin, *Dialogue*, CXXII.
28   Cf. I. Abrahams, *Studies in Phariseeism and the Gospels,* p. 63, n. 2, who refers to Harnack.
29   Josephus, *Ant.*, XX:2.2-4.
30   Tertullian, *Scorp.* 10.10; cf. A. von Harnack, *Mission and Expansion*, I, p. 1.

people of the Jews, and be circumcised.[31] The word of Jesus in Matt. 23:15 would make no sense at all if the Jews never sought to win converts. He said,

> Woe to you, scribes and Pharisees, hypocrites! for you traverse land and sea to make a single proselyte, and when he becomes a proselyte you make him twice as much a son of hell as yourselves.

When in the history of Imperial Rome many decrees were issued prohibiting Jewish proselytizing, these decrees only witness to the zeal and success with which the Jews pursued this effort. An anonymous reference in the Peshita Rabbati, in answer to the question whether God's people would abandon him now that they are scattered (for previously in the homeland already they had served idols), Gods says, "I know that my children will not abandon me; nay more, they will be my martyrs. They will offer their very lives to bring others under my wings." The rabbis were provoked when they saw a country or province that had produced few proselytes.[32]

We conclude, therefore, that the synagogue fellowship was not a homogeneous community of committed believers and worshippers of God. It consisted of God-fearing Jews, some of whom continued to maintain their heritage by faithful adherence to the Torah,[33] others of whom were little more than hypocrites. There was a class of genuine converts from among the Gentiles who had fully committed themselves to the God of Israel and his service. This group was extremely zealous, although it was recognized that some had converted from ulterior motives. Another group with varying degrees of affinity and acceptance of the true faith, who remained on the fringe of the community, was always welcome. This class of people constituted a reservoir for proselytizing of the Gentile world, as Horace witnesses in his famous phrase, *"veluti te Iudaei cogemus in hanc considere turbam.* Once they fixed their eyes on a possible proselyte they surrounded him with attentions, prayers, invitations, enticements of all kinds until he succumbed to the gentle pressure behind them."[34] The pressure seems not to have been quite that gentle at all times and places, for Horace once wrote, "If you won't come willingly, we shall act like the Jews and force you to."[35] Although the Rabbis did not regard these *metuentes* as Jews, they had enormous good will toward them and expressed this fervently and graciously. No doubt this good will served to win at least some to faith of Israel, while the larger part remained on the fringe of the Jewish community,

---

31   See Acts 2:5, 10; 6:5; 13:43.

32   W. G. Braude, *Jewish Proselyting*, pp. 18-19, gives full references from Talmud, Mishnah, and other sources.

33   Even Philo, who said in encouragement to the Gentiles that the transition to Judaism was not one of excessive difficulty, was not free from the letter of the law, even though he allegorized it. Cf. Philo, *De Migratione Abrahami*, 16; *De Paenitentia*, 2.

34   Horace, *Sat.* I, 4, 142-143, quoted by G. Ricciotti, *The History of Israel*, II, p. 200.

35   Horace, *Sat.* I, 4, 133-143; cf. also J. Blauw, *Missionaren Nature*, p. 60.

never undergoing the rites of initiation.[36]

Those who did convert were not always accorded the full rights of the proselyte, however. It is observed by Eichhorn that

> they were thought of as co-religionists but not as being of the same race or nation as born Jews. They were considered to be part of the Jewish religious fellowship, the people of Judaism, rather than as belonging to the Jewish race or the Jewish nation. The Greek term for such religious affinity, used by Josephus, is ὁμόφυλον[37] [homophulon].

We may not conclude from the above that Judaism was a missionary religion in the modern sense during the pre-Christian era. Although there was a definite desire and attempt to win the heathen over to the faith and practice of Judaism, this movement always remained on the fringe of official circles.[38] At no time were professional or specially selected persons trained or employed as missionaries. Whatever attempts were made depended on the initiative of individual believers and originated not in Jerusalem but in the Diaspora, as Martin-Achard says,

> this movement ... retains the form of national propaganda since conversion to the Jewish faith involved adherence to the Jewish nation, that is to say, naturalisation. The Jewish approach to the heathen is both individualistic and nationalistic. This is what distinguishes it from the Christian mission for which providentially it prepares the way. In a certain sense Jewish proselytism is a private enterprise undertaken by individuals and concerned with particular persons ....[39]

Although "Judaism ... was the religion of the people with a mission,"[40] its spread was not occasioned by central authority within the community or from the cultic center. The impetus to witness came from within each community. The rabbis set before their hearers the example of proselyting by their honored men of old. Abraham, Moses, and others were constantly referred to in order to inspire the same zeal in the hearers who were challenged to go out and do as Abraham and Moses. "Orally and by pen the Israelites were educated to do personal work for their God among the Gentiles."[41]

When the Christian mission reached out into the world community it met the Gentile world first of all in the Diaspora synagogue. The command, "To the Jew first," was not a limitation of the Gospel proclamation to one people and

---

36 E. Schürer, *Geschichte*, III, pp. 124-127; W. G. Braude, *Jewish Proselyting*, pp. 136-138.

37 D. M. Eichhorn, *Conversion to Judaism*, p. 47.

38 R. Martin-Achard, *A Light to the Nations*, p. 4, quoting and referring to J. Jeremias, *Jesus' Promise*, pp. 12, 13.

39 R. Martin-Achard, *A Light to the Nations*, p. 4ff.

40 D. M. Eichhorn, *Conversion to Judaism*, p. 49.

41 J. Peterson, *Missionary Methods*, p. 179.

race but a gracious providence by which Christianity would be thrust upon the world scene where God and the nations were already accustomed to meet. The Jewish diaspora provided an at-hand avenue into the Gentile world. Although the members of the Jewish community did not go abroad as emissaries of the faith, many of them served as emissaries among the people who lived around them.

> Judaism was carried to the world by Christianity, but it was a Judaism that was doubly modified: by all that Christianity discarded and by all that its Founder brought into it. Christianity owed to Judaism a deep, inestimable debt, took over from Judaism the conception of her task, exercised the world mission of Judaism to a degree that Judaism has never attained, and made the heritage of Judaism the heritage of the world.[42]

It was observed earlier in this study that the Jewish Diaspora colonies were frequently given considerable authority to govern and determine their affairs and administer the Jewish laws. The synagogue community appears to have been the center of this discipline, especially when it concerned religious matters of Jewish law. Paul's letters of authority to the synagogues of Damascus given by the high priests indicate that this authority extended to the diaspora (Acts 9:1-2). Similarly, Gallio, proconsul of Achaia, refused to adjudicate differences of Jewish law because the Jews had full authority to do so themselves (Acts 18:12-17). Paul was beaten five times by the Jews in the course of his labors (II Cor. 11:24).

Such authority was exercised from Jerusalem in later days. It was not unusual, for Ezra had been given specific authority by Artaxerxes to administer both the king's law and "the law of your God" and to "let judgment be strictly executed ... whether for death or for banishment or for confiscation of his property or for imprisonment" (Ezra 7:25-26). The Jews whom Paul summoned to his place of confinement in Rome tell him, "We have received no letters from Judea about you, and none of the brethren coming here has reported or spoken any evil about you" (Acts 28:21). Any scholar among the Jews could remove religious as well as civic officials for the infraction of legal principles and whose conduct of public affairs did not meet the requirements of Jewish law.[43] The unity of Judaism was promoted by such conditions, a phenomenon quite unparalleled in history.

B. *The Rabbinic Attitudes Towards Proselytes*

The nature and content of the Jewish propaganda can best be seen against

---

42   H. H. Rowley, *Israel's Mission to the World*, p. 99.
43   *JT*, Peah 8:7, 21a; Kid. 76b. Hugo Mantel, *Studies in the History of the Sanhedrin* (Cambridge: Harvard University Press, 1961), pp. 199-202.

the background of the Rabbinic exegesis concerning the proselyte. The Talmud and Mishnah are the main sources for this material. However, these recorded teachings and traditions go back a long time and present a tradition that found its origins in pre-Christian times. The missionary consciousness of the early Christian community was in part at least due to those centuries not mentioned in the Old Testament when the Jewish proselyting movements received their great impetus.

A reading of the Talmudic references to the proselytes makes one aware of the caution which the Rabbis exercised with respect to the legal status of the proselyte. The statement "whoever wrests the judgment of the proselytes is as if he wrests the judgment of the Most High, for it is said, 'And that turn aside the proselyte from his right': the consonants may be read: 'and that turn Me aside' " [44] sets forth the basic criteria by which the rabbis established the position of the proselytes within the community. If the proselyte was robbed, restitution was to be made by the formula: the principal plus an additional one-fifth (Num. 5:7,8).[45] If anyone robbed him, it was the same as though he had robbed an Israelite.[46] The same restitution was to be made to a proselyte woman as to an Israelite in the case of injury by an ox or by other means.[47] A sin offering had to be brought for robbing the proselyte.[48] He had every right to enter the Assembly and to act as judge and witness in court.[49] Anyone kidnapping a proselyte was liable to the death penalty.[50]

Recalling that proselytes were present at Sinai because "their guiding stars were present" (based on Deut. 29:14ff.), the rabbis said that this meant that "the teachings of Judaism and its ennoblement were freely meant for all mankind." [51] "He who brings a Gentile near to God is as though he has created him." [52] Solomon employed large numbers of strangers ("proselytes") "to inform [Israel] that the Holy One . . . brings nigh those that are distant and supports the distant [rejoices over the distant] just as the nigh." [53] God is represented as waiting "for the nations of the world in the hope that they will repent and be brought under his wings." [54] In a number of instances the proselytes are used as an encouragement to Israel to trust God's faithfulness, for if God is faithful to Rechabites and Gibeonites, "how much more will he be faithful to his people?" [55] Gen. 49:5 is understood in terms of the deceit

---

44 Hag. 19.
45 Hal. 758.
46 Naso VIII.1.
47 Bk. 277.
48 Zeb. 224.
49 Nid. 344.
50 San. 566.
51 Shab. 738.
52 Lech Lecha XXXIX.14; Vayesheb LXXXIV.4.
53 Naso VIII.4.
54 Naso X.1.
55 Bemidbar V:3, 9; Jeremiah 35:9.

practiced on the men of Shechem and the guilt of Simeon and Levi who "raised a wall" meaning "the wall of proselytes ... The men of Shechem had been circumcised and future proselytes would take their example from them. Now that the men of Shechem were murdered, the confidence of the proselytes was destroyed." [56] Abraham, Sarah, Jethro, Moses, Rahab (whom Joshua is reported to have married and who bare him daughters but no sons), Naaman, and Nebuzaradan are cited as examples of great people who won proselytes.[57]

The legal status of the proselyte (or his children) was of great concern. The point at issue seems generally to be whether or not all the ritual requirements had been met at the moment of his converting. "A proselyte is exempt from priestly dues if he slaughtered a cow before he became a proselyte, but not afterwards. In cases of doubt the burden of proof rests with the claimant." [58] The statements, "One who becomes a proselyte is like one newly born," and, "the heathen has no father," imply that a completely new existence is now his.[59] The rabbis did not permit a proselyte to marry an Ammonite or Moabite proselyte. Ammonite and Moabite proselytes must marry within their own group.[60]

This new legal status is reflected in the laws of inheritance. A proselyte woman does not have to wait three months to re-marry if her husband was also a believer, for any child conceived before re-marriage would legally be an Israelite.[61] "A proselyte born in holiness [that is, his mother was a proselyte at the time of birth] but not conceived in holiness [his mother was not a proselyte at the time] legally has maternal sanguinity but no paternal sanguinity."[62] "A proselyte has no legal heirs except those born after he became a proselyte." [63] A proselyte son not conceived in holiness is entitled to a gift only, not a legacy.[64] Jeremias refers to the keeping of genealogical records for the Jews as well as for those descended from proselytes. These genealogies were important, for the civil rights of a person were based on them. The highest privilege was to be known as a family which could marry its daughters to priests. Pure ancestry was necessary for membership in the Sanhedrin.[65] The

56 Vayechi XCVIII.5.

57 Meg. 86; Suk. 232; Naso XIV:11; Git, 255, 265; Tzav IX.9; Shemoth I.36; Vayechi II.9; Debarim I.5; Hag. 8. Cf. also S. Sandmel, *Philo' Place*, p. 23ff. B. J. Bamberger, *Proselytism*, pp. 174-217, says, "The very bulk of the material precludes the possibility of extended quotation of the sources." Bamberger contains full references and documentation.

58 Hul. 761; Zeb. 497, 500.

59 Yeb. 131; cf. J. Jeremias, *Jerusalem in the Time of Jesus*, p. 323ff.

60 San. 562; Kid. 381, the latter reference in spite of their favorable attitude towards these nations, as previously noted.

61 Yeb. 216; Ket. 159, 198; B.B. 644-645.

62 Yeb. 673.

63 BK. 636.

64 B.B. 644-645.

65 J. Jeremias, *Jerusalem in the Time of Jesus*, pp. 281-298.

social point of view of the Jewish community in Jesus' day was dominated by the fundamental idea of racial purity.[66]

The property of a proselyte who died without heirs might be seized by a Jew, but his slaves were to be freed.[67] Offerings designated by the deceased must be made, however; if the estate cannot pay for them, they must be made at public expense.[68] In matters such as Sabbath observance, ritual cleanness, offerings, blowing the Shofar, pledges, etc. the proselyte was bound in exactly the same manner as the natural born Israelite.[69]

Regarding his reception into the people of Israel, circumcision and immersion were essential. If he had been circumcised before conversion, at least "a few drops of blood of the covenant" must be made to flow from him.[70] "One does not become a proselyte until he has been circumcised and has performed ablution; and so long as he has not performed ablution he is a gentile." [71] Jews might not be circumcised by Samaritans even when no one else is available because they circumcise in the name of Mt. Gerizim. A heathen might accidentally castrate the Jew, but could perform the surgery if there was no one else available to do so.[72] Circumcised but not immersed proselytes and their children render things ceremonially unclean.[73] Shammai said that being caught in a rainstorm sufficed in place of baptism for the proselyte to eat the Passover if he had been circumcised but not immersed. Hillel would not permit this, for "whoever separates himself from uncircumcision is as one who separates himself from the grave," and demanded that seven days intervene between baptism and Passover.[74] The rabbis taught that Abraham had not circumcised himself at the age of forty-eight when he first recognized his creator "in order not to discourage proselytes who might otherwise think it was too late in life to be circumcised." [75]

Favorable references to the proselyte abound. "The righteous among the Gentiles are priests of God. The saints of all nations have a share in the world to come." [76] "He who repudiates idolatry is a Jew"; however, to "turn away from idolatry" is not synonymous with complete conversion for such persons may not yet have turned away from immoral practices.[77] "A non-Jew who busies

---

66 For a full treatment of this idea see J. Jeremias, *Jerusalem in the Time of Jesus*, p. 270.
67 Git. 164.
68 Men. 311.
69 Shab. 326; R. H. 134, 150; Yeb. 505; Keb. 347; Mak. 115; Ker. 67; Mid. 297.
70 Shab. 679.
71 Ber. 288.
72 A.Z. 132.
73 A.Z. 287.
74 Ed. 32; cf. also J. Jeremias, *Jerusalem in the Time of Jesus*, p. 321.
75 Lech Lecha XLVI.2.
76 Sanh. XIII.2.
77 A.Z. 120; Meg. 74.

himself in the Torah is equal to the High Priest." [78] "Gentiles outside Palestine are not idolaters, for they are only following practices of their fathers." [79]

A change in viewpoint towards the proselyte is indicated by the above. Only the idols of the proselytes were regarded as impure and circumcision alone was sufficient to mark his conversion to Judaism up to the second century B.C. [80] The school of Hillel regarded the proselyte himself as impure. It was said that the impurity of the Gentiles was like the impurity of a menstruous woman. This view dominated Judaism in the time of Jesus and the apostles. [81]

It is particularly helpful against the New Testament background to place together the phrases and images used to describe the change of religion that was effected in the case of the male proselytes by circumcision and immersion, and in the case of the woman proselyte by immersion only. Jeremias has brought these together in a significant paragraph: [82]

> The Gentile who changes his religion, who previously was far from God, has now come near to Him (Ephesians 2:13; Acts 2:39). He was dead Ephesians 2:1), lay, in a manner of speaking, in the grave (I Clem. 38:3), and has been raised from the dead (Colossians 3:1). A new creation has taken place (Galatians 6:15; II Corinthians 5:17). Thereby his past is blotted out, he has entered a completely new existence, is like a newborn child I Peter 2:2), is a νεόφυτος (I Timothy 3:6). All this happened through forgiveness of all his sins being granted to the Gentile on his change of religion (Colossians 2:2). Henceforth he is in holiness (I Thessalonians 3:13).

> These are not just individual points of contact, but the whole terminology of the Jewish conversion theology connected with proselyte baptism recurs in the theology of primitive Christian baptism.

> How powerfully the thought that conversion signified the beginning of a completely new life had penetrated the consciousness of the great mass of the people is proved by the numerous instances in inscriptions and literary sources of changes of name of proselytes. This usage goes far back into the centuries before the introduction of proselyte baptism.

78 Bab. K, 38a.
79 Hullin, 13b.
80 Judith 14:10.
81 Matt. 8:7; John 18:28; Acts 10:28; 11:12; I Cor. 7:14; Gal. 2:12. See also Joachim Jeremias, *Infant Baptism in the First Four Centuries* (Philadelphia: Westminster, 1960), p. 25, henceforth to be cited as *Infant Baptism*. The NEB translates Matthew 8:7 as a question ("Sir, who am I to have you under my roof?") suggesting the idea of uncleanness to Jeremias. K. H. Rengstorf, *TWNT*, III, p. 294, says, "he is not thinking of ritual uncleanness which Jesus as a Jew would incur by entering a non-Jewish house. What he has in view is the majesty and authority of Jesus which left Him above everything human, especially in the non-Jewish sphere."
82 J. Jeremias, *Infant Baptism*, p. 36; pp. 19-37 also.

Sacrifice is another area of interest in the relation of proselytes and Gentiles to Judaism. There was a considerable body of Gentiles who were not proselytes nor adherents of the *superstitio-Judaica* but who participated in the worship of the Temple at Jerusalem and were permitted to sacrifice.[83] A number of persons were alleged to have offered sacrifices. Josephus tells of Alexander the Great, Ptolemais III, Antiochus VII (who during his siege of Jerusalem at the time of the Feast of Tabernacles sent sacrifices into the Temple), Marcus Agrippa (15 B.C., who sacrificed 100 oxen as a burnt offering on behalf of Herod), Vitellius (who came to Jerusalem especially for the purpose).[84] Philo records that Augustus ordered the daily sacrifice of two lambs and a bullock at his expense. It is this sacrifice to which the Jews pointed as a sign of their loyalty to Rome. This sacrifice continued to be offered until 66 A.D. The Ptolemies frequently gave presents to the temple.[85] The expenses for the required sacrifices at the New Temple were to be paid from the king's treasury according to Ezra 6:9ff.[86]

The priest's responsibility in these matters was to see to it that the sacrifice was offered properly and in honor of God. They were not concerned at whose expense the offering was brought. The Old Testament assumed this practise in Lev. 27:26 (the word *ben nechar*, a non-Israelite, is used). Later Judaism specified the acceptable offerings, such as for vows and the free-will offerings, but not the sin or trespass offerings.[87] The Mishnah on Lev. 1:2 says that the word *Adam* is used for man in that place "precisely so as to include proselytes."[88] Josephus says that in A.D. 6 a resolution was passed prohibiting the acceptance of offerings from the Gentiles, but the conservatives maintained, "All our forefathers had been in the habit of receiving sacrifices at the hand of the Gentiles" and if the Jews were the only people among whom a foreigner was not allowed to sacrifice, then Jerusalem would incur the reproach of being an ungodly city.[89] Offering a sacrifice at a temple other than that connected with one's own faith was very often nothing more than an expression by the offerer of a cosmopolitan piety, a mere act of courtesy toward a people, city, or temple, and said nothing about a man's religious creed.[90]

It may be concluded, therefore, that the rabbis approved of proselyting, encouraged it, used the patriarchs and great men of Israel's past as examples to follow, and in their reading of Scripture discovered many references to the proselyte. In all cases, however, the proselyte was bound to become an Israelite

---

83 E. Schürer, *Geschichte*, I:1, pp. 299-305 (E.T.).

84 Josephus, *Ant.*, XIII.8.2; XVI.2.1; XVIII.5.3; *Bell. Jud.*, V.1.s; IV.4.3.

85 Josephus, *Contra Ap.*, II.5, 6; *Bell Jud.*, II.10.4; II.17.2-4; E. Schürer, *Geschichte*, I, p. 302-303 (E.T.).

86 G. C. Luck, *Ezra and Nehemiah*, sub loco.

87 *BT*, Mak. 133; Men. 364-365, 435.

88 Vayyikra II.9.

89 *Bell. Jud.*, II.17.2-4; *Ant.*, XI.1.5; *Contra Ap.*, II.5.

90 E. Schürer, *Geschichte*, I, pp. 299-300 (E.T.).

in every respect. He had to observe the whole law (Gal. 5:3), and he had to demonstrate his sincerity by being baptized and circumcised.

C. *The Reception of Proselytes*

From what classes among the Gentiles did those who constituted the prose-lytes of the synagogue community come? It is well-known that Jewish colonists in the diaspora frequently married heathen women, who were by the fact of their marriage accepted into the Jewish fold.[91] The slave and the stranger were from early times a natural and inevitable means for enlarging the Jewish community. The slave and the stranger actually resident under the roof of a head of a household were foreign in blood but became practically members of that household. The Decalogue makes the stranger the special responsibility of the community (Ex. 20:10). Abraham served as an example in this, since at his circumcision all the males of his household were likewise circumcised at Yahweh's command (Gen. 17:12-13). Later, the slave was offered his freedom at conversion since the Jews were forbidden to own fellow Israelites as slaves.[92] The emancipation of slaves was closely related to the synagogue. The transaction took place in the synagogue, which was also witness and guarantor. The legal notices found in the Crimea from the first century A.D. indicate that one of the conditions of the emancipation was that the slave's freedom depended upon faithful attendance at the synagogue and adherence to its teachings. Derwacter says "this gives the impression that possibly the freedom was granted as a means to proselytism."[93] The Maccabees were not above using force upon those who did not voluntarily convert to Judaism as is shown in their treatment of the Idumeans and Itureans. The former were forced to be circumcised or leave their country by John Hyrcanus. The latter were forced to be circumcised by Aristobulus under the same threat.[94] The Herods required those who married into the family to be circumcised. Alexander Janni conquered parts of Moab and massacred those who refused circumcision.[95]

The greatest success lay with the common people among whom the process of conversion went on throughout the diaspora not affected by the Maccabaean

91 Cf. B. J. Bamberger, *Proselytism*, p. 18, who refers to the excellent study by A. S. Herschberg, *Ha Te Kufah*, vol. XII, p. 132.

92 J. H. Peterson, *Missionary Methods*, p. 140; M. Radin, *The Jews Among the Greeks and Romans*, p. 389, n. 12.

93 F. Derwacter, *Preparing the Way for Paul*, p. 80, who quotes E. Schürer, "Die Juden im bosporanischen Reiche" in *Sitzungsberichte der Akademie der Wissenschaften*, 1897, pp. 200-206, especially p. 203.

94 Josephus, *Ant.*, XIII.ix.1 and xi.3. J. S. Raisin, *Gentile Reactions*, pp. 84ff. and 171ff., reviews and discusses the forcible accretions together with the reasons for them. See also J. Jeremias, *Jerusalem in the Time of Jesus*, p. 320; J. Peterson, *Missionary Methods*, pp. 159-161.

95 Josephus, *Ant.*, XIII.xv.4; XVI.vii.6.

struggle. The large numbers of converts near Antioch mentioned by Josephus, the women of Damascus, the expulsion of the Jews from Rome, the Greeks, Poppaea, the judaizers and semi-converts of Syria – these all witness to the fact that all classes of the society of the Roman world found spiritual refuge in the true faith.[96]

By what ceremony were they admitted to the status of Jew? What was required of the convert? It is worth noting that it is only in Esther 8:17 that the Hebrew word (*mityahadim*) for conversion is used for the first time in the Bible, "which probably indicates that conversion was a practice sufficiently familiar to have a verb to describe it." [97] The word is from a root meaning to worship and is translated in the R.S.V. as "become a Jew". On the basis of the incident recorded in this passage the rabbis sometimes spoke of "Esther proselytes".[98] An earlier phrase in the book of Ruth "to take refuge under the wings of Yahweh, the God of Israel" (2:12) is used in the sense of "to be converted to Judaism."

Only one Scriptural requirement is laid on the *gerim* who wished to identify with Israel in the eating of the Passover and it is limited to the prescription of circumcision (cf. Gen. 17:12,13; Ex. 12:48). It appears that this requirement was the only one made of the convert until approximately the second century B.C. (cf. Judith 14:10). At the time that the Gentile began to be regarded as being personally impure other obligations became associated with his reception into the community of God's people. At what time or in what place (or even whether universally) these new obligations became conditions for admission into the community, it is impossible for us to tell.

We begin with the Talmud which clearly and unequivocally required three conditions for admission: (1) circumcision, (2) baptism, and (3) sacrifice.[99] Maimonides, a great Jewish scholar of the twelfth century (1135-1204), gave a clear and detailed account of the reception of proselytes. His account is really a mosaic of the Talmudic tradition; therefore, it is given in full:[100]

By three things did Israel enter into the Covenant, by circumcision, and

---

96   Josephus, *Bell. Jud.*, VII.3.30; II.8.2; II.20.2; *Ant.*, XVIII.3.5; XX.8.11; *Vita*, 3; *Contra Ap.*, II.11 & 40.

97   Cf. L. Ginzberg, *Legends of the Jews*, VI, p. 480; B. J. Bamberger, *Proselytism*, p. 13.

98   *Biblical, Theological and Ecclesiastical Encyclopedia*, VIII, p. 659.

99   E. Schürer, *Geschichte*, II, p. 319 (E.T.). The Talmudic data can be found in the tractates Yebamoth, Berakoth, Kerithoth, Kethuboth, Shabbath, and Abodah Zarah. We have no information on these matters outside the rabbinic tradition. Cf. H. H. Rowley, *HUCA*, XV (1940), p. 321; G. F. Moore, *Judaism*, I, pp. 331ff., 334; J. Bonsirven, *Palestinian Judaism*, I, p. 29ff. All these authors agree that the tradition that sets forth these requirements is trustworthy.

100   Maimonides, *Isure Biah*, 13 and 14, quoted by Thomas F. Torrance, "Proselyte Baptism," in *NTSt*, I (1954), 150-154. H. H. Rowley, *HUCA*, XV, pp. 320ff. also details the initiation rite.

baptism and sacrifice. Circumcision was in Egypt, as it was written, "No uncircumcised person shall eat thereof" (Exodus XII:48). Baptism was in the wilderness just before giving of the Law: as it is written, "Sanctify them today and tomorrow, and let them wash their clothes" (Exodus XIX:10). And sacrifice, as it is said, "And he sent young men of the children of Israel which offered burnt offerings" (Exodus XXIV:5). And so in all ages when a Gentile is willing to enter into the Covenant, and gather himself under the wings of the Shekinah of God, and take upon him the yoke of the Law, he must be circumcised and be baptized and bring a sacrifice. As it is said, "As you are, so shall the stranger be" (Num. 15:15). How are you? So likewise the stranger (or proselyte) through all generations: by circumcision and baptism, and bringing a sacrifice. And what is the stranger's sacrifice? A burnt offering of a beast, or two turtle-doves, or two young pigeons, both of them for a burnt-offering. And at this time when there is no sacrificing, they must be circumcised and be baptized; and when the Temple shall be built, they are to bring the sacrifice. A stranger that is circumcised and not baptized, or baptized and not circumcised, is not a proselyte till he be both circumcised and baptized: and he must be baptized in the presence of three.... Even as they circumcise and baptize strangers, so do they circumcise and baptize servants that are received from the heathen into the name of servitude .... The Gentile that is made proselyte and the slave that is made free, behold he is like a child new born.

Entrance into the commonwealth of Israel was more than naturalization. It was essentially admission to full covenant status. Therefore, since the completion of these rites made the proselyte in all respects an Israelite, it was understood that his admission should involve all that was required of Israel: circumcision, sacrifice, baptism (cf. Gen. 17:12; Ex. 12:48; 19:10; 24:8; Num. 15:15; Josh. 5:1). These requirements made of Israel "once for all time" were likewise required from the proselyte. When he comes up from waters of baptism, he has entered the covenant.[101] It is certain that all three rites were required prior to 70 A.D.[102]

The meaning and place of circumcision in the covenant with Abraham and Israel has already been traced. Circumcision was required only of males, according to Scripture, and was the *sine qua non* for their conversion. In the case of males who were already circumcised, the rabbis instructed that a few drops of blood must be shed, otherwise the covenant was not complete. In all cases a person already circumcised had to be baptized.[103]

Female converts were only required by the rabbis to offer a sacrifice and to baptize themselves.[104] Some find in this circumstance the explanation for the

101 *BT*, Yeb. 46b, 47b; Ker. 9a; AZ 57a; Shab. 135a; *JT*, Kiddushin iii.14, 54d.
102 See T. M. Taylor, "The Beginnings of Jewish Proselyte Baptism" in *NTSt*, II, no. 3 (Feb. 1956), 193-198, in which Taylor responds to Torrance's article − see note 100 above.
103 *BT*, Shab. 679, AZ 293; Strack-Billerbeck, *Kommentar*, I, p. 105.
104 D. Daube, *The New Testament and Rabbinic Judaism*, p. 106.

greater number of female proselytes in the Jewish communities. In the Christian era there were a number of occasions when the Jews under threat of the death penalty were forbidden to circumcise, indicating a continuing proselyting effort.[105]

The requirement of a sacrifice continued as long as the Temple stood. The rabbis required readiness to offer a sacrifice on the part of the proselyte in the times when the temple remained unbuilt.[106] It was a condition which like circumcision could be waived in cases of necessity.[107] The nature of the sacrifice was that of a burnt offering.[108] An offering by itself was not sufficient, since, as has been shown, the Gentiles were permitted to provide offerings at the Temple. The burnt offering was appropriate for the reception of the proselyte since by the laying on of hands the offering was accepted for him before Yahweh (Lev. 1:3).

Greater controversy has surrounded the question of baptism of proselytes. No little difficulty in resolving the questions raised is occasioned by the fact that there is no positive information regarding the origin of this rite and its original meaning (was it purificatory or an initiatory ritual, e.g.). Baptisms were common in Palestine among tribes living in the Jordan areas. The ancient world was full of religious ceremonies which were expected to effect a spiritual change in those who submitted to them, in some instances even to transform them from men into gods.[109] Earlier scholarship generally held to a late date for the origin of proselyte baptism, but this was usually done in the interest of supporting the thesis of the originality of Christian baptism.[110] Oepke remarks that

105 Joseph Crehan, *Early Christian Baptism and Creed* (London: 1950), pp. 2-4, who holds to a late date for the origin of proselyte baptism. *The Sibylline Oracles,* iv. 164, (probably around 80 A.D.) state that circumcision is not required, only a ceremonial cleansing.

106 *BT,* R.H., 150.

107 F. Derwacter, *Preparing the Way for Paul,* pp. 104-108, discusses the various exceptions respecting the requirement of circumcision with documentation from the sources. Cf. also Jeremias, *Jesus' Promise,* p. 15.

108 Men., 435.

109 For the full treatment of baptismal practices of peoples in the Jordan area, see Richard Reitzenstein, *Die Vorgeschichte der Christlichen Taufe* (Stüttgart: B. G. Teubner, 1967), p. 18ff., who also has a complete survey of the meaning of baptism in various religions. See also the article βάπτω by Albrecht Oepke, *TWNT,* I, pp. 529-535, for a discussion of the meaning of sacral washings in various religions and Hellenism. Oepke concludes that "it is impossible to trace all these customs to a common root" (p. 531). W. F. Albright, *From the Stone Age to Christianity,* p. 377, discusses Reitzenstein's viewpoint. For the lustrations among Italians, Greeks, Syrians, Persians, Indians, Jews, and Gnostic practices see Ernst Lohmeyer, *Das Urchristentum I: Johannes der Taufer* (Göttingen: Vandenhoeck & Ruprecht, 1932); James D. Smart, *The Quiet Revolution* (Philadelphia: Westminster, 1969), p. 21.

110 E. Schürer, *Geschichte,* III, p. 181ff., surveys and criticizes the older treatments. R. Reitzenstein, *Die Vorgeschichte der Christlichen Taufe,* p. 231ff., in the interests of his syncretistic bias contests the earlier emergence of proselyte baptism.

... on inner grounds it is likely that is was already customary in the New Testament period, since the purity demanded of every Jew could not be relaxed in the case of the impure Gentile. Again it is hardly conceivable that the Jewish ritual should be adopted at a time when baptism had become an established religious practice in Christianity. After 70 A.D. at least the opposition to Christians was too sharp to allow for the rise of a Christian custom among the Jews. Proselyte baptism must have preceded Christian baptism.[111]

In addition, the debates between the schools of Shammai and Hillel (contemporaries of Jesus) on the subject of baptism indicate that the practice must have been well established by that time. The Hillelites laid increasing emphasis on proselyte baptism as the crucial point of transition with the intention of making the assimilation of male proselytes comparable to that of the female. The question debated with the Shammaites was concerned with the question whether circumcision or baptism was the point of change. The Hillelites brought a purificatory, levitical sense into baptism, even though they were generally more universalist in spirit. Hillel emphasized the "coming up" aspect of immersion.[112] By the end of the first century A.D. the viewpoint of the Hillel school can be said to have prevailed and is reflected in the Talmud. The fact that the authorities of the Talmud did not know the origin of the rite also indicates its antiquity.[113]

The main characteristic of proselyte baptism can be gathered from the rabbinic sources. These display both similarity and dissimilarity between it and Christian baptism. Rowley has aptly and accurately defined the difference between proselyte baptism and John's baptism in this way: proselyte baptism was "regarded as entrance into a new life; John's baptism was not just into

111 A. Oepke, *TWNT*, I, p. 535. Cf. also Harold Henry Rowley, "Jewish Proselyte Baptism and the Baptism of John" in *HUCA*, XV (1940), 313-334.

112 *Mishnah*, Pes. 8:8; Ed. 5.2; Strack-Billerbeck, *Kommentar*, I, p. 102ff.; George Raymond Beasley-Murray, *Baptism in the New Testament*, (London: Macmillan Co., 1960), pp. 29-30; D. Daube, *The New Testament and Rabbinic Judaism*, p. 108; *BT*, Yeb. 47b; J. Jeremias, *Infant Baptism*, p. 25. A different viewpoint of the schools of Hillel and Shammai is given by Isaiah Sonne, "The Schools of Hillel and Shammai Seen From Within" in *Louis Ginzberg Memorial Volume* (New York: American Academy for Jewish Research, 1945), pp. 275-292, who finds Hillel emphasizes the spirit of the law vs. Shammai and the letter of the law, or immediacy (Hillel) vs. long range values (Shammai). Sonne also considers the position of Geiger that the differences between the schools was political, and of those who hold that these differences were socio-economic. For a specific account of the schools of Hillel and Shammai, relating to the actual training of a Hebrew youth, see Jacob Neusner, *A Life of Rabban Yohanan Ben Zakkai: Ca. 1-80 C.E.* (Leiden: E. J. Brill, 1962), pp. 16-32.

113 George A. Barton, "The Origin of the Thought Pattern that Survives in Baptism," in the *Journal of the American Oriental Society*, 56 (1936), 155-165. Wilhelm Brandt, *Die jüdische Baptismen* (Giessen: A. Toppelmann, 1910), pp. 56-72, has a section containing complete references to proselyte baptism in the Talmud. The book also contains all other ancient sources in full.

a new life but into a new age."[114] The main features of proselyte baptism which are of importance to this study are these:

(1) The proselyte was baptized "in the name of God" and accepted "the yoke of the law."[115] He was instructed in the meaning of what he was about to do. While he was in the water, parts of the Law were read to him and he was interrogated concerning his faith.[116] When he emerged, he was regarded as bearing the yoke of the Law. He had now come "under the wings of the *Shekinah*" and was fully initiated into the faith. This was impressed on him by the witnesses. After the immersion the representatives who first exhorted him said, "Whom hast thou joined, thou blessed one? Thou hast joined him who created the world by the utterance of words, blessed be He, for the world was created solely for Israel's sake and none are called children of God save Israel."[117]

(2) Proselyte baptism was self-administered. The general method seems to have been immersion and could take place almost anywhere except in baths dedicated to idols. Three rabbis, "fathers of baptism," were witnessess.[118] In the case of a woman she was seated in the water to her neck, women assisting her, while two rabbis discreetly secluded behind screens read pertinent sections of the Law to her.[119] Ordinarily a three-fold immersion was practiced. It was regarded as important that the entire person come into contact with the water, and anything that in the least degree broke the continuity was held to invalidate the act: a ring on the finger, a band confining the hair, even a knot in one's hair![120]

(3) Proselyte baptism was distinguished from private ritual ablutions by its public character. It might not take place at night (and hence secretly), and witnesses were present to give it a judicial character.[121]

(4) Infants could be baptized along with the parents, although if males, they like their fathers must first be circumcised. Children of slaves as well as orphans might be baptized.[122] It should be noted that the baptism of infant proselytes

---

114 H. H. Rowley, "Jewish Proselyte Baptism and the Baptism of John," p. 329. For the organization of the material that follows on the main features of proselyte baptism I am indebted to the study of T. F. Torrance, "Proselyte Baptism." See also W. G. Braude, *Jewish Proselytizing*, pp. 77-88.

115 Gerim vii.8; Aboth ii,2, 12; iv.11; Pes. 50b; San. 105b; Nazir 23b.

116 Yeb. 47a,b; Comp. I Peter 3:21.

117 Yeb. 46a, and 48b, referring to Ruth 2:12. See also LXX on Isaiah 54:15. H. H. Rowley, *HUCA*, XV (1940), p 325ff.

118 Keth. 11; Er. 15; Yeb. 47a.

119 Yeb. 47b.

120 Cf. T. F. Torrance, "Proselyte Baptism", p. 151, n. 3; H. H. Rowley, *HUCA*, XV (1940), p. 321ff.; Erub. 4b.

121 Yeb. 46a, 47b; *JT*, Yeb. viii.1.

122 For the presentation and defense of the early practice of baptism of infants see Joachim Jeremias, *The Origins of Infant Baptism*, translated by Dorothea M. Barton (Naperville: A. R. Allenson, 1963); German title = *Die Anfänge der Kindertaufe*. Also see Yeb. 48a; *JT*, Yeb. viii.1; Ketuboth i,2,3,4; iii.1,2.

had a provisional character. The children of proselytes baptized by their parents had the right to exercise their own discretion as to their relationship to the Jewish faith and nation when they attained maturity and were at liberty to renounce their proselyte status. "If an offspring of a proselyte baptized in infancy resolved to turn his back on Judaism, he was not treated as a renegade Jew but was looked on as who had lived all his life as a non-Israelite." Children born after the conversion of their parents to Judaism were not baptized; circumcision sufficed. Heathen slaves bought by the Jew were also circumcised and baptized. His master was required to hold him firmly while he was in the water to clearly distinguish the ceremony from the baptism of the true proselyte.[123]

(5) A forward and backward reference is found in the baptism. Not only is the proselyte free from the pollution of his former life, but all previous relationships are now changed as well.[124]

(6) Participation in the Passover became the criterion whether a man was a proselyte or not, just as in Christianity the right to partake of the Lord's Supper determines whether a person is a confessing member. Accordingly, the Passover season became the usual time in which the baptisms of proselytes took place, and this often in connection with the offering required to be made at the Temple. Baptism in the Pool of Siloam was not a rare occurrence.[125] Not all these items were immediately associated with this rite of baptism. Many grew only gradually, as most such cultic practices do.

The instruction given to candidates for baptism is of special interest to us, since in Matthew 28:18-20 instruction is closely related to Christian baptism. David Daube has detailed the content of this instruction,[126] paralleling it with New Testament practices. The pattern of instruction included these elements: (1) *The test*, whose essence was that a person was asked whether he understood all that was involved in his action requesting instruction for reception as a convert. This indicated knowledge of the fundamentals of the faith. Parallels are found in Matthew 28, "teaching . . . all that I have commanded you" and in Acts 2 where Peter's Pentecost sermon is concerned with the Messiahship of Jesus, the essential element at that moment.[127]

---

123 Strack-Billerbeck, *Kommentar*, I, p. 110ff.; G. R. Beasley-Murray, *Baptism in the New Testament*, pp. 329-334, esp. p. 332; Oscar Cullmann, *Baptism in the New Testament: Studies in Biblical Theology No. 1*, translated by J. K. S. Reid (London: SCM Press, 1951), p. 25; H. H. Rowley, *HUCA*, XV (1940), 321; Yeb. 46a.

124 Yeb. 22a; 48b; 62a; 97b; 98a,b; Bek. 47a; *JT*, Yeb. 4a; Bik. 64a; 65b; *Mishnah*, Yeb. xi.2.

125 G. F. Moore, *Judaism*, I, p. 330; T. F. Torrance, "Proselyte Baptism," p. 152; J. Jeremias, *Jerusalem in the Time of Jesus*, p. 320ff. The Mishnah and Talmud say that the Gentile wishing to become a Jew offered his sacrifice in Jerusalem — see *Mishnah*, Ker. 2.1; *BT*, Ker. 81a.

126 D. Daube, *The New Testament and Rabbinic Judaism*, p. 113ff.; J. Jeremias, *Infant Baptism*, p. 30ff.

127 J. Jeremias, *Infant Baptism*, p. 53, demonstrates that an enquiry into the

(2) *The commandments:* some of the lighter and weightier commandments were read to the applicant. Again the words "all that I have commanded you" of Matthew 28 are a parallel. Other New Testament passages also show that instruction constituted part of the early training of the convert: I Cor. 3:2; I Pet. 2:2; Heb. 5:12ff.; 6:1ff.[128]

(3) *Charity:* the duty of charity was impressed on the candidate. Peter, as shown previously, included frequent references to this duty in his epistles.

(4) *Penalties,* including instruction in the differences between his present and former state: many New Testament warnings also follow the proclamation of duties to the believing community. See Matt. 7:24; Gal. 6:7; Eph. 5:5; Phil. 3:18; Col. 3:25; I Thess. 4:5; Heb. 6:4; 10:25; 13:4; I Pet. 3:12.

(5) *Rewards and the Life to Come:* the entire instruction was set in an eschatological framework as to man's purpose, task, and hope in this world's passing phase. The New Testament is replete with references to the eschatological hope contained in the preaching of the Kingdom of God.

The Christian mission is indebted, in the view of several scholars, to the Jewish scholars for the manuals of instruction prepared by the Jews for the instruction of proselytes. The *Didache* and *Sibylline Books* are regarded as having a Jewish origin and adapted by the early church for its purpose.[129]

We see, then, that the Jewish proselyte was identified with the nation and with Yahweh and his covenant. The manner of his initiation was in harmony with the unfulfilled character of the Old Testament revelation. Proselyte baptism was defined and practiced in accordance with the concept of mission, a matter closely related to the establishment of the Christian rite. Unfortunately this aspect of Christian baptism has often been forgotten and baptism is defined in terms of personal salvation and not of the essential nature of the church and God's universal covenant. Baptism is, as John Piet says, "a mandate for mission."[130] The baptisms of the New Testament relate without exception to missionary baptism, i.e., when Jews and Gentiles were received into fellow-

motivation for changing one's religion was practiced very early. The technical term κωλύειν (forbid, hinder, prevent) is used on a number of occasions in Acts. See 8:36; 10:47; 11:17; also Matt. 3:14 is more than just a simple statement.

128 In Cyril of Jerusalem's instructions to candidates for baptism and newly baptized members, the exposition of the Lord's Prayer was given to the new members after baptism as part of the commentary on the Eucharistic liturgy to which they were now admitted. In Mss. 162 & 700 "thy Kingdom come" reads "thy Holy Spirit come upon us and cleanse us," a reading known to early church fathers Gregory of Nyssa and Maximus Confessor. It is traceable to very early times and reflects the use of the Prayer in the initiation rites of the Christian community. See Thomas Walter Manson "The Lord's Prayer," in *The Bulletin of the John Rylands Library Manchester,* 38 (September 1955), 99-113.

129 Not all scholars take this viewpoint of the *Didache.* For various views see: G. R. Beasley-Murray, *Baptism in the New Testament,* p. 25ff.; D. Daube, *The New Testament and Rabbinic Judaism,* p. 106ff. (chap. 5 = "A Baptismal Catechism"); D. M. Eichhorn, *Conversion to Judaism,* p. 45; F. Derwacter, *Preparing the Way for Paul,* pp. 99-100.

130 J. H. Piet, *The Road ahead,* pp. 69-83.

ship.[131] Further attention will be given to this when the place and meaning of Christian baptism are considered.

D. *The Propaganda*

By the time of Jesus, Judaism had achieved an unequalled integration of religion, race, and culture. Some have called this "particularism" and have seen a conflict in both pre- and post-Christian Judaism, a tension between particularism and universalism.[132] The separation of nation and religion was beyond the grasp of the average Jew. Even the Gentile world considered proselytization as in some sense at least a kind of nationalization. This is necessary to bear in mind since the unique characteristics of the Jewish communities (social, juridical, and religious) were preserved as a result of the existence of the Jews as a separate people among the nations.[133] The emergence of "insular Judaism," as Rowley calls it,[134] was timely. It seems to have gained prominence during the Babylonian Exile as a defense against Babylonian religion and absorption into the heathen world. In Palestine it was motivated by resistance to the laxity that in pre-exilic times admitted pagan influences into Israel and led to the apostacy of the tribes. Ezra's call to put away the foreign women after the Exile is an illustration of this defensiveness (Ezra 9). Ezra was moved to take this action not merely because these women were from the tribes of the land but because the people of Israel had not "separated themselves from the peoples of the land *with their abominations*" (Ezra 9:1). Such drastic action was required because of the aggressive influences of the alien cultures that dominated the land (Ezra 9:11).[135]

In the post-exilic age, which we associate with an insular Judaism, there were not a few writers who had a wider vision, who, in the light of their

131   J. Jeremias, *Infant Baptism*, p. 19.
132   W. O. E. Oesterley, *Judaism and Christianity*, I, p. 112, article by H. Loewe, "Pharisaism," remarks that it would be wrong to stress unduly the connotation of exclusiveness. The Mishnah, he points out, is a Pharisaic compilation and reflects Pharisaic conditions. In the agricultural treatises we find many instances of Jews in partnership with Gentiles. Cf. I, p. 113; II, pp. 41 and 213. See also Otto Eissfeldt, *Partikularismus und Universalismus in der Israelitisch-jüdischen Religionsgeschichte*; a summary of this dissertation can be found in *Theologische Literaturzeitung*, LXXXIX (1954), p. 283.
133   T. J. Meek, *JR*, VII (May 1927), pp. 247-248.
134   H. H. Rowley, *Israel's Mission*, p. 37. I personally feel that the tensions between what is called particularism and universalism in Israel's faith are abstractions. Reality did not fit into such neatly conceived distinctions. We shall use the terms in a very loose sense only to define meaning and not practice.
135   In this and similar circumstances down to the present day we must remember that political and social situations often play a far more determinative role in the practise and expression of the faith than we generally think.

vision of the greatness of God saw men of other races as their brethren, who perceived that the grace of God was far too rich to be exhausted in His goodness to Israel, whose hearts so overflowed with gladness at the mercy of God that they wanted all the world to know it, who felt in their hearts something of the divine compassion as they looked on the world that lived without Him, and who perceived that Israel was called to a mission of service, service that knew no limits, service that should be achieved in testimony and in suffering, and that should be rewarded in the establishment of the Kingdom of God in the world.[136]

Israel was informed of the divine response to the adoration by the Gentiles in the amazing blessing contained in Isaiah 19:25, which places Israel as a third party among the nations in the midst of the world,

> Blessed be Egypt, my people, and
> Assyria, the work of my hands, and
> Israel, my heritage.

In order to feel the full force of a statement such as this, Eichhorn suggests:

> Let the reader imagine some eminent divine today proclaiming, "Blessed is Russia, God's people, and Red China, the work of his hands, and America, his heritage." This does put some strain on the imagination. Yet Isaiah dared.[137]

The particularism of the Jews was not born of disloyalty to this wide vision; it arose from necessity and served a real purpose in God's plan for the fulfillment of his covenant with the nations. It was necessary to preserve the life of Judaism, for God willed to bring life to the world through his people Israel. On Israel's part this was not inconsistent with a real interest in the pagan world or with a desire to lead men now alienated from God to him and to receive them into the fellowship of his people. The defense of her peculiar character as an elect people, a chosen race, had also its role to play in the triumph of the truth. Significantly, "it was the Pharisees and kindred elements in the Diaspora who were the cream of Jewish society, deeply loyal to the faith themselves, austerely loyal in fulfillment of the minutiae of the Law, and ever ready to welcome recruits to share their spirit and devotion."[138]

> We are accustomed to condemn this spirit out of hand, and are rarely willing either to understand it or to consider the conditions which produced it. We

---

136 H. H. Rowley, *Israel's Mission*, pp. 71-75. See also J. Bonsirven, *Palestinian Judaism*, I, p. 24ff., for references to the Talmud and other rabbinic sources to show that particularism did not exclude missionary zeal; H. M. J. Loewe, *Judaism and Christianity*, II: *The Contact of Pharisaism With Other Cultures*, p. 41ff.

137 D. M. Eichhorn, *Conversion to Judaism*, p. 11.

138 H. H. Rowley, *Israel's Mission*, p. 75.

have ourselves entered into a great inheritance for which we did not labor, and we find it easy to speak with contempt of those who never knew our inheritance, because they did not attain the heights on which we believe we stand. Yet it is doubtful if we should have gone farther than they had we begun with what was given them and with the conditions of their day; and it is yet more doubtful if we should stand where we stand today had it not been for that very spirit we so easily condemn in them.[139]

This co-called particularism was vastly more serviceable to the world than the laxity of other parties among the Jews. Pharisaism was not just hypocrisy and self-righteousness (as we often falsely think because we know best its aberrations) but utter loyalty, sometimes even fanatic, to the faith of Israel and to the will of God as understood by them. The converts who were admitted to the fellowship of the people of God did not come to faith as a result of the witness of the lax and compromising parties among the Jews but through the witness of the loyal children of Israel. Persons who are ready to compromise their faith are not the persons who loyally spread it. Only those who value it highly, who love it so much that they are willing to risk their lives for it, are the ones prepared and ready to commend it to others as a very great treasure.[140]

The strength of Judaism, like that of Christianity, cannot be found in the fact that men were faithful in spreading it. The Old Testament messengers confronted the nations with the truth. The key to the success of pre-Christian Judaism and its heir, Christianity, is the fact that they brought a revelation of the truth to men.[141] God witnessed to the success of the spread of the truth, saying:

> From the rising of the sun to its setting my name *is* great among the nations, and in every place incense *is offered* to my name, and a pure offering; for my name *is* great among the nations (Mal. 1:11). [Some versions place this in the future tense.]

The fact that in later generations Judaism rejected its fulfillment in Christ should not be taken to mean that the Old Testament believers were unfaithful. The existence of a class of righteous saints in Jerusalem looking for the consolation of Israel at the time of the birth of Christ (Luke 2) demonstrates a faith-

---

139 H. H. Rowley, *Israel's Mission*, pp. 39, 59-60.
140 H. H. Rowley, *Israel's Mission*, p. 59.
141 It is necessary to emphasize this. However we evaluate the Jewish pre-Christian movements (whether we think of them as passive or aggressive, whether we speak of reception of proselytes or seeking them in mission), this was a movement significant and important in itself. It was a sharing of the truth with the nations, incomplete and unfulfilled as this may have been from our viewpoint today. We cannot say, as F. Hahn does (*Mission in the New Testament*, p. 164), that "Judaism's religious propaganda and efforts to proselytize in the time of Jesus represent only an external preparation for the early Christian mission, without being itself a mission in the real sense."

fulness often forgotten in our evaluation of the religious tenor of the day. Likewise, when James affirmed that from early generations Moses was preached and read in the synagogues, this can only mean that the truth was declared so that "the rest of men may seek the Lord, and all the Gentiles" (Acts 15:21,17). Israel would have forgotten her election and forfeited it if she had existed only for herself.

People come to faith through contact with witnesses.[142] Only limited numbers of Gentiles, however many they might actually have been, ever attended the synagogue services. A large part of the population would at best be indifferent and at worst hostile, but is was nevertheless the responsibility of the believing community. Was there no contact with this large section of the Gentile world? What form did this contact take?

The Jewish mind provided a fair-sized literature that was easily and effectively usable in missionary propoganda.[143] This literary propaganda had its place alongside of the propaganda efforts directed toward certain classes of people, the application of force at certain periods, the open synagogue, the Scripture versions (the LXX especially), and possible personal solicitation such as the aggresive efforts of certain Jews which occasioned the exile of the Jewish community from Rome on a number of occasions: 139 B.C. and the embassage of Simon Maccabeeus, and in 19 A.D. by Tiberius because certain Jews defrauded a rich woman of Rome of gifts for the Temple and for the danger the Romans felt to their religion.[144]

The nature of the propaganda was determined by its purpose. The literature was limited by the field of its reference. Peterson classifies this literature under three categories: (1) the fostering of missionary spirit at home, exhorting the people to share their faith. He includes here the books of Ruth and Jonah, some of Philo's works, and much of the rabbinic literature (admittedly this is often of post-Christian date, however); (2) defensive and propaganda literature. Included here are Tobit, the Sibylline Books, Wisdom of Solomon, e.g.; (3) literature for the instruction of prospective proselytes – the Didache, e.g.[145]

142   G. F. Vicedom, *The Mission of God*, p. 115.
143   There are several well documented surveys of this literature The reader is advised to consult L. Finkelstein, *The Jews*, II, pp. 745-783, article by Ralph Marcus, "Hellenistic Jewish Literature"; F. Derwacter, *Preparing the Way for Paul*, pp. 81-86; J. Peterson, *Missionary Methods*, pp. 161-168; E. Schürer, *Geschichte*, Vol. I, Div. I (E.T.). A very fine discussion from the Jewish point of view is found in Uriel Rappaport, *Religious Propaganda and Proselytism in the Period of the Second Commonwealth* (Jerusalem: 1965), his doctoral dissertation which covers all the Biblical and Hellenistic material on the subject. The book is written in Hebrew, but is available with an English summary. Cf. also B. J. Bamberger, *Proselytism*, who evaluates the bibliographical sources and the significance of the haggadic and halakic materials in a lengthy and detailed introduction.
144   M. Radin, *The Jews Among the Greeks and Romans*, p. 230ff.; D. M. Eichhorn, *Conversion*, p. 44; F. Derwacter, *Preparing the Way for Paul*, pp. 57-60; H. J. Leon, *The Jews of Ancient Rome*, pp. 17, 251.
145   J. Peterson, *Missionary Methods*, pp. 161-165.

The frequent attacks made on the Jews by pagan writers demanded an apologetic. Alexandria seemed to be the center where much of the anti-Jewish literature had its origin.[146] The Jews were often ridiculed for their sabbath observance, their refusal to eat swine's flesh, and their spiritual conception of God.[147] Their defense concerned not only the ridiculousness and absurdity of the charges, but a presentation of the truth. The exclusiveness with which they were charged made it possible to declare the nature and purpose of Israel as the people of God. They would not countenance being called atheists, pointing out the loftiness and reasonableness of their worship of the true God. As is often the case, the matters on which opponents challenge another's religion or faith are the "contact points" between the two faiths, provide a topic in the forum of discussion, and clarify for the believer what those outside that faith judge to be its essential elements, however poorly they may have grasped or understood them.

The apologetic literature demonstrates that the Jews were not satisfied merely to answer the pagan. They carried the war into the enemy's camp. They attacked the polytheism of the heathen, the viciousness of heathen life, the sexual excesses and perversions which are the reproach of the heathen. The literature served a double purpose: (1) to defend the Jews from the attacks of the pagans, and (2) to prove the superiority of the Jews and their religion over other faiths and nations.[148]

What can we say about the content of the literary propaganda? What message did it bring to the non-Israelite? The predominant theme was: forsake idolatry and stop your polytheistic worship.[149] For the Jews the essence of paganism consisted in idolatry; nevertheless, the mere forsaking of idols did not complete a man's conversion for such a man might still cling to his immoral practices. He needed also to turn to God, the true God, the Father of all men.[150] This anti-idolatry note is strong in the Wisdom of Solomon.[151] Philo makes a similar plea in his treatises *De Monarchia* and *De Decalogo*.[152]

146   W. O. E. Oesterley, *Judaism and Christianity*, II: *Contact of Pharisaism With Other Cultures*, esp. pp. 61-111, "Pharisaism and Hellenism" by W. L. Knox, pp. 62-63; G. Ricciotti, *History of Israel*, p. 192-199. Cf. also M. Radin, *The Jews Among the Greeks*, p. 148ff., who makes full reference to the testimony of the classical writers and full use of Reinach, *Textes*.

147   G. Ricciotti, *History of Israel*, p. 192. Roman writers were especially hostile. Tacitus, *History, V.5* (cf. Reinach, *Textes*, No. 175) relates that a number of Jews deported to Sardinia died, and adds, "vile damnum" = "cheap loss." The hostility of Tacitus and Juvenal was not confined to Judaism but included every Eastern influence: Jewish, Christian, Syrian, Egyptian.

148   R. H. Pfeiffer, *History of New Testament Times*, p. 197-230; V. Aptowitzer, *HUCA*, I (1924), p. 300; M. Radin, *The Jews Among the Greeks and Romans*, p. 148ff.

149   F. Derwacter, *Preparing the Way for Paul*, p. 95ff.

150   This is a frequent note of the *Sibylline Oracles* (henceforth to be abbreviated *Sib. Or.*); see III.547-550, 632, 763, 773; IV.163.

151   *The Wisdom of Solomon*, chaps. 13-15.

152   Philo, *De Monarchia*, 1, 2, and *De Decalogo*, 14-16.

A corollary to seeking God and separating one's self from idols is to live according to the will of God. This feature, too, was prominent in the Jewish apologetic. Philo said,

> Those who come over to this worship become at once, prudent, temperate, modest, gentle, merciful, humane, venerable, just, magnanimous, lovers of truth, and superior to all considerations of money or pleasure.[153]

In another place he says,

> Not only the Jew but all the other people who care for righteousness adopt them [the laws of the Jewish religion] .... The Jewish law attracts and links together all peoples, barbarians and Greeks, those who live on the mainland and those who live on the islands .... And its has come to pass that Egypt and Cyrene, having the same government, and a great number of other nations imitate the Jewish way of living, and maintain great bodies of these Jews in a peculiar manner, and grow up to a great prosperity with them, and make use of the same laws with that nation.[154]

Philo may have overstated his case in his enthusiasm. Nevertheless, his words do witness to a new and different sort of life which conversion brought about. In this lay a real danger, not always escaped, for Judaism (and one not always avoided by the Christian church today). It is typical of all religions to think that fellowship of religion is fellowship of culture and people. Judaism could not avoid this, for in the approximately 1400 years of its existence until the fulfillment in Christ the Jewish people were a special sign to the nations. The Christian may never forget his heavenly dimension either. The witness is always a co-worker with God. He seeks to make others be what he has himself become.

> But therein lies the danger: we too "christianize" people; we place them in a society conditioned by our traditions and relate them with strong ties to the tradition. Our duty is rather to bring them to the Lord so that their lives with ours may be determined by Him (Acts 14:21; Matt. 28:19).[155]

153 Philo, *De Paenitentia*, 2. For a complete summary of Philo, see S. Sandmel, *Philo's Place in Judaism*; Sandmel believes Philo represents a Judaism that is as complete a hellenization as possible and yet retaining its loyalty to the Torah; see p. 221. For a complete index of Philo, see Erwin R. Goodenough, *The Politics of Philo Judaeus* (Hildesheim: Georg Olms Verlagsbuchhandlung, 1967), the indices.

154 Philo, *De Vita Moses*, II.5.

155 G. F. Vicedom, *The Mission of God*, pp. 80, 89. J. C. Hoekendijk in "The Call to Evangelism", *IRM*, 39, n. 154 (April 1950), 162-175, esp. pp. 163 and 167, says the following: "We have a distorted view of the Biblical view of salvation. To the drunkard we offered salvation as a way to a better moral rearmament; to the skeptic we offered wisdom. For the one the forgiveness of sins meant ignoring a wild past; for the other, overlooking stupidity." And ... "The call to evangelism is often little else than a call to restore 'Christendom,' *the corpus christianum*, as a solid, well-integrated cultural complex, directed and dominated by the Church. And the sense of urgency is often

The viewpoints referred to above can be illustrated from the stories of the Talmud which relate the attitudes of Shammai and Hillel towards prospective proselytes.[156] A heathen once approached Shammai with the challenge that if he would teach him the whole Torah while standing on one foot, he would become a proselyte. Shammai, angered, repulsed him with a builder's cubit. When the man came to Hillel with the same challenge, Hillel said, "What is hateful to you, do not to your neighbor. That is the whole Torah. The rest is all commentary to it." On another occasion a prospective proselyte told Shammai he would become proselyte on condition that he would be able to be high priest. Shammai, again, repulsed him with the stick. Hillel accepted the man. As he studied the Law he saw how severe the penalties for the born Jew were; how much more for the proselyte? Later these men met Hillel on the street and said, "Shammai's impatience sought to drive us from the world but Hillel's gentleness brought us under the wings of the Shekinah." It is significant that a proselyte would be advised to act according to his heart, implying that if the heart was right, the man would be righteous. Hillel was close to the New Testament conception of the righteous man who is the man that fits God's specifications, the man who is what God wants men to be like.

The ethical and ceremonial continued to exist side by side in Judaism, and when Judaism rejected the Mediator of the covenant, the ceremonial took precedence, while the ethical lost its intended goal. All that could be used to replace it was a doctrine of self-righteousness and works. By the time of Jesus, ritual purity was increasingly emphasized so that Rabbi Simon ben Eleazer observed, "How vastly has *tahara* (ceremonial purity) increased for it was but little aforetime and has now waxed abundant."[157] The Pharisees challenged Jesus with respect to the conduct of his disciples on this very point, asking, "Why don't your disciples follow the traditions of the elders?" (Matt. 15:1-20; Mark 7:1-23).

In this circumstance can be found part of the basic differences which eventually led to the parting of the ways for Christianity and Judaism. Judaism considered loyalty to Torah as interpreted by the elders to be the *sine qua non* of allegiance to its faith and community. For Christianity it is allegiance to, recognition of, obedience to Jesus Christ, the risen Son of God and Lord of all.[158] This undoubtedly helps to explain why in the Christian era the Jewish

nothing but a nervous feeling of insecurity, with the established church endangered, the flurried activity to save the remnants of a time now irrevocably past."

156 BT, Shab. 140. Cf. also I. Abrahams, *Studies in Phariseeism and the Gospels*, p. 28ff.

157 Samuel Solomon Cohon, "The Place of Jesus in the Religious Life of His Day", *JBL*, 48 (1929), parts I and II, 82-108

158 For the Jewish viewpoint see Abraham Cohen, *The Parting of the Ways: Judaism and the Rise of Christianity* (London: Lincolns – Prager Ltd., 1954), esp. pp. 72-80. W. Oesterley, *Judaism and Christianity*, I, p. 266, says, "The men of the Great Synagogue, with Ezra as the second Moses, began the process of what we may call the deification of the Torah."

sources have a great deal to say about Christians, but almost invariably it is Jewish Christians that are the object of castigation. When national survival became the issue, resistance to the church became a national duty. There is an undeniable denationalizing tendency associated with Christianity.[159]

The importance of this religious propaganda for the Christian mission is shown in that in many ways the catechetical, liturgical, and apologetic material could be employed by the church with but little alteration. Von Harnack has stated the relationship in this way:

> By recognizing the Old Testament as a book of Divine revelation, the Gentile Christians received along with it the religious speech which was used by Jewish Christians, were made dependent upon the interpretation which had been used from the beginning, and even received a great part of the Jewish literature which accompanied the Old Testament . . . . The Jewish, that is the Old Testament element, divested of its national peculiarity has remained the basis of Christendom.[160]

Notable among these contributions are the Didache and the Sibylline Books.[161] Unfortunately, Judaism and Christianity, related to each other as promise and fulfillment, went their separate way. This did not have to be.

> What was not inevitable was that the new movement within Judaism (Christianity) should become a separate and hostile movement (to Judaism) . . . The Christian movement was the bursting forth of the life Judaism had treasured and guarded, but, since truth is never in bondage to the metaphors by which it is expressed, the life which in the church burst forth in eager missionary zeal remained at the same time still shut within the shell of the Judaism that repudiated Christianity.[162]

A brief reference to yet one other form of literary propaganda in pre-Christian times is necessary for the sake of completeness: the apocalyptic literature. The literature was varied. One author describes the sequence of ideas in this literature as follows:

> The signs of the Messiah, the birth-pangs of the Messiah, the coming of Elijah, the trumpet of the Messiah, the ingathering of the exiles, the reception of proselytes, the war with Gog and Magog, the Days of the Messiah, the renovation of the world, the Day of Judgment, the Resurrection of the dead,

159 Jakob Jocz, *The Jewish People and Jesus Christ* (London: *SPCK*, 1949), pp.6, 44; I. Abrahams, *Studies in Phariseeism and the Gospels*, II, p. 56ff.

160 A. von Harnack, *History of Dogma*, I, p. 52.

161 W. O. E. Oesterley, *Judaism and Christianity*, I, p. 273; see also Karl Axenfeld, "Die jüdische Propaganda als Vorläuferin und Wegbereiter in der Urchristliche Mission" in *Missionswissenschaftliche Studien: Festschrift zur 70 Geburtstag Prof. Dr. Gustav Warneck.*

162 H. H. Rowley, *Israel's Mission*, p. 87.

the World to Come – all presented in a confused mass of symbols from cows to talking vines.[163]

It is not necessary to survey this literature in detail. The Jewish apocalyptic stressed God's judgment on the enemies of God's people and the restoration of the earthly city of Jerusalem (Messiah was a Restorer in the Jewish apocalyptic).[164] What is significant about the apocalyptic stance of Judaism is that an absolutized hope floated in the air, as it were, not anchored in faith in what had already been fulfilled. When this happens, the real world is denied. A false hope is always isolated from redemptive history and is attached to a corresponding false, ascetic ethic. This is precisely what happened in Judaism. The appearance of the ascetic groups in the pre-Christian period witnesses to this. Even in the New Testament churches this sickly kind of hope was sometimes expressed. The Thessalonians separated hope from Christian redemptive history (II Thess. 3:10) and in connection with this false hope stopped working. Cullmann has demonstrated that it simply it not true (overagainst Martin Werner and Albert Schweitzer) that "primitive Christianity has the same eschatological orientation as does Judaism .... For the primitive church after the death of Jesus the crowning act of this work is the mighty fact of the resurrection of Christ."[165] Loewe discusses the Jewish eschatology from the view-of the judgment and concludes that the eschatology of Jesus' day moved directly into the age to come without the knowledge of a Judgment such as is in the New Testament.[166] The Jewish view saw ultimately only judgment for the Gentiles; in the New Testament there is salvation for all nations. Pre-Christian Judaism had a sense of "mission" but not as a pre-condition of the Messianic Kingdom. Judaism taught that the Kingdom of God would come only when Israel repented, and that only Israel's failure prevented the appearance of Messiah.[167]

One's viewpoint of those "outside" will determine one's relationship to and concern for them. The attitude of late Judaism was uncompromisingly severe. The Gentiles were godless, rejected by God, as worthless in God's eyes as chaff and refuse. They were steeped in vice, given over to all forms of

163 J. W. Parkes, *Foundations*, p. 43, who cites Joseph Klausner, *The Messianic Idea in Israel*, p. 385.

164 George Adam Smith, *Jerusalem* (2 vols.; New York: A. C. Armstrong, 1908), II, p. 537ff. Cf. also James C. De Young, *Jerusalem in the New Testament*. W. O. E. Oesterley, *Judaism and Christianity*, I, pp. 83-104, surveys this literature and the historical background from which it arose.

165 Oscar Cullmann, *Christ and Time*, translated by Floyd V. Filson (Philadelphia: Westminster Press, 1964), pp. 211-212, 85.

166 H. Loewe, *Judaism and Christianity*, II, p. 37.

167 William David Davies and David Daube, editors, *The Background of the New Testament and its Eschatology: Studies in Honor of C. H. Dodd* (Cambridge: University Press, 1956), chapter by O. Cullmann, "Eschatology and Missions," pp. 409-421, esp. p. 414.

uncleanness, violence, and wickedness. Jeremias has shown a change in the Jewish expectation regarding the Gentiles, increasing in severity until Rabbi Eliezer ben Hyrcanus ($\pm$ 90 A.D.) said, "No Gentile will have a part in the world to come." Another said, "Hell is the destiny of the Gentiles."[168] It was extremely important for the development of the Christian mission that Jesus detached "the nationalistic idea of revenge from the hope of salvation", taught that in the final judgment the distinction between Israel and the Gentiles would disappear, promised the Gentiles a share in salvation, and made clear that the redemptive activity and lordship of Jesus included the Gentiles.[169]

Conclusion: there was an active literary apologetic, oftentimes of the nature of propaganda, carried on in the centuries before Christ. This literature represented all aspects of the Jewish life and thought, in the Holy Land as well as in the Diaspora. A part of it was directed towards the Gentile for the purpose of winning him to the faith. Christianity profited greatly from this heritage, although later the Jewish apologetic began to be directed against it. The literary effort of the Jews was more than preparation for Christianity: it was significant in its own right and was a spreading of the truth of God's redemptive work for the world. God had not delayed the calling of the Gentiles; his universal covenant was being proclaimed and men everywhere were welcomed into fellowship with Israel and participation in its assignment and election.

In these efforts to share with the nations the treasures of God's mercy the presence of God in the midst of his people must be seen, for this is a basic theme of the entire revelation of God. Equally important was the fact that his people lived in God's presence and that the world of nations should reckon with this in their life also.

The appearance of God's Son in the flesh coincided with the missionary age *par excellence* of Jewish history.[170] The proselytizing efforts of the Jews did not immediately subside when the Christian mission began but seemed to intensify and continued until long after the anti-Jewish legislation promulgated in the Theodosian code (478 A.D.), in which the death penalty was threatened against both those who allowed themselves to be circumcised and those who performed the operation.[171] Many Jews were converted to the Christian faith, even after the initial success of the Christian mission in the lands of the Diaspora. Numerous conversions continued until the days of the Bar Cochba uprising.[172] The words of Jesus in Matt. 23:15 are now set in their context:

168   J. Jeremias, *Jesus' Promise*, pp. 40-41; Strack-Billerbeck, *Kommentar*, III, pp. 144-154; IV, p. 1066ff.
169   J. Jeremias, *Jesus' Promise*, pp. 43, 49, 51ff.
170   G. F. Moore, *Judaism in the First Three Centuries*, I, pp. 323-353.
171   Marcel Simon, *Verus Israel, Étude sur les relations entre Chrétiens et juifs dans l'empire romain* (135-425 A.D.) (Paris: E. De Boccard, 1948), pp. 315-355. E. Schürer, *Geschichte*, I, p. 674ff.; J. Jeremias, *Jesus' Promise*, pp. 11-12, p. 11, n. 4.
172   J. Jocz, *The Jewish People and Jesus Christ*, p. 6.

Woe to you, scribes and Pharisees, hypocrites! for you traverse land and sea to make a single proselyte, and when he becomes a proselyte you make him twice as much a son of hell as yourselves.

E. *Matthew 23:15 and the Jewish apostolate*

The words of Jesus in Matt. 23:15 constitute one of the most direct as well as interesting testimonies to the Pharisaic-Rabbinic interest in proselytism. The passage is apparently clear, simple, and hardly subject to misunderstanding, and yet it has been twisted and distorted, doubted and believed by both Jewish and Christian scholars. Bamberger says, "For some inexplicable reason the learned have been unwilling to believe that the passage means what it obviously says." [173] The fact is that the passage makes no sense at all if no scribe or Pharisee had never had the smallest desire to make proselytes. Nor would the Roman laws against proselytizing have been necessary if there were no propaganda or conversions. The explusion of the Jews from Rome was in a number of instances occasioned by the proselytizing efforts of the members of the Jewish community there.[174]

The above observations do not remove a very real difficulty with respect to this verse. Unless one takes the position that this is not an authentic word of Jesus, as some have done,[175] he is left with the fact that this statement about the Gentile mission of the Pharisees and their scribes is extremely harsh and is the only utterance by Jesus that is left from an age of unparalleled proselytizing

---

173 B. J. Bamberger, *Proselytism*, p. 267; L. Finkelstein, *The Pharisees*, II, pp. 498-499.

174 See above, footnote 144. Also: F. S. B. Gavin, "Jewish Views on Jewish Missions," p. 13.

175 J. Münck, *Paul and the Salvation of Mankind*, pp. 265-267. A discussion of the various views can be found in B. J. Bamberger, *Proselytism*, pp. 267-273. He cites the following: (1) J. Derenbourg, who says Jesus misrepresents the Pharisaic attitude, the rabbis were not eager for converts, and the Jews did not engage in extensive missionary work; (2) H. Gaetz, who asserts that the progress of the Jewish mission was made without any great missionary zeal, and makes the verse mean "to make one particular proselyte," referring to the Rabbis Gamaliel, Joshua, and Akiba who were present at Rome for the formal reception of Flavius Clemens as a convert. (3) A. Jellinek, citing the remark of R. Haman ("The inhabitants of the cities of the sea are worthy of extermination, and by what merit have they been delivered? By the merit of a single convert, or a single fearer of Heaven whom they produce each year."), says that the Pharisees in order to keep alive the hope that all the heathen would ultimately be converted used to make one convert a year. (4) M. Friedlaner says that it refers to one case only: Izates, The Pharisees are attacked for their narrow fanaticism in seeking to transform every fearer of heaven into a slave of Jewish ritualism. (5) The Int. Crit. Comm. says that Matthew is wrathful against the converts of the Pharisees, not against converts in general. (6) Strack and Billerbeck do not think that the Pharisees were so interested in making converts to Judaism. Bamberger holds that "the Pharisees and Rabbis were eager for converts, highly successful in winning them, and friendly in their treatment of them," p. 274.

activity in Jewish history.[176] All the evidence adduced thus far in this study demands the conclusion that Jesus lived in a time when the Jews, dispersed over the whole world, by spoken word in synagogue, by written word in the Septuagint and apologetic literature, and by their daily life were motivated to some form of witness to their Genitle neighbors. Although Jesus' words are critical of what the Pharisees made of their converts, he does not criticize a mission to Gentiles by them.[177] He denounces their hypocrisy and sanctimonious formalism. Bamberger represents Jesus as saying:

> Now there is nothing inherently wrong in long prayer, tithing herbs, or preserving outward appearances; when these are combined with moral obliquity they are damnable. You go to any lengths to make a convert; then you make him such a legalistic, ritualistic, unspiritual ... individual as yourselves.[178]

The criticism of the Pharisees by Jesus reduces to a severe rebuke of their example to and instruction of their converts, not of their proselytizing zeal. It is in harmony with verse 13 where they are warned because they

> ... shut the Kingdom of heaven against men; for you neither enter your-selves, nor allow those who would enter to go in.

The fact that the whole message of Jesus concerned the proclamation of the Kingdom of God helps us to understand why he expressed himself so strongly on his point. To Jesus the essence and foundation of the Kingdom is its existence as the inbreaking of the Spirit, power and justice of God. The rule of God involves the gift of the Spirit, and the essence of the total experience which is the Kingdom of God is God as Spirit and power. This Kingdom lies behind, surrounds, and gives meaning to the cosmos, and is in its essence the presence of the God of justice who has called the world into being and placed on his creation the judgment of his sovereignty. His jealousy will allow no rival to his will.[179] When Jesus saw in the Pharisees the annulment of God's sovereignty and the enthronement of man-made righteousness, he as the obe-

---

176 J. Jeremias, *Jesus' Promise*, p. 19.

177 J. Jeremias, *Jesus' Promise*, p. 17 n. 4, says that "the woes are not uttered aginst the Pharisees because of their missionary zeal but because they make their converts children of hell." He seeks to demonstrate this from the supposed underlying semitic (Aramaic) sentence structure which he reconstructs.

178 J. Bamberger, *Proselytism*, p. 271.

179 We shall return again to the subject of the Kingdom of God. I am deeply indebted to J. Arthur Baird, *The Justice of God*, pp. 55-58, for this understanding of the Kingdom. Baird also demonstrates that the reason why we do not find more frequent reference to the Spirit in the teaching of Jesus is that Jesus speaks of the Spirit in such terms as πατήρ, θεός, βασιλεία, δύναμις. See also Charles Kingsley Barrett, *The Holy Spirit and the Gospel Tradition* (London: SPCK, 1966), p. 159.

dient Servant of God could only speak in truthful assessment as to what they were doing to themselves and their converts among the Gentiles.[180]

This mission of the Pharisees to which Jesus refers shows that the truth of God was being preached and witnessed to others besides the members of the dispersed communitites of the Jews. What is surprising is that these efforts were so severely criticized by Jesus, since it was men among the earnest, devoted representatives of religion and morality who were the motivating force behind these movements.[181] Jesus' words in Matt. 23:15 also show that the test of a mission is not the zeal with which one pursues others to join him in his faith, but rather what he makes of them after they have been won. Among the things for which Jesus criticized the Pharisees in Matt. 23, three matters stand out: (1) they shut the Kingdom of heaven to men; (2) they themselves failed to enter that Kingdom; and (3) they made "sons of hell" out of their converts. Jesus' own mission and that which he committed to his disciples would have to bear a kind of corrective revolutionary character.[182] He would have to set the mission of God's people in the context of true discipleship lived under the sovereignty of God and summon men to be *his* disciples.

The words of Jesus in Matt. 23:13,15 are unique to his ministry; they are not unique to the New Testament. Assuming that Paul has the proselyting efforts of his contemporaries in mind, his words in Rom. 2:17-24 constitute a parallel to what Jesus said:

> But as for you – you may bear the name of Jew; you rely upon the law and are proud of your God; you know his will; you are aware of moral distinctions because you receive instruction from the law; you are confident that you are the one to guide the blind, to enlighten the benighted, to train the stupid, and to teach the immature, because in the law you see the very shape of knowledge and truth. You, then, who teach your fellow-man, do you fail to teach yourself? You proclaim, 'Do not steal'; but are you yourself a thief? You say, 'Do not commit adultery'; but are you an adulterer? You abominate false gods; but do you rob their shrines? While you take pride in the law, you dishonour God by breaking it. For, as Scripture says, 'Because of you the name of God is dishonoured among the Gentiles.' (N.E.B.).

What Judaism needed was renewal and fulfillment, both of which came in the Person and work of Jesus Christ.

The Pharisees and their kindred elements in the Diaspora were in many

---

180 The words of Jesus in Matthew 23:15 cannot be taken to mean converts from among the Jewish people to the Pharisaic sect and principles, for the word προσήλυτος is used by Jesus, referring to a Gentile convert. The word never has the connotation of a Jewish adherent. Cf. J. Jeremias, *Jesus' Promise*, p. 18 n. 1(2), who opposes this viewpoint of J. Münck, *Paul and the Salvation of Mankind*, pp. 265-267.

181 J. D. Smart, *The Quiet Revolution*, pp. 150-155.

182 *Ibid.*, p. 151.

senses the cream of Jewish society. Deeply loyal to the faith, austerely loyal to the minutiae of the law, and ever ready to welcome recruits to share their spirit and devotion, the Pharisees' main work was practical and sought to bring religion and learning into the life of the people.[183] Oesterley says,

> They never left official Judaism; they captured it .... The Roman Procurator and publican gathered the imperial taxes. They saw to it that the people rendered Caesar his due. But who was responsible for collecting the tithes upon which rested organized religion? Here the Pharisaic brotherhood stepped into the breach. They made tithe-paying a matter of conscience.[184]

How were the ties to Diaspora communities maintained? The answer is found in one final Old Testament institution which we must survey because of its importance later in the Christian church. There is no evidence for a central governing authority in Judaism which sent out missionaries to the world or which directed the Diaspora witness. What was accomplished in the Jewish proselytizing was the direct result of local and/or individual initiative. However, the Diaspora did maintain strong ties with Jerusalem. This is evidenced by the collection of the temple tax,[185] the annual pilgrimages from the Diaspora to the feasts in Jerusalem, and the institution of the ἀπόστολοι (apostles) of Judaism. To understand the promulgation and carrying out of God's universal covenant with men in the Person and work of Jesus Christ ("the apostle and high priest of our confession" – Hebrews 3:1), the so-called "Gentile mission" of Jesus, the apparent limitation of Jesus' labors to the house of Israel, as well as the purpose and meaning of the institution of the extraordinary office of the apostles, requires a review the Old Testament antecedents of this institution.

Contact between the Diaspora communities and Jerusalem was maintained by different means. In reviewing the Diaspora it was observed, e.g., that the commercial trade with far distant colonies brought the latest news from the homeland. In this way, together with accretions to these communities, the Jews of China, e.g., learned of the destruction of the Temple in 70 A.D., memorializing the day. The same was true of the regions of the Yemen, Persia, Africa, India.[186] The letters of Peter and James (Jas. 1:1 and I Pet. 1:1) do not appear unusual either in form or practice in that general letters to Diaspora communities seem to be a common phenomenon. That individuals acting on their own initiative would go to the Diaspora seems to be implied in John 7:35 where the Jews, puzzled at the word of Jesus, "You will seek me and you will

---

183 H. H. Rowley, *Israel's Mission*, p. 71.
184 W. O. E. Oesterley, *Judaism and Christianity*, I, pp. 122, 136. The author specifies many of the practical values for the everyday life and religion of the Jew from the Pharisees.
185 E. Schürer, *Geschichte*, II, p. 324 (E.T.); Strack-Billerbeck, *Kommentar*, III, p. 316ff.
186 See footnote 173, Chap. I.

not find me; where I am you cannot come," ask, "Where does this man intend to go that we shall not find him? Does he intend to go to the Dispersion among the Greeks and teach the Greeks?"

But all of the above is casual, individually motivated. It says nothing about the exercise of central authority nor of official contact. From what is known of the circumstances during the Roman period there were two categories of authorized agents or representatives in the Jewish community: (1) apostles of the central authority to the various communities, and (2) apostles of the communities to the central authority. The origin of the apostolate in Judaism is difficult to trace.[187] Vogelstein connects its development with the Persian State Administration, in which an "apostolate" functioned so effectively and significantly that it was taken over by the Jews in the rebuilding of the Jewish community and was especially taken over by the religious authority in Jerusalem.[188]

There are significant references to such authority under Persian administrators in the Scriptures. King Artaxerxes sent Ezra the scribe out with this commission: (1) to make an investigation of Judah and Jerusalem according to the law of God; (2) to convey the king's gifts of gold and silver for sacrifices to the God of Israel in Jerusalem; (3) to disburse from the king's treasury the expenses necessary for the rebuilding of the Temple; (4) to appoint magistrates and judges; (5) to teach those who do not know the laws of God; (6) to administer God's and the king's laws in the case of disobedience, including punishment with the death penalty, exile, confiscation of goods, or imprisonment (Ezra 7:14-16,20, 25-26). His task and authority in this mission were carefully prescribed by and limited by the king.[189]

The case of Ezra is important because it includes a juridical as well as ecclesiastical function, both of which are prescribed within the laws of the Persian empire. The Elephantine Papyrus (419 B.C.), the Pesach Epistle of Darius II, shows that the Jewish religion was an official religion of the empire, the established religion for Jews everywhere.[190] The Persian administration specified that its apostles' authority was clearly limited only to those matters defined in the letter of authority; that the authority of the apostle ceased at the central seat of the board or authority which authorized the mission (obviously, for there the central authority was exercised and present and no representatives were necessary) and was for a limited period of time, which ended when the

---

187   Some have found its legal institution in II Chronicles 7:7-9 under Jehosaphat.

188   Cf. the significant study by H. Vogelstein, "The Development of the Apostolate in Judaism and its Transformation in Christianity, *HUCA*, II (1925), 99-124. A. H. Godbey, *Lost Tribes*, p. 451ff. traces the meaning of ἀπόστολος in Babylonian and Akkadian terms and usage.

189   On the commission of Ezra I have found G. C. Luck, *Ezra and Nehemiah*, p. 54ff., of very great help Luck designates Ezra as an apostle in the Persian sense of the term.

190   H. Vogelstein, *HUCA*, II, 100.

mission had been completed; and that that authority included the right to appoint associates in the work, whose prerogatives, however, could never exceed those of the apostle himself.[191] These elements are clearly evident in Ezra's commission and will be shown to be significant also as parallels to Jesus' apostleship. Similar circumstances governed the appointment and mission of the community-appoined apostles to the central authority.[192] Among the Jews these apostles of the community (twenty or more in number) collected and brought to Jerusalem the gifts of the communities. A reflection of this function is found in the instructions of Paul to the Corinthians for whom he appointed certified messengers to carry their gifts to the distressed saints in Jerusalem. He and Barnabas had also served such a function.[193] The payment of the temple tax is the one certain relationship of Jerusalem to the Diaspora.[194]

Rengstorf has pointed out that the Jewish institution of the *shali'ah* (apostle) was characterized in all periods by their commissioning with various tasks, at greater or lesser distances, and that authorization is the decisive thing, not the task or the fact of being sent. The rabbis expressed this in this way, "The one sent by a man is as the man himself." The transaction, of whatever nature, could not be properly conducted without a resolute subordination of the will of the representative to the one who commissioned him. Even though this be legal in character it is basically religiously confirmed and oriented.[195]

The task of the apostles of the Sanhedrin to the Diaspora was varied. They regulated the calendar for the Diaspora on the basis of the official decree of the Palestine authority; the new moon was made known to the Syrian diaspora by means of fire signals. These men carried messages of Jewish learning and piety to the diverse Jewish communities and apprised the heads of the San-hedrin of the Jewish situation in the Diaspora. They acted as fund-raisers

191 *Ibid.*, II, p. 100, as well as the study of Karl Heinrich Rengstorf, ἀποστέλλω, *TWNT*, I, pp. 398-406, and ἀπόστολος, *TWNT*, I, pp. 407-447. Rengstorf concentrates on the connection of the Greek apostle with Judaism and believes this connection is very slight. Vogelstein believes that the Jewish apostolate had its roots in the period of Persian sovereignty, not in Hellenistic influences, and that it did not arise independently.

192 Vogelstein further observes that the New Testament word ἐξουσία corresponds exactly to the Hebrew רשׁוּת as a designation for the writ of full authority which was granted by the Persian kings. Cf. also Werner Foerster, ἐξουσία, *TWNT*, II, pp. 562-575. ep. p. 562, who says that ἐξουσία is the right granted by a higher to a lower court to do something or to have the right over something and involves being backed by real, not illusory, power. It includes responsible use of this authority as well.

193 Cf. Acts 11:30; I Cor. 16:3. Rom. 15:26. See also Keith F. Nickle, *The Collection: A Study in Paul's Strategy. Studies in Biblical Theology, No. 48.* (Naperville: A. R. Allenson, 1965). This author reconstructs the history of Paul's collection in chaps, 1, 2, & 5. In chap. 3 (on the temple tax) he shows that Paul's collection was partially patterned after the temple tax, but he also notes that there were immense differences between the two. The offerings of the Corinthians were for the poor, whereas the *shali'ah* collected the temple tax.

194 J. W. Parkes, *Foundations*, p. 105; J. Juster, *Les Juifs*, I, p. 391ff.

195 K. H. Rengstorf, *TWNT*, I, pp. 414-415; Strack-Billerbeck, *Kommentar*, III, p. 2.

for the Sanhedrin's activities. Often they were men who were respected scholars.[196] There is no evidence that they were ever commissioned to carry out a missionary witness. Although these officials are not specifically mentioned in the New Testament, two incidents at least fit their task and duty. Saul of Tarsus' commission to Damascus (Acts 9:1,2) is clearly the kind of commission given the *shali'ah*. The mention of "no letters from Jerusalem" to the Jewish community in Rome (Acts 28:21) is another example. It was previously shown how the authority of the Jerusalem Sanhedrin extended throughout the Empire in matters relating to Jewish law.

A distinctive office of apostle developed in the newly constituted church of the New Testament which had Christ as its head. There was prominent in this development an apostolic board of authority appointed and designated by Christ as his representatives. A four-fold change occured:

> (1) The name apostle was largely used as a designation of the new leaders of the Church instead of the name disciple; (2) The apostolate became a life-long office; (3) The apostles' authority was exercised at the seat of authority (previously, authority ceased there), namely Jerusalem, as well as all areas of their assignment; (4) The apostles now constitute a 'collegiate board of authorities', and with but the sole exception of the introductory verses of Peter's letters it is always used in a collective, not singular sense. The cross of Jesus Christ stands between the disciples and the apostles.
>
> Because Acts tells us that the apostle had to be a witness of the resurrection, the special office ceased with the end of the first generation. Only Paul was specially favored and defends his apostolic office by direct appointment of Christ. ... The only matter Paul is willing to concede to the rest of the apostles is the priority of their commission.[197]

Our survey of the pre-Christian materials is completed. God created man good, but through disobedience man became lost in sin, ever in rebellion against his Creator: in Eden, during the pre-diluvian age, at Babel, down to the present age. But grace was always present and where judgment was poured out grace was active: the waters of the Deluge overwhelmed and destroyed all flesh but bore up the Ark of Noah; the waters of the Red Sea were parted to give access to God's highway on the bottom of the sea, but these same waters returned to destroy Pharoah's host. The issues throughout history were always the same: God's way or man's way.

Redemptive history displays God's continuing concern for his creation. His universal covenant with Abraham was speeded to fulfillment in the establishment

---

196 H. Vogelstein, *HUCA*, II, p. 100; K. H. Rengstorf, ἀποστέλλω, *TWNT*, I, pp. 398-406; Strack-Billerbeck, *Kommentar*, III, p. 2; H. Mantel, *Studies in the History of the Sanhedrin*, pp. 176-202, who also has an extensive bibliography.

197 H. Vogelstein, *HUCA*, II (1925), pp. 117-118; cf. also K. H. Rengstorf, *TWNT*, I, pp. 424-447.

and election of Israel from whom the nations' Deliverer would come. Wherever God's people scattered or were dispersed, they developed inclusive communities where the Gentile world could hear the demands of God and learn the way of renewal by turning to him.

By obedience to its special election from God the people of Israel found their own salvation and with it the breaking down of the middle wall of partition. Whatever character of the mission Israel carried on, her goal and purpose had to be the glory of God. The Old Testament furnished the conditions by means of which the mission of the church flourished. This was not merely preparatory for the Christian mission (to read it as such or to limit it to this would be inaccurate) but was a legitimate mission in its own right, an appeal of God through Israel to the nations.

The presence of believing communities throughout the world brought together in loyalty to the Truth, the availability of the Scriptures in translation and interpretation in the synagogues, the relative simplicity of the synagogue service, the synagogue itself, a comprehensive literary heritage for purposes of apologetic and instruction, centralized ties with Jerusalem which directed Jew and proselyte eyes and hearts to the City of God, a system of administration through *shali'ah* – these are but a few, though major, benefits from which Christianity would profit when the time was fulfilled that God "sent forth his son, born of woman, born under law, to redeem . . . ." (Gal. 4:4.)

> His state was divine,
> yet he did not cling
> to his equality with God
> but emptied himself
> to assume the condition of a slave,
> and became as men are;
> and being as all men are,
> he was humbler yet,
> even to accepting death,
> death on a cross.
> But God raised him high
> and gave him the name
> which is above all other names
> so that *all beings*
> in the heavens, on earth and in the underworld,
> *should bend the knee* at the name of Jesus
> and that every tongue should acclaim
> Jesus Christ as Lord,
> to the glory of God the Father.[198]

198 Phil. 2:6-11, quoted from the *Jerusalem Bible*, Alexander Jones, gen. ed. (Garden City, N. Y.: Doubleday and Co., 1966).

"Consider Jesus ... the apostle of our confessions" (Heb. 3:1). Center stage in the drama of redemption has been reached. A host of messengers have declared what has been going on behind the scenes, the news from within concerning the wonderful works of God.[1] The full revelation of the mystery hidden for generations and ages is about to be made manifest (Col. 1:26). God is about to make known "how great among the Gentiles are the riches of the glory of this mystery, which is Christ in you, the hope of glory" (Col. 1:27). The Light of the Gentiles has come with an illumination that comes not from without but from within, Jesus the Light of the world, who enlightens every man (John 8:12; 1:9; Isa. 49:6).[2] It took nothing less than an angelic choir come down from heaven to reveal to shepherds "the good news of a great joy to all the people" (Luke 2:10). The saints who in that day were looking for the redemption of Jerusalem and for the consolation of Israel (Luke 2:38,25) could never have dreamed in their wildest fancies what God was about to do. Only the Spirit, inspiring aged Simeon, could make even an expectant saint see in the babe Jesus the salvation which God "prepared in the presence of all peoples, a light for revelation to the Gentiles, and for glory to (his) people Israel" (Luke 2:30-32). The eyes of the Gentiles are faced towards Jerusalem. For centuries they have been coming near to the Lord in Zion, the gathering place of Israel and all who believe. God is about to send his apostle to men.

On the facade of the cathedral in Strasbourg there is a well-known sculpture representing Judaism and Christianity by means of two female figures. They are symbols of the Old and New Dispensations. The Old Covenant is pictured as mourning, without a crown, with bandaged eyes. If indeed the Old Dispensation is represented by this figure, the symbolism should rather be that of a person veiled, dazzled by the brightness of the light that has dawned in Christ (I Cor. 3).[3] No corner of this great creation of which we are a part, no place in this world may remain without God's promise of new

---

1 See I Peter 2:9; also Part I, note 125 and section to which this note applies.

2 The verb μεταμορφόομαι is used for the transfiguration of Jesus in Matt. 17:2 and Mark 9:2, meaning a change from within revealing the real Person hid by the form of the servant. On the basis of John 1 also Jesus is the Light that lightens and shines in the world; he is not revealed by the world or spot-lighted by it.

3 W. O. E. Oesterley, *Judaism and Christianity*, I, p. 253, makes use of these figures.

creation through Jesus Christus and the dawn of the day when "we shall be like him for we shall see him face to face" (I John 3:1-3).[4] The mission of Jesus, God's apostle, concerns nothing less than the fulfillment of God's universal covenant of salvation.

A. *Jesus' Baptism*

The baptism of Jesus marked the turning point between his private and public ministries. After his emergence into public view at about the age of thirty, we hear of Jesus for the first time in nearly eighteen years (Luke 3:23). The story is told in all four Gospels, an indication of the importance attached to this event in the apostolic preaching.

The baptismal event in itself is singular. No one else ever received baptism in such an unusual way. Externally, it likely had nothing to distinguish it from that of thousands of other persons who were baptized by John in the Jordan. But no else's baptism was ever marked by the appearance of the Holy Spirit, in some visible form, descending as a dove comes down from the heavens and resting upon Jesus. No one else's baptism became the occasion for the voice of the Father's expressed appoval, "Thou art my beloved Son; with thee I am well pleased."[5] He who would baptize men with the Spirit and with fire was baptized with the Spirit. He received the seal of God's testimony of approval on Himself and the life of obedience he had lived. He had "increased in wisdom and stature, and in favor with God and man" (Luke 2:52). The age of majority had come (Num. 4) for service in the house of the Lord.

1. *The Baptism of John*

It is necessary to have a clear understanding of the baptism of John in order to understand the significance of the baptism of Jesus by John. Various relationships of John's baptism to proselyte baptism and levitical lustrations on the one hand and to Christian baptism on the other have been defended and proposed. These opinions range all the way from the opinions of those who believe that John's baptism bears a close relationship to proselyte baptism and that John required his baptism as an initiatory rite from the Jews who sought entrance to the Kingdom of God to the opinions of others who see no relationship between these two at all.[6] Some find the relationship of proselyte baptism and Christian

4   J. Moltmann, *Theology of Hope*, p. 328.
5   This is the form of the statement in Mark and Luke. Matthew reports the words of the Father as addressed to the audience, not to Jesus.
6   Representative of those who find a close relationship between proselyte and John's baptism are: Beasley, *The Holy Spirit and the Gospel Tradition*, p. 31; Albrecht Oepke,

baptism to be greater.[7] A still different idea is proposed by G. W. H. Lampe who suggests that John derived the conception of baptism from the Old Testament prophecies and not from any existing rite.[8]

Whatever the background, there are certain important and distinctive features of John's baptism emphasized in the Gospels which are more significant for the understanding of its meaning than any alleged antecedents. Some of these distinctive features are:

(1) John's baptism was not self-administered as was proselyte baptism, but like Christian baptism, which was instituted later, it was administered by someone else to the baptismal candidate.[9]

(2) John's baptism was performed as the result of a divine mandate. John's witness concerning Jesus includes this significant statement, "He who sent me to baptize with water . . . ." (John 1:33.) The warrant for his baptism is not found in its alleged connection with proselyte, Essene, Qumram, or Mandaean baptisms, nor in some personal whim or fancy of John. God sent John to baptize and this fact alone substantiates its authenticity.

(3) John's baptism was not purificatory but ethical in reference. It cannot be compared to Levitical washings that were ceremonial. A basic requisite of John's baptism was that something had to happen to the heart of the recipient. He must repent. Those who did not "bear fruit that befits repentance" (Matt. 3:8) were warned about the impending judgment (Matt. 3:8-12).

(4) John's baptism had a directly eschatological reference: "the kingdom of heaven is at hand . . . he who is mightier than I is coming . . . all flesh shall see the salvation of God . . . even now the axe is laid to the root of the trees." His baptism was a preparing of the way of the Lord, the prelude to the revelation of the Christ to Israel.[10] His baptism was more than a symbol of the

βάπτω, *TWNT*, I, p. 537, who says, "The nearest analogies to the baptism of John are the baptisms of official Judaism, and especially proselyte baptism; W. F. Albright, *From the Stone Age to Christianity*, p. 377, who relates this to the Essenes or some similar group. Representative of those who find minimal relationship: G. R. Beasley-Murray, *Baptism in the New Testament*, pp. 25-28.

7 O. Cullmann, *Baptism in the New Testament*, p. 64, writes, "Christian baptism took over the outward operation of the proselyte bath of purification from the Jewish practice of reception"; J. Jeremias, *Infant Baptism*, p. 24, believes that "proselyte baptism is akin to Christian baptism"; E. Lohmeyer, *Das Urchristentum I: Johannes der Taufer*, p. 145; J. Jeremias, *The Origins of Infant Baptism*, p. 27.

8 Geoffrey William Hugo Lampe, *The Seal of the Spirit* (2nd ed.; London: SPCK, 1967), p. 22, and cites Neh. 9:3-7; Dan. 9:4-19; I Sam. 7:6; Micah 7:17-20; Isa. 1:16-20; Jer. 4:14; Ezek. 36:25-27; 40:1ff. See also M. Kline, *By Oath Consigned*, pp. 50-62, who places John's baptism in the context of symbolic water ordeal.

9 Matt. 3:6, 11, 13, 16; Mark 1:5, 9; Luke 3:7, 16; John 1:26. See also G. W. H. Lampe, *Seal of the Spirit*, pp. 24-25. In the New Testament passages cited here the passive form of the verb βαπτίζειν is consistently used; in Jewish proselyte baptism the middle or reflexive is predominant. See A. Oepke, *TWNT*, I, p. 537.

10 Matthew 3:2; Luke 3:16, 6; Matthew 3:10; Mark 1:3; John 1:31.

entrance into a new life, as the rabbis described the significance of the proselyte's baptism ("he is as child newly born"). John's baptism symbolized entrance into a new age.[11]

(5) John's baptism is closely connected with that of Christ. John compared his ministry and that of Jesus explicitly in terms of baptism (Matt. 3:11,12). When both John and Jesus inaugurated their preaching ministry, the theme of each was the same: "Repent for the Kingdom of heaven is at hand" (Matt. 3:2,17).

Meredith Kline calls John the "Messenger of Ultimatum" and relates his baptism to the ancient covenant administration, especially the covenant lawsuit.[12] The covenant lawsuit was instituted whenever a vassal failed to satisfy the obligations of a sworn treaty. The suzerain would then send messengers to the vassal, delivering one or more warnings, reaffirming the conditions of the covenant and demanding explanation of the offenses. If the messenger(s) was rejected, imprisoned, or killed, the legal process then proceeded to declaration of war in accordance with the sanctions of the covenant. The messages of Israel's prophets must be understood in the judicial framework of covenant lawsuit. The prophets of Yahweh enforce in their messages the covenant mediated to Israel through Moses.[13] This judicial process seems to underlie the teaching of the Baptist who is messenger of the covenant to declare the Lord's ultimatum of eschatological judgment. The call to repentance (Matt. 3:2), the warnings of the wrath to come (Matt. 3:7), the axe at the roots of unfruitful trees which have not borne God's first fruits Matt. 3:10; compare with Lev. 19:23-25) are all consistent with this construction of covenant.

The same applies to Jesus' ministry. The succession of rejected messengers in the parable of the vineyard (Matt. 21:33ff.; Mark 12:1ff.; Luke 20:9ff.) in which the Lord of the vineyard demands his due portion, the shameful treatment of the messengers, and finally the murder of the son lead to the vengeance of covenant sanctions. Kline points out that this parable is set in the Gospels in the context of Jesus' counter-challenge to the Jewish authorities with respect to John's baptism, and the Matthew passage is followed by the parable of the

11   See Chap. II, footnote 59 and the section of this manuscript referred to by this note; H. H. Rowley, "Jewish Proselyte Baptism and the Baptism of John," *HUCA*, 15 (1940), p. 329.

12   M. G. Kline, *By Oath Consigned*, pp. 50-62. Kline says that his presentation is one-sided because he wishes to call attention to what he believes is a neglected element in the meaning of baptism. He feels that his emphasis requires a change in the total bearing and the central thrust of the traditional doctrine of baptism.

13   Cf. also W. Brueggemann, *Tradition for Crisis*, pp. 13-105, who treats the covenant context of the prophets of Israel, the prophets and the covenant forms, and the prophets and the covenant institution with special reference to Hosea. It would be interesting to see whether the prophetic word addressed to the nations by these messengers of Yahweh takes the structure of God's universal covenant of Genesis 12 (or of creation) as a basis for God's appeal to the nations.

marriage of the king's son.[14] This occurred in the Passion Week, the element of crisis being the arrival of the Messianic King in God's City and Temple. The interrogative element in this form of covenant administration is found in the question which Jesus used to elicit from the recalcitrants their own verdict of destruction and disinheritance (Matt. 21:40,41). Additionally, it must be noted that Malachi spoke of coming messengers under various figures: "my messenger to prepare the way before me" (3:1), and "the messengers of the covenant in whom you delight." He speaks of Elijah to come (4:5,6) in terms of Sinai's covenant and judgment. Therefore, he concludes,

> One would expect that the baptism of John as the sign of such a mission of ultimatum would portray by its own symbolic form the threatened ordeal of divine judgment ... The baptismal waters of John have been understood as symbolic of a washing away of the uncleanness of sin. But the possibility must be probed whether this water rite did not dramatize more plainly and pointedly the dominant theme in John's proclamation (particularly in the early stage before the baptism of Jesus), namely, the impending judicial ordeal which would discriminate and separate between chaff and wheat, rendering a verdict of acceptance, but also of rejection. The fact is that for such an interpretation of the rite there is ample biblical-historical justification.[15]

Kline speaks of the water-ordeal in relation to the settlement of covenant controversy and believes that "the principle of ordeal comes to expression in every judicial intervention of God in history." [16] The common elemental forces that functioned as ordeal powers were fire and water.[17] Because John stands in the prophetic tradition, his baptism visualizes the coming judgment, a "second Red Sea judgment (and so a water-ordeal)." [18]

> The whole record of John's ministry points to the understanding of this water rite as an ordeal sign rather than as a mere ceremonial bath of purification. The description of John's baptism as "unto remission of sins," which is usually regarded as suggesting the idea of spiritual cleansing, is even more compatible with the forensic conception of a verdict of acquittal rendered in a judicial ordeal .... To seal a holy remnant by baptism unto the messianic kingdom was the proper purpose of the bearer of the ultimatum of the Great King.[19]

14 Matthew 21:23-32; Mark 11:27-33; Luke 20:1-8; Matthew 22:2ff.
15 M. G. Kline, *By Oath Consigned*, p. 54.
16 M. G. Kline, *By Oath Consigned*, p. 55ff.
17 Recall Noah (I Peter 3:21), the Red Sea (I Corinthians 10:2), crossing of the Jordan with reference to water ordeal, and II Peter 3:5-7 with reference to fire, Both are combined by John in his comparison of his baptism and Jesus' baptism (Matthew 3:11).
18 This assertion is made on the basis of Isaiah 11:10-16 (cf. 27:1, 12, 13; 51:10); Zechariah 10:10, 11, says Kline, *By Oath Consigned*, p. 56, see also note 10 on p. 56.
19 M. G. Kline, *By Oath Consigned*, pp. 56-57.

The value of this understanding of John's baptism is that it combines his message and baptism into a unified covenant administration. John's baptism was a symbol to be replaced by the baptism of the Coming One who would baptize men with the elements of divine power in an actual ordeal. Just as men can be immersed in the waters of Jordan and survive, so too they can be freed from the death of sin, the wrath to come. John's baptism, just like his message, introduced (revealed) Jesus to Israel (John 1:31).

2. Jesus' Reception of John's Baptism

What was the meaning of Jesus' baptism by John? On the basis of what Kline has demonstrated concerning John's baptism, it can be more easily understood why Jesus was baptized. The question, "Why did Jesus request to be baptized?" puzzled John and has puzzled the church since. If John's baptism is covenant administration and ordeal, then in the case of Jesus the question of his personal righteousness (and hence no need of repentance) does not enter in. In a sense one can say that the baptism of Jesus was unique. Although it took place in the context of repenting multitudes and converted sinners, for Jesus the necessity of his baptism is to be found not in himself but for the very crowds that came to the baptism by John. Their trial by ordeal would mean death to them if the Lamb of God did not assume for them the place of mediator and surety of broken covenant. Jesus was baptized for their sake, not his own. To demonstrate how fully he was ready to continue in the perfect obedience in life and death that God demanded in his will for man's salvation, Jesus asked to be baptized. He came to "fulfill all righteousness," to undo the disobedience of the covenant breakers and to render for them the obligations they would not and could not do themselves because of their sinful nature. To be baptized meant that he submitted to the symbol of judgment and offered to take the curse of the covenant. At his baptism Jesus is not proclaimed king, but only Servant. His Lordship appears after his resurrection.[20]

But John's baptism only remained a symbol. At a later time Jesus spoke of "a baptism to be baptized with" (Luke 12:50; Mark 10:38), a baptism accomplished in the death of the cross and resurrection to life (Col. 2:10-14). Als Kline says, "When Jesus began his public ministry, God's lawsuit with Israel was in the ultimatum stage."[21] The question of the origin of John's baptism is important in this connection. If John's baptism were akin to proselyte baptism and levitical washing, then its significance would lie in large part in the realm of ceremonial cleansing only, even though in the school of

---

20 O. Cullmann, *Baptism in the New Testament*, p. 10. See also Gerhard Delling, πληρόω, in G. Kittel, *TWNT*, VI, pp. 283-311, especially pp. 285, 290, 292-294, on the meaning of "fulfill" as being to fulfill a demand or claim with reference to the will of God, never to a human demand, to bring into force God's order of salvation.

21 *Ibid.*, p. 63.

Hillel (contemporary to John and Jesus) the idea of the proselyte himself being morally unclean was beginning to supercede the idea that baptism was necessary because of ritual pollution by idols.[22] Oepke states that there is no thought in proselyte baptism of any natural, let alone ethical, death and resurrection, and that it cannot be deduced from the immersions current in Judaism that John conceived of his baptism as a voluntary dying. He prefers to find the origin of this thought of lifegiving inundation in Hellenism. However, it must be observed that on this basis Jesus could not think of a voluntary giving of himself in death, a thought Oepke finds unlikely if the full meaning of proselyte baptism is to govern our interpretation.[23]

It must be concluded, therefore, that Jesus in his baptism identified himself with sinners, not in a ritual of ceremonial purification (which he did not need and whicht would make his baptism meaningless if not hypocrisy), but in the sense of covenant identification and voluntarily assuming the guilt of covenant breakers. Jesus' baptism needs to be taken seriously. The age of promise is about to become the age of fulfillment. The divine declaration of his Sonship, the approval of his Person and life, and the possession of the Spirit all agree in this way with the expectation of the Messiah and follow immediately.[24] Cullmann says "the baptism of Jesus was proleptic, signifying and summing up in a single action the entire mission and saving work of the Servant-Messiah, which was to be unfolded gradually in the course of his life, death, resurrection, and ascension."[25]

3. Baptism by Jesus' Disciples

This discussion is not concerned at this point with the relationship of Christian baptism authorized in Matt. 28, but with the baptism attributed to Jesus' disciples in the early period of Jesus' ministry, during the short while in which John's and Jesus' ministries overlapped. Two matters are of interest: (1) Why did this baptism cease so abruptly, and (2) What did it mean? The witness of the Gospel of John is as follows:

> After this Jesus and his disciples went into the land of Judea; there he remained with them and baptized (John 3:22).

22 J. Jeremias, *Infant Baptism*, p. 25; D. Daube, *The New Testament and Rabbinic Judaism*, p. 108.

23 A. Oepke, *TWNT*, I, pp. 537-538. The connection of proselyte baptism and John's baptism has not been established. The differences are so vast that all one can say is that the Jews were not unfamiliar with various forms of baptism. Possibly the greatest obstacle to relating the two is the fact that proselyte baptism was never administered to those under the sanctions of God's covenant with Israel whereas John's baptism was for the Jews (nothing is said about Gentiles coming to his baptism).

24 G. W. H. Lampe, *The Seal of the Spirit*, pp. 30-39 discusses this fully.

25 O. Cullmann, *Baptism in the New Testament*, p. 45.

Now when the Lord knew that the Pharisees had heard that Jesus was making and baptizing more disciples than John (although Jesus himself did not baptize, but only his disciples), he left Judea and departed again to Galilee (John 4:1-3).

The abrupt termination of the baptism seems to have been occasioned by the accomplishment of the purpose Jesus had in mind: to call the attention of the religious leaders to the continuity of the messages of John and Jesus, to demonstrate to these authorities that John's ministry was only preparatory to the coming of Jesus, and that he, Jesus, was the one to be reckoned with. When Jesus learns that these effects have been accomplished in the minds of the leaders, the baptism-cum-teaching ministry in Judea comes to an end. The import of Jesus' baptismal work was essentially the same as John's. It was, therefore, a symbol of imminent judgment. By permitting his disciples to baptize with John's baptism he puts the stamp of his approval on the validity of John's ministry. Jesus and John moved in the same circle of prophetic and eschatological concepts.[26]

The Gospels indicate that the imprisonment of John was the occasion for the opening of Jesus' new Galilean ministry. Certainly the leaders of Israel felt nothing but contempt for John and refused to say (what they knew well enough) that his authority was from God (Matt. 21:23ff.; Mark 11:22ff.; Luke 20:1ff.). Peter later made it very clear that the beginning of the ministry in Galilee marked the end of the baptism John preached (Acts 10:37), implying the unity of John's baptism and that of Jesus' disciples. To use Jesus' parabolic form of the administration of the covenant ultimatum: John was the last of a long series of messengers the Lord had sent to a rebellious, disobedient people; his last effort will be the sending of the Son. But these wicked men will reject him too. "The time is fulfilled", this Son will proclaim, "and the kingdom of God is at hand; repent, and believe in the gospel" (Mark 1:15). The announcement was made in most explicit terms in his home town, Nazareth, in a synagogue service in which Jesus declared the arrival of the acceptable year of the Lord (Luke 4:19,21).

> In brief, then, the early baptism authorized by Jesus was a sign of God's ultimatum to Israel. When that ultimatum was emphatically rejected, a new phase of the administration of the covenant was entered, Jesus' ministry of baptism ceasing along with the Johannine message of ultimatum which it had sealed.

> The difference between the earlier and later baptisms authorized by Jesus was the difference between two quite distinct periods in the history of the covenant. The later baptism was of course ordained as a sign of the New Covenant; it was not part of the old lawsuit against Israel .... There would

---

26 C. K. Barrett, *The Holy Spirit and the Gospel Tradition*, p. 34.

be a pronounced continuity between Christian baptism and the earlier, Johannine baptism. While, therefore, the baptismal ordinance which Christ appointed to his church would have a significance appropriate to the now universal character of the covenant community and to its new eschatological metaphysic, it would continue to be a sign of consecration to the Lord of the covenant and, more particularly, a symbolic passage through the judicial ordeal, in which those under the rule of the covenant receive a definitive verdict for eternal glory or for perpetual destruction.[27]

It is now understandable why Jesus himself did not baptize. He stood over against John's baptism as the one to be baptized to fulfill all righteousness. When he would baptize men, it would be with the Holy Spirit and with fire. The baptism he would administer could not have the character of promise and symbol; it would have to be fulfillment. This does not mean that the disciples acted outside of his authority. They were indeed Jesus' representatives in what they were doing. But their hands were no different than John's hands and all acted under his jurisdiction. When the Spirit was his to bestow, then the time would be here for Jesus to baptize. Meanwhile, the baptism of John served to unite those who repented into a fellowship, the fellowship of the citizens of the Kingdom of God.[28] Christian baptism would be instituted by Jesus when through his life, death, and resurrection the church is constituted as the locus of the Spirit,[29] and he receives a full commission to be Lord of lords and King of kings.

B. The Kingdom of God

The Bible reveals a God who *commands* man's attention, a Christ who *compels* his allegiance, and a concept of sin and salvation that presents mankind with alternatives it *cannot* ignore.[30] These are all bound together in a unity in the Person of Jesus Christ. The Old Testament formed the background of Jesus' thought; he quoted freely from it, applied specific passages to himself without hesitation, and interpreted it infallibly and authoritatively as no prophet or scribe before or after was able to do. One does not have to search for the theme that unifies his teaching; it is thrust before the reader throughout the whole of the Gospel: the Kingdom of God.

The Kingdom of God constituted the theme of the preaching of the Baptist

---

27 M. G. Kline, *By Oath Consigned*, pp. 64-65.
28 Josephus, *Ant.*, 18.5.2, uses a word for John's baptism which does not just mean "come together for the purpose of being baptized" but "unite by baptism." Cf. C. K. Barrett, *The Holy Spirit and the Gospel Tradition*, p. 32; G. W. H. Lampe, *The Seal of the Spirit*, p. 22, who says John's baptism "inaugurates a collective movement."
29 O. Cullmann, *Baptism in the New Testament*, p. 10.
30 J. A. Baird, *The Justice of God*, p. 13.

and of Jesus. Matthew summarized the message of both in these words, "Repent, for the kingdom of heaven is at hand" (Matt. 3:2,23; Mark 1:15). When Jesus sent out the Twelve, he "sent them to preach the Kingdom of God" (Luke 9:2). The parables and messages of Jesus referred more frequently to the Kingdom than to any other concept or theme. Jeremias states this in the following summary:

> All Jesus' parables compel his hearers to define their attitude towards his person and mission. For they are full of "the secret of the Kingdom of God" Mark 4:11) — that is to say, the certainty that the messianic age is dawning. The hour of fulfillment has come; that is the keynote of them all. The strong man is disarmed, the powers of evil are in retreat, the physician has come to the sick, the lepers are cleansed, the heavy burden of guilt is removed, the lost sheep is brought home, the door of the Father's house stands open, the poor and the beggars are summoned to the banquet, a master whose kindness is undeserved pays wages in full, a great joy fills all hearts. For there has appeared the one whose veiled kingliness shines through every word and every parable — the Savior.[31]

Luke writes (Acts 1:3) that Jesus used the resurrection appearances to the disciple group as opportunities to speak to them further about the Kingdom of God. Reference to the Kingdom repeatedly recurs in the book of Acts. Philip's evangelistic tour in Samaria is summarized in this way: he "preached good news about the Kingdom of God and the name of Jesus Christ" (Acts 8:12). Paul made frequent reference to the Kingdom in his epistles (e.g. Rom. 14:17; I Cor. 4:20; 15:24,50, e.g.). His ministry in Ephesus and Rome are reported as being "preaching about the kingdom of God and teaching about the Lord Jesus Christ" (Acts 28:31; 19:8; 20:25). The whole New Testament message is good news, the good news about the Kingdom of God (Mark 1:14; Matt. 24:14). Small wonder then that at the time of the Great Consummation revealed in Revelation this message is proclaimed: "the kingdoms of this world have become the kingdom of our Lord and of his Christ" (Rev. 11:15).

An extensive literature has developed about this theme in Christian theology.[32] There is no necessity to review this in detail, nor would any purpose be gained by such a study. Nevertheless, some attention must be given to the topic if the background and meaning of the church's commissioning by Jesus Christ are to be understood.

---

31 Joachim Jeremias, *Rediscovering the Parables* (New York: Charles Scribner's Sons, 1966), p. 181, an abridgement of *The Parables of Jesus*, translated by S. H. Hooke (6th ed.; New York: Charles Scribner's Sons, 1963).

32 The literature has become so voluminous that histories and bibliographies of the discussion have been written in recent years. Cf. J. A. Baird, *The Justice of God*, p. 265, n. 1, for some of the principal outlines of opinion.

1. *The Chronological reference*

The majority of studies of the Kingdom of God are occupied with the question of chronology, and seek an answer to the question of the time reference of Jesus' Kingdom concept. It is increasingly common today to interpret and integrate the New Testament teaching concerning the Kingdom in a threefold way as (1) the presence of God's sovereignty in men's lives today, (2) the final consummation of God's purposes, and (3) God's sovereign purpose and presence throughout time and eternity. An analysis of all Jesus' logia concerning the Kingdom according to the audience addressed in terms of the above categories is quite revealing.[33] Taking into consideration the number of times Jesus spoke of the Kingdom we find that Jesus' teaching gives a fairly balanced emphasis on the Kingdom both present and future. If there is any difference, the emphasis is on the present. However, when the audience addressed is taken into consideration, then a remarkable difference appears: only once does Jesus speak to his opponents about the future, eschatological Kingdom (Luke 14:15), and never about both present and future. To his opponents Jesus always stressed the present nature of the Kingdom. Jesus' crisis teaching concerned both love and wrath, but to the opponent group the greatest stress was laid on the wrath. Jesus showed a greater accommodation to the Jewish point of view and Jewish concerns when speaking to the opponent audience. Then the emphasis of his teaching was on repentance, inner purity, forgiveness, righteousness, obedience to the Old Testament commandments to show true religion.

> Whereas he criticized the Twelve for putting *themselves* before the Kingdom, Jesus criticized the opponents for putting *their religion* before the Kingdom of God. They put the traditions of the elders before the justice and mercy of God (Mark 7:3); they put ritual legalism before their concern for men; they put external purity before their own inner righteousness. In this stance they were unable to understand the working of God in and through him.[34]

Because Jesus spoke so little to the opponents regarding the future Kingdom, it would appear that it is in his words to the disciples that his full teaching about the Kingdom must be found. This agrees with what he said to them, "To you has been given the secret of the kingdom but for those outside everything is given in parables" (Mark 4:11), to which Mark adds, "He did not speak to

---

33   The method John Arthur Baird used and the results obtained are found in his book, *Audience Criticism and the Historical Jesus* (Philadelphia: The Westminster Press, 1969), henceforth to be cited as *Audience Criticism*. Baird catalogued all the logia of Jesus according to source, subject and audience to which addressed (from disciple to opponent groups). They were then analyzed by computer. The results are significant and valuable and should advance greatly our understanding of the meaning and method of Jesus. Baird concludes that the logia are genuine words of the Lord and that a consistent picture of Jesus is presented in the traditions preserved through the Gospel editors.

34   J. A. Baird, *Audience Criticism*, p. 133.

them without a parable, but privately to his disciples he explained everything" (vss. 33-34). Whenever he deliberately explained a parable dealing with the Kingdom of God, he did so only to the Twelve or to the larger disciple group.

It is necessary to go beyond a mere analysis of the statements concerning the Kingdom according to their chronological reference. In all categories (present, future, eternal) there is both a horizontal and a vertical dimension added to the chronological reference. While in every case the concept of the Kingdom is the central element in the crisis, man chooses for or against entrance. His reward for obedience is his position in the Kingdom. His judgment for disobedience is exclusion from it. For those who believe two points of reference are important: (1) the point at which a man enters the Kingdom, and (2) the point at the end of the age when for that life the Kingdom is consummated. Manson correctly observes that there really is no sense in asking whether the Kingdom is present or future because it is something independent of such relationships.[35]

> The Kingdom is in essence a symbol for describing the very judgment plan and presence of God, calling men out of the dimension of the physical into that of the spiritual, out of the realm of the temporal into that of the eternal, calling men to live in God's spiritual world and in his spiritual time even as they continue to live in his world of men and in the time of history.[36]

The present time is always filled with the tension of God's imperative: "Repent, for the kingdom of heaven is at hand." When a man comes to occupy the place of the repentant, he is prepared for the "secret of the Kingdom." This is shown by another characteristic theme in Jesus' teaching regarding the Kingdom: the absolute claims of the Kingdom to the total obedience, total priority, total self-abnegation of man. Twenty-five times, Baird says, this emphasis is found in all sources, and all of these are directed to disciple audiences! There is an apparent logic to this, for it would be only with those who made the initial response to Jesus that these total demands would have any meaning.[37] The Kingdom which lies behind, surrounds, and gives meaning to the cosmos is in essence the very presence of the God of justice who has called the world into being and placed upon it the judgment of his sovereignty.

2. The Universal Covenant

Reflecting on the teaching of Jesus with respect to the Kingdom brings the universal covenant of God with mankind to the foreground. Neither John nor

35 T. W. Manson, *The Teachings of Jesus* (Cambridge: University Press, 1945), p. 135.

36 J. A. Baird, *The Justice of God*, p. 141.

37 J. A. Baird, *Audience-Criticism*, p. 119.

Jesus was the first to speak of the Kingdom. The fact that they did not define the Kingdom for their hearers indicates that it was a concept familiar to their day and relates this message to the rabbinic teaching.[38] To grasp what is meant by the Kingdom of God is to come very close to the heart of the Bible's Gospel of salvation. Old Testament theology was not dominated by the expectation of the Messiah. It was rather dominated, as Kuhn has shown, by the fact that Yahweh is King! Past, present, and future! Throughout the Old Testament hope for the full blessing of his Kingship becomes increasingly prominent and hope is set on the fact that Yahweh will show himself to be King.[39] Kuhn also cites some interesting references to the effect that later Judaism used the phrase "God is King" for "God is present." "To accept the yoke of the Kingdom of God" was equivalent to "acknowledge God as one's King and Lord," "to confess the one God as the King and to foreswear all other gods". A part of the same development was that the term Kingdom of God was read in cultic usage "Kingdom of heaven."[40] The triumphal entry of Christ concerned the fulfillment of Zechariah's prophecy, "Behold thy king cometh unto thee." The issue of Jesus' trials and rejection was precisely his Messianic Kingship and what was judged blasphemy because he applied to himself the divine sovereign prerogatives of God.

Thus the call to repentance comes to the man who is set before God and his rule, not as an individual but as a member of a community. Man responds to this call in faith, i.e., obedience. When he does so, he is in touch with the Kingdom of God which comes without his cooperation. The use of the word μετάνοια (metanoia) for what is translated "repentance" is peculiarly fitting.[41] This word deals with the source of man's motives, not with conduct or even the motives themselves. It involves what Tertullian called similarity of mind between God and his people. The thoughts of God are not the thoughts of men, but they must be before man can enter God's Kingdom.[42] Repentance is the reorientation of the personality with reference to God and his purpose. It turns men's faces forward, not backward. Repentance may not be conceived of as

38 Karl Ludwig Schmidt, βασιλεία, in G. Kittel, *TWNT*, I, p. 584, discusses this and points out the similarities and differences between Jesus' teaching and that of contemporary Judaism. Cf. also J. Bright, *The Kingdom of God*, p. 17, who traces the origin of the Kingdom concept in Scripture, pp. 18ff.
39 Karl Georg Kuhn, in G. Kittel, *TWNT*, I, p. 568. Cf. Isaiah 24:33; 33:22; Zephaniah 3:15; Obadiah 21; Zechariah 14:16ff.
40 G. Kittel, *TWNT*, I, pp. 569-571; Strack-Billerbeck, *Kommentar*, I, pp. 173-177.
41 John A. Broadus has called the translation of μετάνοια by "repentance ... the worst translation in the New Testament." Cf. A. T. Robertson, *Word Pictures in the New Testament* (New York and London: Harper and Bros., 1930), I, p. 24. A similar view is presented by John Calvin, *Institutes of the Christian Religion*, III.iii.5,9; III.iv.1. A significant historical and exegetical study of the word has been made by William Douglas Chamberlain, *The Meaning of Repentance* (Philadelphia: Westminster Press, 1943).
42 Tertullian, *De Paenitentia*, IV.

regret, sorrow, introspection or man-made satisfaction for sin; it is the transformation of the mind in preparation for fellowship in the Kingdom of God. It looks ahead in hope and anticipation, not backward in shame and regret or forward with fear. Men enter the Kingdom in joy.

The challenge to repentance as preached by John, Jesus, and the disciple fellowship is the link that unites the universal covenant of God with men to the preaching of the Kingdom of God. Throughout the New Testament the command to all men everywhere to repent (Acts 17:30) is nowhere set forth as a duty for Israel or for the Gentiles alone. Paul defines for Agrippa his commission received from Jesus Christ, in words reminiscent of the message of the Baptist,

> Wherefore, O king Agrippa, I was not disobedient to the heavenly vision, but declared first to those in Damascus, then at Jerusalem and throughout all the country of Judea, and also to the Gentiles, that they should repent, and perform deeds worthy of repentance (Acts 26:19,20).

His words indicate that one and the same message of repentance was brought to Jew and Gentile alike (see also Acts 20:21). One and the same light has been proclaimed to the people and to the Gentiles (Acts 26:23).

Nothing is so comprehensive of mankind's needs and duties as repentance. It includes the revamping of the outlook and outreach of all life, the metamorphosis of the whole man. By means of it a man enters into the purpose and plan of God for his life. In God's universal covenant, the basic elements of which appear in this demand, the creation of all things by God, his uncompromised sovereignty over all things, man as the image of God, and God's continued care and love for his people were central.[43] When man transgressed, God's dealings with mankind were weighted with the potentials for blessing or curse, good or evil, salvation or condemnation. Man has no other duty but to respond in obedience: God always meets him in his grace not with permissible alternatives but with the imperative to believe and obey. To do otherwise is rebellion. Now that this universal covenant is about to be fulfilled and fully ratified in the work and Person of Christ, the unifying theme of the Kingdom of God is what makes the message "good news." Man's condition is not unalterable. God commands repentance: no other theme would do, for God provides the obedience.[44] The Kingdom is for all, and every man is set

---

43 Paul Sevier Minear, *The Images of the Church in the New Testament* (London: Lutterworth, 1960), pp. 119-139, esp. p. 119, henceforth to be cited as *Images*, shows how the Kingdom of God comes as God's creation of a new heaven and a new earth, and discusses the multiple correspondences (parallelisms) between the Kingdom and the Genesis accounts of creation. What is so remarkable is that so many of the New Testament images of the Kingdom of God are chosen from Genesis 1-11 and not from the particular form of the covenant and election of Israel. See also p. 275, n. 8.

44 It is characteristic of God's work to demand the impossible from man. A brief survey of some of Jesus' miracles illustrates this. To the paralytic he said, "Take up your

before God and his rule. All the emphasis of the divine challenge is on the arresting call to mankind to take seriously the implications of the divine dominion.

3. ... And Mission

"This Gospel of the Kingdom must be preached in all the world for a witness" (Matt. 24:14). This significant sign of the end time must be seen not only against the background of the preaching and meaning of Jesus but also of the world which receives the witness. J. H. Bavinck [45] observes that all religions in some way or other endeavor to establish some sort of kingdom of God on earth.

> The ancient Chinese empire was in its way a kingdom of God, ruled over by the divine emperor, welded into a living unity by centuries-old customs, bound together by structure and all-embracing laws .... Until recently the empire of Japan was a heavenly imperium, governed by a divine ruler, who was a descendant of the gods, and who through his divine commands gave stability to the kingdom. The most primitive peoples in Asia and Africa strive in their tribal religion to make the tribe into a sort of kingdom of God .... All are in greater or lesser degree theocratic communities whose intent is to govern all of life in all its expressions, but they can represent this character only in a secularized form. The Kingdom of God which they represent is of this world and roots in this world.

When now the good news of the true Kingdom of God breaks in on the world's history, opposition from the forces of darkness and the false kingdoms can be expected because God's kingdom is diametrically opposed to the principalities and powers of those kingdoms. This understanding of the celestial struggle is also rooted in the New Testament teaching on the Genesis story of the fall of man. The two kingdoms – of Christ and Satan – have separate origins, are as disparate as the treachery and the faithfulness of the men who represent these two humanities: the first Adam and the last Adam. [46] Between these two kingdoms there will be no compromise, no appeasement. The mission of God is often the battleground between them and the place where the battle is joined.

---

bed," which is exactly what the man wanted most to do (Luke 5:18). To the man with the withered hand he said, "Stretch forth your hand," something he could only do if it were normal (Matthew 12:13). To the impotent man who laid for 38 years on the porch, Jesus said, "Walk," an ability he long despaired of regaining (John 5:8). To dead Lazarus, he said, "Lazarus, this way out!" (John 11:43). The illustrations can be multiplied.

45   J. H. Bavinck, *The Impact of Christianity*, pp. 34-36.
46   P. S. Minear, *Images*, pp. 121, 276 n. 9.

Walter Freytag observes that missions were from the beginning seen from the viewpoint of the Kingdom of God and that each of the missionary periods or missionary streams that have emerged reveal a characteristic contraction of the Kingdom of God outlook, if not in doctrine then in the understanding of the meaning and purpose of mission.[47] Specific reference is made to the following:

(1) Pietism narrows the Kingdom down to a purely spiritual and individual-ethical outlook. Mission becomes the salvation of souls; the Kingdom of God becomes the total of those saved out of the world. What Pietism forgets is that Jesus is already Lord over all and that the Kingdom of God exists in right-eousness, peace, and joy (Rom. 14:17ff.). The new world of God has come and the people of God live in it today. They do not fulfill their calling if they seek to convert men out of the world, for conversion is only complete if the men of this world have turned towards the new world of God.

(2) Ecclesiological narrowing of the Kingdom concept defines the goal of mission as the planting of churches that must be self-supporting, self-governing, and self-propagating. The Kingdom of God is narrowed down to the church. This viewpoint forgets that the churches are not the Kingdom of Got but serve as the gathering of the Kingdom community in preparation for the end.

(3) Idealistic-socio-ethical contraction. This approach blends philanthropy and enlightenment and seeks to make the world a better place in which to live. The Kingdom is identified in its coming with increasingly improved world conditions. Freytag observes that missions is not a matter of improving the world but of being fellow-workers with God (Col. 4:11) in his will for man-kind's salvation. This agrees with the thesis of Bowman who said that Jesus' concept of the Kingdom of God is as wide as the human race and his social ethic as wide as the human need. Overagainst those who hold to a social gospel (e.g. Harnack) this author shows that believers are bound to the Person of Jesus as Lord, not just to his teaching. The social gospel does not need a Messiah to mediate the salvation God promised or a community limited by attachment to his Person.[48]

(4) An apocalyptic narrowing is evidenced when mission is pursued in order to hasten the coming of the end, the Second Coming of Christ. In this view-point there is little sensitiveness to a task to fulfill in this world. It is true that the Gospel must be preached to all, but the end does not come in this way. God's people can only be obedient servants who work in the world and for the world while waiting for the coming of the Lord. Making the proclamation of salvation to bring about the Lord's return ignores the NOW of Jesus' work and kingdom.[49]

47 Walter Freytag, "The Meaning and Purpose of the Christian Mission" in IRM, 39 (1950), 153-161; cf. also his "Vom Sinn der Weltmission" in EMM (May 1950), p. 75ff.
48 John Wick Bowman, The Intention of Jesus (Philadelphia: Westminster Press, 1943), p. 195.
49 F. Hahn, Mission in the New Testament, p. 168.

Two things must not be lost sight of: the Kingdom of God exists in this world, in real historical time, under our familiar conditions with their confused mixture of good and evil;[50] also, no one can really know the hope of this coming unless he answers the urgent, present demand to repent and enter the Kingdom today. Living as it does in the time after the death and resurrection of Jesus Christ, the Kingdom community must be aware that the eschatological hour has arrived, that God's saving grace is offered in mercy to all the world and that it is the duty of the Kingdom community to announce to the nations that they too have a part in the Kingdom of God. Those who are in the Kingdom of God are under obligation to be at the disposal of the King for the furtherance of his good purposes. The beneficiaries must become benefactors (Luke 22:25ff.), not in name only but by spending themselves and being entirely expendable in the service of mankind for Christ's sake. The point is that no one who has seen the kingdom from within can rest content while others remain outside. "You received without pay; give without pay" (Matt. 10:8).[51]

> Merely to sing hymns about the coming universal reign of Christ is no more sufficient than the reading of the old prophecies and psalms sufficed for Judaism ... there must be in a real sense the giving of ourselves ... to actual mission ... by which [is meant] aggressive work for the Kingdom, whether at home or abroad.[52]

Man is open for exciting new possibilities for the future. Our world-transforming, future-seeking service to all peoples does not search for eternal order in the existing reality of the world, but for possibilities that exist in the world in the direction of the promised future, as Moltmann suggests. If this world were immutable, the call to obedient molding of it would have no meaning. The world is like a vast container, full of future and of boundless opportunities and possibilities for good and evil.[53] Karl Barth expressed this in this way:

> We are going, then, not to a fantastic Paradise, not to an eternal hallelujah-singing, but toward a revelation of the distinctive quality of our life as believers, the unique element of which is indeed now manifest to the forgiving and healing mercy of God; for to our eyes, and to the eyes of all men and angels, the manifestation of the structure which must consummate the enduring foundation of our faith is still hidden.[54]

50   Charles Harold Dodd, *New Testament Studies* (Manchester: University Press, 1967), p. 56; J. Jeremias, *Jesus' Promise*, p. 39.
51   Thomas Walter Manson, *Only To The House of Israel? Jesus and the Non-Jews* (Philadelphia: Fortress Press, 1964), p. 17, henceforth to be cited as *Only To The House of Israel?*
52   H. H. Rowley, *Missionary Message*, p. 81.
53   J. Moltmann, *Theology of Hope*, pp. 286-289.
54   Karl Barth, *God's Search for Man* (New York: Round Table Press, 1935), p. 193.

And Karl Rahner said,

> In the sphere of secular, wordly living, there is never any period that can be called *the* Christian age, any culture which is *the* Christian culture. ... It is never possible simply to deduce, from Christian principles of belief and morality, any one single pattern for the world as it ought to be ... although in some circumstances it may be true that for the individual there is a very narrow, and limited choice.[55]

C. *Jesus' Relationship to the Gentiles*

The surprising, single utterance of Jesus with respect to the extensive Gentile mission of the Pharisees (Matt. 23:15) is matched only by the equally perplexing instruction Jesus gave his disciples,

> Go nowhere among the Gentiles, and enter no town of the Samaritans, but go rather to the lost sheep of the house of Israel (Matt. 10:5,6),

and by his definition of his apostleship:

> I was sent only to the lost sheep of the house of Israel (Matt. 15.24).

Perplexity deepens all the more when the context of this instruction to his disciples is reviewed, for Matthew says that while on the one hand Jesus instructed them to limit their ministry of preaching that "the Kingdom of heaven is at hand" to the regions of Galilee, he also informed them that they would bear testimony before governors, kings, *and the Gentiles* (Matt. 10:18).

This becomes even more puzzling when the centrality of the Person of Christ in the mission of the church is recalled. Mission is his work through his church, as Mark so clearly reports: "And they (the eleven) went forth and preached everywhere, while the Lord worked with them," or: "Jesus sent out by means of them, from east to west, the sacred and imperishable proclamation of eternal salvation" (Mark 16:20). Without the person of Christ there could be no Christian mission. Yet do not his words seem to contradict this?

It is not satisfactory to say that the church has not stumbled over these words because the missionary meaning of Matt. 28:18-20 and of Acts 1:8 are perfectly clear. Such an approach to the problem does not explain why Jesus spoke as he did concerning his disciples' mission and his own assignment. Nor does it assist us in understanding what on the surface appears to be a rather harsh and uncalled-for answer to an anguished, desperate mother in the regions of Tyre and Sidon, "Let the children first be fed, for it is not right to take the children's bread and throw it to to the dogs" (Mark 7:27). How are these words of Jesus to be understood? Did Jesus intend a Gentile mission or did he introduce such a mission

---

55 Karl Rahner, *The Christian Commitment*, translated by Cecily Hastings (New York: Sheed and Ward, 1963), p. 7.

only after he had died and rose again? Was a universal mission his aim all the time, or did Jesus change his mind and direction when the Jews rejected him?

Whereas it appears that Jesus understood his mission to be temporarily at least to the lost sheep of the house of Israel, he pronounced this "rule" with an attached exception (Matt. 15:24). Additionally, it appears from the very strange passage of Mark 4:10-12 that an even stricter rule was earlier pronounced. He did not initially address himself directly and properly to the whole people of Israel, but only to his disciples.[56]

1. *Only to the House of Israel?*

The problem posed by these statements of Jesus was recognized and discussed very early in the Christian church. Some of the early church fathers used allegory to explain away the difficulty. They took "the way of the Gentiles" and the "cities of the Samaritans" to mean heresy, false doctrine, or pagan behavior. They understood the words of Jesus in a negative sense as though Jesus was warning the disciples about these things. These early fathers overlooked the fact that the command of Jesus was quite positive and was literally fulfilled and understood positively by his disciples.[57]

Tertullian, on the other hand, said that the limitations were not meant for all time but for that single instance only.[58] Eusebius took a similar stance but added that the first task of Messiah was concerned with Israel and that the needs of the Gentiles would be met when the mission to the Jews had been completed. This view is followed also by Calvin.[59] Grotius said that the benefits for the Gentiles from Christ's ministry were only incidental.[60] Bengel says that Jesus gave the disciples enough to do when he sent them to the Jews.[61]

56 See Karl Barth, *Auslegung von Matthäus 28:16-20.* (Basel: Basler Missionsbuch-handlung, 1945). English translation by Thomas Weiser can be found in Gerald H. Anderson, ed., *The Theology of the Christian Mission* (New York: McGraw-Hill, 1965), pp. 55-71.

57 This is the position of Hippolytus, Clement, Origen, Cyprian, and Didascalia. For full textual references to their positions see T. W. Manson, *Only To The House of Israel?*, p. 2 footnotes.

58 Tertullian, *De Fuga in Persecutione*, 6, cited by T. W. Manson, *Only to the House of Israel?*, p. 3, n. 6, from *Ante-Nicence Christian Library* (Edinburgh: T. & T. Clarke, 1868) vol. V, II, p. 11.

59 John Calvin, *Harmony of the Evangelists* (Grand Rapids: W. B. Eerdmans, 1956), I, p. 440, says, "If anyone imagines that this prohibition is unkind, because Christ does not admit Gentiles to the enjoyment of the Gospel, let him contend with God, who, to the exclusion of the rest of the world, established with the seed of Abraham alone his covenant, on which the command of Christ is founded."

60 Grotius, *Annotationes in Vetus et Novum Testamentum* (1641 ed.), I, p. 193ff., cited by T. W. Manson, *Only To The House of Israel?*, p. 4, n. 9.

61 Bengel, *Gnomon* (1855 ed.), p. 67, quoted in T. W. Manson, *Only to the House of Israel?*, p. 4, n. 10.

A variety of solutions are offered in our present day:[62]

(1) The mission to the Gentiles lay outside the horizon of Jesus, even though "the world mission was bound to proceed from Jesus' horizon and spirit;" Jesus never gave any instruction in world mission.[63] This viewpoint ignores the convenantal context in which Jesus' ministry was performed. Although a connection is sought between Jesus' ministry and the church's missionary activity, this is not taken as a matter of direct but only incidental necessity. This explanation fails to take the eschatological meaning of the proclamation of the Kingdom of God into account.

(2) Jesus had a positive view towards Gentiles, was the first Gentile missionary, and during his ministry was in constant touch with Gentiles. Jesus resists the Pharisaic caricature of the Gentile mission. Support for this position is found in the journeys of Jesus into Gentile territory and the fact that Gentiles sought him. Matt. 28:18-20 is regarded as a commissioning of a large body of disciples, the inner circle of the Twelve having been given directions for a Gentile mission during Jesus' lifetime.[64] This position overlooks the fact that it cannot be said on the basis of the Gospel record that Jesus ever undertook any deliberate "missionary" activity among the Gentiles to win them to his cause and viewpoint.

(3) Jesus' lifetime ministry was confined to Israel. Because Jesus envisioned the future inclusion of the Gentiles, he commanded his disciples to undertake a Gentile mission after his resurrection and ascension.[65] Unfortunately, this viewpoint does not discover a unity in the words and mission of Jesus. It is guilty of an error common to such studies, namely, that it concentrates one-sidedly on the disputed problem of Jesus' attitude toward the Gentiles and seeks the solution to the problem by arguing backwards from the attitudes of the early church to the mind of Jesus.

(4) Jesus deliberately confined his and the disciples' mission to Israel, even forbidding his disciples to preach to non-Jews. The Lordship of Jesus Christ becomes a matter of proclamation after his resurrection, but even then it is God who brings in the Gentiles in the last days.[66] What is unexplained on this

62 F. Hahn, *Mission in the New Testament*, pp. 26-29, discusses these in full.

63 The view of A. von Harnack, *Mission und Ausbreitung*, I, p. 39ff. It must be borne in mind that von Harnack does not regard the Matthew 28:18-20 passage as an authentic word of Jesus.

64 This is the view of Friedrich Spitta, *Jesus und die Heidenmission*, pp. 72ff., 190ff., and quoted in F. Hahn, *Mission in the New Testament*, p. 27. It should be noted that Spitta makes Matthew 28:18 refer to a pre-resurrection period, thus removing the problem by supposing two different forms of commission which complement one another.

65 This view is shared by Max Meinert, Heinrich Schleir, Thomas Ohm, David Bosch; cf. F. Hahn, *Mission in the New Testament*, p. 27, n. 3.

66 This is the view of J. Jeremias made most explicit in his *Jesus' Promise*; Helene Stoevesandt, *Jesus und die Heidenmission* (Dissertation: Göttingen), a summary of which is found in *TLZ*, 74 (1949), 242. Stoevesandt disputes the idea of a mission of Jesus to the Gentiles on the ground that Jesus *expected* them to come. The New Testament

position is that while Jesus taught and meant that God would bring in the nations, the disciples went ahead with such a mission anyway. Either the conclusion must be drawn that the disciples correctly understood what Jesus did not, or else that either Jesus or the disciples were in error. If the disciples were in error and Jesus was the correct judge of the purpose of God, the Gentile mission comes dangerously close to finding its basis in a misunderstanding of the purpose of God revealed in prophecy, a conclusion no one would care to draw.

The solution to the problem of Jesus' attitude to the Gentiles lies in the proper understanding of the mission of Jesus. The real question reduces to this: what commission was given to Jesus? Was Jesus the obedient, faithful Servant of Yahweh? And what did this mean for his ministry? To answer this question, recall for a moment what was said earlier and in a preliminary way concerning apostleship.

Apostleship involved commissioning with authority for a specific task in specific areas at a specific time. It included the right to appoint assistants in the work whose authority never exceeded that of the commissioned apostle. Such apostleship was exercised within the limitations of the assignment.

What was meant by the designation of Jesus as "apostle" (Heb. 3:1)? Jesus, it is stated, "was faithful to him that appointed him" (Heb. 3:2), an obvious reference to the work of his ministry. The significance of this statement goes far beyond a mere statement that Jesus did what he was sent to do. It includes the idea of obedient fulfillment of the task assigned him as an apostle of God according to the mind or will and the purpose of God. Jesus' faithfulness was more than that rendered by a servant (such as Moses); his faithfulness was that of a son over God's house. His mission was that of builder of God's house under God, the master builder. The house is the people of God (Heb. 3:1-6). The Person and work of Jesus Christ are here given the seal of approval by God. Whatever the terms of reference of Jesus' ministry, they were obediently fulfilled by Jesus and were not chosen by him but given of the Father who sent him. In the Son, God who sent him speaks and acts. The thought is that of absolute authority on the basis of absolute authorization for word (ἀπόστολος) and work (ἀρχιερεύς).[67]

It is also important that Jesus' ministry be understood as standing in the

church began the Gentile mission because it believed the new age *had* come. When Jeremias speaks of the mission to the heathen as a coming to Jerusalem and that at the sudden coming of the Kingdom Jesus Christ will lead the fulness of the heathen into it, he forgets that Jesus no longer stands in the literal, Old Testament Zion–Jerusalem tradition. Earthly Jerusalem and Zion were only types; the fulfillment came in Jesus Christ. The sanctuary is in heaven, Jerusalem is above; there is a priesthood after the order of Melchizedek and not of Aaron. Cf. G. F. Vicedom, *The Mission of God*, p. 37, for various other views on the question "Did Jesus want mission to the heathen?" J. Blauw, *Goden en Mensen*, p. 109ff., also discusses Harnack's view.

67 G. Kittel, *TWNT*, I, pp. 423-424, 443-445.

context of the old dispensation and on the threshold of the new. This required a deliberate policy on Jesus' part of keeping himself within the historic context of revelation.[68] Jesus brought the time of salvation near and also brought it into connection with himself. Therefore the question of Jesus' assignment is the crucial matter in this discussion, not whether or not he fulfilled a "Gentile mission" by offering salvation to non-Jews.

Jesus was conscious of his apostleship.[69] The consciousness of having been "sent" was frequently emphasized as the decisive point for men's decisions why they should receive him and his message. "He who receives you receives me, and he who receives me receives him who sent me," he said.[70] The phrase "him that sent me" is used so frequently in the Gospel of John as to be almost equivalent to a designation of the deity. The fast that his words were spoken and his miracles performed, not on his own authority but on that of the One who sent him, required believing acceptance of Jesus who was sent ("My teaching is not mine but his who sent me" – John 7:16). To his fellow citizens in Nazareth he did not hesitate to apply the prophetic word to himself because he knew he had been sent to fulfill the Scripture (Isa. 61:1) which said, "he has sent me to preach good news ... proclaim release to the captives ... recovering of sight to the blind ... set at liberty the oppressed ... proclaim the acceptable year of the Lord" (Luke 4:18-21). "God sent ... his son into the world," we are told, "... that the world through him might be saved" (John 3:17). Behind all his words and actions stands God who sent him, who guarantees the right and truth of what he speaks. In him and through him God's work reaches its goal, for his work originates in God's work ("My food is to do the will of him who sent me and to accomplish his work" – John 4:34).

So many of the words of Jesus find their parallels in the nature of the apostolate.[71] He was sent for a specific mission. He represents God the Father

68   J. W. Parkes, *Foundations*, p. 185; J. Blauw, *Missionary Nature*, p. 67ff.

69   The question arises on the basis of Hebrews 3:1, the only place in which Jesus is called an apostle, whether it is correct to apply this designation to him generally. Certainly the frequency with which Jesus uses the word ἀποστέλλειν to describe his relation to God shows that the reality is present. Jesus is "sent," not as a man "but as the Son in whom the Father attests his presence and himself offers salvation or judgment." Cf. G. Kittel, *TWNT*, I, pp. 443-445.

70   Matthew 10:40; Mark 9:37; Luke 9:48; 10:10; John 5:24; 12:44; 13:20.

71   In the Greek two words are used for "send": ἀποστέλλειν and πέμπειν. The latter is used most frequently by John. Karl Heinrich Rengstorf in his article "ἀποϲτέλλω, etc.," *TWNT*, I, pp. 398-447, defines the difference between these words as follows (p. 404): "when πέμπειν is used in the New Testament the emphasis is on the sending as such, whereas when ἀποστέλλειν is used its rests on the commission linked with it. The Synoptists never use πέμπω with reference to God." With reference to the usage in John's Gospel he remarks: "To denote his full authority both to the Jews and to the disciples Jesus uses ἀποστέλλειν, since he thereby shows that behind his words and person there stands God and not merely his own pretension .... He uses the same term (in prayer) to describe his relationship to God .... When Jesus uses πέμπειν in speaking of his sending by God he does so in such a way as to speak of

149

and is identified with him in work and word. He confines himself to the work God assigned him and sent him to do. He appointed assistants to specific tasks and missions, but their authority never exceeded that of the One who sent them, no more than in Jesus' own case (John 13:16). Even the way in which the disciple group came into existence is significant for an understanding of Jesus' assignments to them. They were not a group of volunteers who gathered themselves around Jesus after the manner of the pupils of the rabbis. They became disciples on the initiative of Jesus. This meant for them that obedience to his call was the way of preparation for his service.[72] The special activity of the disciples began when Jesus decided to make them his fellow-workers (Matt. 10:1; Mark 6:7; Luke 9:1). Matthew writes that Jesus "sent them out" (ἀποστέλλειν) while Mark and Luke emphasize the fact that Jesus endowed them with authority (ἐξουσία). They were delegated, in other words, with full authority. They now spoke and acted in the name of Jesus, not their own authority (Luke 10:17).

In Matt. 10:2 the Twelve were called "apostles." The reason is that by Jesus' decision they who were previously disciples were now given authority (ἐξουσία) and were sent out on a specific mission for him. When as Jesus' apostles they later returned and gave their report, their authority ceased; this is an exact parallel to the cessation of apostolic authority at the seat of authority. In the presence of Jesus they were always designated disciples. Their authorization is linked to the Person of Jesus.

> ... The person of Jesus, and his relationship to his disciples in his lifetime, are grossly misunderstood if we assume that "Jesus gathered around Him disciples who should go out to preach the kingdom of God and work miracles," without even considering the concept of the personal authority of Jesus, let alone making this authority, or the concept of God represented by it, the only standard of the conduct of the disciples as such .... At the very best this could produce only a group of philosophical adherents but not a religious fellowship.[73]

Therefore, whatever the nature of the assignment Jesus gave the disciples, they were participating in his work. What they did they did as his representatives. What was the nature of Jesus' assignment?

"I was sent only to the lost sheep of the house of Israel," he said in answer to the repeated pleas of a distressed non-Jewish mother. The meaning of this

---

God as the πέμπειν με." ἀποστελλειν grounds his authority in that of God; πέμπειν affirms the participation of God in his work.

72 K. H. Rengstorf, *TWNT*, I, pp. 424-5, shows the relationship between being a disciple and apostle for the Twelve whom Jesus chose. Discipleship begins in obedience, and only those who belonged to the disciples of Jesus can have any authoritative part in his work. This thought has significance for an understanding of Matthew 28:18-20.

73 K. H. Rengstorf, *TWNT*, I, p. 426, n. 113.

admittedly puzzling and difficult saying has long been a source of perplexity and even embarrassment to Christians. The word seems to stand in such stark contrast to the openness and responsiveness that otherwise characterized his reactions to people's needs. Because we are so accustomed to thinking of his mission and work as being for all men, it is something of a shock when he gives as his reason for ignoring her need an answer that seems based on the fact she does not belong to the house of Israel. If the word were spoken in a gathering of the Twelve to whom Jesus privately explained his mission, we would not be so distressed. But the words were uttered publicly, to a Syrophoenician woman of great faith, who was in desperation because her daugther was demon-possessed, a Gentile who stood at the very door of the Kingdom, ready to enter. Futile attempts have been made in seeking to justify the words of Jesus or to soften their apparent harshness.[74] None of them is really satisfactory, for not the least of the difficulties in this case is that of being unable to place one's self within the context of the revelation and its time, since the full revelation of Scripture and of God's purpose and plan of redemption is enjoyed by the church today.

It is really immaterial whether the borders of Tyre and Sidon are regarded as part of the territory of Israel or not. It would be very difficult to defend the thesis that Jesus' ministry took place exclusively in regions that were purely Jewish. Jesus never lived one hour in an exclusively Jewish territory. Albrecht Alt in his geographical study of all the Galilean places Jesus visited concludes that Jesus never crossed the boundaries of Israel.[75] However, every attempt to answer the question why Jesus spoke the way he did, or whether Jesus ever went outside the political boundaries of Galilee reformulates the basic question illegitimately. The question to be faced is: What was Jesus sent to do? How did he define his own mission in the context of the appeal of a Gentile woman in great need?

Jesus word is, "I was sent to the lost sheep of the house of Israel." A brief review of the commentaries on this passage discloses yet another common error in seeking for the answer to what Jesus meant. Jesus did not say, as some would make him say, "I was sent to Israel." He said, "I was sent to the *lost sheep* of the house of Israel." His word therefore reveals a basic attitude towards the house of Israel, which is regarded by Jesus from a very particular viewpoint.[76]

74 For a brief review of several current explanations see J. Smart, *The Quiet Revolution*, pp. 71-73.

75 Albrecht, Alt, "Die Stätten des Werkens Jesu in Galiläa Territorial-geschichtlich Betrachtet" in *Kleine Schriften zur Geschichte des Volkes Israel* (München: C. H. Beck'sche Verlagsbuchhandlung, 1959), pp. 436-456. See also T. W. Manson, *Only to the House of Israel?*, "Introduction"; Floyd Vivian Filson, *The New Testament Against Its Environment: Studies in Biblical Theology No. 3* (London: SCM Press, 1950), pp. 24-25. For a different viewpoint see Henry Dewsbury Alves Major, Thomas Walter Manson, and Charles James Wright, *The Mission and Message of Jesus* (London: Nicholson and Watson, 1937), pp. 100-101.

76 J. Jeremias, *Jesus' Promise*, p. 26, n. 3, takes the genitive οἴκου Ἰσραήλ as an

The use of the figurative "straying sheep" to denote God's people is common in the Scripture.[77] The scattered, lost, straying sheep are the object of the redemptive work of the Son of Man and of Jesus as King (Ezek. 34 is especially descriptive of this eschatological goal).[78] The people of Israel are like a very badly treated flock in the days of Jesus. They have no shepherd and are "harassed and helpless" (Matt. 9:36; compare with Ezek. 34). Jesus must gather them, teach and feed them (Mark 6:34-37). He is called "the shepherd of the sheep" (Hebrews 13:20).

A particularly clear and descriptive summary of the ministry of the Good Shepherd is found in John's Gospel (10:1ff.). The sheep belong to the shepherd, no matter what their origin (vs. 16). He does not inspire fear in them. He speaks to them and they follow. He even sacrifices his life for them, and they are ready to accept him who rescued them from such great peril (vs. 17-18). Concerning the duty to gather, feed, protect, lead, and die for the sheep, Jesus says, "this charge I have received from my Father." Jesus is obviously concerned here with the old community comprised of the ancient people of Israel in its remoteness from God and the new people of God who with the sheep from Israel will become one flock under one shepherd (10:16).

The designation of the sheep in Matt. 15:24 as "lost" has the strong sense of crisis in it. For one thing, man is an object of value, and both God and his commissioned representative are interested in him. The comparable Jewish expression is "to trifle away one's life," and includes the active element that the lostness is attributable to the will or fault of the one who suffers it.[79] The lostness also consists in the danger of final judgment. Salvation came to the house of Zacchaeus because "the Son of Man came to seek and to save that which was lost" (Luke 19:10). The very obvious relationship of this work of Christ to Old Testament prophecy is in the foreground (cf. Ezek. 34), for the God who scattered the sheep in judgment will once again gather them in grace and mercy, delivering them from their enemies.[80] Jesus becomes the fulfillment of God's promise; he is at one and the same time both the one who gathers and the one to whom the sheep are gathered. The prophets of the Old Testament could only say, "Return unto the Lord" (Jer. 3:12); Jesus says, "Come

explanatory genitive, not partitive. It means therefore "the whole of Israel as a lost and shepherdless flock, including even the religious people, than whom none were more lost (cf. Luke 15:25ff.)." On p. 20, n. 2, he accepts οἶκος in the sense of tribe, lineage, community as a Semitism, and the absence of the article in οἶκου 'Ισραήλ as pointing to an underlying construct state.

77 Isaiah 53:5 = "all we like sheep have gone astray"; Ezekiel 34:5ff.; Jeremiah 23:1ff.; I Peter 2:25 = "you were straying like sheep".

78 On the use of πρόβατον for the people of God see Herbert Preisker and Siegfried Schultz, article "πρόβατον," in G. Kittel, TWNT, VI, pp. 689-692.

79 Cf. the article ἀπόλλυμι by Albrecht Oepke in G. Kittel, TWNT, I, pp. 394-396.

80 Compare Zechariah 14:7 with Matthew 26:31, e.g. See also Ezekiel 34, esp. vss. 6 and 11.

unto me" (Matt. 11:28), appropriating and applying to himself the very invitation a gracious God extended to his people (Isa. 44:22).[81]

It can now be seen why a kind of priority is given to the house of Israel. The election of Israel was never intended to be exclusive but inclusive. Israel's calling was to live under the signs of the promise.

> Its true business is simply to live; its presence in the world is a miracle which in the end must draw the Gentiles to Yahweh ... Between the nations and himself, Yahweh has set Israel. The Old Testament is always referring to the *mediatorial function* of the Chosen People.[82]

The tragedy is that Israel so often wandered, became lost. The glory is that Israel's disobedience to covenant obligation and calling did not cancel her election. Christ came to be God's rallying point and revealed that it is God's will to gather the whole of mankind together round Him through the mediation of His People.[83] The universal goal would be reached by way of a restoration of the servant nation. Upon that restoration Jesus concentrated both his own mission and that of his disciples, but this was only preparatory to the larger fruition when a restored Israel would be the light of the world. Whenever one loses sight of the universality of Jesus' Gospel and the significance of his Person and work for all men, it becomes difficult to grasp the reality of the priority placed upon his earthly ministry and to understand that what Jesus said to the woman in no way contradicts the intrinsic universal intention of his ministry and gospel.

God's call to Abraham to be the father of a great nation belongs in the setting of God's purpose for his whole creation and all mankind. The singling out of one people was for the purpose of the ultimate restoration of all mankind to true life. The covenant with Israel was promulgated not for Israel's sake but as the first fruits of a life under God that must characterize the life of all mankind. Israel needed to be recalled to her true purpose and destiny as the servant people, and then would come through a restored Israel the light to lighten the world.

> And now the Lord says, who formed me from womb to be his servant, to bring Jacob back to him, and that Israel might be gathered to him, for I am honored in the eyes of the Lord, and my God has become my strength — he

81   The Scripture references are illustrations only; any concordance will assist in selecting many parallels. Cf. A. G. Hebert, *The Throne of David*, p. 222; J. Blauw, *Goden en Mensen*, p. 110.

82   R. Martin-Achard, *A Light to the Nations*, p. 77.

83   The observation of A. Lacoque that we must not allow ourselves to overlook the fundamental continuity of the People of God when we make a distinction between the different situations of Israel and the Church in the unfolding of the history of salvation is to the point. The Church can rely in its mission on the Old Testament promises mediated through Israel. Cf. Martin-Achard, *A Light to the Nations*, p. 77, n. 3.

says: "It is too light a thing that you should be my servant to raise up the tribes of Jacob and to restore the preserved of Israel; I will give you as a light to the nations, that my salvation may reach to the end of the earth" (Isa. 48:5,6).

The ministry of Jesus took place in a time of transition. The responsibilities of Israel and the Church differ by reason of the different moments at which God has caused them to intervene in the history of salvation. Israel's business was to live under the sign of the promise. The business of the Church is to tell the good news to the nations, to proclaim that the divine purpose has been fulfilled. Therefore "mission" in the modern sense is distinctly characteristic of the Church and belongs to the final chapter of the history of salvation. But the Church may not forget that God saves people and converts the nations by working in the midst of his own people. It is his interventions that make Israel (and today makes the Church) the light of the world.

Jesus defined his ministry, therefore, in terms exactly corresponding to the terms of God's universal covenant and Israel's election. The duty of God's apostle was to live his life and perform his saving work in terms of the judgment God pronounced on him for the sake and in the place of the lost sheep he was seeking and saving. Gentiles have a share and a claim to this great redemption and may claim the food on the table for themselves, even if it be only crumbs that fall to the ground, either dropped accidentally or thrown away unwanted by the children. "Woman, great is your faith! Be it done for you as you desire" (Matt. 15:28). Gentiles are accepted while the mission on behalf of Israel continues.[84] Later in the history of revelation the apostle Paul showed that the salvation of the Gentiles and Israel are inseparable (Rom. 9-11). The one and the same Lord who challenged the power of Satan by casting out demons from the possessed of Israel has the right to challenge and sovereignly expel demons from those possessed among the Gentiles. He confronts the hostile powers of this world wherever they are found. In working for the salvation of Israel Jesus worked for the salvation of the whole world.[85] "The reason why Jesus came to Israel was precisely because his mission concerned the whole world."[86] His announcement of salvation to Israel was an act of service to the Gentiles in the same way as his vicarious death was for all. It was entirely consistent with the nature of his commission, therefore, that Jesus sent his disciples to the house of Israel.[87] The Gospel is "the

---

84 J. Münck, *Paul and the Salvation of Mankind*, p. 262.

85 F. Hahn, *Mission in the New Testament*, p. 30, remarks that Jesus' act cannot be thought of in terms of conventional boundaries within the people of Israel: the sick segregated on cultic and ritual grounds, prostitutes and sinners boycotted on moral grounds, tax-collectors excluded on religious and national grounds – all received his help and fellowship.

86 J. Münck, *Paul and the Salvation of Mankind*, p. 266.

87 H. Vogelstein, *HUCA*, 2 (1925), p. 115.

power of God for salvation to everyone who has faith, to the Jew first and also to the Greek."[88] John's Gospel contains the most radical and important sentence on this topic: "Salvation is *from* the Jews" (4:22) a word spoken to the Samaritan woman. For today this means that salvation, ministry, life are not to be organized and adapted according to whatever looks most urgent or efficient without reference to Israel. Today's Church is "built up together" (Eph. 2:20,22) with those who were the people of God before and who still are a chosen people. The growth of the Church takes place only where the structure is "joined and united together" (Eph. 2:21; 4:16). This word "together" appears frequently in Ephesians especially and always describes community of the Church with Israel (also when resurrection and enthronement are explicitly mentioned as in Eph. 2:6ff.). In an alienated world of sin, darkness, and error there always was and always will be a people of God. The unfaithfulness of Israel to covenant cannot nullify God's faithfulness (Rom. 3:3-4).

> As brothers of Jews the Christians are given an unchanging constitution and order. They are received into a God-given order of living in God's house. They are dependent upon a Word given and a Spirit promised by God to others first. They are served by, and are called to serve in, a ministry that has preceded their own commission. It is Israel who ., right of God's choice always comes first in questions of truth and righteousness, faith and preaching, fellowship and service.[89]

The same priority also applies in the sphere of judgment, for "there will be tribulation and distress for every human being who does evil, the Jew first and also the Greek ... for God shows no partiality" (Rom. 2:9-11).

Jesus had frequent contact with Gentiles during his ministry. Each recorded instance was an occasion for one of his great signs to be shown. In one case this became the cause of great joy for Jesus because certain Greeks sought him through the disciple Philip. One significant act of Christ must still be considered, one which is directly concerned with the relationship of Israel and the Gentiles and which is directly related to his mission. Attention must turn from the House of Israel to the House of Prayer for all peoples.

2. *The Cleansing of the Temple*

Jesus lived within a circle of crisis and involved the people and leaders of that day in that crisis. The crisis was both communal and individual at one and the same time. Everything Jesus said and did was conditioned by an overwhelming sense that he was sent by the Father and that he therefore must obediently accept God's will for himself and mankind. It is interesting to note that as his life

---

88   Rom. 1:16; 2:9; 3:9, 9; I Cor. 9:20; Acts 13:5; 20:21.
89   M. Barth, *The Broken Wall*, pp. 130-131.

drew swiftly to its close Jesus increasingly appealed to prophecy and applied to his deeds the fulfillment of what God decreed concerning the Son.[90] In the last days in Jerusalem the conscious fulfillment of what was prophesied concerning himself played a significant role in the words and actions of Jesus. His entry into Jerusalem in fulfillment of Zechariah 6:6, the Cleansing of the Temple, and the challenge to his authority, the thirty pieces of silver, the trials, Crucifixion, etc. are all specifically related to prophecy. The summary of this is stated by Jesus himself to the men with whom he walked to Emmaus,

> "O foolish men, and slow of heart to believe all that the prophets have spoken! Was it not necessary that the Christ should suffer these things and enter into his glory?" And beginning with Moses and all the prophets, he interpreted to them in all the scriptures the things concerning himself (Luke 24:25-27).

Isaac Watts said, "In Jesus grace and vengeance strangely join." Not the least significant of the occasions in which this happened was the Cleansing of the Temple.

The importance of this act of Jesus is shown by the fact that all the Synoptists record the event. John also records a cleansing of the Temple, though it appears that the cleansing to which John refers may have taken place early in Jesus' ministry.[91] There is no question that Jesus makes reference to the following prophecies on this occasion:

> And the foreigners who join themselves to the Lord, to minister to him, to love the name of the Lord, and to be his servants, every one who keeps the sabbath, and does not profane it, and holds fast my covenant – these I will bring to my holy mountain, and make them joyful in my house of prayer; their burnt offerings and their sacrifices will be accepted on my altar; for my house shall be called a house of prayer for all peoples. Thus says the Lord God, who gathers the outcasts of Israel, I will gather yet others to him besides those already gathered. (Isa. 56:7)

and,

> Has this house, which is called by my name, become a den of robbers in your eyes? Behold, I myself have seen it, says the Lord. (Jer. 7:11)

90 J. A. Baird, *The Justice of God*, p. 251, calls this "acted parable." I am not certain what meaning he places on the word "parable" and have therefore not used his term. If parable means teaching by means of word or act, I can agree. It would appear to me, however, that the phrase is ambiguous. Jesus' words and works were an actual, historical reality, an element missing in the general meaning of parable.

91 Matt. 21:12-13; Mark 11:15-19; Luke 19:46; John 2:13-22. It is a matter of dispute whether these passages all refer to the same event. If they do, the chronology in John's Gospel becomes a problem. If there are two different occasions on which this happened, one faces the question how these two acts differ from each other, and what they mean.

Bringing these two Old Testament references together in his public outcry against the prostitution of God's house for secularized purposes to the exclusion of those for whom the house was built brings together the same familiar tensions of grace and judgment in one act that was observed in other circumstances as a characteristic of God's dealings. While Isaiah taught that the house of the Lord must be the gathering place for Israel and the Gentiles, Jeremiah revealed that this sanctuary shall pass away. No wonder that Jesus had to speak of the destruction of the Temple in this context![92] Only in this way does it become clear that what Jesus is demonstrating about the earthly sanctuary is expressive of the new gathering place of the whole people of God. The time will come when neither Jerusalem nor Gerizim will be a gathering place (John 4:21) to worship the Father. Jesus himself will be the Temple men will destroy but which Jesus will rebuild in three days (John 2:19).

As to the actual cleansing of the Temple Mark makes it very clear that buyers and sellers of all kinds of merchandise were excluded by Jesus. Their presence in the Court of the Gentiles is attested by Jewish sources from which we learn that the money changers set up their tables three weeks before the Passover, the time when the Temple tax fell due; they were not there the whole year.[93] This was the only part of the Temple to which non-Jews had access; in other words, this was the only place in God's House of Prayer that Gentiles were permitted to use to worship God. Yet their place had been pre-empted by the agents of Annas the high priest for whom these concessions constituted a rich source of revenue.[94]

It is not enough to say that Jesus' action was designed as an objection to the abuses suffered by the common worshippers at the hand of temple authorities.[95] Lohmeyer has pointed out that it is not the Temple that is cleansed but the Court of the Gentiles. In this action Jesus did something quite empty and insignificant, he thinks, from the viewpoint of the devout Jews since that action of Jesus did not touch the Temple proper or its services. Jesus did not interfere with the existing order of the Jewish ritual.[96] It is significant that in this event

92   Matt. 24; Mark 13. John's record of the cleansing includes the same note of judgment, for Jesus replied to the authorities, "Destroy this temple and in three days I will raise it up" (John 2:19-22). John's account relates how the disciples recalled Psalm 69:9 in connection with the action of Jesus, "Zeal for thy house has consumed me, and the insults of those who insult thee have fallen on me."

93   J.T., Sheq. I:3; J. Jeremias, Jesus' Promise, 65, n. 3.

94   JT., Taan. IV.8; Ker. I.7; Chag. 78a; Sheq. I.7; cf. esp. Rosh ha Sh. 31.a, b; Peah I.6; Josephus, Ant., XX.9.2-4, on the family of Anna. See also E. Lohmeyer, Lord of the Temple, p. 37; Ethelbert Stauffer, Jesus war ganz anders (Hamburg: Friedrich Wittig Verlag, 1967), p. 97ff.

95   J. C. De Young, Jerusalem in the New Testament, p. 60.

96   E. Lohmeyer, Lord of the Temple, pp. 39-40; Robert Henry Lightfoot, The Gospel Message of St. Mark (Oxford: Clarendon Press, 1950), p. 63, who also remarks that "the existence of a court for the Gentiles in this area, in the very heart of Judaism, is indeed remarkable." Gottlob Schrenk, article "ἱερός" in TWNT, III, pp. 221-247, esp.

one of the great missionary appeals of Jesus comes to the fore in the very center and stronghold of Judaism and that it was occasioned by Jesus' confrontation with the noxious abuses of an avaricious and worldly priesthood. Here at the Temple where the sacrifices and offerings pictured his atoning death and perfect life he was so filled with zeal for God's house that he of necessity had to restore to the Gentiles their designated place.

This Court of the Gentiles was no ordinary place. Its size together with the splendor of the Temple and its buildings and porches were the marvel of the ancient world. Certain regulations governed this Court. No one with dusty or dirty feet was permitted to pass through it. The Court might not be used as an ordinary thoroughfare. Use of the Court was forbidden to the sick. The Court was definitely a part of the Temple and Jesus seemed to regard it as such, for the robber's refuge which the leaders had made of it he looked upon as a desecration of the entire House.[97] The eschatological destiny of all men revolved around this place. Mt. Zion with its Temple was regarded as the center of the world, and Jerusalem was looked upon as the mother of peoples:

> Thus says the Lord God: this is Jerusalem; I have set her in the center of the nations, with countries round about her (Ezek. 5:5).

The destiny of the City and God's House was that some day it would embrace all nations in the day of fulfillment. The rabbis taught,

> The land of Israel lies in the centre of the world: Jerusalem lies in the centre of the land of Israel; the holy precincts lie in the centre of Jerusalem; the Temple lies in the centre of the holy precincts; the ark of the covenant lies in the centre of the Temple; the foundation stone lies before the ark of the covenant. For, on it the world was founded.[98]

The Cleansing of the Temple is one of the acts of the Lord as the Messianic King in the Father's house. The road of the triumphal entry of the prophesied coming King could not end at Herod's palace or at Pilate's Praetorium. It had to proceed directly from the Mount of Olives to the Temple of God, who alone is sovereign Lord. No longer does Jesus say, "The Kingdom of God is at hand" (or what is almost its sense in the use of the phrase, "God is coming"). The Lord has suddenly come to his Temple. Fulfillment is near. The King has come. And such a King! The exercise of his Lordship begins by renovating and restoring his earthly palace so that any man anywhere at any time can

---

p. 243, says that "Jesus' promise and purpose was to purify the cultus from a profane and calculating spirit." Schrenk objects to the view of Jeremias who stresses the Messianic aspect of the event and to the views of those who find a religio-political interpretation in it.

97   R. H. Lightfoot, *The Gospel Message of Mark*, pp. 62-63.

98   Midrash Tanchuma, ed. Choreb, p. 444.15-18, illustrating Ezek. 5:5. The quotation of this source is found in R. H. Lightfoot, *The Gospel Message of Mark*, p. 64, and E. Lohmeyer, *Lord of the Temple*, p. 22.

obtain unhindered, unimpeded access to him. Even if a man comes empty-handed (recall how Jesus forbade anyone to carry anything through the Court – Mark 11:16), his palace was the place where all men could pray.

Therefore the King pronounces a verdict on the transgressors. Their sin was that they had pre-empted for themselves the place that belonged to the nations, excluded those for whom this Temple stood, and took refuge in the Temple as robbers who go back to the safety of their den. They gloated,

> "This is the sanctuary of Yahweh!" ... Steal, would you, murder, commit adultery, perjure yourselves, burn incense to Baal, follow alien gods that you do not know? and then come presenting yourselves in this Temple that bears my name, saying, "Now we are safe – safe to go on committing all these abominations!" Do you take this Temple that bears my name for a robbers' den? I, at any rate, am not blind – it is Yahweh who speaks.[99]

Mark makes a significant observation regarding this action of Jesus. He observes that Jesus' actions were combined with instruction, that after Jesus had driven out those who sold and those who bought,

> He taught, and said to them, "Is it not written, 'My house shall be called a house of prayer for all nations'?" ... And the multitude was astonished at his teaching (Mark 11:17,18b).

Jesus' words cannot be looked upon as a passionate outburst uttered on the spur of the moment. They are a deliberate address intended to instruct the people concerning the nature of God's Temple and the place of the Gentiles in it. The cleansing is not a plea for a more spiritual worship, but a demand to make room in God's house for Gentiles to come and worship. Only indirectly is this a problem of the Jewish Temple; it is directly a problem of the Gentile nations.[100] This is clearly demonstrated from the prophetic passages which Jesus cites and which without any doubt refer to Gentiles. The Lord has come to his Temple (Mal. 3:1), and he comes in grace and judgment (Mal. 3:1-5). When the time is come that there will be "no temple in the city, for its temple is the Lord God the Almighty and the Lamb," then "in its light will the nations walk; and the kings of the earth shall bring their glory into it ... they shall bring into it the glory and the honor of the nations" (Rev. 21:22,24,26). James said that the house of David (which is Christ and his kingdom) will be rebuilt "that the rest of men may seek the Lord, and all the Gentiles who are called by my name, says the Lord, who has made these things known from of old" (Acts 15:16-18).

---

99 Jeremiah 7:4-11, quoted from *The Jerusalem Bible*.
100 T. W. Manson, *Only to the House of Israel?*, pp. 13-16; R. H. Lightfoot, *The Gospel Message of St. Mark*, pp. 60-69; E. Lohmeyer, *Lord of the Temple*, p. 44ff.; H. Stoevesandt, *Jesus und die Heidenmission*, pp. 89ff.; F. Hahn, *Mission in the New Testament*, pp. 36-37, n. 4.

Abolition of the old Temple and the influx of the Gentiles are inseparably linked together. This great act of Jesus in the Temple is an act of power on the authority given by God, a manifestation to Israel and the Gentiles that the universal covenant of God abolishes all earthly distinctions and barriers. Now that the Gentiles are given their place in the Temple, it is time for the middle wall of partition to be torn down. To believe in Christ and accept him means community, co-existence, a new life, peace (Eph. 2:14).

From the viewpoint of a Jewish audience there was an unheard-of element in Jesus' teachings and actions. Jesus did not proclaim the triumph of Israel over the nations of the world. He emphasized the sovereignty of God over all of life and all peoples. The current attitudes of the Jews of his day towards other people came to the fore in two encounters between Jesus and his contemporaries; these encounters concerned taxes and Roman restrictions on Jewish courts in capital cases. When shown a Roman coin, he said in effect, "If the Pax Romana is worth having, it is worth paying for" (Matt. 22:21). When asked to judge a woman taken in adultery, he did not presume to challenge Roman authority in favor of Moses and said in effect, "The Romans may reserve the right to condemn to death for themselves, but man possesses the capacity to forgive" (John 8:1-11).[101] Therefore, when God's sovereignty is proclaimed Jesus did so in terms of the grave danger to Israel of being excluded by God and the glorious hope for the Gentiles of being admitted to God's Kingdom. For both Jew and Gentile these two poles remain real options in the teaching of Jesus. That Gentiles from East and West would sit at table with the Fathers Abraham, Isaac, and Jacob in the Kingdom of Heaven while the sons of the Kingdom are thrown into outer darkness to weep and gnash their teeth (Matt. 8:11-12) was the exact reverse of current Jewish priorities. It was also the great privilege given to the Gentiles concerning one of whom Jesus said, 'Not even in Israel have I found such faith! . . . Go; be it done for you as you believed" (Matt. 8:10,13).

The implications are tremendous for the Christian mission. No one may under any circumstance claim to have Christ on his side or for himself alone, be the man Jew or Gentile, man or woman, Westerner, African, or Asiatic. In Christ those "who were once afar off have been brought near in the blood" (Eph. 2:13). When Paul wrote of the work of Christ, he said, "He came and preached peace to you who were far off and peace to those who were near," and then, as if thinking of the cleansing of the Temple, he added, "for through him we both have access in one Spirit to the Father" (Eph. 2:17,18).

Small wonder that Jesus reacted as he did to the visit of certain Greeks who had come to the feast and asked to see him (John 12:20ff.). In this request Jesus saw the fulfillment of his mission, though it would mean death, and

101   I am indebted to T. W. Manson, *Only to the House of Israel?*, p. 11ff., for this insight into the contrast of the views of Jesus and his contemporaries.

said, "The hour has come for the Son of Man to be glorified!" Dr. Harry Boer writes concerning this passage as follows:

> The glorification of Christ [in John 7:38,39 and 12:20ff.] refers to his exaltation in and after the resurrection. It was at the resurrection that the Spirit was given to Jesus, and this receiving of the Spirit enabled him to give the Spirit to the Church from which rivers of water would flow to the world. The glorification of the Son of Man [John 12:23] makes possible the transmission of his life through the Spirit to πάντα τὰ ἔθνη whom Jesus saw coming to him in the form of certain Greek proselytes. It means the dawning of the day when the Spirit whom he will send forth will gather the universal Church through the proclamation of her ambassadors.[102]

Before this could happen, however, Jesus would have to undergo both circumcision and baptism.

D. *God's Universal Covenant Ratified*

Events moved swiftly in the closing days of Jesus' life, and all these events centered in him, the Messianic King. Unknowingly, the leaders of the Jews provided the occasion and brought about the circumstances in which Christ fulfilled his sign (σημεῖον) and validated his authority (ἐξουσία). They destroyed the Temple; he raised it again in three days (John 2:18-22). He had already restored the earthly Temple to its proper function. All men were now free to pray in the House of Prayer. Nevertheless there still remained a wall of separation between Jew and non-Jew that needed to be destroyed, never again to be erected. Worship still required sacrifice which meant that non-Jews had first to be identified with the election of and covenant with Israel before they could have free access to the sanctuary of God. A kind of sacrifice needed to be brought so that every man at any time anywhere could draw near to God with empty hands to be filled with an overflowing blessing.

Jesus' death changed forever the status of the Gentiles in relation to the Jews. The ends of the earth both see and share in the salvation of the Lord. Jesus was lifted up and killed by the hands of lawless men acting in ignorance, according to the definite plan and foreknowledge of God (Acts 2:23; 3:17). Why? Because God had said to Abraham, "In your posterity shall all the families of the earth be blessed" (Acts 3:25). God had not forgotten his promises to the people of Israel, however, as Peter said, "God, having raised up his servant, sent him to you [the Jews] first, to bless you in turning every one of you from your wickedness" (Acts 3:26). The time was come when God

---

102 H. R. Boer, *Pentecost and the Missionary Witness of the Church*, pp. 185-186, who refers to F. W. Grosheide.

would make the Servant of the Lord "a covenant of the people" and "the light of the Gentiles" (Isaiah 42:6).

1. *Jesus' Circumcision and Baptism*

When Jesus began his public ministry, God's covenant lawsuit with Israel was in the ultimatum stage. Jesus was baptized by John not for his own sake but to identify himself with sinners and fulfill all righteousness. Jesus' baptism by John was proleptic in character, for it symbolized the judgment ordeal which mankind could escape only if Jesus underwent the ordeal for them: the righteous One dying for sinners, the One giving himself for the many. John's baptism was not the ordeal itself but only symbolized what was man's danger. It was also "acted parable," for it was the sign of God's ultimatum. Who could escape death except someone die in his place?

The baptism which Jesus later authorized as a sign of the universal character of the covenant community has a significance appropriate to the new dispensation with which it was inaugurated. It is a sign of consecration to the Lord of the covenant. Through baptism God accepts men as the servant people of his covenant and under the authority of his Christ. This, it was noted, was one of the basic meanings of circumcision also, as Kline has shown.[103] Circumcision was part of the redemptive, law covenant and involved an administration of God's lordship and the exercise of his sovereignty. Christ, the obedient Servant, was circumcised on the eighth day, in this way being placed within the fellowship of a covenant people elected by God. As a man, he shared Israel's election to service.

> The circumcision of the infant Jesus in obedience to Genesis 17, that partial and symbolic cutting off, corresponded to the ritual of Genesis 15 as a passing of one who was divine under the curse threat of the covenant oath. That was the moment, prophetically chosen, to name him "Jesus".[104]

What he did, he did not for himself but for those whom he came to save. God gave his Son who would come under the judgment knife and suffer the curse as a substitute for sinners. Jesus became Isaac's substitute. Abraham's faith in God's covenant faithfulness was vindicated because Yahweh had provided (Gen. 22:14).

However, it is not the cirmumcision of Christ in accordance with Genesis 17 that saves. For him too the circumcision in the flesh, done with hands, was only a type, not fulfillment. Every type found its fulfillment in some historical

---

103 M. G. Kline, *By Oath Consigned*, pp. 43-49. Kline does not limit the meaning of circumcision only to consecration. He says on p. 47 that it includes malediction, consecration, identification, justification, and spiritual qualification.

104 *Ibid.*, p. 45.

event in the life of Jesus. "That the Scriptures might be fulfilled" is the frequent witness in the Gospels as the life and ministry of Jesus unfolds. So also there was another circumcision which Christ had to undergo, just as he spoke of another baptism with which he had to be baptized.[105] This circumcision Paul calls "the circumcision of Christ" (Col. 2:11). The entire passage reads as follows:

> For in him the whole fulness of deity dwells bodily, and you have come to fulness of life in him, who is the head of all rule and authority. In him also you were circumcised with a circumcision made without hands, by putting off the body of flesh in the circumcision of Christ; and you were buried with him in baptism, in which you were also raised with him through faith in the working of God, who raised him from the dead. And you, who were dead in trespasses and the uncircumcision of your flesh, God made alive together with him, having forgiven us all our trespasses, having canceled the bond which stood against us with its legal demands; this he set aside, nailing it to the cross (Col. 2:9-14).

This passage is crucial to an understanding of what the work of Christ means for Jew and Gentile. If circumcision is the seal of the covenant with Abraham's seed, Israel, and baptism the seal of the universal covenant of God with all mankind (also announced formally to Abraham), and if in addition Jew and Gentile are alike saved in the same work of Christ, there must be a place, a time when both seals meet and find the center of their reference and fulfillment. This happened at Calvary and Joseph's garden tomb. What happened at Calvary was not a symbolic oath-cursing, but the actual carrying out of the curse in the circumcision of God in the crucifixion of his only-begotten Son. There "the body of [Jesus'] flesh by his death" (Col. 1:22) was actually cut off (Col. 2:11 = ἀπέκδυσις) so that "we [Jew and Gentile] might be presented holy and blameless and irreproachable," who once were "estranged and hostile in mind, doing evil deeds" (Col. 1:21,22).

Paul uses the noun ἀπέκδυσις ("removal, stripping off") in Colossians 2:11 to express what happened in the circumcision of Christ. The verb ἀπεκδύομαι is used in Col. 2:15 and again in Col. 3:9. To catch the sense of the word we should translate "fully put off," expressing the exclusion of every possibility of returning again to the former state or condition.[106] Paul means to say, therefore, that Jesus' death was his circumcision. The accompanying sequence of the

105 See Luke 12:50; Mark 10:38; Col. 2:10-14.
106 Thus Albrecht Oepke in G. Kittel, *TWNT*, II, pp. 318-321, article ἀπέκδυω, who regards the verb form used as a middle with the accusative of object. The word is used only these three times in Colossians. The participle in 3:9, he says, is meant imperatively. The middle is used with an active sense; "this is particularly suitable because the usage is figurative and because the One who acts has a personal interest in his action" (p. 319).

experiences of Jesus found in the Philipians 2 passage (circumcision, burial, resurrection) would lend strong support to this interpretation. Additional confirmation comes from the equivalence of baptism with crucifixion, a thought of great importance in Paul's epistles.[107] Christ's death as sin-bearer was the experience of God's wrath against sin, a coming under God's judgment.

The above interpretation of Christ's circumcision as an objective reality experienced by Christ in his death on the cross is not incompatible with the idea that what Paul is speaking about is the subjective experience of the Christian who is in Christ and therefore shares in all that which Christ has done for our salvation. Even on the latter position the thrust of the passage remains, for the believer is still identified with Christ in his death, burial, and resurrection.

> The same pattern emerges in Romans 6:3ff. [where] the first step is called death, whereas in Colossians 2 it is called circumcision. If then Paul calls the Christian's death-experience a circumcision, it is only because he was first of all prepared to call Christ's death a circumcision.[108]

J. B. Phillips combines these two ideas of the objective and subjective sense of the genitive in his clear translation of Col. 2:11,12.

> In Christ you were circumcised, not by any physical act, but by being set free from the sins of the flesh by virtue of Christ's circumcision. You, so to speak, shared in that, just as in baptism you shared in his death, and in him are sharing the miracle of rising again to new life — and all this because you have faith in the tremendous power of God, who raised Christ from the dead.[109]

This circumcision, says Paul, was made "without hands," that is, it was not accomplished in some human symbolization but by God, just as Isaiah had prophecied.

> We esteemed him stricken, smitten by God, and afflicted .... He was cut off out of the land of the living, stricken for the transgression of my people .... It was the will of the Lord to bruise him .... He poured out his soul to death, and was numbered with the transgressors (Isa. 53:4,8,19,12).

The surgical removal of the foreskin in the covenant rite was fulfilled by Christ in "the putting off of the body of the flesh" (Colossians 2:11), i.e., death, crucifixon, the cancellation of the bond "which stood against us with

---

107 See Rom. 6:3-6; Gal. 2:20; 5:24; 6:14.
108 M. G. Kline, *By Oath Consigned*, p. 71.
109 J. B. Phillips, *The New Testament in Modern English* (London: William Collins and Sons, 1958), *sub loco*.

its legal demands; this he set aside, nailing it to the cross" (Col. 2:14).[110]

The Scriptural data teach that Christ was also baptized in his crucifixion and death. The New Testament's exposition of Christ's experience of the ordeal of death and burial, together with the triumph of his resurrection is called his baptism.[111] What must be observed is that the baptism of Christ on the Cross goes beyond the meaning of his circumcision. Both circumcision and baptism involved for Christ the suffering of the curse of God, the cutting off of the body of the flesh. However, that is where the meaning of circumcision stopped. Jesus' death and burial were the fulfillment of the curse sanctions of broken covenant. Circumcision says nothing about the restoration of life, about resurrection. This glorious experience was, however, part of the baptism of Christ in which believers share. A new era of covenant administration was about to begin, inaugurating the time of the "new covenant in my blood" of which Jesus spoke (I Cor. 11:25). His baptism, real and actual in death, resurrection, ascension, established and made possible for all men the blessings of salvation, the universal covenant. It became the basis on which the people of God were constituted a holy nation, a royal priesthood, a people of God's own possession. Because Christ was baptized at Calvary and Joseph's tomb (not a series of unrelated events but one single, comprehensive work of redemption), the believer incorporated into Christ by faith becomes a part of the new community Christ came to establish.

Therefore even the circumcised Jew needed to be baptized. His circumcision was not sufficient to symbolize the completed work and fulfilled covenant. It was not enough for the Jew to be identified with a race or nation of special promise. He needed to be identified as part of the new humanity Christ came to redeem and which God promised to bless. Christian baptism is clearly a re-presentation of the baptism of Christ on the cross and in the tomb.

There is yet one other characteristic of circumcision and baptism that must be pointed out. Circumcision could only point to broken covenant, the cutting off of a man's life in symbolic form, even though that life was spared by the mercy and grace of God. Baptism does not point to unfulfilled but completed covenant, of life restored, indestructible, eternal, in union with Christ (Rom. 6:9-11). He who shares in the death of Christ must of necessity share in his life. The covenant was God's way of bringing mankind back to the source of life in him and into unity with each other, expressed in a common life.[112] The difference between the two covenants may be summarized as being the difference between the administration of condemnation and righteousness. In

---

110 M. G. Kline, *By Oath Consigned*, pp. 72-73, also combines the ancient covenant administration to this verse and to Colossians 2:15 with the legal elements found there. Cf. also Andrew J. Bandstra, *The Law and the Elements of the World* (Kampen: J. H. Kok, 1964), p. 164ff.

111 Rom. 6:1-5; Gal. 6:15.

112 H. Berkhof and P. Potter, *Key Words of the Gospel*, p. 37.

baptism this movement from the one to the other is completed and finalized. "There is therefore no condemnation to them that are in Christ Jesus" (Rom. 8:1). This new covenant in Jesus' blood serves as the necessary basis of the church's life and task. Just as the election and purpose ("mission") of Israel was dependent upon and defined by the Sinai covenant, so also the church's task is grounded in the passion cup. Through his death and resurrection Christ defined the nature of the Church's commission: proclamation of the lordship of Jesus Christ.[113] If covenant is, as was shown earlier, basically a declaration of God's lordship, then baptism as a sign of entrance into it will mean coming under the jurisdiction of the covenant and of the sovereignty of the Lord of the covenant. There is, says Paul, only "one Lord, one faith, one baptism, one God and Father of us all, who is above all, and through all, and in all" (Eph. 4:5).

2. *Acquital by Resurrection*

"Mission to the nations can only be pursued meaningfully on the presupposition of the clear promise and firm belief that everything which was needed for the salvation of all has already taken place."[114] The proclamation of the death of Christ, of Christ crucified, is more than a certain qualification of the Christian's message to the world and of their life in the world. The "crucifixion of the Lord of glory" (I Cor. 2:8) which was the utmost humiliation of the Son of God (Phil. 2:6ff.), is the very beginning, center and source of all that Christians have to attest by word and deed. At the same time, another event stands with this and belongs equally to the heart of the Gospel. This event is equally as unique as the Crucifixion: the resurrection of Christ.

> The Resurrection is the miracle of miracles. We cannot argue for it; we cannot explain it; we cannot prove it. We can only ponder over it and study what the New Testament says about it.[115].

The Biblical teaching about Christ's resurrection connects it inseparably with the Crucifixion. On the one hand, there could be no resurrection except a death occur first. On the other hand, if Jesus had only died and was not raised again from the dead, there is no hope, no faith, no message left to Christ's Church (I Cor. 15). The resurrection of Christ by God's power is the solemn accept-

113 See Paul S. Minear, article "The Covenant and the Great Commission" in N. Goodall, ed., *Missions Under the Cross*, pp. 64-80, esp. p. 75.
114 K. Barth, *Church Dogmatics*, IV:III, p. 874. For a survey of the missionary viewpoint and theology of Karl Barth see I. P. C. Van 't Hof, *Het Zendingsbegrip van Karl Barth* (Hoenderloo: Zendingsstudie Raad, 1946). Van 't Hof affirms that Barth's view of mission cannot be understood apart from his view of the church. He also considers Kraemer's views which he feels are corrective of Barth's.
115 M. Barth, *The Broken Wall*, p. 51.

ance of Christ's sacrifice, for a sacrifice is only good when it is "accepted" by God, when it is a "pleasing odor" to him.[116] A sacrifice, like a prayer offered to God, depends on *God's* acceptance of it.

The resurrection of Christ means that the might and grace of God exhibited in this great act reversed the normal order of life–death to which man is by nature captive and by which he is hopelessly intimidated.[117] The sequence has now become death–life, as Paul wrote in Eph. 2:5, "We who were dead . . . [he] made alive." To say "resurrection" means that there is One, who, though neither detached from, nor strange to, nor unconcerned with the troubles of man's life, is stronger than the laws of nature to which we are subject. It was simply impossible for death to hold Jesus Christ (Acts 2:24).

It is no mere accident that the resurrection of Christ is frequently described in political terms. Christ through resurrection is "enthroned" (Eph. 1:20) on God's established throne. He is to be honored by all as the supreme King and Monarch (Phil. 2:9-11). And obviously, the authority of such a king affects the lives and existence of every one and every thing in his realm. Christ rules over the spirit world, the world of man and over the natural realm. The resurrection and enthronement of Christ reveal the eternal election, pleasure, and plan of God to have Christ rule over mankind through sonship, grace, and redemption. The resurrection means nothing less than that God rules through Jesus Christ.

The acquital which mankind experiences in the resurrection of Christ is related to forgiveness and salvation. We read in Acts 5:30-31, "God . . . raised Jesus . . . . He exalted him by his right hand in order to give Israel repentance and forgiveness of sins." But it was not for Israel alone; "in your seed all the families of the earth shall be blessed." [118] In the Gospel the resurrection always means that chosen men are committed to something new. Their commission and ministry presuppose that they are made new men (II Cor. 5:[17]). They are forgiven, acquitted, sent out, equipped for service. The witness they bring to Jew and Gentile will come from their own experience of their participation in the death, resurrection, and enthronement of Christ.

> We are called to join God's work, not so much by saying there were or are mighty acts of God in this world, but first by being a sign of them so that our message is "not in plausible words and wisdom, but in demonstration of the Spirit and the power" (I Corinthians 2:4), in expectation of new acts in the coming years and of the time of the mightiest completing act of all, which the Father has fixed in his own authority.[119]

---

116   Eph. 5:2; Gen. 8:21; Ex. 29:18; Isa. 53:10; Ezek. 20:41.

117   Cf. Heb. 2:15, "all those who through fear of death were subject to lifelong bondage."

118   Compare Gal. 3:8; Acts 3:25 and Gen. 12:3; 18:18; 22:18.

119   H. Berkhof and P. Potter, *Key Words of the Gospel*, pp. 47-55.

The resurrection of the acquitted sinner with Christ is absolutely necessary or there is no witness, no faith, no reality to Christ's resurrection (I Cor. 15) for any one (Acts 26:23).

The resurrection is pre-eminently the work of God. Markus Barth writes,

> Unless the resurrection is explained as a deed by which God manifests, distinguishes, and describes *himself*, even his love and power, his holiness and righteousness, his mercy and grace — it is not explained at all. Much mental balking before and against the resurrection may have its roots in the fact that the respective critics are unwilling to let God be God on God's own terms. The God of whom the Old and New Testaments speak is the God who raises the Son.[120]

The resurrection becomes the justification of God, his Son, and the sinner. How can this be? This question is brought into sharp focus in the description Paul uses of God's act of justifying sinners. Paul speaks often of justification by faith, but once only he used the daring phrase that "God justfies the ungodly" (or "the godless") — (Rom. 5:4). This statement seems to deny his righteousness or at least to give a strange view of his justice. This seems all the more strange since the justification of the wicked is excluded in Scripture unless there is expiation of their guilt.[121]

But the answer is not hard to find. God is faithful to His covenant. His judgment is based upon events. No person, event, institution of the Old Testament was able to provide a way by which a sinner might be justified (forgiven). God maintained this even in relation to his covenant with Israel. The works of the law did not suffice.[122] The only way that God could justify the ungodly was in Christ Jesus alone. Our acquittal before God lies in his Person, in his history, in his death and resurrection. It does not lie in man's faith in him, for faith says, "Not I, but Jesus Christ in me" (Gal. 2:20). "He was raised for our justification." Jesus Christ is today before God not only as the evidence before the law, nor as an attorney for the defense. He is at one and the same time the legal ground, the advocate, and the proclaimer of man's justification. The One died and rose again for the many.

> The resurrection is the enthronement of the divinely appointed intercessor for the sinners; it is the validation of his ministry; it is the proclamation of his work's accomplishment; it is the ground of all certainty and trust in the victory and regal rule of grace over sin.[123]

There is great urgency for the Church to understand the meaning of the

---

120 M. Barth, *Acquital by Resurrection*, p. 61.
121 Ex. 23:7; Numb. 14:18; Deut. 25:1; Isa. 5:23; I Kings 8:32; Psalm 82.
122 Rom. 3:23, 28; 4:5; 10:3.
123 M. Barth, *Acquital by Resurrection*, pp. 95-96. In the section pp. 67-96 Barth has an excellent treatment of justification and forgiveness by resurrection.

Resurrection. Karl Barth rightly critizes the Church for the character of the Easter hymns with which it celebrates the resurrection of Christ, drawing specific attention to this characteristic in them that they for the most part emphasize the first-born rights of the church and largely ignore its first-born duty, the duty of mission.[124] Jeremias expresses this in this way:

> Easter saw the dawn of the Last Day. The Gentile mission is the beginning of God's final act in the ingathering of the Gentiles. The Gentile mission ... is an anticipation of the visible enthronement of the Son of Man ... *The missionary task is part of the final fulfillment,* a divine factual demonstration of the exaltation of the Son of Man, and *eschatology in process of realization.* It offers the possibility of cooperating with God in his gracious anticipation of the decisive hour of redemption described in Isaiah 25: the Gentiles accepted as guests at God's table (vs. 6), the veil torn from the eyes (vs. 7), and death abolished for ever (vs. 8).[125]

E. *Christ's Enthronement*

John 17, which is often referred to as the high-priestly prayer of Jesus, is actually the report of Jesus Christ, God's great Apostle, to the Father who sent him. His assignment is near its close. Events will move fast to their conclusion. In the hearing of his disciples he makes his report to the Father:

> Father, the hour is come. Glorify thy Son that the Son may glorify thee. For thou hast made him sovereign over all mankind, to give eternal life to all whom thou hast given him. This is eternal life: to know thee who alone art truly God, and Jesus Christ whom thou hast sent.
>
> I have glorified thee on earth by completing the work which thou gavest me to do; and now, Father, glorify me in thine own presence with the glory which I had with thee before the world began (John 17:1-5, NEB).

Later in this report to the Sender, the Apostle, Jesus Christ, continues:

> I have delivered thy word to them, and the world hates them because they are strangers in the world as I am ... As thou hast sent me into the world, I have sent them into the world ... But it is not for these alone that I pray but for those who through their words put their faith in me; may they all be one: as thou, Father, art in me, and I in thee, so also may they be in us, that the world may believe that thou didst send me. The glory which thou gavest me I have given to them, that they may be one, as we are one; I in them

---

124   K. Barth, *Church Dogmatics*, IV:III, 304.
125   J. Jeremias, *Jesus' Promise*, pp. 74-75; R. Martin-Achard, *Light to the Nations*, p. 1.

and thou in me, that they may become perfectly one. Then the world will learn that thou didst send me, that thou didst love them as thou didst me (John 17:13-23).

Reading the entire chapter in the light of what has previously been said about the apostleship of Jesus Christ, places his mission and that of his followers in a more meaningful light. Jesus Christ is ready for a new assignment. His church will from now on live in a new condition and circumstance (they will be scattered, each to his own home – John 16:32). A change has taken place, however, for the scattered sheep will neither be shepherdless nor will they be separated – the Great Shepherd will keep them as one flock. When his circumcision and baptism on Calvary are completed, he will rise without the robes of his humiliation,[126] ready to baptize his own with the Spirit and with fire as he takes them into partnership in his assignment. "All power," he said, "has been given unto me." It is characteristic of John's Gospel (which places the greatest emphasis on the apostleship of Jesus) that the hour of the Gentiles comes into its fullest expression after the death and resurrection of the Son of God. Jesus said that the grain of wheat must first fall into the earth and die before it will bear much fruit (John 12:24); he said this in the context of the Greeks who came to the feast to worship. When he is lifted up, he would draw all men to himself (John 12:32). Jesus speaks of the "other sheep" that will be brought into the fold in relation to his laying down his life for them (John 10:15,16). He will give eternal life to mankind when his work is finished (John 17:1,2).[127] The resurrection from the dead was the enthronement of the Son of God. What does he say about his kingship? his program? the assignment to his subjects? To answer these questions requires a study of Matt. 28:18-20 and related passages.

1. The Promulgation of the Universal Covenant

Scholars such as O. Michel, J. Jeremias, E. Käsemann, E. Lohmeyer have given detailed attention to the teaching of the New Testament regarding the enthronization of Jesus Christ.[128] They have also shown that the New Testament

126 It is outside the scope of this study to enter into detail concerning the matter of Jesus' garments as mentioned in Scripture. Clothes were a mark of man's shame and guilt (Genesis 3:21). The sign of Christ's humiliation which conclusively pointed out God's Son was that a babe was lying in a manger in Bethlehem, wrapped in swaddling clothes (Luke 2:12). When men wished to put him to an open shame in his crucifixion, they took away his garments (John 19:23-24). Though men wrapped him with clothes at burial, a sign of his complete triumph and of the fulfillment of the curse was that he left his grave clothes behind in the tomb (John 20:5-7).

127 J. Jeremias, *Jesus' Promise*, pp. 37-38.

128 See the following: Ernest Käsemann, "Kritische Analyse von Phil. 2:5-11," *ZThK*, 47 (1950), p. 346ff.; O. Michel, *Der Brief an die Hebräer*, p. 116ff.; O. Michel, "Der

data must be understood against the background of Dan. 7:9-14.[129] Daniel has a vision of God in heaven, where "the court sat in judgment and the books were opened" (vss. 10,26). From the throne "a stream of fire issued" (vs. 10) by which the horn making kingdom-claims in rebellion against God is consumed and destroyed (vss. 11,26). The Son of Man and the vindicated saints of the Most High receive an everlasting kingdom.[130] Then,

> there came one like a son of man, and he came to the Ancient of Days and was presented before him. And to him was given dominion and glory and kingdom, that all peoples, nations, and languages should serve him; his dominion is an everlasting dominion, which shall not pass away, and his kingdom one that shall not be destroyed (Dan. 7:13,14).

This service of the nations to the Son of Man is part of his enthronement. The parallels of the Daniel 7 passage to John 17, Matt. 28:18-20, et al., are quite obvious.

Oriental enthronement patterns included these elements: (1) exaltation, (2) presentation (or declaration of exaltation), (3) enthronement (or the transfer of dominion).[131] These elements, found in parallel coronation hymns and ritual among the Egyptians, are clearly traceable in varied New Testament passages.

I Timothy 3:16

1. Exaltation "He was manifested in the flesh, vindicated in the Spirit, seen by angels"

2. Presentation "preached among the nations, believed on in the world"

3. Enthronement "taken up into glory"

Philippians 2:9-11

1. Exaltation "God has highly exalted him"

2. Presentation "and bestowed on him the name which is above every name"

Abschluss des Matthäusevangeliums," *Evangelische Theologie*, X (1950/51), pp. 16-26; Ernst Lohmeyer, *Das Evangelium des Matthäus* (Göttingen: Vandenhoeck & Ruprecht, 1967) in Werner Schmauk, ed., *Kritisch-exegetischer Kommentar über das Neue Testament*. Passages considered as relating to the enthronization are: Matt. 28:18-20; Phil. 2:5-11; I Tim. 3:16; Heb. 1:5-14; Rev. 4, 5; Dan. 7:9-14, 26-28. See also R. P. Marten, *Carmen Christi*, p. 235.

129 See in addition to the above references, W. Freytag, *IRM*, 39 (1950), pp. 153-161; Werner Schmauk, ed., *In Memoriam Ernst Lohmeyer* (Stüttgart: Evangelisches Verlagswerk, 1951), pp. 22-52, article by Ernst Lohmeyer, "Mir ist gegeben alle Gewalt," esp. p. 34; J. Blauw, *Missionary Nature*, p. 83.

130 M. Kline, *By Oath Consigned*, p. 58, n. 13, points out that the total structure of this passage follows the pattern of a judicial ordeal. We would have then the fulfilling of the ordeal sanctions of the covenant against transgressors.

131 See O. Michel, *Der Brief an die Hebräer*, p. 116ff.; J. Jeremias, *Jesus' Promise*, p. 38.

| 3. Enthronement | "that at the name of Jesus every knee should bow, in heaven and on earth and under the earth, and every tongue confess that Jesus Christ is Lord, to the glory of God the Father" |

Hebrews 1:5-14

1. Exaltation	"Thou art my Son, today I have begotten thee .... I will be to him a father and he shall be to me a son .... Let all God's angels worship him"
2. Presentation	"thy throne, O God, is forever and ever, the righteous scepter is the scepter of thy kingdom; thou hast loved righteousness and hated lawlessness; therefore, God, thy God, has anointed thee with the oil of gladness beyond thy comrades .... For it was fitting that he, for whom and by whom all things exist, in bringing many sons to glory, should make the pioneer of their salvation perfect through suffering. For he who sanctifies and those who are sanctified have all one origin. That is why he is not ashamed to call them brethren, saying, 'I will proclaim thy name to my brethren, in the midst of the congregation I will praise thee' "
3. Enthronement	"Sit at my right hand, till I make thy enemies a stool for thy feet"

Lohmeyer in reference to Philippians 2:9 has shown that "the exaltation has to do with the cosmic lordship of Christ who is installed as Lord of the universe and not simply as cultic Lord of the church." He believes that the second part of this hymn must be placed in a soteriological setting: Christ is Lord over all the world, and it is through him that God works out his purpose.[132] Christ becomes the "criterion and Judge of all history, and the arbiter of all destiny." In this early Christian hymn the supreme name is bestowed on Jesus, the glory of God is shared with Jesus (and it is not diminished but enhanced in the process). For, when every tongue confesses that Jesus is Lord, this will be done "to the glory of God the Father." No angel or man by any act or deed can exalt him so highly as God has already done.[133]

Otto Michel, who is followed by Jeremias, believes that this triple-action coronation formula also applies to Matt. 28:18-20, and analyzes the text as follows:[134]

| 1. Exaltation | (the assumption of all power by the Risen One) "all authority in heaven and on earth has been given to me" |

132 Ernst Lohmeyer, *Philipper*, p. 97; R. P. Marten, *Carmen Christi*, p. 235. Wilhelm Bousset, *Kyrios Christi* (Göttingen: Vandenhoeck & Ruprecht, 1967), pp. 75-104, holds that the title "Lord" has cultic significance.

133 J. McDowell Richards, ed., *Soli Deo Gloria: New Testament Studies in Honor of William Childs Robinson* (Richmond: John Knox Press, 1968), article by F. F. Bruce, "Jesus is Lord", pp. 23-36.

134 O. Michel, "Der Abschluss des Matthäusevangeliums," *Evangelische Theologie*, X (1950/51), p. 346ff.

2. Presentation	(the injunction to proclaim his authority among all nations) "Go therefore and make disciples of all nations, baptizing them in the name of the Father, and of the Son, and of the Holy Spirit, teaching them to observe all that I have commanded you"
3. Enthronement	(the word of power) "Lo, I am with you always, to the close of the age"

This last word of power "is to be understood," says Jeremias, "in the light of Luke 10:19 and Mark 16:17ff.: the Son of Man displays his royal power in his guardianship of his messengers." [135]

This application of the enthronement pattern to Matt. 28:18-20 has not been uncritically accepted, and F. Hahn warns "not to rush to bring Matt. 28:18ff. one-sidedly into connection with the passage." [136] There are some significant data that must be observed that distinguish this passage and make it unique among the selection of enthronement texts with which it is grouped.
1. In this passage Christ himself speaks, whereas in the other passages the Spirit through the inspired author gives expression to the faith of the Church. It is not unlikely that in some of the enthronement passages of the epistles remnants of the liturgy and hymns of the early Church have been preserved. In them *the Church* declares to the world what it knows and believes concerning Jesus Christ and God's acts through him. In Matthew 28 *Jesus* speaks to his Church.
2. Prophetic references such as are found in I Timothy and especially in Hebrews 1 are entirely absent from the Matthew selection. There is good reason

135 J. Jeremias, *Jesus' Promise*, p. 39; F. Hahn, *Mission in the New Testament*, p. 64ff. It must be remembered that Jeremias and Hahn (as also von Harnack) do not regard Matt. 28:18-20 or the Mark passage as authentic words of Jesus, but view these passages as editorial insertions of a later date. A. von Harnack, *Mission and Expansion*, p. 37; Joachim Jeremias, *The Prayers of Jesus* (London: SCM Press, 1967), p. 36. The major difficulty with their position is that these men have failed to see the unity of these words in relationship to the universal covenant and the apostleship of Jesus Christ. See also G. R. Beasley-Murray, *Baptism in the New Testament*, pp. 77-92; R. P. Marten, *Carmen Christi*, pp. 235-242. J. Firet draws the right conclusion when he says that the conclusion of Matthew's Gospel is not an appendix that has no relationship to the Gospel, but it is the point from which the Gospel goes forth; it is the *raison d'être* of the church; J. Firet, *Het agogisch moment in het pastoraal optreden* (Kampen: J. H. Kok, 1967), p. 82. K. Barth, *An Exegetical Study of Matt. 28:16-20*, p. 67, says "the Great Commission is truly the most genuine utterance of the risen Jesus" and "these texts . . . do not mean that this event was subsequently interpreted or construed, much less invented by the faith and the piety of the Church. They unequivocally refer to an event which laid the foundation of, and gave shape to, the faith of the emerging community" (p. 57). In conclusion, we must maintain that the passage gives us a clear summary *e mente Jesu.*

136 F. Hahn, *Mission in the New Testament*, p. 65; on p. 65, n. 4, Hahn notes the objections of Trilling, *Das wahre Israel*, p. 32ff., to the application of the enthronement pattern, although Hahn accepts the pattern because the authority of Jesus is brought into connection with the lordship over heaven and earth.

for this, and this reason is related to the above observation regarding the one who does the proclamation. In Matthew Jesus summons his church to the task of proclamation. He, as their Chief Prophet, speaks in his own right, for the period of his obedient service, fulfilling all that God in the Scriptures required of him, is now ended. He now summons the believing community to join in that proclamation. In a sense, the other passages are the community's obedient response.

3. Christ includes a sacramental element in the words of Matthew 28. This is entirely lacking (and it would even be difficult to formulate some construction that would include it in harmony with the contents of the hymnic sections) in the other passages. The reason for this difference is to be found in the nature of the passage: in the epistles Jesus Christ is being *proclaimed* as Lord; in Matthew he *acts* as Lord.

4. The audience reference is also distinct. The command to make disciples (the principal verb in Matt. 28:18,19) is addressed to the believing community. In the epistles the believing community addresses the world in witness and thereby confronts the world with the challenge to discipleship.

5. The words of Matthew 28 are concerned with the establishment of a community, a new, all-embracing community comprising people of all nations. This does not come to expression in the epistolary passages. The focus of attention in the epistles is the glory of God's acts in exalting Jesus Christ; in Matthew this is implied, of course, but the center of reference is what Christ Jesus will do through and for his Church.

6. A comparison of the passages in the Gospels and the Acts parallel to Matthew 28 give no indication of enthronement, hymnic form. Although one might attribute this to the editorial work of the writers of these books, the forms of these commissions differ sufficiently to make impossible a generalization such as Michel makes.[137] These parallel passages do lend themselves to a covenantal interpretation, as we shall show.

Several years ago it was my privilege to be an official guest at the opening of Parliament in Ceylon.[138] In his throne-speech the newly elected Prime Minister made continual reference to "my government," specifying in detail along what lines the nation would be governed, what policies the government would initiate and fulfill, as well as what duties were expected from the citizens. This "throne-speech" was quite distinct in character from the actual investiture with authority which had preceded and by which the Queen of the

137 The passages in mind are Matthew 28:18-20 and parallels in Mark 16:15-18; Luke 24:46-49; John 20:21-22; Acts 1:3-8. J. Hahn, *Mission in the New Testament*, p. 63ff., writes in part about difficulties in harmonizing the view of Michel with enthronization, although he does accept the thesis.

138 The author was at the time Moderator of the Presbytery of Ceylon and President of the General Consistory of the Dutch Reformed Church of Ceylon, serving as a collegiate minister of that church and as missionary of the Christian Reformed Church in America (1956-1960).

British Commonwealth had recognized the Prime Minister's appointment. This distinction defines the difference between the Matthew 28 passage and the texts from the epistles. Matthew 28 is the throne-speech of the enthroned Lord, not the proclamation of his enthronement.

To define the actions and words of Matt. 28:18-20 in this way only is not sufficient, however. The passage (with its parallels) must be considered as the promulgation of the new covenant in Jesus' blood, the full inauguration, implementation, and revelation of God's universal covenant with mankind. Since covenant is basically the administration of God's lordship in which he consecrates a people to himself under the sanctions of divine law, are there found here all the covenantal elements which would allow the conclusion that this sovereign administration of the Kingdom of God is indeed a covenant and the same as God's universal covenant?

The passage does contain all the covenantal elements. There is the *divine oath* sworn to maintain the established relationship: "I am with you always, to the close of the age" (vs. 20). *Personal conmitment* in terms of consignment under Christ's authority is clearly prominent: "When you go, make disciples, baptizing ... teaching ..." (vs. 19). An *oath sign* is present: baptism, and includes God's part and man's part in its signification. An *authority or ownership relationship* is clearly understood in baptizing "in/into the name". And what clearly relates this to all covenant administrations that have preceded is the fact of the *divine initiative* so prominent in the passage.

> The incorporation of disciples into the jurisdiction of the New Covenant by the baptismal confession of Jesus Christ as Lord is in clear continuity with the tradition of the initiatory oath of allegiance found in Old Testament covenantal engagements (and their extra-biblical counterparts).[139]

The unity of Matthew 28 with other covenant administrations is clearly seen by means of a comparison of the elements basic to covenant as found in each of them. In an earlier part of this study it was demonstrated that the form of the covenants God promulgated in the Old Testament finds parallels in the Hittite suzerain–vassal treaties of those days. Three elements were basic in these covenants: (1) a preamble, spoken by the sovereign, which was intended to inspire confidence and gratitude and to dispose the vassal to attend to the covenant obligations and which might take the form of specifying the name of the sovereign and/or mentioning one of more of his great works on behalf of his subjects; (2) declaration of the fundamental demand(s) expected from the vassal, involving complete consecration and commitment to the sovereign to the exclusion of all other alien alliances or purposes – demands which were

139 M. G. Kline, *By Oath Consigned*, p. 80. It is a well-known fact that the confession of Jesus as Lord was made in early baptism. See J. Crehan, *Early Christian Baptism and Creed*; R. P. Marten, *Carmen Christi*, p. 292.

usually specified in such a way that meeting them would lead to the highest good and greatest benefit for the vassal; (3) the promise of the sovereign to covenant fidelity as lord of the covenant, administrator of its conditions, and fulfiller of the promises.[140]

All God's covenants are declarations of his lordship, manifested especially in his gracious acts for his people in the past and present, and to be manifested in the execution of the promises (or threats) included in the covenant. In the specifically soteric forms of the covenants in Scripture this sovereignty is related to God's sovereign grace which infallibly effects his redemptive purposes in Christ, which purposes are accompanied by the divine guarantees assuring the realization of the blessing sanctions of the covenant. Since there is a unity in all of God's work of redemption for Israel and for mankind, it is not unlikely that a similarity of form in the way God's redemptive covenants are administered is also present. The following comparisons will be helpful in setting this in focus and showing the unity of the covenants. In a previous discussion it was noted that the covenants with Israel were instituted by God in service of the universal covenant. Therefore they must lead to and find their fulfillment in the universal covenant, which – like all covenants – now assumes a new form of administration since the conditions of its promulgation are found in the fulfillment in Christ, whose circumcision on the Cross fulfilled and completed the covenant with Israel and whose baptism in death and resurrection accomplished everything for our redemption (John 19:28-30).

The crucial question is whether Matt. 28:18-20 may be equated with the "new covenant in my blood" of which Jesus spoke in institution of the Supper (I Cor. 11:25). The phrase "new covenant" occurs first in Jer. 31:31-37. Jeremiah's prophecy mentions two features of this covenant which will characterize it and differentiate it from the previous covenants. First, *this new covenant will abrogate the old*. It will be a covenant "not like the covenant which I made with their fathers when I took them by the hand to lead them out of the land of Egypt" (vs. 32). It will stand in sharp contrast with the old; its distinctive feature will be that God's law will be written on the heart rather than on tables of stone (vs. 33; compare II Cor. 3:3). This change is very significant. The suzerain–vassal treaties on which the Sinai covenant was patterned provided for two copies of the covenant to be made, one of which was deposited in the temple of the god of the suzerain, the other was deposited in the temple of the god of the vassal. In the case of Israel both copies were placed in the Ark of the Covenant since this was God's place of residence.[141] In the New Covenant this will be written in the heart, for there God dwells in the

---

140 Many of these treaties and covenants had other identifiable and important distinguishing elements besides these three. These were selected as being central to the covenant structure. Detailed analyses of this covenant form can be found in W. Brueggemann, *Tradition for Crisis*, and M. G. Kline, *The Treaty of the Great King*. Both of these works contain excellent bibliographies of other studies on this subject of covenant form.

141 M. G. Kline, *The Treaty of the Great King*, pp. 16-22.

Spirit sent by the Son. The fellowship of believers is now in Christ "a dwelling place of God in the Spirit" (Eph. 2:22). The apostle Paul gives this significant description of the Church in the context of the preaching of peace by Christ to Jew and Gentile alike and of the spiritual house in process of building whose foundation is the prophets and the apostles (Eph. 2:17-22). However, this new covenant is clearly specified as *a writing of the law!* It will be, therefore, a new form of law covenant (Jer. 31:33).[142] Second, *the New Covenant will consummate the Old.* This new covenant will belong to the administrative pattern of periodic covenant renewal and be inclusive of the promise of the establishment of an eternal, personal relationship of God to men (vss. 33, 36), based on forgiveness and experienced in fellowship (vss. 33b, 34bb). Former covenants could be and actually were broken by Israel (vs. 32) and have been made obsolete (Hebr. 8:73). The New Covenant, mediated by Christ and more excellent than the Old, would be enacted on better promises. The promise of God, "I will be their God and they shall be my people," (Jer. 31:33) connects this with the old (Gen. 17:7) and was made in the word of Jesus, "I am with you always." God refers to his great work as Creator (a feature prominent in the Universal Covenant as we have seen) to guarantee this, "If this fixed order [of the heavens and the laws established for the heavenly bodies in their creation] departs from before me, then shall the descendants of Israel cease from being a nation before me" (vss. 35, 36). If, then this new covenant abrogates as it consummates, this very discontinuity is expressive of its profound, organic unity with the Old Covenant.[143]

The writer of Hebrews (see chapter 8) relates this passage in Jeremiah to the completed work of Christ on earth and his continuing ministry from heaven. Jesus said that the New Covenant was in his blood, which was poured out for many (I Cor. 11:26; Jer. 31:34; Heb. 8:12). A disciple of Christ cannot drink of Christ's covenant without proclaiming the Lord's death (I Cor. 11:26). Covenant and proclamation are two ways of describing the same divine deed. The New Covenant, therefore, is the basis of the words of Jesus in Matt. 28:18-20. Just as the mission of Israel was made explicit in Israel's election and deliverance through the covenant at Sinai, so the task of the new people of God is appointed by Christ to his disciples and is for all nations. Through his enthronement they are told of their mission under his covenant. The crucified, risen Lord visited them and spoke as their King. His visits always mean vocation, commission.[144]

---

142 M. G. Kline, *By Oath Consigned*, p. 175, n. 25, notes in this connection the fact that Jesus is spoken of in the New Testament as a new and greater Moses, and refers to C. W. Davies, *The Setting of the Sermon on the Mount* (Cambridge: 1964), p. 25ff., and T. F. Glasson, *Moses in the Fourth Gospel* (Naperville: A. R. Allenson, 1963), to which I have not had access.

143 M. G. Kline, *By Oath Consigned*, p. 76.

144 Paul S. Minear, "The Covenant and the Great Commission," in Norman Goodall, *Missions Under the Cross*, pp. 64-80.

	GOD'S UNIVERSAL COVENANT		GOD'S COVENANT WITH ISRAEL		
	Genesis 12	Matthew 28	Genesis 15	Genesis 17	Exodus 20
PREAMBLE	The LORD (Yahweh) said	All power has been given unto me in heaven and on earth	Fear not . . . I am your Shield	I am God Almighty	I am the LORD (Yahweh) your God who brought you out of the land of Egypt
DEMAND	Go from your country and your kindred and your father's house . . . (Go) to the land that I will show you	When you go, make disciples of all nations . . . baptizing . . . teaching all that I have commanded you	He believed the LORD and he counted it to him as righteousness	Walk before me and be blameless	Thou shalt not . . . . Thou shalt . . .
PROMISE	I will make you a great nation . . . I will bless you . . . I will make your name great . . . I will bless/curse those who bless/curse you	I am with you always, to the end of the age	Your reward shall be great . . . To your descendants I will give this land	I will establish my covenant . . . to be a God to you and to your descendants . . . I will give to you the land of your sojournings	He (will) establish you as his people . . . He (will) be your God . . . (Deut. 29:13)

THE NEW UNIVERSAL COVENANT PROMULGATED BY JESUS CHRIST, GOD'S APOSTLE

	Matthew 28	Mark 16	Luke 24	John 20	Acts 1
PREAMBLE	All power has been given unto me in heaven and on earth (18)	(the testimony of the resurrection) (9)	It is written that the Christ should suffer and on the third day ese from the dead (46)	Peace be with you	He presented himself alive by many proofs... it is not for you to know times or seasons which the Father has fixed by his own authority (3, 7)
DEMAND	Go therefore and make disciples of all nations, baptizing them into the name of the Father, and of the Son, and of the Holy Spirit, teaching them to observe all that I have commanded you (19, 20)	Go into all the world and preach the Gospel to the whole creation (15)	Repentance and forgiveness of sins should be preached in his name to all nations, beginning in Jerusalem. You are witnesses of these things (47-48)	As the Father has sent me, so send I you (21)	You shall be my witnesses, in Jerusalem and in all Judea and Samaria and to the end of the earth (8)
PROMISE	Lo, I am with you always, to the end of the age (20)	These signs will accompany those who believe: in my name they will cast out demons; they will speak in new tongues; they will pick up serpents, and if they drink any deadly thing it will not hurt them; they will lay their hands on the sick and they will recover (18)	I send the promise of the Father upon you, but stay in the city until you are clothed with power from on high (49)	Receive the Holy Spirit (22)	You shall be baptized with the Holy Spirit (5)... You shall receive power when the Holy Spirit is come upon you (8)

2. *Commissioning of the Disciple Fellowship: Matthew 28:18-20*

With the enthronement of Christ and his announcement of it to the disciple group the redemptive program of God entered a new age. The promulgation of the new covenant for all nations revealed the new commission for God's Apostle. Whereas formerly he dwelt among men in the form of a servant, having been made like unto us in all things, he will henceforth reign as Lord of lords and King of kings. Peter proclaimed, "Let all the house of Israel know assuredly that God has made him both Lord and Christ, this Jesus whom you crucified" (Acts 2:36); "this Jesus God raised up . . . exalted at the right hand of God" (Acts 2:32,33).

The writer of the book of the Hebrews heralded similar glad tidings:

> Thou didst make him for a little while lower than the angels, thou hast crowned him with glory and honor, putting everything in subjection under his feet. Now in putting everything in subjection to him, he left nothing outside his control (Hebrews 2:7-8a).

This new assignment with full authority over all to be exercised until the end of the age is also a part of the apostleship of Jesus Christ and will have its end. Paul conveys this revelation in connection with the study of the resurrection of those who belong to Christ (who is himself the firstfruits),

> Then comes the end, when he delivers the kingdom to God the Father after destroying every rule and every authority and every power. For he must reign until he has put all his enemies under his feet. The last enemy to be destroyed is death. "For God has put all things in subjection under his feet." But when it says, "All things are put in subjection under him," it is plain that he is excepted who put all things under him. When all things are subject to him, then the Son himself will also be subject to him who put all things under him, that God may be everything to every one (I Cor. 15:24-28).

All this is in harmony with the meaning of apostleship. Authority is delegated to Christ from the central authority (i.e. by God the Father). It is exercised within the defined (unlimited in this case) boundaries set by God. It includes a time reference when the assignment terminates (the end of the age). There is a return of authority to the one who commissions at the end. The commissioned one during the assignment remains subject to the One who commissioned him.[145] The Apostle is able to enlist and assign others to his task, but the task

---

145 An interesting parallel to I Cor. 15:27 and the subjection in the present age of Jesus Christ to God who commissioned him can be found in the story of Joseph and his commission by Pharoah. "You shall be over my house, and all my people shall order themselves as you command; only as regards the throne will I be greater than you . . . . I am Pharoah, and without your consent no man shall lift up hand or foot in all the land of Egypt" (Gen 41:40, 44).

remains his. All is to be done to the glory of God the Father. There recurs here all that we have learned previously about apostleship. Seen in this light the commissioning of the disciple fellowship for the task of making disciples to himself [146] is the excercise of Jesus' sovereignty as Lord over God's Kingdom.[147] The throne-speech of the Enthroned Lord clearly defined his authority as given by God and exercised over the world and the redeemed community. He received this authority by delegation: "all authority *has been given* unto me." How must the throne-speech itself by which the new (universal) covenant was announced and the Kingdom program declared be understood?

PREAMBLE: "All power has been given unto me in heaven and on earth" (Matt. 28:18). "You shall receive power when the Holy Spirit has come upon you" (Acts 1:8).

The authority (ἐξουσία) which the formerly abased, humbled, crucified, but obedient Servant of God now exercises is nothing less than the authority of God himself. It is not the nature of authority to perform an action without any hindrances that is central to the thought, but the giver and the bearer of that authority. Christ's rule in harmony and free agreement with the Father is in the fore, and this presupposes responsible use of that authority to exercise a right over all things. It includes the right and power to give effect to God's will. Nothing will or can take place, even in a fallen world, which would compromise his authority or take place outside of it.[148]

This proposition is basic to the task of Christ. He is called upon to defeat all principalities and powers that are in rebellion against God. His authority and power must extend to all spheres and over all things, the world of men and angels as well as the natural realm. The Kingdom of God is everywhere opposed by the powers of evil. Vicedom has pointed out how great is the force of demonism in its struggle against God's King and Kingdom. He says,

> Everything can be demonized. The satanic element lies in this: the demonic power depends entirely on God and what he has created. It possesses nothing that does not come from God. Whatever is demonized and turned against God [sex, technology, power, nationalism, piety, e.g.] is always but a distorted image of the glory of God.[149]

146 J. L. Koole, *De Joden in de Verstrooiing*, p. 106.

147 H. Vogelstein, "The Development of the Apostolate in Judaism and its Transformation in Christianity," *HUCA*, II (1925), p. 115, comes very close to defining Christ's apostleship in relation to the commission of Matt. 28:18-20. His study is invaluable for a clear understanding of the meaning of this office.

148 Werner Foerster, ἐξουσία, in G. Kittel, *TWNT*, II, pp. 562-575; J. Blauw, *Missionary Nature*, p. 85.

149 G. F. Vicedom, *The Mission of God*, p. 18; Karl Heim, "Die Struktur des Heidentums," *EMM* (1939), p. 17. All sin is of this character. We must use the blessings God has given to us for good purposes to pervert them in our use to evil ends. The vineyard (Isaiah 5) brought forth worthless, rotten grapes by prostituting every good deed and purpose of the gardener.

God's people need not fear: "We are more than conquerors through him who loved us" (Rom. 8:37), the reality of which the NEB makes very explicit in its translation, "In spite of all, an overwhelming victory is ours through him who loved us."

Heaven and earth stand under the same Lordship of God, both as Creator (Col. 1:16; Eph. 1:10) and as covenant Lord (Matt. 11:25). They are the sphere of God's absolute dominon. No entity can possess autonomy, for only God is supreme. "All things" in heaven and earth are drawn into the work of reconciliation and peace. Heaven and earth are taken up into the saving event in Jesus Christ. All power has been placed in the hands of the risen Christ exclusively by the Resurrection. All thought of decay and destruction is excluded because the power of the Resurrection consisted in the overthrow of death (Acts 2:27).[150] The unity of the redemptive work and of the creative role of Christ are strongly emphasized in Colossians 1:13-20. A new interrelation of heaven and earth has been effected by God's saving action in Christ.[151] This triumph of the Resurrection becomes the heart of the Gospel proclamation (Rom. 1, e.g.).

There is no activity in which men engage which so impresses man with the sense of his personal helplessness than missionary work. In bringing the Gospel to the world the witness for Christ knows how utterly impossible it is for him to change the heart of a man. As soon as he begins his labor he immediately experiences the opposition of the forces of evil. Though this is humbling, neither is there any work in which we are supported by such overwhelming promises.[152] To feel this, recall his promises: "all power has been given to me .... I am with you always." Man counts but little in his own sight and right. The least of the apostles once reviewed his labors (in the light of the resurrection of Christ) and gave this testimony:

> By the grace of God I am what I am, and his grace toward me was not in vain. On the contrary, I worked harder ... though it was not I, but the grace of God which is with me (I Cor. 15:10) .... Let him who boasts, boast of the Lord (II Cor. 10:17).

The work and the message of the Christian mission may never be abstracted from either the activity or the authority of Christ. They are its only validation. J. H. Bavinck observed concerning this important concept,

> Missions claim the kingship of God over all of life. Jesus Christ is Lord of everything. The whole of life ought to be subject to the royal authority of

150 Peter in this passage applies to Christ the prophecy of Psalm 16:10 and takes this to mean that the victory of Christ over death was so complete that his body did not decay while in the tomb.

151 See Helmut Traub and Gerhard von Rad, οὐρανός, in G. Kittel, *TWNT*, V, pp. 497-536.

152 J. H. Bavinck, *The Impact of Christianity*, p. 41.

Him who has redeemed us by his precious blood .... God is King is the heart of our message. This means that all earthly powers, the power of ancestral morals, the power of fear of demons and sinister forces, the power of fleshly lust and human egotism are destroyed and God is worshiped as the only King, whose will ought to be only norm for our thinking and living.[153]

Blauw has pointed out that in all the Gospels the command of Christ is concerned with authority: Matthew emphasizes *royal* authority (28:18-20), Mark, *liberating* authority (16:15-18), Luke, *forgiving* authority (28:44-53); John emphasizes the continuity between Jesus and those sent (20:21).[154] It is considerations such as these which set the mood of our faith, as D. T. Niles wrote:

> Some months ago I stood inside the imposing temple to Meenatchy Amman at Madurai in India and as the bells tolled and as the worshippers prostrated themselves I found myself saying, "The kingdoms of this world are become the kingdoms of our Lord and of His Christ." In some such way the Christians of the early Church must have reacted as they faced the temples and the powers of the Greco-Roman world. That is the mood of our faith ... which says, "This is the banner under which we march" rather than "This is the opinion which we hold." [155]

DEMAND: "Go, therefore, and make disciples of all nations, baptizing them in the name of the Father, and of the Son, and of the Holy Spirit, teaching them to observe all that I have commanded you" (Matt. 28:19).

This instruction is the distinctive turning point, the great change of direction in the proclamation of salvation. All limitations previously in effect are removed. "All power ... everywhere ... all nations ... all that I have commanded" – it is impossible to conceive of anything more inclusive than this.[156] The Jewish proselyting efforts, significant movements in their own right, never reached these heights. Surely the Jews had gone everywhere in their dispersions, but the purposes for going were not to "make disciples." They had indeed practiced baptism, but it was not in the name of the Triune God. They had faithfully conveyed the Torah to men and brought them under the wings of the Shekinah, but they had never been able to preach an accomplished redemption or the fulfillment of the Law. Their message was reinforced by symbolic, typical ceremonies such as circumcision and sacrifice, not the accomplished reality. On the one hand the Christian church inherited a wonderful legacy from its past. On the other hand the Christian mission was radically "new" and different.[157]

---

153 J. H. Bavinck, *The Impact of Christianity*, p. 30.
154 J. Blauw, *Missionary Nature*, p. 88.
155 D. T. Niles, *Studies in Genesis*, p. 13.
156 J. Blauw, *Missionary Nature*, p. 85ff:, does in fact analyze Matthew 28:18-20 in terms of the four "alls" contained in this passage.
157 I cannot agree with A. H. Godbey, *The Lost Tribes*, p. 451, who says that "the

The mission carried on by Jesus' disciples included both Jew and Gentile. It included a relocation of the center of God's acts from Israel with Jerusalem and the Temple to the body of Christ.[158] When Christ said, "I am with you," he presented to the believing fellowship and to the world the locus of his presence on earth: his disciples. The full significance of this is seen in the fact that the Gospel begins with the prophecy "Immanuel, God with us" (Matt. 1:23) and ends with the promise of Christ with us (Matt. 28:20).[159]

It should be noted that the command of Jesus in Matt. 28:19 finds its center in "make disciples of all nations." Three participial clauses modify this main verb (μαθητεύω) used transitively here. These participial clauses are: (1) πορευθέντες (used also in Mark 16:15) = "having gone," in the sense of "when you go"; (2) βαπτίζοντες = "baptizing"; (3) διδάσκοντες = "teaching." They elaborate the command to make disciples; the disciples are to help other nations to become what they are, disciples of Jesus.[160]

There has been and still is current a popular misrepresentation of this command of Christ. The emphasis is placed on the going, whereas actually the emphasis is on the task of making disciples, for that is the primary verb. Even if one takes πορευθέντες in the sense of an imperative, this does not change the main verb or the central commission.[161] What is tragic about this wrong emphasis so frequently attributed to the command of Christ is that the entire demand is isolated from the whole witness of the Bible, and the *"going* into all the world"* becomes the fulfillment of what Christ demands. Obviously, not everyone can go into all the world, but each can start from where he is. Do we live in Jerusalem where Christ was rejected, or in Judea where he was crucified outside Jerusalem's walls, or in Samaria where he was not wanted, or in some uttermost part of the world where he is not known? There disciples must be made for him.

This verb πορεύομαι was frequently used by Jesus to describe his mission. Jesus' work was a movement toward his people, and when this verb is used in the New Testament to describe his journeyings, it emphasizes a certain divine

missionary activity of the early church was simply the missionary activity of the Judaism of the time in its personnel, its agencies, its technical terminology, its organization, in the communities to which it appealed and in the relations of those communities to the pagan world". See also J. Blauw, *Missionary Nature*, p. 63, for a balanced viewpoint of the relationship of the two missions; also p. 97ff.

158 J. Blauw, *Missionary Nature*, p. 98ff.

159 C. H. Dodd, *NTSt.*, p. 61.

160 K. Barth, *Church Dogmatics*, IV:iii.2, p. 860.

161 This is the sense that J. Blauw, *Missionary Nature*, p. 86, gives to the word, calling πορευθέντες a *"participium aoristi."* He says, "The fact that this *participium* is put first places the emphasis on going and travelling. One will have to pass Israel's boundaries consciously and intentionally in order to fulfill the order." It would appear more logical to say that the going is first simply because it temporally and logically precedes baptizing and teaching. It cannot take to itself the emphasis that belongs on the main verb.

necessity in his wanderings (δεῖ; Luke 13:33, 9:51). His wandering life is a renunciation of self for the sake of his own. In the metaphor of the shepherd Jesus showed how the shepherd both goes out and searches (πορευθεὶς ζητεῖ = Matt. 18:12) and also goes before the flock to protect and provide for it (John 10:4). This becomes a model for the disciples of Christ (Matt. 10:6), or as Hauck/Schultz say, "A technical term in the missionary command . . . The disciples go with the preaching of judgment of salvation to the whole world."[162] The command taken in this sense means that the disciples are to be apostles of God's Great Apostle, Jesus Christ, who not only came unto his own but whose coming was for a purpose, "to seek and to save the lost" (Luke 19:10). The going to the world must correspond to his assignment, for in his commission the disciple finds the path of his obedience. "As the Father has sent me, so send I you" (John 20:21).

Therefore, "make disciples of all nations" remains the center and heart of covenant obedience. By it the disciple displays that he lives under the Lordship of Jesus Christ, for the word πορεύομαι carries the connotation of going to a task or goal.[163] "Missions is the summons of the Lordship of Christ."[164] Behind this command to "make disciples" (μαθητεύω) there is the thought that one can become a disciple of Jesus only on the basis of a call that leads to discipleship. This is precisely how men were made disciples of Jesus in his day. The Gospels record that Jesus took the initiative and called men to himself.[165] It is Jesus who finally decides whether a man enters into discipleship. Therefore, he is the One who gives form and content to the relationship. His method of claiming Lordship over men was to call them to follow him.[166]

Andrew Young has written "An Everlasting Covenant" and in it he describes a conversation between Nicodemus and the disciple John as follows:[167]

Nicodemus: But tell me why! Why did you follow him?

John: I think it was our feet that followed him.
           It was our feet, our hearts were too afraid.
           Perhaps indeed it was not within our choice;
           He tells us that we have not chosen him
           But he has chosen us. I only know
           That as we followed him that day he called us,

162 See Friedrich Hauck and Siegfried Schulz, πορεύομαι, in G. Kittel, *TWNT*, VI, pp. 566-579, esp. p. 574.4, 5.

163 *Ibid.*, p. 573.

164 J. Blauw, *Missionary Nature*, p. 84.

165 Karl Heinrich Rengstorf, μανθάνω, μαθητής, *et al.*, in G. Kittel, *TWNT*, IV, pp. 390-461, shows that this is fundamentally different from the disciples of the rabbis to whom the pupil links himself and seeks out the teacher, and that everything depended on Jesus' Person, not his teaching. Faith is the controlling factor in the case of Jesus' disciples (p. 447). H. Vogelstein, *HUCA*, II (1925), 112.

166 J. W. Bowman, *The Intention of Jesus*, p. 156.

167 Quoted by D. T. Niles, *Studies in Genesis*, p. 107.

We were not walking on the earth at all;
It was another world ...

Nicodemus: Perhaps it was some miracle he did.

John: It was indeed; more miracles than one:
I was not blind, but he gave me sight;
I was not deaf, but he gave me hearing;
Nor was I dead, yet he raised me to life.

The Person of Jesus is central. Discipleship involved acceptance of his authority, inwardly by believing in him and outwardly by obeying him. There is a supremely personal union implied everywhere in the New Testament when the word μάθητης (disciple) is used.[168] There can be nothing in the life of the disciple that is apart from the Lord and his life. The disciple is drawn into fellowship with him with all they have and are. His call to discipleship cuts across every human consideration, for he challenges those (and who really is excepted?) who seem to have none of the necessary qualifications for disciple-ship: tax-collectors, open sinners, even Gentiles and the common rabble that knew not the Law. The disciple fellowship was not created because Jesus needed the disciples, but men and women needed him, and until he called them, they were not even aware of this need!

> The circle of disciples is really a microcosm of the Judaism of the times. In it we find all the powers and thoughts of the people, even their divergence. In its own way it thus bears witness to the fact that Jesus sought to do it service with a full realization of the relationships around him, and that this was a service to the people as it was, not as he imagined it to be. The calling of the disciples shows Jesus to be a sober realist. But is also shows him as the One who is ready obediently to bear all that may result when he comes to a people which, while it is conscious of its election, no longer perceives why it is called, and undertakes to tell this people afresh what is its obliga-tion to God.[169]

That is why discipleship is so fitting as a description of what Jesus desires to do for men. He wishes to bring men into the position of conscious relation to the will of God revealed in him. The personal attachment men acquire to him shapes the whole life of the man who obediently responds to the call. Under these conditions the Word develops his true and binding force because the disciple is committed to him who is himself completely committed to the will of the Father.

Mark uses the phrase "herald the Gospel" (16:15) as a parallel to "make disciples" because this is precisely the content of the "good news": Christ died for those who were enemies; in his blood men are brought nigh. When one

---

168   P. S. Minear, *Images*, pp. 145-148; K. H. Rengstorf, *TWNT*, IV, pp. 442, 445b.
169   *Ibid.*, p. 452.

responds to his personal call, "Follow me," he will have to say to men, "Follow him with me." There are no limitations, because race, nation, language, social position matter nothing before God. Jesus says, "Tell all nations that they must be my disciples." [170] This disciple fellowship has not been established for itself. It has been brought into existence for those who are yet outside of that fellowship. The believer's function in this world is the same as Christ's: he is called to confront men with the same demands of the Creator as those to which he himself responded by Christ's enabling grace. Vicedom states this very forcibly, "Because God wants missions to the heathen, we are the church. Otherwise we make ourselves lords of the Gospel and abuse the ministry of reconciliation." [171] The social patterns of the nations become new by the power of the Gospel.

The Gospel that is heralded is Christ. This proclamation takes place with full authority and power. Signs and wonders accompany the message (Mark 16). Joy reigns where this is proclaimed (Acts 8:8). What is spoken it not a word of man but the living, eternal Word of God. Hence, to evangelize men is to offer men salvation (I Pet. 1:23-25). Friedrich has shown that there was current in Jesus' day a Messianic expectation that was connected with the coming of Messiah's Kingdom and evangel which looked for the full manifestation of Yahweh as King. This message was for the Gentiles also, but it was first for the Jews and then for all men. [172]

Because through proclamation the divine intervention in men's lives takes place, true preaching it not just preaching about Christ. It is Christ preaching. He declares to men an event; through him the Kingdom of God comes. His word is efficacious because he speaks from God and the Spirit of God rests upon him. Jesus Christ did not bring a new doctrine that demanded intellectual acceptance. He brought a message that demanded faith. At the heart of the New Testament *kerygma* stands the Lordship of God. Preaching is not a lecture on the nature of his Kingdom. Men must repent (μετάνοια), not just because they are bad but because the Kingdom is at hand. Man must be changed

170   The position of Dennis Eric Nineham, *Studies in the Gospels: Essays in Memory of R. H. Lightfoot* (Oxford: Blackwell, 1955), "The Gentile Mission in Mark and Mark 13:9-11," pp. 145-146, is not acceptable. Citing first divergent opinions from ancient times to show the variant understanding of the words εἰς πάντα τα ἔθνη ("among all the people" or "unto all people"), he says, "If the Gospel were preached in all the synagogues of the Diaspora, the hearers would probably regard the prophecy as adequately fulfilled. There is, strictly speaking, no mention of preaching the Gospel to all nations."
171   G. F. Vicedom, *The Mission of God*, p. 82.
172   Gerhard Friedrich, εὐαγγέλιον and εὐαγγελίζομαι, in G. Kittel, *TWNT*, II, pp. 707-737; see esp. pp. 707, 715, 720, 725, 735. Karl Barth believed that the working of these miracles was declared to be obligatory; see Karl Barth, "Interpretation of Matthew 28:16-20" in Gerald H. Anderson, *The Theology of the Christian Mission* (New York: McGraw-Hill, 1965), p. 55ff. Herman Ridderbos, *The Coming of the Kingdom*, trans. by H. De Jongste (Philadelphia: Presbyterian and Reformed Publ. House, 1952), p. 373. J. C. Hoekendijk, *Kerk en Volk in de Duitse Zendingswetenschap*, p. 223ff.

because God is coming, his rule is near. Repentance creates the possibility of participation in God's great work and Kingdom. It is salvation history that must be heralded, and this proclamation is itself an event of salvation. The proclamation is the decisive action and through it the Kingdom of God comes. Those who enter are disciples, ready to live under the sovereignty of God and the terms of his covenant of salvation.[173] The connection between proclamation and commission is made very clear by the apostle Paul, who asked, "And how can men preach unless they are sent?" (Rom. 10:15). ἀποστέλλειν and κηρύσσειν are decisively united in the New Testament.

> A preacher is an agent of someone who is higher whose will he loudly and clearly makes known to the public. Without calling and sending preaching is a self-contradiction and even a deception. It holds out something that has no reality. If there is no sending, the preaching of Christ is propaganda, not mission.[174]

Three words are used in the Gospels to designate to whom and where the Gospel is to be preached. (1) Matthew says, πάντα τα ἔθνη (28:19) = "all the nations." This phrase, when used in the sense of the Gentiles, is often used with no sense of the plurality of the nations; that is, it is used non-sociologically. It designates, then, all the individuals who do not belong to the chosen people.[175] The significance of this designation is that the community of the Gentiles (together with the Jews) has taken over the place of Israel as the locus of the redemptive work of God. The church is now the "holy nation" (ἔθνος), God's own people (λάος) – I Pet. 2:9.[176]

> In regard to the world of nations this means that the church, in so far as she has taken the place of Israel, represents the salvation which has come in Christ, just as in the Old Testament Israel could in anticipation represent the salvation of the world. But the difference is that the church no longer anticipates; she remains a symbol of the hopes of the Kingdom in the fulness of the nations. *Missions* comes into view when this hope takes the form of proclamation on behalf of Christ.[177]

173 A very stirring and inspiring treatment of κηρύσσω is given by Gerhard Friedrich in G. Kittel, *TWNT*, III, pp. 683-696 (κῆρυξ) and pp. 697-714 (κηρύσσω); see especially pp. 710-712.

174 *Ibid.*, p. 713.7.

175 Karl Ludwig Schmidt, ἔθνος, in G. Kittel, *TWNT*, II, pp. 364-372. It is not necessary to go into detail on the distinctions between the Old Testament and New Testament terms. Those interested may consult Ronald Kenneth Orchard, *Out of Every Nation* (London: SCM Press, 1959), p. 48ff.; for a summary of various views see G. F. Vicedom, *The Mission of God*, p. 97ff., who criticizes the view of Hoekendijk that "all nations" means humanity without their national involvement. Daniel 7:14 certainly understands all peoples, nations as meaning all men, including the Jews; see E. Lohmeyer, *Das Evangelium Matthäus*, p. 417.

176 See J. Blauw, *Missionary Nature*, p. 130.

177 J. Blauw, *Missionary Nature*, p. 80.

But humanity is not viewed as "a world-wide census of individuals, but as the separate peoples that, taken together, comprise mankind as a whole. Each people maintains its discrete unity."[178] What Jesus had in mind was not nations in the sense of ethnic, social units. The word is obviously used in a religious sense, mankind in its separation from the Creator and Redeemer God.[179]

(2) Mark says (16:15) that the believing community must go εἰς τὸν κόσμον ἅπαντα ("into all the world") and must preach πάσῃ τῇ κτίσει ("to the whole creation"). The κόσμος (cosmos) specifies the inhabited world, the theatre of human life and history, oftentimes in the New Testament in the sense of salvation history as this works out in the fallen creation. In some passages the κόσμος is looked upon as the locus of revelation in Christ (I John 4:4). When the κόσμος is reconciled and redeemed in Christ, then it becomes the βασιλεία τοῦ Θεοῦ (the Kingdom of God).[180]

(3) The word κτίσις ("creation") has as its background the thought that Yahweh is the Creator of all things and that the world is absolutely dependent on him. As a creature man owes God obedience and the goal of his life has been appointed to him by the Creator. In the preaching of the Gospel the Creator confronts the creature with the purpose of his having been created. "This confrontation of Creator and creature . . . makes the creature a creature of will. To be a creature is to be willed, and to be willed is to be willed for a goal." God is creatively at work wherever his action is effective for man's salvation.[181]

No limitation is placed on the proclamation. The extensive character of the power and authority of Christ is exercised by him immediately as he claims the whole world and creation for himself as the sphere of his redemptive work and sovereignly sends his witnesses everywhere into that world. Wherever his disciples go, they go not only at his command but in his authority for there is nothing that does not belong to him. When they are instructed to teach men all that he has commanded, the intensive range of that authority over all life and over the whole man comes into view. In these thoughts lies the justification

178 P. S. Minear, *Images*, p. 69, and other references as found in the index regarding the people of God, etc. Also F. Hahn, *Mission in the New Testament*, p. 125.

179 German mission studies have been dominated for the past 100 years by the concept of τὰ ἔθνη. J. C. Hoekendijk, *Kerk en Volk in de Duitse Zendingswetenschap* (Utrecht: 1948), details this development. See also Gustav Warneck, *Evangelische Missionslehre* (2nd ed., Gotha, 1902), part III, p. 249ff. H. R. Boer, *Pentecost and the Missionary Witness of the Church*, pp. 160-164, also believes that τὰ ἔθνη must be thought of in a religious sense and fears that if the ethnic (anthropological) and not the soteriological sense is allowed to dominate, the soteriological elements "will be crowded into a corner and the Christian family threatened with the loss of its covenantal character and tend to be viewed as a Volk in microcosm", p. 164. See also R. K. Orchard, *Out of Every Nation*, p. 48ff., and G. Bertram, *Juden und Phönizier*, p. 50ff., both of whom hold that the concept "people" or "nation" has a religious significance.

180 Hermann Sasse, κόσμος, in G. Kittel, *TWNT*, III, pp. 867-898.

181 Werner Foerster, κτίσις, in G. Kittel, *TWNT*, III, pp. 1000-1035.

of the comprehensive approach in missions. There are no boundaries recognized by Christ to his sovereignty, and in the end all things in heaven and on earth will be subject to him. Therefore, the Christian may not think of his task primarily from the viewpoint of task, but he must think of it in terms of the existence of Christ's own in the world where it is his pleasure and will that they shall be. That is the area of their assignment and of his. It is not just heaven that belongs to them. "All things are yours . . . and you are Christ's; and Christ is God's," said the apostle Paul (I Cor. 3:21,23). The world and all its relationships come under the domain and the claim of Christ.

The participles "baptizing" and "teaching" describe the way by which disciples are made. The believers are commissioned to make disciples *by* baptizing men and putting them under instruction. Once the witness has been received and believed (reception by faith is implied in becoming a disciple), the recipient is brought under the promises and sanctions of the covenant through baptism and instruction.[182] Since the covenant is a declaration of God's Lordship, then the baptismal sign of entrance into it becomes a sign of coming under the jurisdiction of the covenant and particularly under the covenantal dominion of the Lord. Baptism is the sign of consecration and discipleship in the New Covenant. Its meaning is life, the new life, that has been made possible by their participation in the death and resurrection of Christ. Matthew 28:19 means consignment under the authority of Christ. In this passage baptizing the nations takes its place alongside of teaching them Christ's commandments, both of which are descriptive of the manner in which disciples are to be made.[183] An interesting and significant parallel can be found in John 4:1 where Jesus teaches the multitudes, making disciples and baptizing. In the New Testament the confession of Jesus as Lord is closely related to baptism.[184] Such confessions were closely related to baptismal liturgies in the early church.[185]

Further confirmation for the covenant basis of baptism can be found in the meaning of the phrase in/into the name of the Triune God, which from Old Testament analogies signifies an authority or ownership relationship.[186] Some examples from the rabbinic literature illustrating the meaning of the phrase "into the name" will help us to understand how this term was understood by the people of Jesus' day.[187]

(1) Heathen slaves were compelled to receive baptism on their entry into a

---

182 G. R. Beasley-Murray, *Baptism in the New Testament*, pp. 88-89, discusses this fully.

183 M. G. Kline, *By Oath Consigned*, p. 79.

184 Acts 2:38; 8:16; 19:5; Rom. 10:9; I Cor. 1:13; I Peter 3:21.

185 Vernon H. Neufeld, *The Earliest Christian Confessions* (Grand Rapids: Eerdmans, 1963), p. 6ff.

186 Deut. 28:9, 10; Isa. 63:19. The Aaronitic blessing in Num. 6:22-27 involved placing God's name on his people.

187 Strack-Billerbeck, *Kommentar*, I, p. 1054ff.; G. Beasley-Murray, *Baptism in the New Testament*, p. 90ff.

Jewish household and were to be baptized "in the name of slavery." Similarly, when they were set free they were to be immersed "in the name of freedom." Such baptisms set the man in the relationship which was in mind in its performance. The analogous thought in Christianity would be that being baptized in the name of the Father, the Son, and the Holy Spirit sets the one baptized in a definite relationship to God. The Father, Son, and Holy Spirit become to the baptized person what their names signified.

(2) Offerings were said to be made in the name of six things: in the name of the offering, the offerer, God, the altar fires, the sweet savor, and the good pleasure before God. This also defines the purpose one has in view. The offering in made with respect to its intention, for the benefit of the offerer, for the sake of God, with regard to the sacred fires (that they were properly kindled, e.g.), in view of the sweet savor, and for the delight it yields to God. From this point of view Christian baptism, if analogous, would take place for the sake of God, making the baptized person over to God.

(3) An Israelite might circumcise a Samaritan, but a Samaritan might not circumcise an Israelite because Samaritans circumcised "in the name of Mount Gerizim," i.e., with the obligation of venerating the God of the Samaritans who is worshiped there.

The above illustrations serve to enforce the meaning of Scripture that Christian baptism grounds a relation between the Triune God and the person baptized. The baptized person must affirm this through his confession to the God in whose name he is baptized. This is consistent with the Biblical usage where by giving someone a name, one establishes a relationship of dominion and possession toward him.[188] On the basis of I Cor. 6:11 the name of Jesus is seen to mean the whole content of the saving acts revealed in Jesus Christ. "In the name of the Lord Jesus Christ and in the Spirit of God" the Corinthians are washed, sanctified, and justified. In I John 5:13 those who believe are said to have life "in the name of the Son of God" (εἰς τὸ ὄνομα τοῦ υἱοῦ τοῦ Θεοῦ), that is, by entry into his sphere of action, His Person (John 20:31). Therefore, in Matt. 28:19 baptism into the name means that the subject of baptism, through fellowship with the Son who is one with the Father, receives forgiveness of sins and comes under the operation of the Holy Spirit.[189] Baird has pointed out that the theme of forgiveness is reserved in the teaching ministry of Jesus for the disciple audiences. Faith, forgiveness, healing and discipleship go together, and forgiveness is the mark of the true servant of the Kingdom of God.

---

188 Hans Bietenhard, ὄνομα, in G. Kittel, *TWNT*, V, pp. 242-281, esp. p. 253.

189 J. A. Baird, *Audience Criticism*, p. 120, para. 10. The logia to which Baird refers occur in all the sources. G. R. Beasley-Murray, *Baptism in the New Testament*, p. 80, says "that in all its forms the commission has to do either with baptism or with the remission of sins. These are but two forms of the same thing, for in the world of the New Testament ideas baptism and the remission of sins are inseparably associated."

The place where this change takes place for the believers is their baptism. Just as the Philippians, so they at baptism have

> ... renounced the old nature of Adam's likeness and received the new nature of Christ's image imprinted upon them. They confessed their allegiance to the new Man as Lord of all, as they invoked his name and passed into his kingdom. All that is involved in being "in Christ" (as by nature they were all "in Adam") is concentrated in the baptismal rite, with its imprinting of a new image and of a change of lordship.[190]

In the New Testament baptism is also represented as a seal in the sense of a mark of ownership or authority.[191] Believers will pass through very troubled times before the end of the age will come. This seal of union with Christ and ownership by him will be their hope and strength in that hour.[192] In this sense the participation in Christ's redemption and its benefits gives the believer security based on a divine oath and promise. God's people are sealed with a sign that marks them as God's own, assures them of salvation in the day of wrath and judgment, and protects them from divine condemnation and the powers of evil.[193] Paul says they have been "sealed for a day of redemption."

Baptism is an act of confession of Christ before the world and shows that the believer is willing to be joined to the Lord and separated from his previous life (or in the case of religion, from the old religious community). This is exactly the way a heathen community regards Christian baptism today. The heathen do not generally object to hearing the Word of God, and are quite ready many times to make room for Christ alongside their deities. But when one of their fellowship permits himself to be baptized, then the community becomes hostile. The reason is not hard to find because baptism is public recognition of the fact that there is another Lord whose commandments receive priority over everything else in the life of the believer. The community of the baptized appears dangerous to worldly government from this viewpoint. Vicedom observes that western Christians are often hesitant to recognize this external side of baptism as important.[194]

This must be taken seriously by the church in its prosecution of its witnessing task. The nature of the process by which one becomes a believer is easily forgotten. Christians are tempted to make themselves the norm for others, forgetting that the norm for the new life of the new-born disciple is determined

---

190   R. P. Marten, *Carmen Christi*, p. 293. See also O. Cullmann, *Baptism in the New Testament*, p. 50.

191   G. W. H. Lampe, *The Seal of the Spirit*, pp. 8-18; O. Cullmann, *Baptism in the New Testament*, p. 45. Lampe mentions branding and marking of cattle, slaves, prisoners, soldiers.

192   Eph. 1:13; 4:30; II Tim. 2:19; Rev. 7:2; 14:1; 22:4.

193   G. H. Lampe, *The Seal of the Spirit*, p. 16.

194   G. F. Vicedom, *The Mission of God*, pp. 126, 140.

by his new relationship to God, not by someone else's experience. The new-born disciple's obedience to Christ may be imperfect and insight will need to be given and received on many things, but the fundamental step was taken when Christ was accepted as his Lord. Baptism equips every believer with the gifts needed for the service of the Lord and with the same rights as well as obligations.

> By undergoing baptism the new converts come to belong to Christ; they are made his property, entered in the Name of the Messiah as members of his people; and through their participation in the Anointed they share in his anointing, the gift of the Holy Spirit, the sign that the Messianic age has already dawned.[195]

Moltmann says that "baptism is ahead of itself," by which he means that when men are baptized into the past death of Christ, they are sealed for the future that is being brought by the Risen Christ. It is only as an eschatological church that the baptizing Church has the right to perform the act of baptism, i.e., its title to this judicial and creative act derives from its openness towards that to which it is only on the way as yet. Christianity is to be understood as the community of those who on the ground of the resurrection of Christ wait for the Kingdom of God and whose life is determined by that expectation.[196] Baptism demarcates the congregation of the New Covenant. There was an Abraham at the head of the covenant community marked by circumcision. The Head of the new body is Christ who is confessed as its Lord. Therefore, in its mission the Church requires the confession of that Lordship before it administers the sign and seal of cove-nantal incorporation. This has primacy; it is not, however, exclusive. The person so baptized must live under Christ's authority. In his baptism he is "consigned by oath to the Lord of redemptive judgment," by active commitment and passive consecration.[197] Baptism is the sign which Christ places upon those who are incorporated into the life and work of his Church.

The second element involved in making disciples is teaching. The verb "to teach" (διδάσκειν), says Rengstorf, is a word "peculiarly fitted to express God's presenting His will to His people in order to subject them to this will and to fashion it accordingly."[198] This is characteristic of Jesus' ministry also. He constantly called for a decision from men either for or against the will of God. His goal was to bring the whole man in line with the purposes of God. In Matt. 28:19 Jesus makes the teaching of all that he has commanded a per-petual command for his Church. In being obedient to what he has commanded them, they become the agents to pass on that will and commandment to still others. Not the least of the implications of this is that the new disciples will be

---

195   O. Cullmann, *Baptism in the New Testament*, p. 52.
196   J. Moltmann, *Theology of Hope*, p. 326.
198   Karl Heinrich Rengstorf, διδάσκω, in G. Kittel, *TWNT*, II, pp. 135-148.
197   M. G. Kline, *By Oath Consigned*, p. 102.

taken into a similar task and an unbreakable chain formed to the end of the age. This includes not just proclamation concerning Jesus but proclamation of Christ.

The total dominion over the whole of creation must come to expression in a total dedication and submission to what Jesus commanded. One's obedience is determined by his relationship to Jesus Christ himself, not by conformity to an impersonal commandment.[199] Therefore, "all that I have commanded you" includes not merely the thought of the content of the proclamation but, what is more central, it refers to the total scope of one's obedience and commitment to the Lord of the covenant. Nothing in all life's relationships lies outside the area of subjection to him. It is as though Christ is saying through the witnesses in all ages, "You have been made the object of salvation; prove it now true that you know it."[200] There is a clearly defined unity with baptism in this, for in baptism it is not the convert's faith that is being sealed (i.e., guaranteed as genuine), but their actual persons, and they are "sealed with a view to a day of redemption," as Lampe so effectively shows.[201] The purpose for which the Lord of the covenant calls to his service is so that God's purposes may be accomplished through him and his people. His perfect love proves that he lays no heavier burden of obedience on them than what he had himself perfectly fulfilled. Because the will of the Sender is supreme, the mission to which he calls and appoints is spared every caprice and whim and human inclination. This is extremely important for the Christian mission because mission is not propaganda. Propaganda only serves to make others like ourselves. There has been much in proclamation such as the transmission of tradition and of culturally conditioned traits that have no bearing on the true disciple relationship. "Every man has a right to draw so near to Jesus Christ that he does not have to become a Westerner before he can understand him." The Lordship of Jesus Christ is established over the whole redeemed creation when his sovereign will is obeyed. Therefore we dare not "Christianize" people but we must "missionize" them, as Vicedom says, that is, "we must seek to bring them to the Lord so that their lives will be determined by him."[202] A missionary situation is created the moment a man professes Jesus Christ as Lord.

This is essentially what the Gospel meant to the Jews. Peter said, "Let all the house of Israel know assuredly that God has made him both Lord and Christ, this Jesus whom you crucified" (Acts 2:36). "If the Christian Church has no Gospel for the Jews, it has no Gospel for the world. The Gospel of the Lordship of Jesus Christ spells out God's love for the world."[203]

PROMISE. "Lo, I am with you always, to close of the age" (Matt. 28:20).

199 J. Blauw, *Missionary Nature*, p. 86.
200 O. Cullmann, *Baptism in the New Testament*, p. 49.
201 G. W. H. Lampe, *The Seal of the Spirit*, p. 8.
202 G. F. Vicedom, *The Mission of God*, p. 80.
203 J. Jocz, *Christians and Jews*, p. 48.

"Promise" in the Bible carries a specific connotation that differs from the common usage of the term. The general, everyday use of the term refers to the coming of a reality that does not yet exist and and sets the heart of a man on the future. This element is not lacking in divine promises, but there is more: the present circumstances are determined by what is possible to the God of promise. We do not have to wait for the development of the expected future out of the framework of the potentialities inherent in the present. History for the Christian is not just the movement toward future potentialities but is also a fulfillment in the present by the God of promise of what he has guaranteed. [204]

Looked at in this way the promise element in the universal covenant takes on a special significance.

> Christian eschatology, which seeks to span the inexhaustible future of Christ, examines the inner tendency of the resurrection event, asking what rightly can be and must be expected from the risen and exalted Lord. It enquires about the mission of Christ and the intention of God in raising him from the dead ... It is not that time brings his day and it is not that history proves him right, but he guides time to his day.[205]

History may not be viewed as though it were merely the unfolding of a divine plan for the ages. History in the Biblical sense is the consciousness of a divine commission in this present age when men are confronted with the peculiar tensions created by their confrontation with the Lordship of Christ. Will man obey or continue in disobedience? Will he believe or continue in rebellion?

The words of Jesus, "I am with you always," are in exact correspondence with his own commission and that which he gave his disciples. He did not mean to say merely that the work of mission will continue under his authority to the end of the age. He rather promised to be the fulfiller of the covenant, his disciples working with him rather than he working with his disciples. He would direct all things and exercise all power to the consummation of the age. Therefore, discipleship does not mean obedience to his command to preach, baptize, and instruct all nations. It means orientation of the whole life of the believer to the goal of Christ's own commission. The temporal and geographical components of mission (end of the age, ends of the world), as Blauw calls them,[206] are subsumed under the promise and goal.

The promise "I am with you always" is really quite astounding. It is another illustration of Jesus' applying to himself the divine prerogatives. In Hag. 1:13 we read, "I am with you, says the LORD." The promise of the divine presence (and identification with his people) is a keynote in the Old Testament revelation and finds its most striking, symbolic expression when Israel is called the

204 For a discussion of the nature of promise see J. Moltmann, *Theology of Hope,* p. 102ff.

205 *Ibid.,* p. 194.

206 J. Blauw, *Missionary Nature,* p. 110.

"apple of God's eye" (Deut. 32:10; Ps. 17:8).[207] Much attention has been given to the phrases "I am," "I am he," etc. as used by Jesus.[208] Jesus deliberately used these expressions of divine self-revelation in the boldest declarations concerning himself, for he means to say by them, "Where I am, there God lives and speaks, calls, asks, acts, decides, loves, chooses, forgives, rejects, suffers and dies."[209] The rabbis understood this phrase in this way, for in the Hagaddah exposition of Deuteronomy 26:5ff. regarding the Passover, the words "I am" are used to denote the personal presence of the redeeming God on that occasion.[210] Conscious of his unity with the Father and aware that the world would hate and persecute his people just as it hated and put him to death, Jesus promises to fulfill this covenant by his own act and presence. When at the end of the age evil men will wax worse and worse, when anti-Christ will set himself up in the temple of God, then in the darkest hour the Church can triumphantly say, "He is with us!" – in Jerusalem, Judea, Samaria, the uttermost part of the world. The promise means more than divine presence; it means the divine activity.

3. The Baptism by Christ

The universal covenant had been announced. The basis on which it was founded was laid in the death and resurrection of Jesus. The Mediator of the New Covenant had ascended into heaven, far above all principalities and power, to rule until all things are put his feet. A community of disciples has been commissioned to work with Him. That community needed only the qualification for its task.

"He who is coming . . . will baptize you with the Holy Spirit and with fire," John had said (Matt. 3:11). Jesus had promised, The Father will send the Holy Spirit in my name" (John 14:26), and, "Before many days you will be baptized with the Holy Spirit . . . and you will receive power after the Holy Spirit has come upon you" (Acts 1:5,8). What was this baptism with the Holy Spirit and what did it mean?

Recall that Jesus in his ministry did not baptize, though John had clearly related the work of Christ to baptism. He permitted his disciples to baptize for a very short while, a baptism which we have earlier paralleled with John's baptism (John 4:2). It may legitimately be presumed that at least some of Jesus' disciples

---

207 The apple of the eye is 'ishon (אישון), the "little man" of the eye; i.e. the pupil. One sees God's people reflected in his eyes, for his eyes are focused on them as the object of his love and care.

208 See e.g., Ethelbert Stauffer, *Jesus and His Story* (New York: Alfred A. Knopf, 1960), pp. 174-198; D. Daube, *The New Testament and Rabbinic Judaism*, p. 325ff.

209 E. Stauffer, *Jesus and His Story*, p. 194.

210 D. Daube, *The New Testament and Rabbinic Judaism*, p. 325.

had received the baptism of John, having previously been John's disciples. However, the baptism of John did not suffice as a substitute for Christian baptism, for in Acts 19:1-7 a group of disciples who knew only John's baptism were baptized in the name of the Lord Jesus, receiving at that time the Holy Spirit. The crucial question which determined the procedure concerned the reception of the gift of the Spirit: "Did you receive the Holy Spirit when you believed?"

The significance of the outpouring of the Holy Spirit on the disciple fellowship is that the pouring out of the Spirit is the baptism of that fellowship by Jesus. Nowhere is it stated that this nucleus of believing followers received Christian baptism with water. They did not need to receive it. They experienced the full reality when Christ himself baptized them with fire and the Spirit at Pentecost. They did not need to receive the symbolization. Significantly, in every New Testament passage where the gift of the Holy Spirit comes to men, this is always related with water baptism in the name of Jesus or in connection with the profession of faith in him.[211] Paul is the only apostle of whom it is reported that he was baptized with water (Acts 9:18), at which time Ananias told him that God had sent him to Paul so that Paul might be filled with the Holy Spirit (Acts 9:17). The Holy Spirit is the bond that unites the ascended Lord to his followers and the agent through which they become his members.[212] Those who were baptized with fire and the Spirit on Pentecost emerged from this baptism by Christ vindicated as the people of the new covenant. The redemptive, universal covenant was inaugurated by the ascended Lord of that covenant. Those who were baptized by the Spirit-baptized apostles were likewise vindicated as the redeemed community for they also shared in the forgiveness of sins and the gift of the Holy Spirit as well (Acts 2:38). Peter's address calls specific attention to this fulfillment of the universal promise, "It shall be that whoever calls on the name of the Lord shall be saved" (Acts 2:21). This Gospel was for the Jews first, and therefore the challenge had to be presented to them: "Let all the house of Israel know assuredly."

In the previous consideration of the baptism of Jesus by John one element was purposely omitted in order to give attention to it in this connection. In defining the meaning for Jesus of the baptism of John in the Jordan, it was noted this was according to the word of Jesus "a fulfilling of all righteousness." In being baptized by John Jesus accepted the penalty of broken covenant in place of his people. No attention was given at that time to an equally important and significant part of the entire episode, namely that there was in a sense a dual baptism administered that day, both of which are related to (although they are seemingly related only in a temporal sense) but quite distinct from each other. The one baptism was administered by John; the other was a baptism of the Son by the Father. The ritual of the first involved the prophetic voice of a commissioned servant and forerunner, John, through

211   Acts 2:36; 5:32; 8:16-18; 9:17; 10:44-48; 19:5, 6.
212   I John 3:24; 4:13. See also O. Cullmann, *Baptism in the New Testament*, p. 51.

whom the coming of the Lamb of God to take away the sins of the world was announced to the community; the second involved the testimony of the Father, "This is my beloved Son." The one was a baptism with water; the other a baptism with the Spirit. The first took place in the swift-flowing waters of the Jordan; the second took place on the shore after Jesus had come out of the water (Matt. 3:16). John's baptism involved some sort of word spoken by men as they were baptized, but no human voice sounded in the baptism with the Spirit.[213]

This was the Servant's commissioning, his inauguration as God's Apostle. The witness of the Father and the gift of the Spirit testify that the judgment which Christ took upon himself to fulfill was not for himself but for others. God said, "My Son, in whom I am well pleased." "He had done no violence, and there was no deceit in his mouth ... yet ... he was numbered with the transgressors and he bore the sins of many" (Isa. 53). It is a misreading of the narrative to say it was through John's baptism that the Spirit was given to Jesus, the Christ. The two baptisms (with water and with the Spirit) were coterminous, but they remain quite distinct. The Spirit was given to Christ after he had placed himself under the sanctions of the covenant which his people had broken. He was led by that Spirit, and everything he did, said, and wherever he went was through the Spirit. Significantly, the narrative illustrates the control of the Spirit and his qualifying gift when we were told (immediately after the testimony concerning his baptism) that the Spirit drove him into the wilderness to be tempted by Satan (Matt. 4:1). He said to his fellow citizens in Nazareth not many weeks later, "The Spirit of the Lord is upon me because he has anointed me to preach ...." (Luke 4:18).

This does not mean that the two incidents, though distinct, are unrelated. There is a close connection between Jesus' reception of John's baptism and the baptism with the Spirit. He was declared to be the Son of God with power (Rom. 1:4); he accepted his appointment to be the Obedient Servant, the Lamb of God; the qualifying Spirit was given to him for the task that lay ahead of him. Only when he had through the symbolic curse of the water ordeal placed himself within the covenant context could he receive the Spirit for his work. From now on "God is encountered where He Himself confronts the community, that is, in the Son, or, for the individual, in the Spirit in whom this encounter with the Son takes place."[214] The visible manifestation of the Spirit, the audible accreditation by God the Father, and the fact that this took place at the public announcement of the Messiah (with whom the Rabbis connected the endowment of the Spirit) all stamp this incident as the beginning of the new

---

213   See Mark 1:5, "They were baptized by John in the Jordan river *while they were confessing their sins*" (I have tried to convey what I believe is the meaning of the Greek text by this translation).

214   See πνεῦμα, article by Kleinknecht, Baumgartel, Bieder, Sjoberg, and Schweizer, in G. Kittel, *TWNT*, I, pp. 332-455, esp. p. 401.

age of God. Otto Procksch[215] says that it is the baptism of Jesus which marks the beginning of the new age of the Spirit in the full sense. The Spirit was obviously not yet poured out on believers, although on one occasion before Pentecost Jesus did say to the disciples, "Receive the Spirit."[216] Until Pentecost the Spirit is linked exclusively with Christ. His words clearly indicate that his possession of the Spirit and the pouring out of the Spirit by him were made possible by the gift of the Spirit to him by his Father.[217]

If these considerations are kept clearly in mind some otherwise vexing questions cease troubling. For one thing, an important aspect of the significance of Pentecost is that through the Holy Spirit the ascended Lord is inseparably united to his followers and it is the Spirit who accomplishes this.[218] John wrote, "By this we know that he abides in us, by the Spirit which he has given us" (I John 3:24); also, "By this we know that we abide in him and he in us, because he has given us of his own Spirit" (I John 4:13). The Spirit who comes upon converts to the faith is the same Spirit which descended on Jesus at his baptism and with which he was anointed.[219] In the controversies within the apostolic church regarding the reception of the Gentiles the confirming evidence that Gentiles share in the fulness of the salvation in Christ was found in the fact that when they were baptized they shared in the gift of the Holy Spirit. As a rule, baptism in the name of the Lord Jesus confers the Spirit. The account of Acts 10:44-48 shows that baptism may follow the gift of the Spirit, but baptism was still necessary. This is a record of an extraordinary event in that God was demonstrating through Cornelius that nothing God has cleansed may any longer be rejected. Peter defended his action of baptizing Cornelius and his household in this remarkably clear expression.

> As I began to speak, the Holy Spirit fell on them *just as on us at the beginning.* And I remembered the word of the Lord, how he said, "John baptized with water, but *you shall be baptized with the Holy Spirit.*" If then God gave *the same gift* to them as he gave to us when we believed on the Lord Jesus Christ, who was I to withstand God? (Acts 11:15-17).

The Jerusalem Church drew the same conclusion as Peter, "Then to the Gentiles also God has granted repentance unto life" (Acts 11:18). The reference to the Spirit, baptism, repentance, and life in this short narrative conclusively demonstrates that the Church regarded this as a complete sharing in the fulness

215 *Ibid.*, p. 401; Otto Procksch, ἅγιος, in G. Kittel, *TWNT*, I, pp. 88-114, esp. pp. 103-104.

216 See John 20:22.

217 See Acts 2:33 where the granting of the Spirit to men is made possible by God's act of fulfilling the promise of the Spirit to the Son. Jesus can be said to have *possessed* the Spirit in fulness during His lifetime and to *dispense* the Spirit to the community after the resurrection (Luke 24:49). See πνεῦμα article in *TWNT* cited above, p. 405.

218 O. Cullmann, *Baptism in the New Testament*, p. 51; G. W. H. Lampe, *The Seal of the Spirit*, p. 51.

of salvation by Jew and Gentile. The result of the controversy was that it settled once for all the basic question whether Gentiles became Christians by way of Judaism. Such questions as circumcision and the Gentiles' relationship to the keeping of the Law would arise in a later context (see Acts 15 and the Council of Jerusalem), and the apostle Paul would have continuing difficulties with persons who were of the party of the concision; nevertheless, the direction of the Christian mission was definitively set by God in the home of a Roman centurion, and Jesus Christ brought the first of the Gentile families into the redeemed fellowship when he gave his Spirit to a Roman.[220]

The accomplished work of Christ is the ground and foundation of Christian baptism. By baptism men are made to participate in the death and resurrection of Christ, share in the Spirit with whom Christ equips his people, and become members of the redeemed covenant community. The completion of the work the Father had sent him to do made it possible for believers to be baptized in his name and in the name of the Spirit. The baptism by which men are baptized and made partakers of Christ and his commission corresponds in many respects to that baptism which the Lord himself received. Just as there were two aspects to his baptism(s) [death and resurrection, and the bestowing of the Spirit], so our baptism involves participation in his finished work and commission to apostleship today. The Christian who has sacramentally died and risen with Christ to the new life in the Spirit is anointed in the Messiah upon whom the unction of the Spirit came. The baptism of the Christian is the mark of his incorporation into the body of Christ and of his participation in the baptism and anointing of Christ. The disciples proclaim to the world that this participation can be theirs in the same way as it has become theirs: repentance towards God and faith in Jesus Christ.

It is in this way and in this way alone that Judaism finds its fulfillment. All the prophets and Moses testified that the Christ had to suffer and enter into his glory (Luke 24:26). When the Jew is baptized into Christ he does not reject the election and calling of Israel. Instead, this election finds its end in the obedience to the sovereign Lord of the New Covenant, and he finds himself through grace made a member of the new people of God, the new humanity.

---

219   See Acts 10:38 where the temporal sequence in the summary of Jesus' life goes this way: baptism by John – anointing of Jesus by the Spirit – ministry of Jesus – death – resurrection, etc. See also Acts 10:44; 1:8; 4:27.

220   G. R. Beasley-Murray, *Baptism in the New Testament*, p. 85; F. V. Filson, *Three Crucial Decades*, p. 118. The antagonism of the Jews to Paul continues into our present day. Samuel Sandmel, *We Jews and Jesus* (New York: Oxford University Press, 1965), p. 79, expresses this as follows:

> "A man named Saul,
> Later called Paul,
> Came and spoiled it all."

In his book, *Christ Finds a Rabbi*, George Benedict wrote:

> What has Christ done for you that you are willing to turn your back on
> Judaism and your face to Christianity? I will tell you. But first, please notice,
> that I have *not* turned my back on Judaism. On the contrary, I am carrying
> Judaism forward with me. I cannot turn my back on my mother, but I can
> give her my arm to help her walk with me while my life lasts.[1]

In this unique way the author sums up his relationship to the community of
Israel into which he was born and the new covenant community into which he
was re-born by the grace of Christ. His experience is from a certain viewpoint
an illustration of what God accomplished in the gathering together under one
head, Jesus Christ, both Jew and Gentile. There was a great re-grouping of
mankind in the presence of Christ in whom God calls us to meet him. Christ
has taken the place of the city Jerusalem, but the situation is still the same: it
matters not whether this be the Jerusalem here on earth (as in the Old Testament) or the Jerusalem that is above where Christ is at God's right hand. God
is eager that men should come to him where he is. And he is present through
Christ in the body called the Church. This gathering of mankind through the
mediation of his people constitutes the heart of the Church's commission. God
converts the nations by working in the midst of his people.

> The Church does its work of evangelization in the measure in which its Lord
> gives it life; when it lives by him its very existence is effectual. In contra-
> distinction to what has sometimes been believed, mission has nothing in
> common with any sort of political or commercial enterprise; it is entirely
> dependent on the hidden activity of God within his Church, and is the fruit
> of a life really rooted in God.[2]

What is the character, the nature of this new people of God? What does God
intend to do for mankind through the redeemed community commissioned by
the universe's sovereign Lord? How must this commission be conceived of

---

1 George Benedict, *Christ Finds a Rabbi* (Philadelphia: Bethlehem Presbyterian
Church, 1932), p. 263.
2 R. Martin-Achard, *A Light to the Nations*, p. 79.

today? The redeemed community's relation to the world (which is the field of its labors in Christ and the arena in which disciples are to be made) has not been defined. The baptism of believers is the sign which Christ through his Church places upon his disciples and by which they are ordained to do his work in this world.[3]

A. *The New People of God*

Any consideration of the nature of the new People of God and its constitution must take account of the bond that exists between Israel and the Christian Church. Attention also needs to be given to the social dimensions of the perfect work of God whereby all tensions and contrasts have been resolved and all have been made one in Jesus Christ. Finally, it is necessary to ask whether the definitions of the People of God under which the Church has been operating since the times of the Reformation are still serviceable today, and if they are found to be inadequate, how they must be re-defined in order to set the commission from Christ in its proper focus for today? For in the great and inscrutable wisdom of the sovereign Lord his people have come into his Kingdom for *this* time and age.

1. *Israel and the Church*

The establishment of a fellowship of disciples drawn from all peoples, Jews as well as Gentiles, involved in the redemptive work of Christ meant that the insiders and outsiders of God's house now stand in a unique relationship to each other. Since it was made very clear in the Apostolic Church that Gentiles did not become Christians via Judaism, the creation of this fellowship required a re-definition of Israel's relation to God and of the Gentiles' access to Him. At the same time, the relationship Israel has to the Gentiles had be defined anew.

The New Testament epistles give consideration to this new phenomenon. Whereas in the Old Testament the nations of the world are often described from the viewpoint of their hostility and enmity to God and his people, this note is almost entirely lacking in the New Testament. Instead, enmity and opposition to the Church are from the time of the establishment of the Church set in the focus of Old Testament prophecies that would seem to refer only to the Gentiles. The disciple fellowship rejoiced over the release of Peter and

3 Increasing attention has been given in late years to baptism as an ordination. Foremost among those who place this significance on baptism is Markus Barth, *The Broken Wall*, p. 186. See also George W. Webber, *The Congregation in Witness* (New York and Nashville: Abingdon Press, 1964), p. 101.

John, quoted Psalm 2:1 in explanation of the rage of the enemies, but included in the list of those who "were gathered together against the Lord and against his anointed" not only Herod and Pilate with the Gentiles but also *the peoples of Israel* (Acts 4:25-27)!

Perhaps the clearest expressions of the new relationships that obtain in Christ between Jew and Gentile are found in Paul's writings.

> Remember, that you [Gentile Christians] were at that time separated from the Commonwealth [πολιτείας] of Israel, and strangers [ξένοι] to the covenants of promise, having no hope, and without God in this world. But now in Christ you [Gentile Christians] who once were far off have been brought near in the blood of Christ. For he is our peace, who has made us [Jews and Gentiles] both one, and has broken down *the dividing wall of hostility*, by abolishing in his flesh the law of commandments and ordinances, that he might create in himself *one new man* in place of the two, so *making peace*, and might reconcile us both to God in one body through the cross, thereby *bringing the hostility to an end*. And he came and preached peace to you who were far off and peace to those who were near; for through him *we both have access in one Spirit* to the Father. So then you are no longer strangers [ξένοι] and sojourners [πάροικοι], but you are fellow citizens [συμπολῖται] with the saints and members [οἰκεῖοι] of the household of God (Eph. 2:12-19; italics and bracket insertions are mine).

Paul describes "the mystery that was hid in Christ," not made known to other generations but now revealed by the Spirit, as being this:

> ... the Gentiles are fellow heirs, members of the same body, and partakers of the promise in Christ Jesus through the gospel (Eph. 3:4-6).

The great mystery which Christ has revealed is the fellow-citizenship of Gentiles with Israel. He was saying here what must have seemed incredible to Jewish ears: he told Jew and Gentile alike that the center of God's acts has been re-located from Israel to a new people created in Christ from both Jews and Gentiles.[4] He makes very clear in Romans 4 that the line of descent runs from Abraham via Christ to the world of Gentiles, and Abraham is himself the prototype of the Gentile Christians.

Salvation has meaning, therefore only if it is all-inclusive and embraces all mankind. God is sovereign over all and established his universal covenant with mankind, announcing this through Abraham and fulfilling it in Christ. The unity of Israel and the Gentiles belongs to the very signs of Messianic fulfill-

---

4 We must be careful in our statement of this proposition so that we do not lose sight of the continuing place of the Jews in God's purpose. To say God has relocated his work among the Gentiles, as Johannes Blauw has done (see his *Missionary Nature*, p. 98), must be taken to include Israel or it is only partially true. (For Paul's emphasis see Gal. 3:8, 26-28; Rom. 3:29-30, 4:11-13, 18; 10:4-21; 15:8-13).

ment. Whether one considers the Old Testament viewpoint of the nations versus Israel or the New Testament viewpoint of the nations (including unbelieving Israel) versus the Church, humanity displays its most visible brokeness at the point of its separation from God's people. The coming of Christ and the re-constitution of the People of God in the mission to the nations was the great and decisive turning point of Israel's destiny as the People of God.[5] The whole argument of Paul in the letter to the Ephesians turns on this one significant truth: Jesus is not really the Messiah if Jews and Gentiles remain separate.

It is to be deeply regretted that the emphasis in Christian missions has shifted so very far away from the sense of duty and responsibility to the Jews. While propaganda for the conduct of Christian mission emphasizes "the uttermost part of the earth," it frequently neglects "Jerusalem and Judea." Perhaps modern theology of mission has developed a blind spot here as a result of failure to appreciate the new relationships that obtain in Christ.[6]

It must be remembered that according to the Scriptures Israel is the apple of God's and mankind's eyes. God keeps his people as the apple of his eye (Gen. 32:10). The man who touches them is a fool who "touches the apple of his eye" (Zech. 2:8). In no place in Scripture is this unique position of Israel abrogated by God. Even though the Jew may have rejected God's salvation, "God has not rejected his people!" (Rom. 11:1). Even though "hardening has come upon part of Israel, until the full number of the Gentiles come in" (Rom. 11:25), there is a future time coming when it will be said, "All Israel is saved" (vs. 26). The Gentiles may never forget that they were grafted in, they who were once wild olive shoots, to share the richness of the olive tree whose Root supports them (Rom. 11:17-21). Those who believe in Christ cannot have peace with God and with each other unless they have peace with Israel and approach God together with Israel (Eph. 2:16-22).[7] They may not proudly think that

5   See J. Jocz, *Christians and Jews*, pp. 44-45.

6   Unfortunately some leading scholars have not helped the Church to return to a balanced, full-orbed theology of Jewish missions. R. Niebuhr evoked quite a controversy when he declared that the cross and the resurrection need not necessarily be the only condition of an approach to God (see "Christianity Today", 8 Dec. 1958; also J. Jocz, *Christians and Jews*, p. 9). Even Markus Barth, who has done such great service in defining Israel's distinctiveness, gives an unsatisfactory description of the nature of missions to the Jews in *Israel and the Church* (Richmond: John Knox Press, 1969), esp. pp. 105-117. Additionally, one need only review the curriculum and courses of our theological seminaries to note the lack of concern for the Jews.

7   In the present day this question is receiving considerable attention, especially among the Christians of Europe. The return of the Jews to Palestine, the establishment of the state of Israeli, the Six Days War, Arab-Jewish relations and the resulting polarity among the world of nations are forcing the church to re-examine the issues involved. A few significant discussions on this subject are: *Kerk en Israel Onderweg*, (n.p.; n.d.), articles reprinted from *De Heerbaan*, 22 (1970), pp. 65-192; *The Conflict in the Middle East and Religious Faith*, the report of the Middle East Advisory Committee of the British Council of Churches (April, 1970); Generale Synode der Nederlandse Hervormde Kerk, *Israël: volk, land en staat* ('s Gravenhage: Boekencentrum N.V., 1970). Even a brief

God did not have a people until he saved them, repeating the error of Job's friends (Job 12:2). Though his house was not full, there was a household of God at all times and we entered by sovereign grace (Luke 14:22-23). In Eph. 2:1-10 Paul specifically mentions that Jew and Gentile (notice his use of the words "we" and "us") needed the rich mercy and love of God in order to be saved. God has always been loving and merciful; he did not become this when for the first time the rooms of the Father's house welcomed in feasting and banqueting prodigal Gentiles who had squandered all their treasures in riotous living. What is so important to observe is that everyone who is saved is redeemed in no other way than by the One God whose will and plan for man is the same for all in all ages.

The passing of 1900 years has not changed the situation one bit. If Ephesians became near when God abolished the wall of enmity, nothing less has happened today. The members of Christ's body are also "no-more-strangers" and "no-more-sojourners" only because God has made them members of the household that once was Israel.

> To belong to the household of God means to live in brotherhood and fellow-citizenship with these Jews who unwittingly bear testimony to the true nature of God and man. Only "in Christ" do we come to see and appreciate why we live in such close solidarity with the Jews. And only "in Christ" do we discover that our solidarity with the Jew is proof of any serious concept of brotherhood. The privilege and the tension of solidarity with Israel test the depth of our brotherly emotions, words, and deeds. No Christian ethics can by-pass this solidarity with Israel.[8]

The growth of the Christian Church takes place only where the real nature of the structure of the Church is taken seriously, where the whole of the Body of Christ is "joined and united together" (Eph. 2:21) and "grows into a holy temple in the Lord." Barth observes that the word "together" occurs nowhere so frequently or in such daring combinations as in the Greek text of Ephesians, and points out that it always describes community of the Church with Israel, also when resurrection and enthronement with Christ are explicitly mentioned.[9]

God's universal covenant was and is with *all* men. This cannot be properly understood unless it is borne in mind that God and his purpose are first in covenant action; only then does a people emerge as the manifestation of his

review of these recent publications demonstrates both the crying need for theological understanding of the question of Israel and the nations, as well as the lack of clarity and unanimity among the Christian churches on the questions raised by today's events. See *Kosmos & oecumene*, IV (10/11), pp. 313-322, "Heilshistorische betekenis van Israel" by B. van Iersel, and pp. 323-329, "De kerken en het joodse volk" by F. Stein. See also M. Barth, "Jesus, Paulus und die Juden", *Theologische Studien*, Heft 91 (Zürich: EVZ-Verlag, 1967); *The Broken Wall*, p. 126.

8 *Ibid.*, p. 129.

9 *Ibid.*, p. 131.

purpose. God creates this society of his people by his sovereign choice. The believing fellowship is his people only because he dwells within them and moves among them.[10] This means that any definition of this people must come from God whose sovereign grace and mercy makes them his people. Paul Minear observes that the galaxy of images that oscillate in the New Testament around the concept "people of God" served in a distinctive way to place the New Testament Church in the setting of the long story of God's dealings with his chosen people. In doing so an enduring solidarity with Israel was asserted. The early Christians did not date the beginnings of a "people of God" from any other point than the covenant activities of God with Abraham and with Israel at Sinai. Among the names that belonged peculiarly to the Old Testament People of God and their history and which were adopted in the New Testament for the Church, he lists the following: Israel, a chosen race, a holy nation, the twelve tribes, the patriarchs, the true circumcision, Abraham's sons, exodus, David's house and kingdom, remnant, the elect.[11] In every case the community's existence, like that of Israel of the Old Testament, is qualified in its creation by God's call and promise. These designations link the New Testament community intimately and inseparably to the whole course of Israel's history and emphasize the truly frightening alternative of being outside rather than within the household God has created. It is in Paul's letter to the Ephesians (note especially 1:3-10) that we see most clearly the relationship of God's creation, covenant, election, faithfulness to the fathers and his redemptive purpose in Christ to unite all things, in heaven and earth in him.

The importance of this for the Church today can be seen in the fact that the designations which the believing community used to identify itself were of a kind that delineated its responsibilities to the electing, covenanting God's purposes. The Church of Christ does not define itself in terms of the world in which it lives. It finds its definitions in the purposes of God for it. This makes a great difference in the way in which we conceive of the place and task of the Church in the world is thought of. The Church is a messianic community ("I am with you") belonging to and dwelling in (discipled, baptized, taught) its living Lord whose sovereign rule marks the beginning and the end of the new age in which it was created to live to his glory and service.

Unfortunately and tragically Church and Synagogue have faced each other in uneasy tension for centuries. The earliest tensions between emerging Church and Judaism arose within the Synagogue.[12] This encounter has often taken the form of hostility whose origin has not always been from the side of the Jews. The

10 Ex. 19:5; Deut. 7:6; 14:2; Ps. 135:4; II Cor. 6:16; Heb. 8:10; Rev. 21:3.
11 P. S. Minear, *Images of the Church*, pp. 70-82. The cultic tradition also provides a series of images as the Holy City, Jerusalem, the Temple, priesthood, sacrifice, aroma, festivals; pp. 89-104.
12 Note the opposition to Stephen in Acts 6:9ff. The story of opposition to Paul in his missionary labors is well known, as told in Acts. See I Thess. 2:14ff.; Gal. 2:13ff.; II Cor. 11:24ff.; Phil. 3:2ff.; Rom. 2:17ff.; 9:1ff.

Church may never forget, however, that the faithlessness of men did not nullify the faithfulness of God (Rom. 3:3). Whatever Israel did with its privileges and opportunities in covenant and election – killed its prophets, stoned those sent unto her, refused to be gathered to its Messiah (Matt. 23:37), boasted in its own works, formulated the Law in terms of man-made statutes, and crucified the Lord of glory (I Cor. 2:8) – the Gentile Christian is an heir by way of adoption into the household of God and is served by a ministry that preceded his own commission. The Church is built on "the foundation of apostles and prophets" (Eph. 2:20). To initiate such re-orientation of mission effort to take account of the Church's solidarity with and responsibility to Israel will require some boldness and serious work. But it is inescapable. The Church is not saved apart from Israel, and any boasting that finds its origin in that branches were broken off the olive-plant of God so that the wild olive branches might be grafted in, is excluded (Rom. 9).

> What the Christians owe to Israel, what they learn from Israel, and what they hope for Israel, this they also apply to their conversation with every man (Rom. 12:19-21).[13]

This duty to Israel remains a part of the responsibility of the Christian Church today. Unfortunately, it is largely ignored in wide circles so that to the Jew the name "Christian" bears the strong overtones of division, persecution, discrimination, suffering. Markus Barth describes the continuing community of the Church and Israel in this way,

> It is not fellowship with fellow men in general that we need primarily and absolutely for our knowledge of salvation and for receiving and rendering service inspired by God. Essential for the growth and building of the Church are the Jews who lived before us and the Jews who live with, among, and around us now. And indispensable is our being joined and knitted and built together with them. The criterion whether we are honest, thorough, uncompromising when we acknowledge that we need fellow man in order to stand before God lies in our relationship to the Jews. The "King of the Jews" is theirs before he is ours. He is theirs, before he is theirs *and* ours. After being "made one" (Eph. 2:14), "both of us have access to the Father in one Spirit" (Eph. 2:18). No access is open, no Holy Spirit is available and operative, that would admit either one of the two without the other to the throne of grace. Access to "our Father" is given to both the prodigal who enters the Father's house and the older brother who has never left it. The Father shows one and the same love for both (Luke 15:11-32). To "the Hebrews" it was written, but by Gentiles, too, it is still to be read, that "since we have a great high priest, let us approach the throne of grace" (Heb. 4:14,16; cf. Rom. 5:1ff.; Eph. 3:12). Not only Christ, the chief cornerstone, but also the foundation

13   M. Barth, *The Broken Wall*, p. 139.

walls of the Church bear witness to the community with Israel. The Church is "built upon the foundation of apostles *and prophets*" (Eph. 2:20).[14]

In the books of Ephesians, Romans, and Acts it is shown that God has not repudiated Jerusalem and the Jewish people, as though God rejected Israel by sending the Church to the Gentiles. Whereas Paul becomes the apostle to the Gentiles, Peter's ministry is towards the circumcision (Gal. 2:7). Old Israel was not cut off from a place in the New Israel of God, as though a curse lay upon the ancient covenant people. It is important to see this in the development of the early Church, the story of which is told in Acts.

Observe, first of all, that the book begins and ends with the proclamation of the Gospel to the Jews first. At Pentecost in Jerusalem's Temple the new age of the Spirit was inaugurated and the first persons invited to receive forgiveness and the Spirit were citizens of the commonwealth of Israel. In addition, not a few priests also were joined in obedient faith to the believing community (Acts 6:7). At the close of the book the apostle Paul, a prisoner under house arrest in Rome, who was so eager to impart some blessing to the Roman Church, first called together the leaders of the Jewish community. He appealed to them to accept the Gospel. Not a few were convinced (Acts 28:24).

Another important thing to note is that Jerusalem is never out of mind. To Jerusalem the apostles always returned. Jerusalem may add to its long list of crimes of murder of the prophets the murders of Stephen and James; it may seek also the life of Paul; nevertheless, Jerusalem's continuing importance indicates that salvation is both from the Jews and also among them. :re were brethren in Jerusalem just as there were brethren in all the world.

The oneness of Jew and Gentile is constantly in the focus of Luke's purpose in the description of the progress of the Gospel. Such events as constituted turning-points in the relationships between Jew and non-Jew are carefully documented and described. On Pentecost men heard in their own tongues the good news of salvation; whereas once men said they would not scatter and fill the earth (Babel) and God scattered them by confusing their languages, this is reversed when the Spirit comes. Stephen's preaching is memorialized in a beautiful and lengthy summary of his address to the Sanhedrin, the burden of his address being as severe criticism of the narrow nationalism and idolatrous perversion of law that caused men to reject God's great deeds in Christ. A eunuch, excluded by law from full participation in the Temple service, is admitted a full member without limitation into the new People of God (Acts 8:38; Isa. 56:3). This man was an Ethiopian, and not of the stock of Abraham. Cornelius and his house received the Holy Spirit (Acts 10:44ff.). The Council of Jerusalem sealed the unity of believing Jew and Gentile in Christ, the fulfillment of the law for both. Paul's conversion story is told three times, with variations and differing emphases; yet the basic fact that he was appointed

14 *Ibid.*, p. 132.

directly by God for the service of the Gentiles is never lost sight of. The mandate of the Risen Lord goes far beyond the geographical boundaries of the Holy City and the Promised Land; it transcends the racial boundaries of Jewish descent and blood; the narrow royal hopes of ancient Israel are shown to be utterly without foundation when the Son of God established the Kingdom and rules as David's royal Son.

It is the Holy Spirit who causes the heralds of the Gospel to speed more swiftly than chariots (Acts 8:39) and uses the Word of God which is sharper than any two-edged sword and who establishes and brings about the Kingdom, not the chariots, horses, and swords of men. What is so very clear is that the proclamation of the Gospel of the Kingdom did not herald a new form or administration of nationalism but the creation of one new People of God from among the Jews first and then also from among the Gentiles. The covenant promises of God are shown to be for all, not for the Jew only even though it may be for the Jew first. Conversely, the Gospel is not now for the Gentile only, even though a hardening in part may have overtaken Israel.

The light of covenant grace, once focused on Jerusalem, now shines from heaven to lighten all the Gentiles together with the people of Israel. The last days have come, foretold by prophets (Acts 2:17-18; 3:24). The Day of the Lord is at hand (Acts 2:20; 17:31). When finally, the Gospel is preached in both Jerusalem and in Rome, two cities, two capitals, united by faith in the one Gospel of Jesus Christ, then the day has come when it is clearly shown that the purpose of God was to grant repentance unto life to the Gentiles also (Acts 11:18). When this Gospel of the Kingdom is preached in all the world for a witness, the day will finally dawn when the Son of Man will come for all things will have been united into one (Matt. 24:14).

2. *The Church and the Reconciled World*

The call to all the nations to become disciples was something new in the history of salvation. Jesus Christ made himself the center of the new fellowship created through the Spirit and develops this fellowship by permeating it with his continued presence in it. Even the desire to become a part of that fellowship originates in the call of Jesus Christ so that men must answer him and not his servants who extend the invitation in his name.

Not the least of the dangers that the Church continually faces is that of identifying itself with the world. It is a feature common to all non-Christian religions that the fellowship of culture and people is identified with fellowship of religion. Vicedom observes that all countries seek to guarantee the unity of their people through unity of religion.[15] Bavinck affirms that in one way or

15 G. F. Vicedom, *The Mission of God*, 89. Even in the U.S.A. where a peculiar form of separation of church and state has evolved and is promoted, most often on a

another every religion in an attempt to establish a Kingdom of God. The Church can avoid this pitfall only if it realizes that it is on the side of God and through him is fully directed to the world. Every true church is an outpost of the Kingdom of God, placed in a particular spot in the world, to bear witness to the Lordship of Jesus Christ.[17]

How does the New Testament express the Church's relationship to the world which is the arena both of its existence and of its witness? It is impressive that in studying the New Testament to find the answer to this question one soon discovers that the Bible confronts the Church with a political perspective in a developed form. The legal and juridical effects of the resurrection of Christ are described by Paul especially. When God raised Jesus Christ from the dead, he "made him sit at his right hand ... above all rule and authority and power and dominion, and ... put all things under his feet ... that at the name of Jesus every knee should bow ... and every tongue confess ... Jesus Christ as Lord" (Eph. 1:20-22; Phil. 2:10,11). The Resurrection is a political event of universal import. From beginning to end the Bible is full of political images: covenants, kingdoms, rulers, judges, and a Messiah who heralds the establishment of the Kingdom of God's rule on earth. Webber speaks of "the politics of God" when he relates these images to the affirmation by Jesus Christ of his absolute sovereignty.[18] The separation of men's lives into secular and sacred is false, therefore, for men are called to be God's people in the midst of God's world. Even baptism can be looked upon as a kind of political event, for in it Jesus Christ marks the person baptized as a citizen of the Kingdom, a member of the redeemed fellowship, one who lives under the Lordship of Christ.

The New Testament shows most clearly that there is a oneness in Christ that breaks down every political, social, racial, moral, sexual barrier. The oneness of Jew and Greek, slave and free man, male and female is found in and guaranteed in Christ (Gal. 3:26-28); excluded in Christ are such divisions as circumcised and uncircumcised, barbarian, Scythian (Col. 3:11). This is the development that should be expected on the basis of God's universal covenant. The purpose of God is to unite all things in Christ; this is his plan for the ages (Eph. 1:9-10). When we are told that "the dividing wall of hostility" has been broken down (Eph. 2:14), this means that Jesus Christ has something to say about and to do with and toward whatever divisions exist in our society: the

quite irrelevant basis, the unity of the state is basically maintained by appeal to a kind of irreligion and secularism which is itself basically religious, and a commitment to a religious standpoint.

16 J. H. Bavinck, *The Impact of Christianity*, p. 34.

17 George W. Webber, *God's Colony in Man's World* (New York & Nashville: Abingdon Press, 1960), p. 29.

18 See M. Barth and V. Fletcher, *Acquital by Resurrection*, p. 99ff.; George W. Webber, *The Congregation in Mission* (New York & Nashville: Abingdon Press, 1964), p. 55ff.; P. S. Minear, *Images of the Church*, p. 233; M. Barth, *The Broken Wall*, p. 111.

differences between races, nations, peoples. Jesus Christ has broken down every barrier, division, and frontier between men. But what is most wonderful of all – he has reconciled men to God.

The implication of this is that no one can claim Jesus Christ for himself alone. In him segregation and separation are abolished. Color of skin, differences of age, sex, language – all are done away. The multitude of the redeemed comprises people of every language, race and people (Rev. 11:15). To proclaim Christ is to proclaim peace and reconciliation. To teach men to obey all that he has commanded is to convey one and the same message to all. There is not one Gospel for one people and a different Gospel and duty for another. The Church is true to its responsibility only when in conformity with Christ's great work of reconciliation it disciples all men and gives them opportunity to experience that Christ's reconciliation of men's differences is greater, stronger, and able to break all hostilities in our fallen society. The alternatives which men face are to live as the new creation in harmony with God and one another through the Spirit, or to exist in eternal isolation from God and man.[19] Unfortunately, Christ's work is often repudiated by the actions and attitudes of those who claim to share his reconciliation. When the peace Christ proclaimed and which in turn is declared by any of his witnesses is deprived of its social, national, racial, or economic dimensions and is reduced and distorted so that only the individual believer's peace with God is of concern, Christ is denied. However, when through his believing disciple others are called in Christ's name to share the blessings of discipleship and to live together under his Lordship, then the uniting, reconciling action of Christ will become a reality. The secret of the Church's relation to the world in which it lives is a dialectic or tension between transcendence and relevance at one and the same time.[20] *Transcendence*, because the Church is the only institution (or better, fellowship) in this world which did not arise from the created order of things. The Church arose exclusively out of the redemptive order, and her function is to transmit to the world the call to share in this through obedience and faith. The Church must do this both in word and by life. To enable the believing community to do this, Christ baptized his Church with the Holy Spirit.[21] It is the duty of the Church to show to the world that peace among men is the necessary corollary to peace with God and that such peace comes in believing obedience to the covenant God so faithfully maintains. *Relevance*, because the Church, while it is not of the world has been

19   C. S. Lewis in his book, *The Great Divorce* (New York: Macmillan Co., 1954), has most effectively pictured the terror of being closed in to one's own self in the pitiful conversation of the lost soul who says, "I don't know what I want!" or of another who has been given everything his wish commanded only to find a terrifying loneliness in the succession of empty houses he has abandoned as his soul was left unsatisfied forever and he moved house after empty house away from his fellow men.
20   Langdon Gilkey, *How the Church Can Minister to the World Without Losing Itself* (New York, Evanston, & London: Harper and Row, 1964), p. 56.
21   See H. R. Boer, *Pentecost and the Missionary Witness*, p. 213.

sent into the world and lives out her obedience there. Paul Minear in his treatment of the images of the Church in the New Testament calls attention to the significant fact that the images which describe the Church are drawn from the everyday, ordinary life with which its members were so very familiar.

> What a profusion of images! This is due in part to the fact of sheer numbers, but also to the diverse origins of the analogies: in home life, in wedding customs, in farm and lake, in city streets and temple, in kitchen and in courtroom, in ancient legends and contemporary events.[22]

Therefore, no part of life can be left untouched by Christ or left separated from his influence, no more than that any part of society may remain beyond his call to discipleship. Every part of life can even be employed to illustrate the Kingdom of God and the Kingdom life of man under God's sovereign rule. The Gospel of the Kingdom is obviously applicable to all spheres in life.

3. A Note on Reformation Definitions of the Church

The challenges the Church faces, the failures with which it is charged, and the new, swiftly evolving forms of society it experiences and with which it must interact demand a response from the Church as to how it conceives of its place in society. The conviction is frequently expressed that the Reformation definitions of the Church, as found in the 16th century confessions and catechisms, no longer serve adequately to express what the Church is. Nor do these confessional statements define what the task of the Church is in terms of God's purpose in its establishment.[23] These confessions reflect conditions existing in the medieval days and period. This is true of Roman and Protestant definitions.[24] In the 16th century all of society was regarded as in some sense Christian. As a result, definitions of the Church from that period tend to justify the existence of one church or one tradition overagainst all others. Although the Reformation was characterized by reflection on the nature of the Church (and this for the first time in the history of the Church), the definitions tended to be passive in form and static.[25] The Church was frequently looked upon as a

22 P. S. Minear, *Images of the Church*, p. 221.

23 Among the recent discussions of this subject among Reformed people in the U.S.A. mention must be made of J. H. Piet, *The Road Ahead*, pp. 21-29. See also Colin Wilbur Williams, *Where in the World?* (New York: National Council of Churches of Christ, 1963); M. Richard Shaull, "The Form of the Church in the Modern Diaspora", *Princeton Seminary Bulletin*, 57 (March 1964), pp. 3-18, esp. 15.

24 A review of the major confessional statements from the Reformation can be found in J. H. Piet, *The Road Ahead*, pp. 21-29.

25 C. W. Williams, *Where in the World?*, p. 44; J. H. Piet, *The Road Ahead*, pp. 33-34; Colin Wilbur Williams, *What in the World?* (New York: National Council of Churches of Christ, 1964), p. 52ff.

local group in a geographical setting and place doing certain religious acts. The Church did not reflect upon its purpose as God's established people in his world, used by God to approach the world that he would redeem. The Church was not looked upon as the place where Jesus Christ relates as the living Lord to humanity, saved and unsaved.

The passive character of the marks of the true Church can be illustrated from the Belgic Confession, article XXIX:

> The marks by which the true church is known are these: if the pure doctrine is preached therein; if it maintains the pure administration of the sacraments as instituted by Christ; if church discipline is exercised in punishment of sin.[26]

From this viewpoint the Church becomes only the place where certain things are done, as Piet observes, and it is not looked upon as a group which God has called into existence to do something.[27] The marks of the Church need to be placed decisively within the framework of the Church's mission. This is where they were first set, for in Acts 2:42 the teaching, fellowship, breaking of bread, and prayers of the newly formed Spirit-filled and Spirit-enlarged disciple fellowship is described within the missionary context of the Pentecost story from which it cannot be extracted. "As the apostles were driven out of the upper room and set on the road to the uttermost parts of the earth, the life of fellowship was one in which there was a constant breaking down of the boundaries of the world – nation, race, language, class, culture."[28] The 16th century definitions emphasize the maintenance of an established pattern within the established church.

This may not be taken to mean that the efforts of the fathers and the heritage received from them are not appreciated. On the contrary, it is doubtful whether their spiritual children today would have done as well as they. And it may not be forgotten that many among them counted these truths so dear that they willingly sacrificed their possessions and often their lives rather than deny the truth. However, times and circumstances have changed. The heathen, the pagan, the "not-my-people" are no longer oceans away, but all around the disciples today. They are neighbors to eachother. Their children play together. They meet at work, in the shopping centers, on the beaches. And unfortunately, at this critical point where the Church of Christ is dispered in the world (a minority, it must be remembered) confessional statements are silent where they ought to be most articulate.

26 *The Psalter Hymnal of the Christian Reformed Church* (Grand Rapids: Christian Reformed Publishing House, 1959), p. 15.

27 J. H. Piet, *The Road Ahead*, p. 24.

28 C. W. Williams, *What in the World?*, p. 52.

The Reformation definitions take little or no account of the New Testament viewpoint which points the Church outside of itself. Having become disciples under Christ's Lordship, the disciples are immediately commanded to make disciples. The direction is ever outward. This finds illustration in the parables of Jesus. The net is cast into the sea in order to be drawn in again (Matt. 13:47). The seed is broadcast in order to gather an abundant harvest (Matt. 13:1-8). The leaven is kneaded into the meal to leaven the whole loaf (Matt. 13:33). The light is set on the lampstand in order to give light to the house which would otherwise be in darkness (Matt. 5:15). The mustard seed is planted and birds come to make nests in the resulting tree (Matt. 13:31-32).

It is true that Christ did not give his Church a distinct missionary office. There was no need to do so. He gave his people a ministry that leads to missionary service, a ministry of the divine word in its fulness as the whole counsel of God. When, however, this pastoral office, because of dogmatic restrictions, serves only the welfare, administration, and self-support of the Church, it is humanly limited in a self-centered way.[29] The Church has been called into existence to live under the Lordship of Jesus Christ and to proclaim that Lordship to the world. The Reformers rightly judged that in the corporate fellowship of that church preaching, the sacraments, and mutual discipline are essential. They could not have anticipated how radically society would be altered and the world's peoples be thrown into such close relationships so that today men are immediately affected by what happens in other parts of the globe and can be instantaneously hearers and observers of events as they take place almost anywhere here on earth. What is the "new" character of the People of God that has emerged or must emerge in our time? In what ways is the Church today closer to the New Testament times than to the times of the Reformers? What does this "new" situation have to say to the Church as it engages in Christ's mission to the world?

B. *The New Diaspora*

Dietrich Bonhoeffer wrote to his god-son, D. W. R., that by the time the boy will have grown up, the form of the Church will have changed beyond recognition.[30] Even with this prophetic insight Bonhoeffer could hardly have predicted the radicalness of the changes, the causes leading up to them, and the consequences that have resulted from them. The concept of a *Corpus Christianum* in a society regarded as in some sense Christian has been every-where abandoned. The Church is definitely a minority everywhere. The growth

29 See G. C. Vicedom, *The Mission of God*, pp. 90-91.
30 Dietrich Bonhoeffer, *Letters and Papers From Prison*, translated by Reginald Fuller (London: SCM Press, 1967), p. 166, in section entitled "Thoughts on the Baptism of D.W.R.". J. Richard Shaull, *The Form of the Church in the Modern Diaspora*, p. 5.

of scientism and secularism, the "under-ground church," changing forms of ministry, social involvement, drug culture, music, race problems – these are but a few of the concomitant changes and results faced by the church today. Many question whether the institutional church can survive while others raise the question whether it ought to.[31]

After 1500 years of Christian history the Church in Western lands has been forced by circumstances to come to grips with its character and purpose. No longer being able to find security in the State as its protector and guarantor, it finds that the modern state is often its enemy. Instead of being able to find support for its positions in custom, civil law, tradition, public opinion and institutional forms, it finds its positions threatened instead and abandoned for some unworkable humanism where every man does as he pleases, where the moral dimension of anything man does is in actual fact denied. The Church is living in a diaspora, a dispersion. The new diaspora means that God has spread his people everywhere in a non-Christian and alien world.[32]

The term "diaspora" means the scattering of God's people in the midst of a hostile environment. This was the form of existence of the Jewish people during their exiles. The Hebrew equivalents translated "diaspora" (διασπορά) in the LXX all have the sense of the process of "leading away, deportation, or exile, or of the state of those led away, deported, or exiled."[33] They are used with reference to the Assyrian, Babylonian, and other deportations suffered by the Jews who looked on exile as the divine judgment or curse (Isa. 53:8; Jer. 23:24; Ezek. 22:15). But since, as was previously shown, voluntary emigrations to all parts of the world characterized the Jewish people, the term began to take on the sense of all Jews who lived throughout the world. Only after 70 A.D. and the destruction of Jerusalem did the Jews really become a "homeless" people, and the diaspora became something different from what it had been previously.

The word is used in the New Testament also. In John 7:35 the Jews use the term in a specifically Old Testament sense when they ask whether Jesus expected to go to the dispersion among the Greeks.[34] Elsewhere in the New Testament

31 The inaugural address of Johannes Verkuyl, *De Taak der Missiologie en der Missionaire Methodiek in het Tijdperk van Saecularisatie en Saecularisme* (Kampen: J. H. Kok, 1965), is the clearest and most definitive expression of the relationships of mission and the secularism and secularization of our age that I have found.

32 A number of authors have dealt with the concept "diaspora". For a survey of these viewpoints consult the following: J. Richard Shaull, "The Form of the Church in the Modern Diaspora"; F. A. Norwood, *Strangers and Exiles*; Lewis S. Mudge, *The Crumbling Walls* (Philadelphia: Westminster Press, 1970), p. 159ff.; P. S. Minear, *Images of the Church*, p. 62ff.; C. C. West and D. Paton, *The Missionary Church*, article by D. M. Paton, "The Uitlander in No Man's Land: The Church in the World", pp. 43-57. For a Roman Catholic viewpoint see Karl Rahner, *The Christian Commitment*.

33 See article διασπορά by Karl Ludwig Schmidt in G. Kittel, *TWNT*, II, pp. 98-104, esp. p. 99.

34 The word "Greeks" (Ἑλληνισταί) is difficult to interpret. It may simply mean

the word is used in James 1:1 and I Pet. 1:1. Here again, one's understanding of the term is dependent on one's viewpoint as to the recipients of the letters. If they are Jewish Christians, the term is used in its normal sense and the reference is to the Jewish diaspora. If they are written to Gentile Christians, it has a figurative, Christian sense.[35] Regardless of what position one takes relative to the meaning of the texts, the persons addressed are Christians and are in fact said to be living in dispersion. The term was commonly used, however, among the post-apostolic fathers in reference to the Christian church.[36]

Minear prefers to take the term "diaspora" and view it in relation to other images such as "exiles," "citizens," "ambassadors." He points out that the scattering of the sheep of the flock ends with their being gathered by Messiah, and that Caiaphas prophesied that "Jesus should die ... to gather into one the children of God who are scattered abroad" (John 11:51-52).[37] The idea of gathering rather than scattering is more frequently emphasized in the New Testament (Mark 6:34ff.; Matt. 26:31-33; 28:16-20). Minear also observes that the master image was the exodus of Abraham from Haran and the exodus of Israel from Egypt, "kinds of exile that always followed upon God's election and always sought the fulfillment of his promise (Heb. 11:8-28). It was this kind of pilgrimage that became a necessary corollary of promise and election to early Christians. They had been chosen as a company of exiles; their common election made them tent-dwellers and created among them a fellowship in the Promised Land as their goal."[38] Perhaps because the term diaspora had become a technical term among the Jews and a sense of pride accompanied its use is sufficient explanation why it did not find immediate and widespread employment in the early church. Schmidt remarks that the diaspora of Israel made it impossible for the Jews to be exterminated at one stroke.[39]

The Christian Church was born in diaspora. The sheep, scattered when the Shepherd was smitten (Matt. 26:31; Zech. 13:7), were gathered again by the living and risen Savior in Galileee (Matt. 26:32), as he had assured them. The

Jews residing among the Greeks, or it may mean the Greeks themselves, in which case the word Greeks would be almost equivalent to the meaning "Gentiles". See K. L. Schmidt, Διασπορά, in *TWNT*, II, pp. 101-102; also article Ἕλλην by Hans Windisch in G. Kittel, *TWNT*, II, pp. 504-516; see also Marcel Simon, *St. Stephen and the Hellenists* (London, New York, Toronto: Longmans, Green, and Co., 1956). Strack-Billerbeck, *Kommentar*, II, p. 548, take John 7:35 to mean dispersed Jews among the Greeks.

35 See the discussion in G. Kittel, *TWNT*, II, p. 102.

36 *Ibid.*, p. 104; P. S. Minear, *Images*, p. 62, 272 n. 28, where Minear refers to the essay of W. C. Van Unnik, "Ecclesia," *Aangeboden aan J. N. Bakhuizen van den Brink* (The Hague: Martinus Nijhof, 1959), pp. 33-45. Van Unnik "demonstrated the rarity of direct allusions to the church as the Diaspora, and the danger of exaggerating this element in early Christian thinking."

37 P. S. Minear, *Images*, pp. 60-63, esp. p. 62.

38 *Ibid.*, p. 62.

39 See G. Kittel, *TWNT*, II, p. 100.

first great ingathering was from Jews and proselytes from around the Mediterranean basin who had come from the lands of the Diaspora to the feast in Jerusalem (Acts 2:9). It was only a short while after the beginning of the Christian Church that a great scattering of the followers of The Way took place in the persecutions that followed hard on the death of Stephen (Acts 8:1). The apostles remained in Jerusalem, however, while believers sought refuge in the regions of Judea and Samaria. There was a new aspect to this dispersion, however. The forced exiles from the Promised Land in the days before Christ were scattered abroad as God's judgment against their sins (Lev. 26:33; Jer. 13:24; Lam. 4:16; Ezek. 24:6). The purpose of the scattering abroad of the Early Church is different: this is not a scattering of a people without unity; it is a dispersion of a fellowship with whom Christ promises to remain to the end of the age. The New Testament Church was scattered in the service of the Gospel, for "those who were scattered went about preachting the word" (Acts 8:4). The Church was founded in Judea and Galilee and Samaria (Acts 9:31) as a result of evangelization and persecution. By that time converts could also be numbered in Lydda, Joppa, Damascus, Caesarea, and even in the court of Queen Candace of Ethiopia (Acts 8:27).

The Christian Church still lives in diapora. But it is a diaspora with a purpose. There is a kind of irreversible direction in the course prescribed for the Church. The whole program of God is moving toward the creation of a reality which will be in accordance with the promise. The Lord of the harvest is petitioned to "thrust out laborers into the harvest" in order to gather in the grain from fields that are already white (Matthew 9:38). The whole diaspora of the Church can only be understood in terms of its apostolic mission – a going forth from its central authority under commission, and to return again when at the end of the age the mission of the Great Apostle is completed. The Church's diaspora is its being sent out by Christ. The gathered ones go out to gather yet others. The significance and purpose of the Christian diaspora is to be found in its mission dimension. The seed that is scattered bears thirty, forty, even one hundred times more grains at harvest.

The use of the term "diaspora" is not new in ecumenical circles, but it is being used in different ways. To some the term describes the scattering of the Christians in the world during the week as over against their gathered life in the Church on Sunday. It also is taken to mean not only that the individual Christian is dispersed but that the Church too is in a diapora situation.[40] Hans Ruedi-Weber expresses the opinion that the Church between Christ's ascension and second coming has two forms of existence: that of ecclesia (the assembly), and that of the diaspora (the dispersion).[41] Karl Rahner looks upon the concept

---

40   Thus M. R. Shaull, "The Form of the Church", p. 5.
41   Hans Reudi-Weber in C. C. West, et al., The Missionary Church, pp. 109-110, article, "The Marks of An Evangelizing Church."

of the diaspora as an essential, a "must," which he equates with "necessity" in the sense of the New Testament term δεῖ. He says,

> Insofar as our outlook is really based on today and looking towards tomorrow, the present situation of Christians can be characterized as that of a diaspora; and this signifies, in terms of the history of salvation, a "must," from which we may and must draw conclusions about our behavior as Christians .... Christianity exists *everywhere* in this world and everywhere as a *diaspora*.[42]

However, Rahner also says that the desire of the church must always be not to be a diaspora, that this remains the obligation of every Christian, and is a desire which cannot fail to inspire apostolic activity of witness, both passive and active. "When the church begins to be a church of *all* the heathen, she also begins, everywhere, to be a church *among* the heathen."[43] This is not necessarily a setting down obstinately in spite of everything, for he speaks out strongly against "a kind of obstinate, pseudo-heroic apostolate that refuses to shake the dust from its feet and go into another city when the message falls on deaf ears."[44] The work of Christ is always a sign of contradiction and persecution, and Christ's victory is coming when in judgment he gathers up world history into its wholly unpredictable and unexpected end. Surrounded by non-Christians and hence living in a culture, state, amidst political movements, economic activity, arts, and science which are not conducted simply and solely by Christians, the Christian today finds his faith under constant attack from without. The negative influence such a culture exercises on the Christian's life brings it into almost unavoidable conflict with his Christian morality.

But it is also true that among the dangers that confront the Church in its diaspora situation is that it is tempted to withdraw from involvement in society into itself. When this happens, Christianity is no longer a religion which is a matter of choice and growth. The challenge to discipleship confronts those who can boast a heritage from the fathers as well as those who are not a people of God. Each person must be won to live his life under the Lordship of Jesus. The Church in this way becomes a church of positive missionary spirit, not waging battles in areas where its energies are wasted, but called to live and witness in the community where it has been set. The temptation is to look with desperation and even fright for some way to maintain our old systems, find refuge in new techniques and evangelistic movements, while the authentic forms of existence for the Christian community which ought to be developing in its dispersion escape it.

The global trend to increasing secularization of life has led to an unprecedented secular diaspora as well. The number of technicians, educators, artists, scientists who constitute this secular diaspora has had an effect on the Christian

---

42 K. Rahner, *The Christian Commitment*, p. 14.
43 *Ibid.*, pp. 18-19.
44 *Ibid.*, p. 14.

mission. Unfortunately, in such a secularizing society the Church has often adopted the secular models for its missionaries. Even though the individual disciples in their secular callings must work in a way appropriate to their calling, they cannot be said to fulfill their Lord's sovereign will nor to be living in obedience to him unless they have an underlying and intentional spiritual purpose. The task of every dispersed believer is clearly ethical, spiritual, theological, whatever the form of the work he does.[45]

It is regrettable that the lesson has not yet been learned that for this task unshakable faith in the promises of our Lord is required. It is his promise, "I am always with you," that makes alle the difference and which changes the basic idea of diaspora from that of being scattered into that of being gathered. From the viewpoint of the world and society the Church is indeed "everywhere." The Kingdom of God (which is not to be taken in the sense of the Church) appears everywhere when the seed is broadcast over all kinds of soil; the purpose of the scattering in every one of the parabolic illustrations Jesus uses to illustrate this truth is to gather again unto himself. The great harvest will take place when he comes again. It is this rootlessness from the present world and their vital union as a living, fruit-bearing branch to the vine that gives the disciples their unity. If no place on earth is truly home, if the Christian community like Abraham lives in tents "in the land of promise, as in a foreign land" (Hebr. 11:9), if final loyalty is to no earthly power, then the real citizenship of the Christian is in the Kingdom of God, and the Church by its very nature is composed of tent dwellers.[46] The characteristic of the People of God seldom comes to expression in the traditional, historic established forms which the Church has evolved and under which it has chosen to live. The present-day parish structure of the Church is almost entirely determined by the dimension of *place*, as Hans Ruedi-Weber has shown. Today, however, the deciding factor is looked upon as *work*, which in many cases no longer coincides with the dimension of place. The evolvement of (or return to) mobile charismata similar to those of the Early Church is proposed by Weber as a partial solution to this challenge.[47]

However, from the viewpoint of the work of Christ the People of God are not scattered but joined to Christ. The sheep *are* in the fold. If the believing community had no center, it would likely be impossible to survive. Because

45 These thoughts are more fully developed by David M. Stowe, "Changing Patterns of Missionary Service in Today's World", *Practical Anthropology*, XVII (May-June 1970), 107-118. In a recent report on Puerto Rican families in the Northeastern sector of the United States I found a sociologist using the term diaspora to mean "migration, scattering" in a purely secular sense.

46 F. A. Norwood, *Strangers and Exiles*, p. 58; P. S. Minear, *Images*, pp. 61-62. It was at Willingen that the church was first designated as the Pilgrim People of God which lives in tents and carries out its ministry until he comes.

47 In "The Marks of an Evangelizing Church," C. C. West, *The Missionary Church*, pp. 101-116.

Christ is its shepherd, the flock is free from harm and inviolate from ravenous wolveh in sheep's clothing. This is a covenant relationship, confirmed in an oath sworn by God in his own Name, for there is none greater than he.

C. The New Crisis

The believing community today is frequently divided around two poles. There is a segment wihtin the Church that wants the Church to become deeply involved in the issues of the day. Some of these people are recklessly ready to sacrifice the traditions, heritage and forms of the Church in attaining this involvement, writing off the traditional churches as irrelevant and stultefying. Another segment of the people of God cherishes traditional forms and formulations so much that any proposed change is looked upon as disorderly and threatening, as a denial of the faith and abandonment of the purposes of God in Christ for his people. The result is a polarization within the Church which tragically limits its effectiveness and the accomplishment of its task. When Christians attack one another, they uselessly expend time and energy which is not being directed to their central task.

The way out of the dilemma posed by this unfortunate polarity must lie in the direction of a proper, Scripturally oriented understanding of our responsibility and opportunity for the exercise of a prophetic ministry to the present age. The Church does not exist for itself, nor may it be made synonymous with the Kingdom of God. There is no way of getting so involved in our world as by missions. Certain false assumptions must be discarded when believers move forward along those those lines. For one thing, they do not have to invent a new message different from the old. There is only one Gospel, just as "there is only one Name under heaven, given to men, whereby we must be saved" (Eph. 4:5; Acts 4:12).

> We are not called to say something never said before or to do something never done before. To be sure, we are called to be imaginative and creative, but we do not have to create something out of whole cloth.[48]

In addition, the message the Christian proclaims is not his private faith. He has the support of a great community that has preceded him and into whose labors he has entered (John 4:38) as well as the great company of witnesses (Heb. 12:1). His ministry is grounded in the commission received from Christ himself, and whatever results from his faithful labors will be brought forth by him to the glory of God (II Cor. 2:14-17). The true disciple has the responsibility and the urgent task of handling the tradition received from Christ ("whatsoever I have commanded you" – Matt. 28:19) in ways which address it relevantly to the new crisis situation.

48 W. Brueggemann, *Tradition for Crisis*, p. 124.

There are, as assumed above, certain basic, unchanging elements in this task. The Lordship of Yahweh over all creation must be continually asserted. Security and life are found in God alone. When men are either individually or collectively confronted with God's claims, a crisis of decision is created. The options must be spelled out in terms of obedience to and rejection of God's claims over men. Men must be compelled to choose, to come in that God's house may be full. God never leaves man a valid option not to choose life; God's appeals and call are always imperatives for man. The tradition received through prophets and apostles is as indispensable for today's people of God in their proclamation as it was for Jesus in his day when he announced the arrival of the Kingdom of God.

This should not be construed, however, to mean that the old order must be saved in its entirety at all cost. Whatever is said to men, whatever "burdens" are placed on them, must first be judged in terms of whether or not these are the things Christ himself commanded. This calls for careful discernment. The child of God exposes false discernments. How much more glorious would many past and present chapters of redemptive history have been if only the Church had heeded this good counsel and sought in the Holy Spirit "to lay upon [men] no greater burden than these necessary things" (Acts 15:28). Under such circumstances the Church could not be accused at is has been by Mgsr. Ivan Illich of Cuernavaca, Mexico, of cultural imperialism in its missionary work. Fr. Illich crusades continually for the withdrawal of all North American missionary personnel from Latin America because they are "ultimately salesmen for the middle class American way of life." [49] And with John Mackay we are

> ... deeply impressed with statements from China lamenting the fact that we did not in time give the Chinese Church a theology and a true doctrine of the missionary obligation. The first full-orbed doctrine which the Chinese have received is Marxism. We did not give them a doctrine of the church in the purpose of God. Let us not make the same mistake in other parts of the world while there is still time. [50]

It is time also to reconsider our ecclesiastical imperialism in missionary efforts. It is not uncommon to defend withdrawal from evangelistic responsibilities on the basis of mission theories which insist on self-support, self-government, and self-propagation, only to replace this with an insistence on the duty to provide leaders for the emerging church by means of schools and seminaries established for this purpose. What has not always been admitted is that this is the one sure way that is left to guarantee a large measure of control over much of the future development of these churches. Therefore, while nationals are trained in Western-oriented courses in theology, liturgy, and polity, they have not been provided the means whereby the Church itself can

49 D. M. Stowe, "Changing Patterns of Missionary Service," p. 112.
50 N. Goodall, *Missions Under the Cross*, p. 139.

speak relevantly to its own situation and day.[51] This is a tragic injustice to the Spirit of God who is given "for the common good" (I Cor. 12:7). The one ought not to be done and the other left undone.

> It was practically a disenfranchisement and subordination of the younger churches that they were not trained for the spreading of the Kingdom of God and admitted to it by the mission. They were deprived of doing mission work as if the Kingdom of God were dependent on the proof of a certain level of culture! In this way the mission had to appear as the prerogative of the older Christianity and therewith as the churchly expansion of the Western world.[52]

The irony of the situation is that such a misconstruction of the missionary task is a serious failure to grasp the point of the tradition. The Church's effectiveness is determined by the fact whether it makes disciples who serve in the Kingdom for such a time as this or whether it makes of itself a ghost town where history has stopped since the demise or departure of the last citizen. The more parochial notions of what is really essential are not always in correspondence with the world of crisis in which the Church lives and to which it ministers.

The real task of the witness of Christ is to enable men to be obedient within the context of covenant, to make the covenant relevant, and to let the tradition touch today's situation in a life-giving way. This is not always easy since the implications of covenant life are not always clear and it cannot always be said with the kind of definiteness we would like what the covenant life must be like in the present. The record of the past is crystal clear concerning God's gracious and liberating deeds in the past; to assert the same thing as positively in the present is difficult. One witnesses God's continuing work of grace when he walks the way of obedience. The stipulations of the covenant are one of its gracious elements; God has not left his people in the dark concerning his expectations from them in their covenant life.

God declares what we must do if we would walk in covenant with him.

---

51 The author served from 1956-1960 as a missionary in Ceylon and served the emerging churches in the Northcentral and Northwestern Provinces. One thing deeply impressed me: how irrelevant so much of traditional Reformed Theology was to these people and their situation, and how seldom this theology spoke to their real needs. E.g., the questions that concern Satan, the demons, angels, charms, etc. are not of great concern, nor do they receive much attention in the West. These were living issues to the Christians of these areas, surrounded as they were by animism and the continual fear of the spiritual realm. Among the greatest joys that we experienced was to proclaim to men the victory of Christ over the powers and see the shackles of slavery to elemental spirits broken by Christ. This is a chapter of Reformed Theology that has still not been written, and perhaps which cannot be written by the West. When the "Five Points of Calvinism" were preached to these people, they often responded with the question, "What's the issue?" Missionaries and pastors were scratching where it didn't itch!

52 G. F. Vicedom, *The Mission of God*, p. 134.

Now the believing community is quite aware of the demands of God, but these have gotten confused with romantic morality and pietistic individualism. God's demands have been perverted so that they do not go beyond being good and staying pure. But the demands of God which come out of our tradition do not stress goodness so much as involvement. They do not speak of churchly obligations but of investment in the secular community.[53]

In the complexities of life today the gifts of every person in the believing fellowship are essential in the functioning of the whole. The community of faith is constituted of prophet-members, some of whom are set apart by ordination for special functions and possess skills and training peculiar to these functions. But every Christian is set apart in his baptism and is provided with all the skills needed for today's challenges. Karl Rahner insist on the fact that any Christian is

> ... an apostle by the nature of his Christianity, and at all times and in all places. Any Christian can be an apostle on the basis of any Christian situation. All that is essential is that he should have a right discernment of his own actual Christian situation. This means apostolate as the identification of our Christian existence with our present situation, whatever that may be.[54]

When it is understood that God is at work in and with his people (Phil. 2:13; Mark 16:20) and is continually present as the Lord of life and action, everything must be brought under his control and sway: education, work, recreation, theology, also mission. The task of mission is to bring home to all men everywhere his claim on them and to challenge them to walk the road of discipleship. Men must be approached with a comprehensive message so that the whole of man's life may be lived to God. The essence of the total experience which is the Kingdom of God is God as power and Spirit. The rule of God over men involves the gift of the Spirit. The divine purpose in calling his people to make disciples is nothing less than the divine will to transmit to men the life and power of the Spirit. Mission is essentially transmission ("make disciples, baptize, teach"). Unfortunately all too often a particular culture, creedal formulations, church polities, denominational expressions, hymns and liturgies, one's brand of Christianity have been transmitted when the witnesses should have concentrated on preaching Jesus Christ and discipleship in him. These other things have their place and cannot be escaped because they are part of the heritage of the Church. Not to value that heritage would be to discredit the blessings which have come through them. But the transmission of heritage is not *the* goal of the missionary task. The task is to make disciples. Whatever else that is done must serve this one great purpose. But since Christ does not

53 W. Brueggemann, *Tradition for Crisis*, p. 139.
54 Karl Rahner, *The Christian in the Market Place*, translated by Cecily Hastings (New York: Sheed and Ward, 1966), p. 3; German title = *Sendung und Gnade*.

live in abstraction but in his people, the task of the missionary becomes that of creating the conditions in which the believing community can experience the fulness of the life of the Spirit, of making real the blessings of God's universal covenant.

Both as individuals and as society mankind is still faced with the fundamental issue: God meets man as his Creator in history, and man must choose whether he will live in covenant fellowship with his God. As man faces God he hears God speak, "Where are you?" In grace God tells him where he can be; he tells and assures him that life is possible in place of death. He announces that a gracious covenant by which he wills to restore man to full fellowship has been fulfilled in Christ. And every man chooses. God says,

> Therefore choose life that you and your descendants may live, loving the LORD your God, obeying his voice and cleaving to him; for that means life to you (Deut. 30:19,20).

> Get yourself a new heart and a new spirit! Why will you die, O house of Israel? For I have no pleasure in the death of any one, says the LORD God; so turn and live (Ezek. 18:30,31).

BT	=	Babylonian Talmud
EMM	=	Evangelische Missions Magazin
HUCA	=	Hebrew Union College Annual
IRM	=	International Review of Missions
JAOS	=	Journal of the American Oriental Society
JBL	=	Journal of Biblical Literature
JE	=	Jewish Encyclopedia
JR	=	Journal of Religion
JT	=	Jerusalem Talmud
LXX	=	Septuagint
NEB	=	New English Bible
NTSt	=	New Testament Studies
RSV	=	Revised Standard Version
SBTh	=	Studies in Biblical Theology
TLZ	=	Theologische Literaturzeitung
TWNT	=	Theological Dictionary of the New Testament
ZATW or ZAW	=	Zeitschrift für die Alttestamentliche Wissenschaft
ZThK	=	Zeitschrift für Theologie und Kirche

Bibliography

For the convenience of English readers the English translations of foreign publications have been included wherever possible. Only those works actually cited in the footnotes are listed here.

Aalen, Sverre. *Die Begriffe "Licht" und "Finsternis" im Alten Testament, im Spätjudentum, und im Rabbinismus.* Oslo: I Kommisjon hos. J. Dybwab, 1951.

Abrahams, Israel. "How Did The Jews Baptize?", *Journal of Theological Studies,* XII (1961), pp. 609-612.

——. *Studies in Phariseeism and the Gospels.* 2 vols. New York: Ktav, 1967.

Albright, William Foxwell. *From The Stone Age to Christianity.* 2nd ed. London: Oxford University Press, 1946.

Alt, Albrecht. "Asenath, The Wife of Joseph: A Haggadic, Literary-historical Study," *HUCA,* I (1924), pp. 239-306.

——. "Die Deutung der Weltgeschichte im Alten Testament," *ZThK,* 56 (1959), pp. 129-137.

——. "Die Stätten des Werkens Jesu in Galiläa Territorialgeschichtlich Betrachtet," *Kleine Schriften zur Geschichte des Volkes Israel,* Vol. II. München: C. H. Beck'sche Verlagsbuchhandlung, 1959.

——. *Führung zum Christentum durch das Alte Testament.* Leipzig: Dorffling und Franke, 1934.

——. *Where Jesus Worked.* London: Epworth, 1961.

Anderson, Gerald H., ed. *The Theology of the Christian Mission.* New York: McGraw-Hill, 1965.

Axenfeld, Karl. "Die jüdische Propaganda als Vorläuferin und Wegbereiter in der urchristliche Mission," *Missionswissenschaftliche Studien: Festschrift zur 70. Geburtstag Prof. Dr. Gustav Warneck.* Berlin: Verlag Martin Warneck, 1904.

Bachli, Otto. *Israel und die Völker.* Zürich: EVZ, 1962.

Baeck, Leo. *This People Israel: The Meaning of Jewish Existence.* New York: Holt, Rinehart, and Winston, 1964.

Baird, Joseph Arthur. *Audience Criticism and the Historical Jesus.* Philadelphia: The Westminster Press, 1969.

——. *The Justice of God and the Teaching of Jesus.* Philadelphia: The Westminster Press, 1963.

Bamberger, Bernard Jacob. *Proselytism in the Talmudic Period.* New York: Ktav, 1939.

Baron, Salo Wittmayer. *A Social and Religious History of the Jews.* 3 vols. New York: Columbia University, 1937.

Barrett, Charles Kingsley. *The Holy Spirit and the Gospel Tradition.* London: SPCK, 1966.

Barth Karl. *Auslegung von Matthäus 28:16-20.* Basel: Basler Missionsbuchhandlung, 1945. E.T.: Anderson, Gerald H., ed. *The Theology of the Christian Mission.* "Interpretation of Matthew 28:16-20." Translated by Thomas Weiser. New York: McGraw-Hill, 1965.

———. *God's Search for Man.* New York: Round Table Press, 1935.

———. *Kirchliche Dogmatik: IV - Die Lehre der Versönnung-3.* München: Chr. Kaiser Verlag, 1932ff. E.T.: *Church Dogmatics.* Vol. IV, parts 1-3. *The Doctrine of Reconciliation.* Translated by G. T. Thomson, *et al.* Edinburgh: T. and T. Clark, 1936ff.

Barth, Markus, *Israel and the Church.* Richmond: John Knox Press, 1969.

———. "Jesus, Paulus und die Juden," *Theologische Studien,* Heft 91. Zürich: EVZ-Verlag, 1967.

———. *The Broken Wall.* Chicago: The Judson Press, 1963.

Barth, Markus, and Fletcher, Verne F. *Acquital By Resurrection.* New York, Chicago, and San Francisco: Holt, Rinehart, and Winston, 1964.

Barton, George A. "The Origin of the Thought Pattern That Survives in Baptism," *JAOS,* 56 (1936), pp. 155-165.

Battenhouse, Henry Martin. *The Bible Unlocked.* New York, London: The Century Co., 1928.

Bavinck, Johan H. *Inleiding in de Zendingswetenschap.* Kampen: J. H. Kok, 1954. E.T.: *An Introduction to the Science of Missions.* Translated by David Freeman. Philadelphia: Presbyterian and Reformed Publishing Co., 1964.

———. *The Impact of Christianity on the Non-Christian World.* Grand Rapids: W. B. Eerdmans, 1949.

Baynes, Norman H. *Israel Amongst the Nations.* London: SCM, 1928.

Beasley-Murray, George Raymond. *Baptism in the New Testament.* New York: St. Martin's Press, 1962.

———. *Baptism - Today and Tomorrow.* New York: St. Martin's Press, 1966.

Benedict, George. *Christ Finds a Rabbi.* Philadelphia: Bethlehem Presbyterian Church, 1932.

Berkhof, Hendricus, and Potter, Philip. *Key Words of the Gospel.* London: SCM Press, 1964.

Berkouwer, Gerrit C. *De Verkiezing Gods.* Kampen: J. H. Kok, 1958. E.T.: *Divine Election.* Translated by Hugo Bekker. Grand Rapids: W. B. Eerdmans, 1960.

———. *De Sacramenten.* Kampen: J. H. Kok, 1966. E.T.: *The Sacraments.* Translated by Hugo Bekker. Grand Rapids: W. B. Eerdmans, 1960.

Bertholet, Alfred. *Die Stellung der Israeliten und die Juden zu den Fremden.* Freiburg und Leipzig: J. C. B. Mohr, 1896.

Blauw, Johannes. *Goden en Mensen.* Groningen: J. Niemeijer, 1950.

———. *Gottes Werk in dieser Welt.* München: Chr. Kaiser Verlag, 1961. E.T.: *The Missionary Nature of the Church.* New York: McGraw-Hill, 1962.

Boer, Harry R. *Pentecost and the Missionary Nature of the Church.* Franeker: T. Wever, 1955.

Bonhoeffer, Dietrich. *Briefe und Aufzeichnungen aus der Haft.* München: Kaiser

Verlag, 1970 (1st ed., 1951). E.T.: *Letters and Papers From Prison.* Translated by Reginald Fuller. 3rd ed. London: SCM Press, 1967.

Bonsirven, Joseph. *Le Judaisme Palestinien au Temps de Jesus Christ.* 2 vols. 2nd ed. Paris: Aubier, 1934. E.T.: *Palestinian Judaism in the Time of Jesus Christ.* Translated by William Wolf. New York: Holt, Rinehart, and Winston, 1964.

Bousett, Wilhelm. *Kyrios Christos.* Göttingen: Vandenhoeck und Ruprecht, 1967.

Bowman, John Wick. *The Intention of Jesus.* Philadelphia: Westminster Press, 1943.

Brandt, Wilhelm. *Die jüdische Baptismen oder das religiöse Waschen und Baden im Judentum mit Einschluss des Judenchristentums.* Giessen: A. Töpelmann (vormals J. Rickers), 1910.

Braude, William Gordon. *Jewish Proselyting in the First Five Centuries in the Common Era.* Providence: Brown University, 1940.

——. *Rabbinic Attitudes Towards Proselytization.* Providence: Brown University, 1940.

Bright, John. *Early Israel in Recent History Writing.* Chicago: A. R. Allenson, 1956.

——. *The Kingdom of God.* Nashville: Abingdon-Cokesbury, 1953.

British Council of Churches. *The Conflict in the Middle East and Religious Faith.* Report of the Middle East Advisory Committee of the British Council of Churches, April 1970. [British Council of Churches; 10 Easton Gate; London S.W. 1.]

Browne, Laurence Edward. *Early Judaism.* Cambridge: University Press, 1968.

Brueggemann, Walter. *Tradition for Crisis.* Richmond: John Knox Press, 1968.

Buber, Martin. "Das Königtum Gottes," *Werke.* Vol. 2. München: Kösel Verlag, 1964, pp. 485-723. E.T.: *The Kingship of God.* Translated by Richard Scheimann. New York & Evanston: Harper and Row, 1967.

——. *The Prophetic Faith.* Translated by Carlyle Witton Davies from the Hebrew. New York: Macmillan, 1949.

Bultmann, Rudolf Karl. *Das Urchristentum im Rahmen der antiken Religionen.* Zürich: Artemis Verlag, 1949. E.T.: *Primitive Christianity in its Contemporary Setting.* Translated by R. H. Fuller. New York: Meridian Press, 1956.

Cadoux, Cecil John. *The Historic Mission of Jesus.* London: Lutterworth, 1941.

Caemmerer, Richard Rudolph, and Leuker, Erwin L. *Church and Ministry in Transition.* St. Louis: Concordia, 1964.

Calvin, John. *Institutionem Christianae Religionis.* Libri IV. Amstelodami: Joann. Jac. Schipper, 1667. E.T.: *Institutes of the Christian Religion.* Ed. J. T. McNeill. Translated by Ford L. Battles. 2 vols. London: SCM, 1961.

——. *Commentarii in quator Evangelistas.* [3 tom. (1 vol.)]. Amstelodami: Joann. Jac. Schipper, 1667. E.T.: *Commentary on a Harmony of the Evangelists: Matthew, Mark, and Luke.* Translated by William Pringle. 3 vols. Grand Rapids: W. B. Eerdmans, 1956.

Case, Shirley Jackson. *The Evolution of Early Christianity.* Chicago: University of Chicago Press, 1960.

——. *The Social Origins of Christianity.* Chicago: University of Chicago Press, 1923.

Causse, Antonin. *Israël et la Vision de l'humanité.* Paris: Libraire Istra, 1924.

——. "La Sagesse et la Propaganda Juive a l'Epoque Perse et Hellenistique,"

Werden en Wesen des Alten Testaments, ZAW, 66 (1936).

——. *Les Disperses d'Israël*. Paris: Libraire F. Alcan, 1929.

Charles, Robert Henry. *Religious Development Between the Old and New Testaments*. Rev. ed. London: Oxford University Press, 1945.

—— *The Apocrypha and Pseudepigrapha of the Old Testament*. 2 vols. Oxford: The Clarendon Press, 1963.

Cohen, Abraham. *The Parting of the Ways: Judaism and the Rise of Christianity.* London: Lincoln-Prager Ltd., 1954.

Cohon, Samuel Soloman. "The Place of Jesus in the Religious Life of His Day," *JBL*, 48 (1929), pp. 82-108.

Cook, Stanley Arthur. *The Old Testament*. New York: Macmillan Col, 1936.

Cullmann, Oscar. *Die Tauflehre des Neuen Testaments - Erwachsenen und Kindertaufe.* Zürich: EVZ Verlag, 1948. E.T.: *Baptism in the New Testament*. Translated by J. K. S. Reid. London: SCM Press, 1953.

——. *Christus und die Zeit*. Zürich: EVZ Verlag, 1962. E.T.: *Christ and Time*. Translated by Floyd V. Filson. Philadelphia: The Westminster Press, 1964.

——. *Heil als Geschichte: Heilgeschichtliche Existenz im Neuen Testament.* Tübingen: J. C. B. Mohr, 1965.

Dahl, Nil Alstrup. *Das Volk Gottes*. Oslo: I Kommisjon hos. Jacob Dybwab, 1941.

Daiches, Samuel. *The Jews in Babylonia in the Time of Ezra and Nehemiah According to the Babylonian Inscriptions: Jews College Publication 2.* London: Jews College, 1910.

Dalbert, P. *Die Theologie der hellenistisch-jüdisch Missionsliteratur unter Ausschluss von Philo und Josephus.* Hamburg: Völksdorf, 1954.

Danby, Hebert. *The Mishnah*. London: The Oxford Press, 1938.

Daube, David. *The New Testament and Rabbinic Judaism.* London: Athone Press, 1956.

Davies, William David. *Paul and Rabbinic Judaism.* London: SPCK, 1958.

Davies, William David, and Daube, David, eds. *The Background of the New Testament and its Eschatology: Studies in Honor of C. H. Dodd.* Cambridge: University Press, 1956.

Delafosse, Michael. *The Negroes of Africa*. Port Washington, New York: Kennikat Press, 1968.

Derwacter, Frederick Milton. *Preparing the Way for Paul*. New York: Macmillan, 1930.

De Young, James C. *Jerusalem in the New Testament*. Kampen: J. H. Kok, 1960.

Dinur, Ben Zion. *Israel and the Diaspora*. Philadelphia: Jewish Publishing Society of America, 1969.

Dodd, Charles Harold. *New Testament Studies*. Manchester: University Press, 1967.

Drazin, Nathan. *The History of Jewish Education from 515 BCE to 220 CE.* Baltimore: Johns Hopkins Press, 1940.

Ehrman, A., ed. *The Jerusalem Talmud*. 11 vols. Jerusalem: El-'Am, 1965.

Eichhorn, *David Max. Conversion to Judaism: History and Analysis.* New York: Ktav, 1966.

Eichrodt, Walther. "Gottes Volk und die Völker," *EMM*, 86 (1942), pp. 129-145.

——. *Theologie des Alten Testaments.* 2 vols. Leipzig: Hinrichs, 1939. E.T.: *Theology of the Old Testament*. Translated by J. A. Baker. 5 vols. Philadelphia: Westminster Press, 1961.

Eissfeldt, Otto. "Partikularismus und Universalismus in der Israelitisch-jüdischen Religionsgeschichte", summarized in *Theologische Literaturzeitung*, LXXXIX (1954), p. 283.

Ellul, Jacques. *The Meaning of the City*. Translated by Dennis Pardee. Grand Rapids: W. B. Eerdmans, 1970. French title: *Sans feu ni lieu*.

Emmerich, E. "Die Juden," *Theologische Studien und Kritiken*, VII (1939), p. 20ff.

Epstein, Isaac. *The Babylonian Talmud*. 34 vols. London: The Socino Press, 1952.

———. *The Response of Rabbi Simon B. Duran as a Source of the History of the Jews of North Africa*. London: Jews College, 1930.

Filson, Floyd Vivian. *The New Testament Against Its Environment*. London: SCM Press, 1950.

———. *Three Crucial Decades*. Richmond: John Knox Press, 1963.

Finkelstein, Louis. "Origins of the Synagogue," *Proceedings of the American Academy for Jewish Research*, I, (n.d.), pp. 49-59.

———. *The Jews: Their History, Culture and Religion*. 2 vols. 2nd ed. New York: Harper, 1955.

———. *The Pharisees*. 2 vols. 3rd ed. Philadelphia: Jewish Publication Society of America, 1962.

Finn, James. *The Jews of China*. London: Wertheim, 1843.

Firet, J. *Het agogisch moment in het pastoraal optreden*. Kampen: J. H. Kok, 1968.

Foerster, Werner. *Herr ist Jesus*. Gütersloh: C. Bertelsmann Verlag, 1924.

Frey, Jean Baptiste. *Corpus Inscriptionum Judaicarum*. Vol. I: *Europa*. Paris and Rome: Pontificio Instituto Di Archeologia Cristiana, 1936.

Freytag, Walther. "The Meaning and Purpose of the Christian Mission," *IRM*, XXXIX (1950), pp. 153-161.

———. "Vom Sinn der Weltmission," *EMM* (1950), pp. 67-75.

Gartenhouse, Jacob. *The Influence of the Jews Upon Civilization*. Grand Rapids: Zondervan, 1943.

Gavin, Frank Stanton Burnes. "Jewish Views on Jewish Missions," *Papers for Jewish People*, XXXI. Jewish Religious Union, n.d., pp. 5-43.

———. "Rabbinic Parallels in Early Church Orders," *HUCA*, VI, 1929, pp. 55-67.

———. *The Church and Foreign Missions*. Milwaukee: Morehouse, 1933.

———. *The Jewish Antecedents of the Christian Sacraments*. New York: Ktav, 1969.

Gelin, Albert. *Les Idées Maîtresses de l'Ancien Testament*. Paris: Editions du Cerf, 1966. E.T.: *The Key Concepts of the Old Testament*. Translated by George Lamb. New York: Sheed and Ward, 1955.

Generale Synode der Nederlandse Hervormde Kerk. *Israël: volk, land, en staat*. 's Gravenhage: Boekencentrum N.V., 1970.

Gilkey, Langdon. *How the Church Can Minister to the World Without Losing Itself*. New York, Evanston, and London: Harper and Row, 1964.

Ginzberg, Louis. *Legends of the Jews*. Translated from German manuscript by Henrietta Szold. 7 vols. Philadelphia: The Jewish Publication Society of America, 1909-1928.

———. "The Religion of the Jews in the Time of Jesus," *HUCA*, I (1924), pp. 307-321. New York: Ktav Publishing House, 1968.

Glover, A. Kingsley. "The Jews of the Extreme Eastern Dispersion," *The Menorah Monthly*.

IV (March 1888), pp. 239-249: "The Jews of India"

IV (April 1888), pp. 359-365: "The Jews of the Chinese Empire"

IV (May 1888), pp. 436-441: "The Jews of the Chinese Empire"

IV (June 1888), pp. 520-524: "The Jews of the Chinese Empire"

V (July 1888), p. 10-19: "Manuscripts of the Jews of China and India"

Gnilka, Joachim. "Der Missionsaufrag des Herrn nach Mt. 28 und Apg. I," *Bibel und Leben,* IX (1968).

Godbey, Allen Howard. *The Lost Tribes a Myth.* Durham, N.C.: Duke University Press, 1930.

Goodall, Norman, ed. *Missions Under the Cross.* New York: Friendship Press, 1953.

Goodenough, Erwin R. *The Politics of Philo Judaeus.* Hildesheim: Georg Olms Verlagsbuchhandlung, 1967.

Grayzel, Solomon. *History of the Jews.* 2nd ed. Philadelphia: Jewish Publication Society of America, 1968.

Green, Michael. *Evangelism in the Early Church.* Grand Rapids: W. B. Eerdmans, 1970.

Hahn, Ferdinand. *Das Verständnis der Mission im Neuen Testament.* Neukirchen-Vluyn: Neukirchen Verlag, 1963. E.T.: *Mission in the New Testament.* Translated by Frank Clark. Naperville: A. R. Allenson, 1965.

Harnack, Adolf von. *Die Mission und Ausbreitung des Christentums in den ersten drei Jahrhunderten.* 3 vols. 2nd ed. Leipzig: Hinrichs, 1915. E.T.: *The Mission and Expansion of Christianity in the First Three Centuries.* Edited by James Moffatt. New York: Harper and Bros., 1961.

——. *Lehrbuch der Dogmengeschichte.* 3 vols. 4th ed. Tübingen: J. C. B. Mohr, 1909 E.T.: *The History of Dogma.* Translated by Neil Buchanan. 7 vols. London: Williams and Norgate, 1894.

Hebert, Arthur Gabriel. *The Throne of David.* London: Faber and Faber, Ltd., 1941.

Hebley, Johannes Adrianus. *Het Proselitisme: Verkenning van een Oecumenisch Vraagstuk.* 's Gravenhage: Boekencentrum N.V., 1962.

Heerban, De. Articles from Vol. 22 (1970), pp. 65-192, also published as a separate volume under the title: *Kerk en Israël Onderweg* (n.p.; n.d.).

Hempel, Johannes. "Die Wurzeln des Missionswillen im Glauben des A.T.," *ZAW,* 66 (1954), pp. 244-272.

Herzfeld, Levi. *Handelsgeschichte der Juden des Altertums.* Braunschweig: J. H. Meyer, 1879.

Hirsch, S. A. "The Temple of Onias," *London Jews College Jubilee Volume.* London: Luzac and Co., 1906.

Hoekendijk, Johannes Christian. "The Call to Evangelism," *IRM,* 39 (1950), pp. 162-175.

——. *Kerk en Volk in de Duitse Zendingswetenschap.* Proefschrift. Utrecht: 1948.

Hof, I. P. C. van 't. *Het Zendingsbegrip van Karl Barth.* Hoenderloo: Zendings-studie-Raad, 1946.

Homrighausen, E. G. "Evangelism and the Jewish People," *IRM,* 39 (1950), pp. 318-329.

Janssen, Enno. *Juda in der Exilszeit.* Göttingen: Vandenhoeck und Ruprecht, 1956.

Jeremias, Joachim. *Abbs. Studien zur neutestamentlichen Theologie und Zeit-geschichte.* Göttingen: Vandenhoeck und Ruprecht, 1966. E.T.: *The Prayers of Jesus.* London: SCM Press, 1967.

——. *Die Abendmahlsworte Jesu.* 3rd ed. Göttingen: Vandenhoeck und Ruprecht, 1960. E.T.: *The Eucharistic Words of Jesus.* Oxford: Blackwell, 1955.

——. *Die Anfänge der Kindertaufe: eine Replik auf Kurt Alands Schrift: Die Säuglingstaufe im Neuen Testament und in der Alte Kirche.* München: Kaiser Verlag, 1962. E.T.: *The Origins of Infant Baptism.* Translated by Dorothea M. Barton. Naperville: A. R. Allenson, 1963.

——. *Die Gleichnisse Jesu.* Zürich: Zwingli Verlag, 1947. E.T.: *The Parables of Jesus.* New York: Scribner, 1963.

——. *Jerusalem zur Zeit Jesu.* 2nd ed. Göttingen: Vandenhoeck und Ruprecht, 1958. E.T.: *Jerusalem in the Time of Jesus.* SCM Press, 1969.

——. *Jesus Verheissung für die Völker.* Münster: W. Kohlhamer Verlag, 1953. E.T.: *Jesus' Promise to the Nations.* London: SCM Press, 1967.

——. *Die Kindertaufe in den ersten vier Jahrhunderten.* Göttingen: Vandenhoeck und Ruprecht, 1958. E.T.: *Infant Baptism in the First Four Centuries.* Philadelphia: Westminster Press, 1960.

——. "The Gentile World in the Thought of Jesus," *Studiorum Novi Testamenti Societas,* III (1952), pp. 18-28.

Jerusalem Bible. Jones, Alexander, ed. *The Jerusalem Bible.* Garden City: Doubleday and Co., 1966.

Jocz, Jakob. *Christians and Jews: Encounter and Mission.* London: SPCK, 1966.

——. *The Jewish People and Jesus Christ.* London: SPCK, 1949.

Johnson, Aubrey Rodway. *Sacral Kingship in Ancient Israel.* 2nd ed. Cardiff, Wales: U. P., 1967.

Josephus, Flavius. *The Works of Flavius Josephus* with an English translation by H. St. J. Thackeray, a.o. 9 vols. London: Heinemann, 1958-1965.

Juster, Jean. *Les Juifs dans l'Empire Romain: leur condition juridique, economique, et sociale.* 2 vols. New York: B. Franklin, 1965.

Käsemann, Ernst. "Kritische Analyse von Phil. 2:5-11," *ZThK,* 47 (1950), p. 346ff.

Kasting, Heinrich. *Die Anfänge der urchristlichen Mission.* München: Chr. Kaiser Verlag, 1969.

Kilpatrick, George Dunbar. "The Gentile Mission in Mark," in *Studies in the Gospels: Essays in Memory of R. H. Lightfoot.* Oxford: U. P., 1955.

Kittel, Gerhard. *Theologisches Wörterbuch zum Neuen Testament.* 8 bde. Stüttgart: W. Kohlhammer Verlag, 1932ff. E.T. *Theological Dictionary of the New Testament.* Translated by Geoffrey Bromiley. 8 vols. Grand Rapids: W. B. Eerdmans, 1965ff.

Kittel, Rudolph, ed. *Biblia Hebraica.* Leipzig: J. C. Hinrichs, 1906.

Kline, Meredith G. *By Oath Consigned.* Grand Rapids: Eerdmans, 1968.

——. *The Treaty of the Great King.* Grand Rapids: Eerdmans, 1963.

Knak, Siegfrid. "Neutestamentliche Missionstexte nach neuer Exegese," *Theologia Viatorem,* V (1954), pp. 27-50.

Knox, Wilfred Lawrence. "Abraham and the Quest for God," *Harvard Theological Review,* 28 (1935), pp. 55-60.

Kohl, Kaufmann. "The Jews and Commerce," *The Menorah Monthly,* III (1887), pp. 211-217, 391-398.

——. *The Origins of the Synagogue.* New York: Macmillan, 1929.

Koole, Jan Leunis. *De Joden in de Verstrooiïng.* Franeker: T. Wever, n.d.

Kraft, Charles Franklin. *Genesis: Beginnings of the Biblical Drama.* New York:

Women's Division of Christian Service, Board of Missions, The Methodist Church, 1964.

Labuschagne, C. J. *Schriftprofetie en volksideologie*. Nijkerk: Callenbach, 1968.

Lampe, Geoffrey William Hugo. *The Seal of the Spirit*. 2nd ed. London: SPCK, 1967.

Landsberger, Franz. "The Sacred Direction in Synagogue and Church," *HUCA*, XXIV (1957), pp. 181-204.

Latourette, Kenneth Scott. *History of the Expansion of Christianity*. Vol. 1: *The First Five Centuries*. New York and London: Harper and Bros., 1937.

Lauterbach, Jacob Z. "The Pharisees and Their Teaching," *HUCA*, VI (1929), pp. 69-139.

Leeuw, Gerardus van der. *Phenomenologie*. Haarlem: F. Bohn, 1948.

——. *Religion in Essence and Manifestation*. London: G. Allen and Unwin, 1938.

Leipoldt, Johannes. *Jesu Verhältnis zu Griechen und Juden*. Leipzig: G. Wigand, 1941.

Leon, Harry J. *The Jews of Ancient Rome*. Philadelphia: Jewish Publication Society of America, 1960.

Levy, Isaac. *The Synagogue: Its History and Function*. London: Vallentine, Mitchell, 1964.

Lewy, Julius. "Origin and Signification of the Biblical Term 'Hebrew,'" *HUCA*, XXIV (1957), pp. 1-13.

Lightfoot, Robert Henry. *The Gospel Message of St. Mark*. Oxford: Clarendon Press, 1950.

Loewe, Herbert Martin James. *Judaism and Christianity*. New York: Macmillan Co., 1937.

Lohmeyer, Ernst. *Das Evangelium des Matthäus*. Göttingen: Vandenhoeck und Ruprecht, 1967.

——. "Johannes der Taufer," *Das Urchristentum I*. Göttingen: Vandenhoeck und Ruprecht, 1962.

——. *Kultus und Evangelium*. Göttingen: Vandenhoeck und Ruprecht. E.T.: *Lord of the Temple*. Translated by Stewart Todd. Richmond: John Knox Press, 1962.

——. "Mir ist gegeben alle Gewalt (Eine Exegese von Mt. 28:16-20)," in *In Memoriam Ernst Lohmeyer*, Werner Schmauk, ed. Stüttgart: Evangelisches Verlagswerk, 1951.

Löwenthall, Rudolph. "The Jews of China," *Chinese Social and Political Review*, XXIV, no. 2. Peking: 1940.

Luck, G. Coleman. *Ezra and Nehemiah*. Chicago: Moody Press, 1969.

Major, Henry Dewsbury Alves; Manson, Thomas Walter; Wright, Charles James. *The Mission and Message of Jesus*. London: Nicholson and Watson, 1937.

Manson, Thomas Walter. *Only to the House of Israel? Jesus and the non-Jews*. Philadelphia: Fortress Press, 1964.

——. "The Lord's Prayer," *Bulletin of the John Rylands Library Manchester*, 38 (1955), pp. 99-113.

——. *The Teachings Of Jesus*. Cambridge: University Press, 1945.

Mantel, Hugo. *Studies in the History of the Sanhedrin*. Cambridge: Harvard University Press, 1961.

Marten, Ralph P. *Carmen Christi: Philippians 2:5-11 in recent interpretation and in the setting of early Christian worship.* London: Cambridge U. P., 1967.

Martin-Achard, Robert. *A Light to the Nations.* Naperville: A. R. Allenson, 1962.

Mattuck, Israel Isidore. *Why the Jews Have No Missionaries.* London: Jewish Religious Union for Liberal Judaism, 1933.

Mays, James Arthur. *Amos.* Philadelphia: Westminster Press, 1969.

Meek, Theophile. "The Interpenetration of Cultures as Illustrated by the Character of the Old Testament Literature," *JR,* VII (1927), pp. 244-262.

Mendelssohn, Sidney. *The Jews of Africa.* London: Kegan Paul, 1920.

——. *The Jews of Asia.* London: Kegan Paul, 1920.

Menes, A. "Tempel und Synagogue," *ZAW,* I (1931), pp. 268-276.

Michel, Otto. "Der Abschluss des Matthäusevangeliums," *Evangelische Missionszeitschrift,* X (1950/51), pp. 16-26.

——. *Der Brief an die Hebräer.* Göttingen: Vandenhoeck und Ruprecht, 1966.

——. "Menschensohn und Völkerwelt," *Evangelische Missionszeitschrift,* II (1941), pp. 258-265.

Midrash, *Midrash Rabba.* Translated under the editorship of H. Freedman and M. Simon. 10 vols. London: Socino Press, 1939.

Minear, Paul Sevier. *And Great Shall Be Your Reward.* New Haven: Yale University Press, 1941.

——. *The Images of the Church in the New Testament.* London: Lutterworth, 1960.

Mirsky, Samuel Kalman. *Jerusalem as a Religious Center.* New York: Mizrachi Organization of America, 1950.

Moltmann, Jürgen, *Theologie der Hoffnung: Untersuchungen zur Begründung und zu den Konsequenzen einer christlichen Eschatologie.* München: Kaiser, 1964. E.T.: *Theology of Hope.* Translated by James W. Leitsch. New York and Evanston: Harper and Row, 1965.

Moore, George Foot. *Judaism in the First Five Centuries of the Christian Era.* 3 vols. Cambridge: Harvard University Press, 1927-30.

Morgenstern, Julius. "Jerusalem - 485 B.C.," *HUCA,* XXXI (1954), pp. 1-30.

Mudge, Lewis S. *The Crumbling Walls.* Philadelphia: Westminster Press, 1970.

Mulder, Harm A. *De Synagoge in de Nieuwtestamentische Tijd.* Kampen: J. H. Kok, 1969.

——. "Ontstaan en doel van het vierde evangelie," in *Gereformeerd Theologisch Tijdschrift,* 69 (1969), pp. 233-258.

——, "Theophilus de Godvrezende," in *Arcana Revelata: Een bundel Nieuw-Testamentische studiën aangeboden aan Prof. Dr. F. W. Grosheide ter gelegenheid van zijn 70e verjaardag.* Kampen: J. H. Kok, 1951, pp. 77-88.

Münck, Johannes. *Christus und Israël: eine Auslegung von Röm. 9-11.* Aarhus: Universitetsforlaget und Köbehavn: Ejnarmunksgaard, 1956. E.T.: *Christ and Israel: An Interpretation of Romans 9-11.* Translated by Ingebord Nixon. Philadelphia: Fortress Press, 1967.

——. *Paulus und die Heilsgeschichte.* Aarhus: Universitetsforlaget, 1954. E.T.: *Paul and the Salvation of Mankind.* Translated by Frank Clark. Richmond: John Knox Press, 1959.

Nestle, Eberhard, ed. *Novum Testamentum Graece.* 25th ed. Stüttgart: Würtembergische Bibelanstalt, 1963.

Neufeld, Vernon H. *The Earliest Christian Confessions.* Grand Rapids: W. B. Eerdmans, 1963.

Neusner, Jacob. *A Life of Rabban Yohanan Ben Zakkai*. Ca. 1-80 C.E. Leiden: E. J. Brill, 1962.

Nicholson, Ernest Wilson. *Deuteronomy and Tradition*. Philadelphia: Fortress Press, 1967.

Nickle, Keith F. *The Collection: A Study in Paul's Strategy*. Studies in Biblical Theology No. 48. Naperville: A. R. Allenson, 1965.

Niles, Daniel Thambyrajah. *Studies in Genesis*. Philadelphia: Westminster Press, 1958.

Nineham, Dennis Eric. "The Gentile Mission in Mark and Mark 13:9-11," *Studies in the Gospel: Essays in Memory of R. H. Lightfoot*. Oxford: Blackwell, 1955.

Norwood, Frederick Abbott. *Strangers and Exiles: A History of Religious Refugees* 2 vols. New York: Abingdon Press, 1969.

Noth, Martin. *Überlieferungsgeschichte des Pentateuch*. 2 aufl. Darmstadt: Wissenschaftliche Buchgesellschaft, 1960. E.T.: *Laws of the Pentateuch*. Translated by D. R. and A. P. Thomas. Edinburgh, London: Oliver and Boyd, 1966.

Oepke, Albrecht. "Internationalismus, Rasse, und Weltmission im Lichte Jesu", *Zeitschrift für Systematische Theologie*, X (1932), pp. 278-300.

Oesterley, William Oscar Emil, ed. *Judaism and Christianity*. London: The Sheldon Press, 1937.

    I: *The Age of Transition*. W. O. E. Oesterley, ed.

    II: *The Contact of Pharisaism with Other Cultures*. E. Loewe, ed.

    III: *Law and Religion*. Erwin I. J. Rosenthal, ed.

Oracles, Sibylline. *Oracula Sibyllina*. With a translation from the Greek by Milton Terry. New York: Hunt and Easton, 1890.

Orchard, R. K. *Out of Every Nation*. IMC Research Pamphlets No. 7. London: SCM Press, 1957.

Parkes, James William. *The Conflict of the Church and the Synagogue*. London: The Socino Press, 1961. Cleveland and New York: World Publishing Co., 1961.

———. *The Foundations of Judaism and Christianity*. London: Vallentine, and Chicago: Quadrangle, 1960.

Peterson, John. *Missionary Methods of Early Judaism in the Early Roman Empire*. Dissertation. Chicago: Chicago Divinity School, 1946.

Pfeiffer, Robert Henry. *History of New Testament Times*. New York: Harper, 1949.

Philo Judaeus. *The Works of Philo Judaeus*. With an English translation by F. H. Colson, R. Marcus and G. H. Whitaker. 11 vols. London: Heineman; New York: Putnam, 1953-1962.

Piet, John H. *The Road Ahead: A Theology for the Church in Mission*. Grand Rapids: Eerdmans, 1970.

Pilchik, Ely Emanuel. *Judaism Outside the Holy Land: The Early Period*. New York: Bloch Publishing Co., 1964.

Pritchard, James B. *Palestinian Figurines in Relation to Certain Goddesses Known Through Literature*. New Haven: University Press, 1943.

Rad, Gerhard von. *Das erste Buch Mose*. 4th. ed. Göttingen: Vandenhoeck und Ruprecht, 1956.

———. "Die falschen Propheten," *ZAW*, X (1933).

———. *Führung zum Christentum durch das Alte Testament*. Leipzig: Dorffling und Franke, 1934.

——. *Theologie des Alten Testaments:* Bd. I - *Die Theologie der geschichtlichen Überlieferungen Israëls.* München: Chr. Kaiser Verlag, 1962. E.T.: *Old Testament Theology.* Vol. I: *The Theology of Israel's Historic Traditions.* Translated by D. M. G. Stalker. Edinburgh: Oliver and Boyd, Ltd., 1962.

——. *The Problem of the Hexateuch and Other Essays.* London: Oliver and Boyd, 1966.

Radin, Max. *The Jews Among the Greeks and Romans.* Philadelphia: Jewish Publication Society of America, 1915.

Rahner, Karl. *Sendung und Gnade.* Innsbruck: Tyrolia Verlag, 1959. E.T. by Cecily Hastings.
  I: *The Christian Commitment.* New York: Sheed and Ward, 1963.
  II: *The Christian in the Marketplace.* New York: Sheed and Ward, 1964.
——. *The Christian of the Future.* London: Burns and Oates, 1967.

Raisin, Jacob Salmon. *Gentile Reactions to Jewish Ideals.* New York: Philosophical Library, 1953.

Rappaport, Uriel. *Religious Propaganda and Proselytism in the Period of the Second Commonwealth.* Jerusalem: 1965. [Doctoral dissertation; Hebrew with English summary].

Reinach, Theodore. *Textes d'auteurs grecs et romains relatifs au Judaïsme.* Paris: E. Laroux, 1895; and Hildesheim: Olms, 1963 (reprint).

Reitzenstein, Richard. *Die Vorgeschichte der Christlichen Taufe.* Stüttgart: Teubner, 1967.

Ricciotti, Giuseppe. *History of Israel.* Translated from the Italian by Clement Della Ponta and Richard T. A. Murphy. 2 vols. 2nd ed. Milwaukee: Bruce Publishing Co., 1958.

Richards, J. McDowell, ed. "Jesus is Lord" by F. F. Bruce. *Soli Deo Gloria: New Testament Studies in Honor of Wm. Childs Robinson.* Richmond: John Knox Press, 1968.

Ridderbos, Herman. *De Komst van het Koninkrijk.* Kampen: J. H. Kok, n.d. E.T.: *The Coming of the Kingdom.* Translated by H. de Jongste. Philadelphia: Presbyterian and Reformed Publishing House, 1962.

Rosen, Georg. *Juden und Phönizier: das antike Judentum als Missionsreligion und die Entstehung der jüdischen Diaspora.* Tübingen: J. C. B. Mohr, 1929.

Rowley, Harold Henry. *Israel's Mission to the World.* London: SCM Press, 1939.
——. "Jewish Proselyte Baptism and the Baptism of John," *HUCA*, XV (1940), pp. 313-334.
——. *The Biblical Doctrine of Election.* 3rd ed. Chicago: A. R. Allenson, 1952.
——. *The Faith of Israel: Aspects of Old Testament Thought.* Philadelphia: Westminster, 1957.
——. *The Missionary Message of the Old Testament.* London: Carey Press, 1945.

Sandmel, Samuel. "Abraham's Knowledge of the Existence of God", *Harvard Theological Review,* XLIV (1951), pp. 137-139.
——. *The First Christian Century in Judaism and Christianity.* New York: Oxford University Press, 1969.
——. ed. *Old Testament Issues.* New York: Harper and Row, 1968.
——. *Philo's Place in Judaism: A Study of Conceptions of Abraham in Jewish Literature.* Cinncinnati: Hebrew Union College Press, 1956.
——. *We Jews and Jesus.* New York: Oxford University Press, 1965.

Schilder, Klaas. *Christus in zijn Lijden.* Vol. I: *Christus aan den Ingang van zijn Lijden.* 2nd ed. Kampen: J. H. Kok, 1949. E.T.: *Christ in His Suffering.* Vol. I. Translated by Henry Zylstra. Grand Rapids: W. B. Eerdmans, 1938.

Schmauk, Werner, ed. *Kritisch-exegetischer Kommentar über das Neue Testament: Das Evangelium Matthäus.* Göttingen: Vandenhoeck und Ruprecht, 1967.

————. "Mir ist gegeben all Gewalt," *In Memoriam Ernst Lohmeyer.* Stüttgart: Evangelisches Verlagswerk, 1951.

Schmökel, Hartmut. *Jahwe und die fremden Völker.* Breslau: Maruschke and Berendt, 1934.

Schonfeld, Solomon. *The Universal Bible: Pentateuchal Texts Addressed to all Nations.* London: Sidgwick and Jackson, 1955.

Schürer, Emil. *Geschichte des jüdischen Volkes im Zeitalter Jesu Christi.* 5 vols. 4th ed. Leipzig: J. C. Hinrichs, 1909. E.T.: *The History of the Jewish People in the Times of Jesus Christ.* Translated by S. Taylor and P. Christie. 5 vols. Edinburgh: T. and T. Clarke, 1890ff.

————. "Die Juden im bosporanischen Reiche," *Sitzungsberichte der Akademie der Wissenschaften* (1897), pp. 200-206.

Shaull, J. Richard. "The Form of the Church in the Modern Diaspora", *Princeton Seminary Bulletin,* LVII (1964), p. 3ff.

Shoemaker, Samuel M. *With the Holy Spirit and With Fire.* New York: Harper and Bros., 1960.

Simon, Marcel. *St. Stephen and the Hellenists in the Primitive Church.* London, New York, Toronto: Longmans, Green, and Co., 1958.

————. *Verus Israel, Étude sur les relations entre Chrétiens et Juifs dans l'Empire Romain (135-425 A.D.).* Paris: E. De Boccard, 1948.

Singer, Isidore, ed. *The Jewish Encyclopedia.* 12 vols. New York and London: Funk and Wagnalls, 1901.

Slouschz, Nahum. *Travels in North Africa.* Philadelphia: Jewish Publication Society of America, 1927.

Smart, James D. *The Quiet Revolution.* Philadelphia: Westminster, 1969.

Smith, George Adam. *Jerusalem.* 2 vols. New York: A. C. Armstrong, 1908.

Smith, William Robertson. *Lectures on the Religion of the Semites.* New York: Meridian Press, 1956.

Sonne, Isaiah. "The Schools of Hillel and Shammai Seen From Within," *Louis Ginzberg Jubilee Volume.* New York: American Academy for Jewish Research, 1945.

Stauffer, Ethelbert. *Christus und die Caesaren.* Rev. ed. Hamburg und München: Friedrich Wittig, 1966. E. T.: *Christ and the Caesars.* Translated by K. and R. Gregor Smith. Philadelphia: Westminster Press, 1955.

————. *Jerusalem und Rom im Zeitalter Jesu Christi.* Bern: Francke, 1957.

————. *Jesus, Gestalt und Geschichte.* Bern: Francke, 1957. E.T.: *Jesus and his Story.* Translated by Richard Winston. New York: Albert A. Knopf, 1960.

————. *Jesus war ganz anders.* Hamburg: Friedrich Wittig Verlag, 1967.

Stoevesandt, Helene. *Jesus und die Heidenmission.* Dissertation: Göttingen, 1949. Summary in *TLZ,* 74 (1949), col. 242.

Stowe, David M. "Changing Patterns of Missionary Service in Today's World," *Practical Anthropology,* XVII (1970), pp. 107-118.

Strack, Hermann Leberecht, und Billerbeck, Paul. *Kommentar zum Neuen Testa-*

237

ment aus Talmud und Midrasch. 6 bde. München: Beck, 1922-1956.

Street, T. Watson. *On the Growing Edge of the Church.* Richmond: John Knox, 1963.

Strizower, Schifra. *Exotic Jewish Communities.* London and New York: Thomas Yoseloff, 1963.

Taylor, T. M. "The Beginnings of Proselyte Baptism," *NTSt*, II (1956), pp. 193-198.

Tcherikover, Victor. *The Jews in Egypt in the Hellenistic-Roman Age in the Light of the Papyri.* Tel Aviv: 1960. [Hebrew with English summary].

——. *Hellenistic Civilization and the Jews.* Translated from the Hebrew (*ha-Yehudim veha-Yevanim ba-tekufa ha-Helenistit*) by S. Appelbaum. Philadelphia: Jewish Publication Society of America, 1959.

Tippett, R. H. *Verdict Theology in Missionary Theory.* Lincoln, Illinois: Lincoln Christian College, 1969.

Torrance, T. F. "Proselyte Baptism," *NTSt*, I (1954), pp. 154-160.

Torrance, Thomas. *China's First Missionaries: The Ancient Israelites.* London: Thynne and Co., Ltd., 1937.

Unnik, W. C. van. "De achtergrond en betekenis van Handeling 10:4 en 35," *Nederlands Theologisch Tijdschrift*, III (1949), pp. 336-354.

——. "Het Jodendom in de Verstrooiing," *Het Oudste Christendom en de Antieke Cultuur.* 2 vols. Haarlem: H. J. Tjeenk Willink, 1951.

Van Ess, Leander, ed. *Vetus Testamentum Graece.* Leipzig: J. C. Hinrichs, 1906.

Verkuyl, Johannes. *Breek de Muren Af!* Baarn: Bosch and Keuning, 1969.

——. *De Boodschap der Bevrijding in deze Tijd.* Kampen: J. H. Kok, 1970.

——. *De Taak der Missiologie en der Missionaire Methodiek in het Tijdperk van Saecularisatie en Saecularisme.* Kampen: J. H. Kok, 1965.

Vicedom, Georg Friedrich. *Die Taufe unter den Heiden.* München: Kaiser Verlag, 1960.

——. *Gebet für die Welt: Das Vater-Unser also Missionsgebet.* München: Chr. Kaiser, 1965. E.T.: *A Prayer for the World.* Translated by Gilbert A. Thiele. St. Louis: Concordia, 1967.

——. *Missio Dei.* München: Kaiser Verlag, 1958. E.T.: *The Mission of God.* Translated by Gilbert A. Thiele. St. Louis: Concordia, 1965.

Vogelstein, Hermann. "Die Entstehung und Entwicklung des Apostolats in Judentum," *Magazin für die Wissenschaft der Judentums*, 49 (1905), pp. 427-449.

——. "The Development of the Apostolate in Judaism and its Transformation in Christianity," *HUCA*, II (1925), pp. 99-124.

Vos, Clarence J. *Woman in Old Testament Worship.* Delft: Judels & Brinkman, 1968.

Waszink, Jan Hendrik; Unnik, W. C. van; Beus, Ch. de.; eds. *Het Oudste Christendom en de Antieke Cultuur.* 2 vols. Haarlem: H. J. Tjeenk Willink, 1951.

Webber, George W. *The Congregation in Mission.* New York, Nashville: Abbingdon Press, 1964.

——. *God's Colony in Man's World.* New York, Nashville: Abingdon Press, 1960.

Weber, Otto. *Bibelkunde des Alten Testaments.* Tübingen: Furche Verlag, 1947.

West, Charles C., and Paton, David M., eds. *The Missionary Church in East and West.* London: SCM Press, 1959.

White, William Charles. *The Chinese Jews: A Compilation of Matters Relating to the Jews of Kai-feng Fu.* Toronto: Toronto University Press, 1966.

Williams, Colin Wilbur. *What in the World?* New York: National Council of Churches of Christ, 1964.

———. *Where in the World?* New York: National Council of Churches of Christ, 1963.

Williams, Joseph John. *Hebrewisms in West Africa.* New York: Biblo and Tannen, 1967.

Wright, George Ernest. *The Old Testament Against Its Environment: Studies in Biblical Theology No. 2.* Naperville: Alec R. Allenson, 1955.

Zimmerli, Walther. "Verheissung und Erfüllung," *Evangelische Theologie,* 12 (1952), p. 38ff.

Index of Scripture References

242

243

244

General Index

of Yahweh — 56, 176
see also "enthrone-
ment"
Lord's Supper — 176
Lydda — 217
Lydia — 89
Lydia-Caria — 71

M

Maccabees — 102, 113
Macedonia — 72
Madurai — 183
Malabar — 61, 63
Malachi — 132
Marcus Agrippa — 101
Mark, ending of the Gos-
pel — 2
Marks of the Church —
212-214
Media — 65, 66
Median Bible — 86
Mediterranean — 67, 93,
217
Medo-Persia — 65, 71
"Megillah" — 85
Mehuzah, synagogue of—
79
Melchizedek — 35, 148
Mercenaries, Jews as —
68
Messenger of the cove-
nant
Jesus Christ as — 56,
131-132
"Metuentes" — 94
Mexico — 221
Mikdash ma'at — 79
Migrations — 43, 67, 70-
71
Mishnah — 4, 69, 89, 91,
93, 97, 110
"Missio Dei" — 9
Mission
Jesus mission to Gen-
tiles — 145-160
to Gentiles — 169
Missionaries, heathen—68
Missionary appeal of the
O.T. — 49, 57
Missionary consciousness
of the O.T.
general — 95, 112, 123,
127
prophets — 7, 49, 53-
54, 57
Missions: Jewish
in O.T. — 123, 127, 154

modern attitudes to-
wards — 3
Mithradaites — 72
"Mityahadim" — 103
Moab — 65, 98, 102
Morocco — 71
Moses — 14, 16, 95, 98,
113, 116, 148, 160, 177
chair of — 62
Mt. of Olives — 158
Murashu — 66
Mystery
in Christ — 203
Religions — 6
(μαθητεύω) — 185-186

N

Naaman — 98
"Nachri" — 44
Nahum — 66
Nations — 16, 18, 50, 56,
188
and missions — 188-190
summoned to Christ —
51, 57
Naturalization—104, 109,
110
Nazareth — 135, 149
Nebuzaradan — 98
"Nechar" — 44
Negro — 69
Nicodemus — 185
Nile — 67, 70
Nineveh — 66
Noachian laws — 90
Noah — 126
N. T. mission conscious-
ness — 4
Nubia — 67

O

Oath form, in covenant—
175
Offerings — 104, 105, 191
Old Testament
antecedents to Christian
mission — 2, 5, 58
missionary conscious-
ness (see under "Mis-
sionary conscious-
ness")
relation to N. T. — 8,
35, 128, 136, 152
Onias — 68
Ophir — 59
Ordeal
baptism as — 131-134

crucifixion as — 163-
165
fire — 132
judicial — 171
water — 131-133
Orestes — 47

P

Pagan
apologetic — 74-75, 92,
110-120
cults in Palestine — 43
Ezra and paganism —
110
paganism — 110-112,
142, 192
Paganus — 88-89
Pahlavi, Scripture in—86
Palestine
migrations from — 67,
70, 71
modern problem — 43
occupation by Israel —
42-43
Pamphylia — 72
Parables — 137, 139, 156
Parthia — 61
"Partes infidelium" — 4
Particularism — 47, 110-
112
Passover — 99, 103, 108,
196
and Christ — 52
Paul — 52, 72, 89, 93, 96,
122, 125, 126, 137, 141,
154, 160, 196, 208
"Pax Romana" — 5, 160
Peacock — 59
People of God
names for — 206
new people of God —
202-214
Peking — 62
Peloponnesus — 72
Pentecost — 11, 93, 196-
200
Peregrini — 71
Persia — see Iran
Persian, Scripture in — 96
Person of Christ, central-
ity in mission — 186
Peshita Rabbati — 94
Peter — 93, 135, 197
Pharaoh — 16, 126, 180
Pharisees—79, 82, 83, 111,
112, 116, 120-124, 135
Gentile mission of —

twin brooks series BOOKS IN THE SERIES